The Sociology of Health and Illness

Third Edition

The Sociology of Health and Illness

Third Edition

SARAH NETTLETON

polity

First edition published in 1995 by Polity Press
Second edition published in 2006 by Polity Press
This third edition first published in 2013 by Polity Press
Reprinted 2013 (twice), 2015, 2016, 2017, 2018

Polity Press
65 Bridge Street
Cambridge CB2 1UR, UK

Polity Press
350 Main Street
Malden, MA 02148, USA

ISBN-13: 978-0-7456-4600-8
ISBN-13: 978-0-7456-4601-5(pb)

A catalogue record for this book is available from the British Library.

Typeset in 9.5 on 12 pt Utopia
by Servis Filmsetting Ltd, Stockport, Cheshire
Printed and bound in Great Britain by MPG Books Group Limited, Bodmin, Cornwall

For further information on Polity, visit our website: www.politybooks.com

Contents

Figures and Tables

Acknowledgements

Table 1.1, 'Interaction of two schemes for organizing medical sociology', reprinted by permission of John Wiley and Sons from Clive Seale, 'Mapping the field of medical sociology: a comparative analysis of journals', *Sociology of Health & Illness*, 30, 5: 677–95.

Table 2.1, 'Medical cosmologies: an extension of Jewson's (1976) diagram', reprinted by permission of Sage Publication Ltd from S. Nettleton, 'The Emergence of E-Scaped Medicine', *Sociology* (© BSA Publications Ltd, 2004).

Figure 7.1, 'Age-standardized limiting long-term illness: by NS-SEC and sex, 2001'; Table 7.1, 'Life expectancy at birth by gender and social class, 1972–1976, 1987–1991 and 2002–2005'; and Table 7.2, 'Age-standardized mortality rates by seven-class NS-SEC for males and females aged 25–64, 2001, 2005 and 2010', reprinted by permission of National Statistics website: <www.statistics.gov.uk>. Crown copyright material is reproduced with the permission of the Controller of HMSO.

Table 7.3, 'National Statistics Socio-Economic Classification', reprinted with permission of Polity Press Ltd. © M. Bartley, *Health Inequality: An Introduction to Theories, Concepts and Methods*, Cambridge: Polity, 2004.

Figure 8.1, 'Strategies of occupational closure: a conceptual model', reprinted with permission of Routledge, Taylor and Francis. © A. Witz, *Professions and Patriarchy*, London: Routledge, 1992.

Figure 10.1, 'Strategies of health promotion', reprinted with permission of Routledge, Taylor and Francis. © A. Beattie, 'Knowledge and Control in Health Promotion: A Test Case for Social Policy and Social Theory', in J. Gabe, M. Calnan and M. Bury (eds), *The Sociology of the Health Service*, London: Routledge, 1991. Reproduced by permission of Taylor and Francis.

Thanks are due to the staff at Polity Press, and especially Jonathan Skerrett, who have been supportive over the years and for their help with the production of this third edition. Many thanks, too, to Ian Tuttle for his copy editing and constructive suggestions and changes.

Preface to First Edition

The aim of this book is to introduce some of the key contemporary debates within the sociology of health and illness. The text does not attempt to give an exhaustive account of all aspects of the field of study, but rather aims to outline some recent developments and tries to articulate how these relate to contemporary changes in health and health care within the UK. It attempts to integrate the core tenets of traditional medical sociology with some of the fresh insights of the more current sociology of health and illness literature.

The book has been written for both undergraduate and postgraduate students of sociology who opt to study the area of health and illness in greater depth. It is hoped that it will also be of value to students in the adjacent disciplines of social and public policy, cultural studies and the health sciences. Health professionals studying the social sciences will also find the book of use.

The text covers a diverse range of topics. Chapter 1 sets out the parameters of the sociology of health and illness and draws attention to recent analytical and conceptual shifts within the field. Chapter 2 focuses on medical knowledge and outlines those approaches that have claimed that this knowledge is socially constructed. Chapter 3 focuses on lay knowledge and beliefs about health and then discusses the concepts of lifestyles and risk that are of increasing relevance to contemporary health policy. Moving from health to illness, chapter 4 examines the extensive literature on the experience and meanings of illness for both sufferers and significant others. The experience of illness highlights the centrality of the body to social action and the study of society more generally. Chapter 5 delineates the growing literature on the sociology of the body and argues that an adequate sociology of health and illness must include analyses of the body. Having explored both medical and lay knowledges of health and illness, chapter 6 outlines those approaches that study the nature of lay and professional interactions. Shifting from social interpretations of health and illness, chapter 7 is more explicitly concerned with the impact of society upon bodies. A key issue in the sociology of health and illness is the extent to which levels of mortality and morbidity are mediated by socio-structural variables such as class, gender and 'race'. The formal organization of health care, and health care professionals, is addressed in chapter 8, where it is argued that these can only be understood in relation to wider societal shifts. This argument is also developed in the final chapter, which discusses three contemporary strands of health policy: health promotion, community care and the rise of consumerism. It is suggested that they are part and parcel of a new paradigm of health and health care. The dimensions of this new paradigm, that patients are treated as 'whole' persons who have a valid and worthwhile contribution to make to their health and health care, constitute a theme which runs throughout the text.

In writing this book, I became somewhat overwhelmed by the breadth of the subject and the amount of work produced by sociologists of health and illness. Making decisions about what to exclude proved to be more difficult than deciding what to include! Three substantive areas in particular receive less attention than some might consider to be appropriate. These are: the sociology of mental health; the sociology of informal health care; and the sociology of death. During the last few years, a number of textbooks have been published which comprehensively deal with mental health (Prior, 1993; Pilgrim and Rogers, 1993; Busfield, 1994). The nature of informal health care, caring for others and self-care, is touched upon in a number of chapters, especially chapters 3 and 4. However, a more extensive elaboration of the issues associated with informal health care can be found elsewhere (Stacey, 1988; Ungerson, 1990; Finch and Mason, 1992; Bornat et al., 1993). Death has also received the attention of sociologists of health and illness who have drawn attention to the social organization of death and the extent to which it has become medicalized (Prior, 1989; Clark, 1993). Although I could try to construct coherent reasons for the relative exclusion of these topics, the truth is that within a text covering such a broad area, one has to make painful choices about what to include and what to exclude. Nevertheless, as I have already suggested, this book was not intended to cover exhaustively *all* substantive topic areas; rather, the intention was to illustrate the full range of analytic sociological approaches to the subject. This said, the alert reader will probably have already noted that the chapters are organized by substantive topic. Each topic tends, though not exclusively, to lend itself to a particular analytic approach. For example, whilst the study of the experience of illness tends to adopt interpretative and phenomenological approaches, the study of health inequalities largely relies on structural analyses. In sum, this book attempts to provide the student with an understanding of sociological approaches *of* health and illness. It does not attempt to offer any unified theoretical perspective or synthesis of approaches, but instead it aims to equip the reader with an appreciation of the rich variety of perspectives which are invaluable to any comprehensive study of the complex issues associated with health and illness.

Writing a textbook proved to be much more difficult than I ever imagined. It certainly would never have seen the light of day without the support of a number of people to whom I am extremely grateful. Aileen McAllister, Ulla Gustafsson, Deborah Michael and my parents have given me encouragement and friendship which have kept me going. Nicki Thorogood has also been very supportive and made useful comments on chapter 5. Neil Small read and made very helpful comments on chapter 3, Anthony Giddens looked over earlier versions of three draft chapters, made helpful suggestions and gave me the confidence to keep up with the project. Indeed, all the staff at Polity Press have been very helpful.

Sarah Nettleton
York

Preface to Second Edition

Drafting this second edition has been an illuminating exercise. Research and academic literature in the sub-discipline of the sociology of health and illness has burgeoned. This is in part because of significant technological innovations in relation to medicine and the growing popularity and cultural salience of health. Developments associated with the 'new genetics', information communication and technologies and e-health, and within the neurosciences in particular, are reconfiguring and 'reordering' experiences of health, illness and the body. The sociological implications of these are clearly outlined by Brown and Webster (2004) in their book *New Medical Technologies and Society*. Nevertheless, I have tried to capture some of these debates by way of exploring illustrative examples in the text. Indeed, more than 300 new references have been woven into the book even though the overall structure and order of the chapters remain unchanged.

Chapter 2 outlines a range of perspectives which share the premise that medical knowledge is to a greater or lesser degree socially contingent. The salience of the information society is new here and the implications for the social production and reproduction of medical knowledge are captured in the notion of e-scaped medicine. Two recent examples which pertain to health, risk and lifestyles are added to chapter 3 - namely the MMR debate and food. These examples throw light on subjective perceptions of risk and how these are negotiated with political pronouncements on risk and safety. The illustrative example of HIV/AIDs has been rewritten, and I am grateful to Graham Hart and Paul Flowers for pointing me in the direction of fascinating and important literature in this area. Over the last decade there has been a growing literature on illness narratives, and chapter 4 now includes a discussion of this. Chapter 5, which deals with the sociology of the body, has been revised and includes debates on visualization techniques - most notably the visible human project, and the debates associated with reproductive technologies are extended to include issues of embryonic stem cell research. Chapter 6 on professional–patient interactions has been updated with more recent examples in the literature, and now includes discussion of sociological critiques of 'compliance' and 'concordance'. Chapter 7 has been revised and updated not only in terms of the data on health inequalities, but psycho-social and life-course perspectives have also been added. This chapter now uses Klinenberg's (2002) excellent book *Heat Wave* (a Durkheimian analysis of the reasons for deaths during a Chicago heat wave) as an illustrative device to introduce readers to the key concepts and perspectives which help to explain the social patterning of mortality and morbidity. Debates about the possible decline of the power of the medical profession have intensified on both sides of the Atlantic in recent decades and analyses of these changes are updated in chapter 8. The salience of consumerism, information technologies and new forms of governance are examined, and the work of a range of commentators on these issues is discussed. Even in the face of the changes that have occurred since this book was first published in the 1990s, the notion of a new paradigm of health set out in chapter 10 still has analytic purchase. Indeed, the three strands of it - health promotion, community care and consumerism - remain important dimensions of contemporary policy. These issues remain, albeit in an updated form. However, in addition, policies and practices associated with increased use of e-health informational technologies, 'evidence-based medicine' and consumer informatics are also introduced by way of illustration. It is suggested that these are features of the new paradigm of medicine and health - namely e-scaped medicine - that we outlined in chapter 2.

In revisiting this text I have, however, been struck by the degree of continuity as well as change. Many core sociological concepts developed within this field of study endure and are instructive for our analyses of these apparently dramatic changes. Concepts such as 'sick role', 'stigma', 'medicalization', 'illness behaviour', 'surveillance', 'risk', 'professionalization' - to name but a few - remain valuable analytic tools for the social scientist who is keen to gain an appreciation of the social implications of health, illness and medicine. The aim of the book is to equip students with analytic tools to make sense of changes in relation to health and health care rather than present a series of 'hot topics' that would invariably 'date'.

As with the first edition, many important substantive issues are not discussed. Revising this book rekindled uncomfortable memories of being haunted by thoughts of commentators listing important omissions. Indeed, there are topics which really ought to have more attention. But one has to make assessments about what to take out and leave in - and no doubt there are many who would have made different judgements.

I was first introduced to medical sociology as an undergraduate student at the University of Newcastle in the late 1970s and early 1980s. My tutor in this subject - Ann Holohan - was an inspirational teacher and a committed researcher. Although the world has changed a lot since then, much of what she taught me remains salient today. Ever since then, I have found the sociology of health and illness to be a fascinating and illuminating area of study. My prime aim in writing and revising this book is therefore to try to share some of the insights that have been gained from this subfield of sociology and, I hope, generate interest and enthusiasm amongst students.

Sarah Nettleton
York

Preface to Third Edition

The second edition of this book involved a significant rewrite with a significant expansion of the bibliography which reflected the volume of work in the field and the changes in health care. It was overhauled. The first edition was published in 1995 and so a decade had lapsed before the second edition. It is the case that this third edition prepared only five years after the previous one has been more modified and updated. It does, however, include a new chapter. It no longer seemed viable to have a book on the sociology of health and illness without including a chapter on health technologies given the pace of innovation and change, and given the breadth of sociological literature published in this area. As with previous editions, the hardest part of writing a textbook is deciding what to leave out. One invariably senses medical sociologists peering over one's shoulder whilst writing, cautioning that important topics, recent innovations and key works have been overlooked. Of this I am guilty to be sure. But in defence, the aim of this book remains intact, and this is to communicate and encourage a critical and analytic approach to the study of health, illness and disease. I have worked in this field since I was an undergraduate student in Newcastle in the late 1970s and early 1980s. Over time I have been struck by the enduring value of many of the classic studies and concepts in the field. But these are matched too by new and innovative research that continues to excite, most especially in the journals such as *Sociology of Health and Illness, Social Science & Medicine, Health, Health Risk & Society, Journal of Health & Social Behaviour* and *Social Theory and Health.*

Sarah Nettleton
York

1 Introduction: The Changing Domains of the Sociology of Health and Illness

Introduction

Fifty years ago, the mention of health and illness would probably have invoked thoughts of hospitals, doctors, nurses, drugs and a first aid box. Today, however, it would probably conjure up a much broader range of images which could well include healthy foods, vitamin pills, aromatherapy, alternative medicines, exercise bikes, health clubs, aerobics, walking boots, running shoes, therapy, sensible drinking, health checks, and more. Health, it seems, has become a ubiquitous motif in our culture. Health and illness receive considerable attention from the media: television, radio, newspapers, magazines and videos all devote considerable space and time to health-related issues. Information and knowledge about health and illness are thus no longer just the property of health 'experts'. Everyone has at least some experience and knowledge. This book is about the contribution that sociology can make to contemporary understandings of health, illness and the human body.

Although many of the concepts dealt with in this book may have rather grand-sounding names, they all attempt to come to terms with issues and experiences that will be familiar to many readers. The sociology of health and illness is not confined to the narrow domain of the formal institutions of medicine. It is concerned with all those aspects of contemporary social life which impinge upon well-being throughout the life-course.

From before the moment that we are conceived to the time that we die, social processes impinge upon our health and well-being. The social locations of our parents will affect our life chances. Our birth may be mediated by technology and controlled by health professionals. The beliefs about health and illness held by our peers and by those with whom we live will shape our own experiences and understandings. Our contact with health professionals (dentists, doctors, pharmacists, opticians, health promoters, practice nurses and so on) is likely to become a routine fact of our lives. Our self-identity may be shaped by our experiences of illness and our interactions with both formal and informal institutions of health care. Our attitudes towards our bodies will be influenced by the discourses of health promotion and consumer culture. Our experiences of death and dying will be affected by our socio-cultural context. We may come into contact with new technologies of health care, either through our own illnesses or through having children. We may have to face the ethical and moral dilemmas central to the blurring of the beginning and ending of life. We may work in organizations (the NHS is one of the biggest employers in Europe) either directly or indirectly associated with health work. We will all carry out health work, which may take the form of caring for elderly relatives, children, partners, friends, and of course ourselves. It is the sociological analysis of topics such as these that provides the basis for this book.

The development of the sociology of health and illness has to be understood in terms of its relation to the dominant paradigm of Western medicine: *biomedicine*. Many of the central concerns of the sociology of health and illness have emerged as reactions to, and critiques of, this paradigm. This chapter therefore briefly outlines the main features of biomedicine and some of the main challenges that have been made against it. The history and the main theoretical underpinnings of the sociology of health and illness are also briefly considered, in order to provide a contextual backdrop to the rest of the book. The chapter concludes by highlighting the centrality of shifting conceptualizations of the body in *both* contemporary medicine and sociology – a theme which recurs at various points throughout the text. We shall see that just as the social and cultural parameters of health and illness have shifted and broadened, so too have the domains of their sociological study.

Medicine and the biomedical model

Modern Western medicine rests upon what has become known as the biomedical model. This model is based on five assumptions. First, that the mind and the body can be treated separately; this is referred to as medicine's *mind/body dualism*. Second, that the body can be repaired like a machine; thus medicine adopts a *mechanical metaphor*, presuming that doctors can act like engineers to mend that which is dysfunctioning. Third, and consequently, the merits of technological interventions are sometimes overplayed, which results in medicine adopting a *technological imperative*. Fourth, biomedicine is *reductionist*, in that explanations of disease focus on biological changes to the relative neglect of social and psychological factors. Finally, such reductionism was accentuated by the development of the 'germ theory' of disease in the nineteenth century, which assumed that every disease is caused by a specific, identifiable agent – namely a 'disease entity' (such as a parasite, virus or bacterium). This is referred to as the *doctrine of specific aetiology*.

The biomedical model, which has dominated formal medical care in the West since the end of the eighteenth century, is neatly summed up by Atkinson (1988: 180) in the following way:

> It is reductionist in form, seeking explanations of dysfunction in invariant biological structures and processes; it privileges such explanations at the expense of social, cultural and biographical explanations. In its clinical mode, this dominant model of medical reasoning implies: that diseases exist as distinct entities; that those entities are revealed through the inspection of 'signs' and 'symptoms'; that the individual patient is a more or less passive site of disease manifestation; that diseases are to be understood as categorical departures or deviations from 'normality'.

Students of sociology and social policy will no doubt quickly recognize the limitations of this approach to health, disease, illness and healing. The body is isolated from the person, the social and material causes of disease are neglected, and the subjective interpretations and meanings of health and illness are deemed irrelevant.

A further assumption inherent in Western medicine is that it is based on an objective science, which in turn involves empirical observation and induction. Medicine thus claims to offer the only valid approach to the understanding of disease and illness. Secure in its approach, medicine has scribed its own history (Shryock, 1979; D. Rhodes, 1985; BMA, 1992), such that its development is presumed to be one that has resulted in an increasingly accurate knowledge of disease. With this knowledge it claims to have achieved a whole series of successes: it has eradicated certain diseases; it has eliminated erroneous ideas and practices; and it holds the promise for further advancements for the control of existing and any new diseases. Thus medicine's own history is one of progress. The development of medicine is presumed to involve a move from speculation to a coherent scientific discipline. This is typified by D. Rhodes (1985: 3):

> The general course of the history of medicine is from massive speculation - without allowing it to be much influenced by fact, as observed or derived from experiment - to narrower and narrower smaller hypotheses, potentially testable by observation and experiment. There is a move too from supernatural to natural explanations of phenomena; and it all takes a very long time, with the old clinging to the new, impeding its progress and having to be discarded as time passes, so that novel and fruitful ways of looking at events may emerge and be tested. In short medicine is one aspect of the development of scientific method being applied in one of the most difficult areas of nature.

This type of account is a *Whig history*: that is, one which sets out the achievements of the past and details how they have contributed to present success in a linear and progressive manner. Events such as discoveries or inventions in medicine are assessed in terms of the contributions they have made to contemporary medical science. Commenting on this type of medical history, the sociologist Eliot Freidson (1970a: 13) wrote:

> Unfortunately, most historians of medicine have been concerned solely with documenting discoveries of those isolated bits of information that we now consider to be scientifically true. Looking back from our present-day perspective of 'modern science', the historian is inclined to pass through the centuries picking out the 'valid' elements of medical knowledge and assembling a chronology of truths that add up to become present day scientific medicine.

Today such Whig accounts of, and approaches to, medicine are, for many, no longer acceptable. The sociology of health and illness has sought to offer alternative ways of interpreting medicine, health and healing. Much of this understanding has come about through criticisms of the biomedical model, some of which are considered below.

Challenges to biomedicine

During recent decades the institution of medicine and the biomedical model have increasingly been challenged by critiques emerging from both popular and academic sources. These criticisms have been intensified within the context of the escalating costs of health care. Medicine is not a homogeneous institution, and criticisms of the biomedical model and medical practice are voiced within medicine as well as outside it. Striking at the heart of biomedicine is the challenge to its effectiveness. It has been argued, from within both medicine (Engel, 1981) and sociology, that medicine's *efficacy* has been overplayed. McKeown (1976), a professor of social medicine, for example, demonstrated by way of historical demographic studies that the decline in mortality which has occurred within Western societies has had more to do with nutrition, hygiene and patterns of reproduction (essentially social phenomena) than it has with vaccinations, treatments or other modes of medical interventions (see chapter 7). Drawing on this type of evidence, authors have pointed to the fact that pouring resources into medical technologies has resulted in diminishing returns (Powles, 1973). Taking this further, Illich (1976) has argued that biomedicine does more harm than good. Rather than curing and healing, medicine actually contributes to illness through the iatrogenic effects of its interventions, such as the side-effects of drugs and the sometimes negative clinical consequences of surgery.

Antibiotic resistance is a contemporary example of this (Humphrey, 2000). Seen as a wonder drug in the 1940s – a 'magic bullet' that contributed to the control of infectious diseases and made surgery safer – today the over-use of antibiotics has led to an increase in antibiotic-resistant organisms. It is estimated that over half of the 50 million prescriptions for antibiotics issued annually in the UK are inappropriate, the iatrogenic consequence being experienced by both individuals and the population. As Humphrey puts it: 'Looked at through Illich's eyes, resistance can be seen as the Aesclapian thunderbolt – the inevitable dark side of the miraculous treatment, hastened in its release by the medical profession's use of the antibiotic miracle' (Humphrey, 2000: 355).

The move to develop what is known as 'evidence-based medicine' is the institutional and policy response to these critiques. There is a move to evaluate all medical and health care interventions to ensure they are the most effective in terms of both treatment outcomes and value for money. However, this turn to evidence-based practice is not immune from sociological scrutiny (see chapter 10).

Not only are there harmful physical effects of biomedicine; Illich also draws attention to the fact that people have become de-skilled and are dependent on so-called medical experts. Self-care and care of one's own family and friends thus became regarded as inferior to that provided by trained health professionals. As we shall see, there has been a popular reaction against this process, as people increasingly try to take more control over their own health (see especially chapters 3, 4, 8 and 10). In addition, more recently there has also been a political reaction to this view, with policy makers and practitioners keen to both acknowledge and capitalize on lay people's ability to care for themselves and for others (Department of Health, 2010).

A second criticism of biomedicine is that it fails to locate the body within its socio-environmental context. In fact, an alternative to the biomedical model is often referred to as the 'socio-environmental model' of medicine (Engel, 1981). Focusing on the biological changes within the body, biomedicine has underestimated the links between people's material circumstances and illness. The privileging of the biological over the social is evident in our contemporary preoccupation with genetic influences on health and illness. Genetic explanations, for example, are popular and compelling. Conrad (2002) draws on Dubos' (1959) influential book *Mirage of Health* to suggest that, like the germ theory of disease, which was privileged in the nineteenth century, contemporary genetic theories rest on the assumptions of the doctrine of specific aetiology, a focus on the internal rather than the external environment, and the metaphor of the body as a machine. As such, 'the public depiction of the new genetics aligns perfectly with the old germ theory model' (Conrad, 2002: 78). He reminds us of the dangers inherent in presuming that the causes and treatment of disease reside within the body of the individual. Too much attention to the genetic determinants of health can detract from the social and environmental factors which significantly influence our life chances. The sociology of health and illness has repeatedly demonstrated that health and disease are socially patterned. Health status is clearly the consequence of factors other than biology, and this is evidenced by the fact that it does not occur at random. Patterns of mortality and morbidity, or a person's 'life chances', are related to social structures, and vary according to gender, social class, 'race' and age. Thus the biomedical model fails to account for the *social inequalities in health* (see chapter 7).

Medicine has also been taken to task for the way in which it treats patients as passive objects rather than 'whole' persons. A tradition within medical education was that when students entered medical school, one of their first tasks was a human dissection. This sets the agenda for their training, wherein their object of study is the body and not the person. In order to try to address the concern, more attention is now given to communication skills and the behavioural sciences within the medical curriculum, and a human dissection is no longer the first encounter for medical students. Critiques of biomedicine recognized that lay people have their own valid interpretations and accounts of their experiences of health and illness. For example, the medical practitioner and former editor of the prestigious medical journal *The Lancet*, Richard Horton, presents a powerful argument in his book *Second Opinion* (2003), which calls on medicine to place the concept of 'human dignity' at its core. For treatment and care to be effective, he argues, health practitioners need to be sensitive to the perceptions, feelings and concerns of their patients. The sociology of health and illness argues that socio-cultural factors influence people's perceptions and experiences of health and illness, which cannot be presumed to be simply reactions to physical bodily changes (see chapters 3 and 4).

Perhaps the most powerful criticism in this respect has come from women, especially from the women's health movement in reaction to medicine's approach to childbirth. The institution of medicine took control of childbirth out of the hands of women in the nineteenth century (Oakley, 1976; Donnison, 1977; Kent, 2000) and managed to ensure, despite the lack of any sound evidence of benefit (Tew, 1990), that by the 1970s virtually all babies were born in hospital. Thus, what is fundamentally a woman's experience was removed from the domestic domain to the public one of the hospital, wherein a male-dominated branch of medicine – obstetrics – had control. Moreover, what is perhaps more remarkable is the way in which pregnancy and childbirth came to be treated as 'illness' and were therefore subjected to a whole array of technological interventions. In this respect the experience of having a baby was *medicalized*; that is, a normal life event came to be treated as a medical problem which required medical regulation and supervision. Women have effectively exposed and challenged the way in which medicine came to control their bodies more generally (see chapter 6). The have produced health literature by women and for women (Boston Women's Health Book Collective, 2011) and have developed forms of medical care which are based on alternative philosophies to those espoused by the dominant institutions of medicine (Foster, 1995; Annandale, 2009).

A fifth challenge to biomedicine is the assumption that through its scientific method it identifies the truth about disease. By contrast, sociologists have suggested that disease, medicine's prime object of study, is *socially constructed* (see chapter 2). It is argued, therefore, that disease categories are not accurate descriptions of anatomical malfunctionings, but are socially created; that is, they are created as a result of reasonings which are socially imbued. Medical belief systems, like any others, are contingent upon the society which produces them. Furthermore, there is a correspondence between modes of organization, technological forms and medical knowledge. It is evident that technology and practices co-construct knowledge of the body (Jewson, 1976) (see chapter 9). Indeed, the apparent 'facticity' of medicine means that values may be transformed into apparent facts (K. White, 2009). For example, the belief that women were unsuited to education in the nineteenth century was supported by medical evidence.

A corollary to challenging biomedicine's scientific basis is to question its presumed superiority in relation to other forms of healing. Medicine has questioned the basis of alternative medicines, arguing that they are 'unscientific', and therefore incorrect (BMA, 1992). However, another view, which suggests that all knowledge is contingent, would imply that alternative medicines are of equal validity. It would appear that the decline in faith in biomedicine is not limited to sociologists. More and more people are opting to seek help from, and are being successfully treated by, alternative practitioners (BMA, 1993; Cant and Sharma, 2000; Barcan, 2011) (see chapter 8).

The final challenge is the claim that the boundaries of the medical profession are best viewed as the outcome of socio-political struggles rather than being based on the demarcations of scientific knowledge, as the Whig histories imply. That is, what counts as legitimate medical knowledge and practice is decided through social processes rather than being shaped by natural objects of which the profession has an accurate knowledge. Similarly, the division of labour between health professions is socially negotiated and is mediated by gender, 'race' and class (see chapter 8). It is these socio-political processes, mediated by social structures, that have permitted the continuation of *professional medical dominance*. In turn, this medical dominance has contributed to the perpetuation of capitalist and patriarchal structures, and led to the eclipse of healing activities which take place beyond the boundaries of formal health care. Such divisions and social relations are challenged in a variety of ways in the contemporary context.

The structure of the sociology of health and illness

Following our review of the challenges to biomedicine, we can begin to appreciate the scope of the sociology of health and illness. The study of health, illness and society will invariably cover a wide and diverse range of topics. These include the analysis of medical knowledge, lay perceptions of health and illness, the experience of health and illness, social and cultural aspects of the body, the analysis of interactions between patients and health professionals, the patterned nature of health and illness in relation to the wider social structure, and the social organization of both informal and formal health care. A number of authors have pointed to the disparate nature of the substantive content of the sociology of health and illness (Freund et al., 2002), and others, recognizing this eclecticism, have attempted to impose some conceptual organizing principles which might help to provide a degree of coherence to the field. Turner (1995: 4–5), for example, suggests what might be described as a *levels of analysis* approach. He argues that a comprehensive sociology of health and illness must involve the study of health and illness in society at three levels: the 'individual level', which examines perceptions of health and illness; the 'social level', which examines the social creation of disease categories and health care organizations; and the 'societal level', which examines health care systems within their political context. Other authors have organized and structured the contents of the sociology of health and illness within different sociological approaches or paradigms. For example, Clarke (1981) has distinguished between positivists (whose aim is to discover causal laws), activists (whose aim is to diagnose societies' ills and propose solutions), and naturalists (whose aim is empathetically to interpret the meaning of situations). K. White (1991, 2009) has organized contemporary developments in the field in terms of Parsonian, Marxist, feminist and Foucauldian/Fleckian perspectives – all of which we shall meet in this book in due course. Gerhardt (1989), however, has provided the most extensive attempt to structure the content of the sociology of health and illness. She classifies its content within four theoretical paradigms: structural functionalism, symbolic interactionism, phenomenology and conflict theory – again, positions we shall meet throughout this book. This 'social theorizing about social theorizing' is not simply a reified activity of value to theorists, but also enables us to appreciate the frameworks which inform and are embedded in empirical research (Armstrong, 2000).

It is generally acknowledged that one of the reasons for the rapid growth of the sociology of health and illness (it forms the largest sub-branch of sociology in both the UK and the USA) is its relationship, albeit an uneasy one, with both sociology and with medicine. In relation to the latter, this problematic relationship can perhaps be best understood by the tension between sociology *in* medicine and the sociology *of* medicine (R. Strauss, 1957). Sociology *in* medicine refers to sociological research which serves the needs and interests of medicine. Research agendas are professionally and institutionally determined, and sociologists work to provide solutions to medically defined problems. This characterized much medical sociology in the 1950s and 1960s, when medicine was keen to understand and improve the dynamics of the doctor–patient relationship, to improve patient compliance, to prevent patients from presenting 'trivial' health matters to their doctors, and to identify social factors which may have contributed to disease. The sociology *of* medicine, by contrast, represents a shift towards a more critical approach wherein the lay rather than the medical view of health and illness is privileged; the dominance of medicine is recognized; the boundaries of the medical profession are questioned; and the functionings of medical organizations are scrutinized. It is out of this critical medical sociology, which challenges the legitimacy of modern medicine, that the sociology *of* health and illness has developed. Clive Seale (2008) combined both Turner's 'levels of analysis' schema discussed above with Strauss's 'in' and 'of' distinction to produce a table which provides a useful map of the field with illustrative conceptual and substantive topics in each cell (see table 1.1).

What is striking about these organizational devices is that they are all derived from sociology more broadly, and do not relate to anything that is inherent in the substantive concerns of the sociology of health and illness itself. Furthermore these theoretical mappings of the contents of the sociology of health and illness counter

Table 1.1 *Interaction of two schemes for organizing medical sociology*

	In medicine/health	*Of medicine/health*
Individual level	• Health behaviour • Lay beliefs • Lay referral • Compliance • Social support and stress/ psycho-social perspectives	• Social construction of disease categories/medical knowledge • Discursive or narrative construction of self and identity • Sociology of body
Social level	• Social causes of disease • Social epidemiology • Evaluation of health care effectiveness • Managerial effectiveness and efficiency • Health promotion and education • Health inequalities	• Medical dominance/power/ interprofessional rivalry • Conflict perspective on lay–professional relationship • Medicalization • Managerialism as an ideology or discourse
Societal level	• Improving the effectiveness and efficiency of policies and government initiatives • Building social capital in the community	• Capitalism/globalization and health care systems • Health social movements • Social construction of the community via disciplinary surveillance/governmentality

Source: Seale (2008: 678).

charges that it constitutes an overly empiricist field of study, and as such has little to offer its parent discipline (Turner, 1992, 1995: 1; Gerhardt, 1989: xxiii). However, it is important to remember that sociology itself is an inherently fragmented discipline, in spite of the many attempts to impose clear and coherent structures upon it (Johnson et al., 1984). It is therefore inappropriate to make this charge against the sociology of health and illness. Furthermore, tensions between empiricism and theoreticism have long existed within sociology. It is undoubtedly the case, however, that the sociology of health and illness has a strong empirical tradition, of which it is proud. Horobin (1985: 104), for example, articulates the view of many when he argues that the sociology of health and illness has

> had a healthy bias towards practical issues largely because of its uneasy symbiosis with medicine and its separation from academic sociology. It is fashionable to criticize this research output on grounds that it lacks theoretical or conceptual sophistication, takes capitalism for granted or simply that it is much too trivial. I believe such criticism conveniently ignores the dynamics of the research process and in its condescension fails to give due credit for the considerable proportion that is interesting and meaningful.

As Taylor and Ashworth (1987) point out, all sociological research involves taking on a theoretical position, albeit implicitly. Empirical work always involves making certain assumptions regarding the nature of social reality and the best manner in which to understand it. Thus, when engaging in research, a theoretical position will invariably be taken. Furthermore, empirical research in itself contributes to the nature and existence of the wider discipline.

Although we have seen that many of the substantive concerns of the sociology of health and illness have developed out of tensions between sociology and biomedicine, there also exists an alternative view regarding the origins of the field. This suggests that rather than developing in *reaction* to medicine, sociology and medicine share *common* origins. As Foucault (1980a: 151) has argued:

> Countless people have sought the origins of sociology in Montesquieu and Comte. That is a very ignorant enterprise. Sociological knowledge . . . is formed rather in the practices like those of doctors.

Thus, both sociology and medicine are concerned with the empirical study of human bodies. This account of the origins of medicine clearly elevates the status of empirical studies, for it is such research that confirms both the existence of the object of study currently (human bodies) and the disciplines (medicine and sociology) themselves.

The body and the sociology of health and illness

As we have already seen, Turner (1992: 154) has taken the sociology of health and illness to task for not having any unifying theoretical structure. He states that 'It is not clear that . . . [it] . . . has any specific integrating theme or powerful theoretical structure, which is able to give the field some coherence and direction.' He does suggest, however, that the sociology of health and illness has the potential to 'become the leading edge of contemporary sociological theory' (1992: 163). This, he argues, is because the sociology of health and illness is the most appropriate place to develop a *sociology of the body*, which, in turn, may provide the possibility of an increasingly sophisticated theoretical sociology. For example, through addressing questions about the constitution of disease, the sociology of health and illness is fundamentally challenging assumptions about the ontology of the body. Further, the sociology of health and illness involves the study of people's interpretations of their bodily experiences and concerns the social aspects of the regulation of bodies. Certainly, studies concerned with the sociology of the body do appear to have proliferated in recent decades, both within and beyond the sociology of health and illness (Jacobus et al., 1990; Scott and Morgan, 1993; Shilling, 2003), and it does appear likely that the body, neglected for so long by sociologists, is coming to form an important dimension of sociological debates (Turner, 1992, 1996; Featherstone et al., 1991; Shilling, 2003). The object of medicine, and the object of sociology, is thus the body. But this is not the passive anatomical frame that was the focus of biomedicine, but the body that is capable of social action and interpretation.

Medicine and the sociology of health and illness: some common interests

In many ways the concerns of both the sociology of health and illness and medicine are different today from what they were thirty years ago. It is argued here that

DISEASE	→ HEALTH
HOSPITAL	→ COMMUNITY
ACUTE	→ CHRONIC
CURE	→ PREVENTION
INTERVENTION	→ MONITORING
TREATMENT	→ CARE
PATIENT	→ PERSON

Figure 1.1 Contemporary transformations in health and medicine

sociology and medicine now have much more in common. Medicine has changed, and this has been brought about, in part at least, as a result of challenges from the social sciences. It is also because the nature of illness itself is changing, as is society's response to it. The second half of the twentieth century has seen a significant shift in the disease burden; there has been a move from predominantly acute, life-threatening infectious diseases to chronic, non-life-threatening conditions such as cancer, circulatory diseases, heart conditions and diabetes mellitus. Moreover, life expectancy is increasing, and these chronic conditions are more prevalent in an ageing population. There has therefore been a need for a move from interventionism to surveillance, and from curing to caring. By definition, chronic conditions are not amenable to successful intervention, and so medicine is limited to ameliorative responses. The causes of the contemporary disease burdens have also changed, and many are now considered to be preventable. Lifestyle factors such as smoking, stress and exercise are now presumed to be important determinants of health at an individual level, and housing conditions, income, unemployment and poverty at a structural level. Increasingly, both medicine and sociology have come to focus on health, and not just illness and disease. This is evidenced by the recent proliferation of elaborate and extensive health promotion programmes (see chapter 10). The organizational responses to physical and mental health are increasingly located within the community, rather than in the institutional confines of a hospital. These developments within health and medical care will be discussed at various points throughout the book, but are briefly summarized in figure 1.1, in order to give a crude indication of the range of transformations with which we shall be dealing. Indeed, some authors have suggested that, collectively, they represent a move towards a new paradigm of health care which will supersede the biomedical model. This will be discussed in more detail in the final chapter of this book.

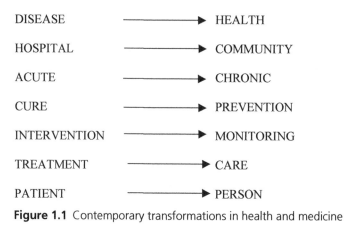

When we reflect upon these changes, we can glean that there is a growing overlap between medicine and sociology: the distinction between the concerns of the former and of the latter is becoming increasingly blurred. It may well be that the changes in our understanding and responses to health and illness are a consequence of the tensions that have long existed between the two disciplines. It would appear that these tensions have led to reformulations of their objects of study. Medicine has increasingly come to acknowledge the thinking person who resides within a social context, and sociology has come to accept the physical as well as the lived body as central to its study. These developments have been, in part, the effect of critical evaluations of the dominant discourse of medicine. This, as we have seen, has involved challenging the basis of medical knowledge and presenting the content and nature of alternative accounts of health and healing. In turn, these debates (which are not confined to sociology) have had significant consequences for medical practice and health care. Furthermore, the challenge to biomedicine, and more formal alliances between the social sciences and medicine, have resulted in significant shifts in health policy. For example, the proscription of health behaviours must now acknowledge lay people's opinions and accounts, health care must move from the domain of the hospital and into the community, professionals must be less paternalistic and more consumer-oriented. Sociological agendas and research are increasingly found within the pages of medical journals. Furthermore, as we have suggested above, a number of medical practitioners are making use of sociological analyses of socio-economic transformations which occurred at the turn of the millennium, the shift from industrial to information-based economies and societies being one of the most profound (see chapter 6). Currently, there are many opportunities for engaging in critical sociological analyses of health and medical matters and there are exciting developments in a number of substantive areas of study such as innovative health technologies, globalization, inequalities, contested health and medical knowledge, and embodied sociology (Nettleton, 2007). Turner (2004) and Seale (2008) both argue that an important direction for sociology of health and illness is to focus on societal and global matters and ensure a critical engagement with the health consequences of globalization, migration and citizenship. Ideally, a strong sociology is one that integrates both the global and the local and the political and personal. Macro level analyses are crucial, but these must not lose sight of the personal, lived experience of the individual. This is what makes this field of study so exciting and valuable. A critical sociology of health and illness amalgamates the public and the private, the political and the biological and the macro with the micro. This sociology *of* medicine approach is the one adopted throughout this text. Indeed, in the next chapter we question the very basis of medical knowledge itself, which, as we will see, is bound up with politics and the organizational practices of medicine and health care.

FURTHER READING

There is now an excellent collection of books on the sociology of health and illness – too many to list here, but highlights include:

Albrecht, G. L., Fitzpatrick, R. and Scrimshaw, S. C. (eds) (2000), *The Handbook of Social Studies in Health and Medicine*, London: Sage. This is an excellent text; it spans the full range of issues within the sociology of health and illness. Every chapter is comprehensive and accessible.

Annandale, E. (1998), *The Sociology of Health and Medicine: A Critical Introduction*, Cambridge: Polity Press.

Blaxter, M. (2010), *Health*, 2nd edn, Cambridge: Polity Press.

Cockerham, W. (ed.) (2010), *The New Blackwell Companion to Medical Sociology*, Oxford: Wiley-Blackwell.

Porter, R. (1997), *The Greatest Benefit to Mankind: A Medical History of Humanity from Antiquity to the Present*, London: HarperCollins. An accessible, thorough and entertaining history of medicine.

White, K. (2009), *An Introduction to the Sociology of Health and Illness*, 2nd edn, London: Sage.

It is worth regularly looking through the following journals: *Sociology of Health & Illness*; *Social Science & Medicine*; *Health: An Interdisciplinary Journal for the Social Study of Health, Illness and Medicine*; *Social Theory & Health*; and *Health Risk & Society*.

2 The Social Construction of Medical Knowledge

Introduction

It is often presumed that there is a distinction between disease and illness. Disease is taken to refer to pathological changes within the body which find expression in various physical signs and symptoms. Illness, on the other hand, is taken to refer to the individual's subjective interpretation and response to these signs and symptoms. It was once the case that whilst disease remained the exclusive province of practitioners of medical science, illness, and more especially the *experience* of illness, could be examined by sociologists. However, this demarcation was challenged, and what were formerly treated as 'natural' categories - disease and the body - are now seen to fall within the scope of the sociology of health and illness. Essentially, sociologists have argued that these 'natural' categories are the products of social activities and do not simply reflect invariant biological realities. This is not to say that people do not suffer from bodily dysfunctions, nor does it deny the realities of pain and distress; what it does argue is that *all* knowledge (including medical and scientific) is socially contingent. It is argued that medical knowledge is *socially constructed*. This chapter will provide an overview of the origins, parameters and variants of social constructionism, and will outline some of the tensions surrounding it. It will conclude by considering some of the implications of the approach for medical practice and health care within contemporary society. First, however, let us set the scene by considering an example.

The social construction of bodies: an example

If we were to be transported back in time to a prosperous small town in Germany called Eisenach during the early 1700s, we would find the way in which the inhabitants described their bodies somewhat alien to us. This is of course because their understanding of the workings of the body was very different from that of today. However, Duden (1991) has argued that the difference between 'us' and 'them' would be not only in our understanding of the workings of the body, but also in how it was actually *experienced*. She contends that the body we know today is fundamentally different from the body that we would find in the early eighteenth century. Striking up a dialogue about our bodies with these eighteenth-century inhabitants could therefore prove to be extremely difficult, as we would essentially be describing two very different objects. The body found in the 1700s has little in common with the modern body with which we are familiar. For example, we would probably find the following story about a court lady who had swallowed some pins rather odd:

> [she] was standing in front of a mirror with a bunch of pins in her mouth when she was startled by a prince who approached her from behind and slapped her on the back, whereupon all the pins fell into her throat. However, she felt no pain from the pins, and on the third day she passed all of them through her urine. (Cited by Duden, 1991: 70)

Duden argues, therefore, that the body is a cultural construction, and that how it is understood and, perhaps more importantly to her thesis, how it is actually *experienced* must be related to the historical context in which it resides. In her book *The Woman beneath the Skin,* she examines the works of Johann Storch, a doctor who practised in Eisenach during the first half of the eighteenth century. Dr Storch documented in meticulous detail over 1,800 'cases' with which he dealt. From his writings Duden is able to gain an insight into both the accounts given to Dr Storch by the women he treated and his medical practice. From this she pieces together a picture of women's bodies as they were experienced in the early 1700s.

According to Dr Storch's medical notes, most illnesses and treatments were related to the general idea of internal and external bodily fluids or 'flux'. Fluids – such as blood, milk or pus – both moved around the inner body and were at times excreted from it. Bodily fluids were all essentially the same, but they could be transformed in terms of their form, colour or consistency. For example, milk could resemble other excretions:

> The wife of a princely footman, twenty years of age, lay sick after first childbirth with 'cold sweat', 'heat', and a feverish rash. Over the course of several days she suffered repeatedly from loose bowels and complained about the 'drying up of the milk'. She had frequent diarrhea 'that looked whitish like milk'; later the diarrhea came out 'white, like curdled cheese'. (Duden, 1991: 107–8)

The main concern was that the flow of fluids should not be obstructed. For example, if a woman's 'menses' were impeded, this could result in illness, but this would not become a problem if the matter was secreted from the body in another form, such as 'loose bowels' (1991: 109). 'Inner flux' was the most common form of complaint presented to the doctor. It related to a multitude of ailments such as headaches, ringing in the ears, rheumatism, loss of sight and so on. The problem with 'inner flux' was that when fluids did not move, they became hard and viscous and began to stagnate. Treatments involved making sure that the 'flux' could escape from the body. Storch had two main treatments. One was to apply 'blister-raising plasters' which were designed to divert fluids so that they might be drawn out of the body. A second was 'fontanels', which were small artificial wounds through which the fluids could drain. Duden (1991: 132–3) cites the following example of the treatment of flux with a plaster:

> The wife of a shoemaker, forty years of age, 'has had an oozing and sometimes foul-smelling sore under the breast for many years. Having dried up in February 1721, it moved to an untoward place, namely to the genitals, *ad muliebra.*' The pains, especially when passing urine, were so intense that the woman tried to soothe them with cold washes. This bottled up the flux, upsetting the stomach and the guts, causing great anxiety in the stomach and the lower body. During the next years whenever the flux, having returned to its old place, dried up, she immediately requested help, 'for fear of dangerous ill effects'. Storch gave her sudorifics and a mustard plaster. She

> placed the plaster under her breast, it dissolved the skin, and already within an hour 'the flux could be lured out again, and the women soon felt . . . relief'.

The woman died thirteen years later, and the cause of death was this: after she had fallen down the cellar stairs, the flux under the breast subsided and failed to return, whereupon all the matter got stuck in her head.

Diseases and ailments associated with inner flux were usually caused by mishaps or emotional upsets. Anger, fright and delusions had a direct impact on the body, and the 'badness' which such experiences induced had to be expelled from it (Duden, 1991: 144–5). For example, if a woman had a quarrel with her husband, it would be as well that this should be followed by some form of bodily secretion. In this respect the experience of the body and the social environment were inextricably linked. As Duden (1991: 145) puts it, 'People were bound into social relations down to their inner-most flesh.'

What strikes Duden as remarkable is the very different bodily experiences of the early 1700s compared with those of today. Rather than treating Storch's work as a source of ideas that are now known to be incorrect, or that can be rationalized in relation to the prevailing medical ideas of the day, Duden argues that they provide us with an insight into the actual bodily experiences of the women living in a given time and place. When carrying out her research into these cases, she reflects how she began to question her own certainties about her own body, and that in order to undertake the work she had to shed many of her assumptions.

> The first step toward understanding the complaints of the women of Eisenach was therefore to realize that my own certainties about the body are a cultural bias, one which perhaps I would even learn to transcend. I had to create some distance to my own body, for it was clear that it cannot serve as a bridge to the past. (Duden, 1991: vii)

The way in which Duden experiences her own body is influenced by the ideas of human anatomy and physiology that were established by the end of the eighteenth century (Foucault, 1976). She is arguing also that the history of medical knowledge does not involve the gradual unfolding of the 'truth' about the body and disease, but that these categories are contingent on their social, cultural and historical context. In other words, they are socially constructed.

Social constructionism

The social constructionist debate, which is now considered to form a crucial perspective within the sociology of health and illness (Bury, 1986; Lupton, 2000; Conrad and Barker, 2010), emerged in the context of an increasingly critical sociology of health, illness and medicine. As we discussed in the previous chapter, the second half of the twentieth century saw a surge of criticisms of biomedicine and the assumptions inherent in medical practice in general. The values and activities of the medical profession were considered to be congruent with the patriarchal and capitalist society in which they were located. One aspect of medicine that came under particular critical scrutiny was that of psychiatry and the practice of hospitalizing people who were deemed to suffer from mental illness (Goffman, 1961; Rosenhan, 1973). From this there materialized an anti-psychiatry movement, which argued that much of mental illness was simply a social construction, created by psychiatrists who acted as powerful agents of social control (Ingleby, 1980). For example, labelling someone as schizophrenic enabled psychiatrists to deem that person unfit to participate fully in social life (Szasz, 1970). Thus the application of diagnostic categories was called into question, and the application of medical knowledge was acknowledged to be a political rather than a technically neutral enterprise.

The social constructionist debates surrounding psychiatry anticipated the more general application of such ideas to other forms of medicine. For instance, Freidson (1970a), when examining the profession of medicine, questioned the assumption on which doctors' autonomous, and so extremely powerful, position in society was based. For Freidson the key problem was the *application* of medical knowledge. Whilst medicine might be based on an objective science, the application of medical knowledge was not. By way of an analogy, he pointed out that the engineer might know how to build a road, but it does not follow that she or he should decide where to build it. So too with medical science; the doctor may know how to treat kidney failure, but decisions surrounding the use of the technological equipment should lie beyond the doctor's remit. Although Freidson focused on illness rather than disease, he was adamant that the medical profession's knowledge and evaluation of it was mediated by the social and political circumstances in which doctors practised. This placed them in a very powerful position, as they were able to define what counted as illness. He notes (Freidson, 1970a: 206) that 'by virtue of being the authority on what illness "really" is, medicine creates the social possibilities for acting sick'. Thus the medical profession does not only legitimate what counts as sickness, but is also able to create the very possibility of illness. Freidson's work has been immensely influential in the sociology of health and illness, not least for drawing attention to the inherently social nature of medical practice. However, whilst Freidson exposed the social values that interfered with the application of medical knowledge, he did not challenge the presumed scientific basis of that knowledge when it came to disease.

The social construction of everyday knowledge and reality was also the focus of phenomenological sociology popularized by Berger and Luckmann in the late 1960s. Berger and Luckmann (1967) argued that everyday knowledge is produced creatively by individuals and is oriented towards particular practical problems. 'Facts' are therefore created by way of social interactions and people's interpretations of these. From this perspective, to understand beliefs about disease, people's commonsense notions of it need to be examined. P. West (1979), for example, illustrates how epilepsy is the product of interactions between professionals and patients. Medical anthropologists also emphasize the constructed nature of knowledge, and argue that medical belief systems are like any other belief systems (Comaroff, 1982), in that they are culturally specific, and their content and practices are social in origin. Comaroff (1978: 247) wrote that Western medicine, like any other healing system, must be viewed 'as a problematic socio-cultural system whose substance cannot be taken for granted'. That medical knowledge has come to be widely accepted, she argues, can be assigned to its symbolic significance rather than its content. Thus medical belief systems should be treated as no different from, and no more legitimate than, religious belief systems (Young, 1980). Similarly, sociologists of science (Woolgar, 1988) have suggested that the scientific basis of medicine itself requires analysis.

Debates within social constructionism

Wright and Treacher (1982: 9) argue that 'social-constructionists begin by taking as problematic the very issues which appeared self-evident and uninteresting to earlier writers'. Constructionists are interested in issues such as the problematic nature of medical knowledge; the fact that medicine is based on a natural science, and has therefore become epistemologically privileged; that diseases are presumed to be natural entities; and the claim made by medicine that in order to advance it must distance itself from any social, and therefore 'unscientific', influences. The literature on social constructionism is diverse, but we might usefully examine it under six headings: the problematization of reality; the social creation of medical 'facts'; medical knowledge and the mediation of social relations; the application of technical knowledge; medicalization; and a sociology of diagnosis.

The problematization of reality

The problematization of reality implies that disease entities are not simply real but are products of social reasoning and social practices. To call a set of symptoms 'bronchitis' does not mean that a discrete disease exists as an entity independently of social context, but that this is how medical science, in a given time and place with the aid of laboratory tests and theories, has come to define it. To be sure, the bronchitis sufferer will experience pain and suffering, but the interpretation of it will vary between time and place. Thus, in a critical review of the approach, Bury (1986: 137) observes that constructionists contend that 'the objects of medical science are not what they appear to be; the stable realities of the human body and disease are in fact "fabrications", or "inventions" rather than discoveries'. Whilst 'discovery' would imply that the disease entity existed all along just waiting to be deciphered, the notion of 'fabrication', by contrast, implies that the disease was established through certain types of investigation that confirmed its reality. Likewise, the body itself, as was illustrated in the example above, must invariably be contingent on the prevailing descriptions of it. For example, reflecting on his medical training and subsequent work as a social-constructionist, Armstrong (1983a: xi) usefully notes:

> At first it seemed strange to me how the apparent obviousness of disease and its manifestations inside the body had eluded scientific discovery for so long. How had pre-Enlightenment generations failed to see the clearly differentiated organs and tissues of the body? Or failed to link patient symptoms with the existence of localised pathological processes? Or failed to apply the most rudimentary diagnostic techniques of physical examination? My disbelief grew until it occurred to me that perhaps I was asking the wrong questions: the problem was not how something which is so obvious today had remained hidden for so long, but how the body had become so evident in the first place. In dissecting and examining bodies I had come to take for granted that what I saw was obvious. I had thought that medical knowledge simply described the body . . . [however] . . . the relationship is more complex . . . medical knowledge both describes and constructs the body as an invariate biological reality.

Studies comparing modern anatomical drawings with those from the Middle Ages have found that they reflect prevailing world-views: whilst the early drawings were found to represent energy and vitalism, those from more recent times depicted the body as a mechanical object (Fleck, 1935a). Indeed, the structures and functioning of the anatomy are often understood in ways that mirror ideas about the wider society and economy (Martin, 1989).

The social creation of medical 'facts'

If medicine's prime objects - disease and the body - are not 'stable realities', then how are ideas about them created? In this section we will consider two responses to this question: first, the argument that all scientific 'facts' about the world are products of the scientific communities from which they emerge, and second, that our presumed stable realities are in fact realized within variable discursive contexts. The first response focuses on work within the sociology of science, and the second on ideas which have been influenced by Michel Foucault.

Sociologists of science have argued that scientific 'facts' are the product of social processes, and that such ideas are contingent upon the scientific communities (Kuhn, 1962), or 'thought collectives' (Fleck, 1935b; Lowy, 1988) which produce them. Within a given 'thought collective', Fleck argues, new incumbents are trained how to see and interpret what they are looking at. For instance, within the context of the medical school, Atkinson (1981, 1988) has described how students, on clinical ward rounds, are coached into interpreting the signs and symptoms of disease. By way of an ethnomethodological study, Atkinson (1988: 200) reveals how biomedical knowledge is 'socially accomplished', and how it is achieved through the interactions between teachers, students and patients.

Similarly, within what might seem like the more 'objective' context of the scientific laboratory, Atkinson (2002) carried out an ethnography of haematologists in both the UK and the USA. Haematologists, like many medical specialists, use various imaging technologies (e.g., ultrasound, magnetic resonance imaging (MRI) and x-rays) in their routine practice to scrutinize the inner frame of the body. Atkinson observed how these specialists went about examining blood samples that were sent to their laboratories for investigation. His analysis of their activities reveals the way in which the haematologists interpret their observations of blood samples, and how they are 'schooled' in ways of seeing. 'Seeing is not straightforward' (2002: 22), Atkinson notes, because 'there is nothing natural about the haematologists' or pathologists' descriptions, and nothing given about the descriptive categories or their use. On the contrary, the language of the pathological gaze is, like any other specialized register, a socially shared collection of conventions' (2002: 24). Novice pathologists and haematologists are taught how to look for certain shapes, images and fragments, the shape, size and colour of which are not readily obvious to the untutored eye. In fact, what is actually seen is debated, discussed and negotiated even between trained clinicians.

According to Kuhn (1962), scientists work within dominant paradigms, or frameworks of knowledge, which comprise an accepted set of concepts and theories about the world. For example, as we have seen in chapter 1, the dominant medical paradigm within contemporary industrial societies is that of biomedicine. Significant changes in scientific knowledge occur only when the beliefs of a given scientific community can no longer be explained within the existing paradigm. If this occurs, there is a 'scientific revolution', and a new framework of knowledge comes into being. As one paradigm replaces another, the displaced ideas and theories are said to be 'incommensurable' with the new ones. This means that the most recent ideas are correct and that the 'old' beliefs are taken to be outmoded and false. Similarly, if scientists are concurrently working within different paradigms, they are unable to communicate with each other, as they see the world from fundamentally different perspectives. It is for this reason that ideas about disease and healing which fall outside the dominant medical paradigm are treated as bizarre and may be rejected. For example, experiments on homoeopathy have been treated with ridicule because homoeopathic treatments cannot possibly be explained within the conventional medical paradigm, and so, if they are effective, this is put down to good luck (Davenas et al., 1988; Vines, 1988).

Fleck (1935b), however, has shown that these thought styles are not necessarily wholly resistant to more 'popular' ideas about disease. To illustrate this point, he tells the story of the development of a blood test – the Wassermann serological test – which was developed for the diagnosis of syphilis. He argued that scientists persisted with the idea that syphilis could be diagnosed by a blood test because, beyond the scientific community, there was a popular notion of 'syphilitic blood'. Thus, as Lowy (1988: 147) explains, 'In this way the old popular idea of "syphilitic blood" when transposed to a new thought collective – bacteriologists and immunologists – allowed the development of an important innovation: the Wassermann test.'

The interaction of 'popular' and scientifically acceptable ideas in medicine has increasingly been acknowledged (Herzlich and Pierret, 1987; Brown and Zavestoski, 2004). Thus the emergence of scientific facts is related to both the scientific community and the social context in which the community resides. This may also be linked to the social interests of the scientists themselves. For example, C. Lawrence (1979: 20) revealed how eighteenth-century Scottish medical thought, with its unique and influential emphasis on the 'nervous system', was attributable to 'the social interests and the self-perceptions of the improving landed class that came to dominate Scottish culture'. Bartley (1992) has suggested that in contemporary society, professional and technical interests are likely to be of greater significance in the development of scientific ideas. Technical interests are the interests 'of occupational subgroups in creating a continuing market for the specific techniques and forms of expertise of which they can claim "ownership" ' (Bartley, 1990: 372). Scientific developments may therefore be linked to their marketability, rather than to the results of objective experiment. This is increasingly recognized as the pace of innovation in medical technologies has accelerated (see chapter 8). Thus it is argued that a sociology of medical knowledge must not merely consider the socio-economic context in which knowledge is created, but must also examine the communities in which it is embedded.

A second approach to examining the social creation of medical 'facts' is that of *discourse analysis*; that is, the claim that medicine's objects are created through the language and practices which surround them. This approach is neatly summarized by Prior (1989: 3) in his study of the discourses surrounding death:

> familiar objects of the social world (whether they be death, disease, madness, sexuality, sin or even mankind itself) are . . . realized only in and through the discursive elements which surround the objects in question. . . . As the discourse changes, so too do the objects of attention. A discourse, moreover, is not merely a narrow set of linguistic practices which reports on the world, but is composed of a whole assemblage of activities, events, objects, settings and epistemological precepts. The

> discourse of pathology, for example, is constructed not merely out of statements about diseases, cells and tissues, but out of the whole network of activities and events in which pathologists become involved, together with the laboratory and the other settings within which they work and in which they analyse the objects of their attention.

This notion of discourse was developed by Foucault (1976) in his study of medicine. He found that it was within the discursive practices of eighteenth-century medicine in Paris that our contemporary notion of disease was developed. At this time, teaching, research, treatment and observation all took place for the first time in the hospital. The body was the prime focus of these medical activities, and came to be the main site of disease. Thus, within the discourse of what came to be called 'pathological medicine', disease was formulated as a discrete phenomenon which was located in the workings of the bodily structures. This conceptualization of disease within the anatomy was the product of what Foucault called the *gaze*. The gaze implies a 'way of seeing', or indeed smelling and/or touching; it was through the medical gaze that things became visible to the doctor, and, once seen, an object formulated as a discrete entity could be observed and analysed. The medical gaze, however, is not a static way of looking; on the contrary, its flexibility constantly permits new objects to come into view. For example, contemporary medicine is increasingly taking patients' interpretations and their experiences of their symptoms into account, rather than just focusing on their anatomy and physiology (Armstrong, 1984; Arney and Bergen, 1984; Nettleton, 1992).

Thus we can see that this approach, which we might call the *Foucauldian approach*, has argued that the body, disease and contemporary medical discourse are inseparable. Disease came to be located within the body around the time of the French Revolution, when a specific notion of disease emerged alongside the development of pathological anatomy. Consequently, the biological basis of disease, which, as we have seen, was for so long presumed to be unequivocal and therefore beyond the scope of the sociology of health and illness, has now become central to the discipline. Just as Foucault described how the pathological basis of disease came about in the eighteenth century, so, more recently, Foucauldians (Armstrong, 1983a; Arney and Bergen, 1984) have argued that since the Second World War, Western medicine has been undergoing another 'revolution', in that disease is now located not merely in the anatomy but in the body of a 'person', which invariably resides within a wider social context.

Medical knowledge and the mediation of social relations

A third dimension of the social-constructionist debate is the proposition that medical knowledge mediates social relations. Disease categories may be applied to reinforce existing social structures, and their application may give social relations the appearance of being 'natural', in that the language of disease is assumed to be objective, and so its social origins become invisible (Taussig, 1980). For example, women in the nineteenth century who wanted to further their education were sometimes labelled as suffering from hysteria (Smith-Rosenberg, 1984), and Figlio (1982) found that a condition suffered by coal miners towards the end of the nineteenth century, called 'miners' nystagmus', was the product of debates and compromises that were struck between employers, employees, insurance companies, doctors and lawyers. Similarly Bloor (2000) describes how miners in South Wales adopted a number of political and legal strategies to influence the establishment of a disease called pneumoconiosis (miners' lung) which the miners, in the 1920s and 1930s, maintained was caused by exposure to silica in coal mines. The miners succeeded in transforming their 'local knowledge' or 'lay epidemiology' (see chapter 3) into scientific orthodoxy by working with, paying and in some cases even duping scientists. Furthermore, they did not simply accept scientific claims of the time, but they were instrumental in shaping their content. Thus disease categories are not simply a product of scientific analysis, but also the outcome of social and political struggles.

This mediation of social relations by medical knowledge is nowhere more evident than in the analysis of gender relations in the nineteenth century. For example, Shuttleworth (1990) has shown how doctors linked aberrations in the menstrual flow to mental disorder. Her examination of nineteenth-century medical discourse revealed that:

> The fashionable diseases of mid-nineteenth-century England were . . . marked by a crucial gender distinction: While male health was believed to be based on self-control, women's health depended on her very *inability* to control her body. Any exertion of the mind, whether of intellectual effort, or fierce emotion, might prove fatal, it was suggested in creating a stoppage of menstrual flow. Women should therefore concentrate on dulling the mind, allowing the processes of their body to proceed unimpeded by mental obstruction. (Shuttleworth, 1990: 57)

From perspectives such as this it is perhaps no surprise that during the nineteenth century medicine developed a whole set of theories and diseases associated with sexuality and reproduction. It was during this period that the private and public domains were being relentlessly policed, and that women's demands for equality, for example through the suffrage movement, were being openly condemned. The use of medical knowledge and its application to women's health and illness are not, however, limited to the nineteenth century. Medical practitioners still use their position to reinforce traditional family values (Porter, 1990: 201–2) and depoliticize the causes of illness by providing technical solutions to problems such as depression (N. Crossley, 2003), which, or so it is argued, are in reality social in origin (Brown and Harris, 1978).

As Bury (1986: 143) notes, medical knowledge may also be 'seen to mediate *changing* social relations'. For instance, Jewson (1976) proposed the thesis that the content of medical knowledge has been variously determined by those who control its means of production. From the eighteenth century, he argues, this control has shifted from the patient to the hospital doctor, and then to the medical scientist. Jewson identified three types of 'medical cosmology' (that is, 'the essential universe of medical discourse') which are linked to the social organization of medical practice. The first cosmology, from the 1770s to 1800s, was *bedside medicine*, wherein the doctor had a close interpersonal relationship with his or her client, who, being the doctor's patron, exerted considerable influence on the doctor's theories of disease. Thus at this time medical knowledge tended to be heterogeneous as doctors developed their own styles to suit their paying clients. The second cosmology, from the 1800s to the 1840s, was *hospital medicine*, wherein patients were located in the hospital. This meant that doctors, rather than patients, took charge, and a coherent theory of disease based on the localization of pathology was developed. Finally, from the 1840s to the 1870s, medical knowledge was developed within *laboratory medicine*, wherein scientists controlled the mode of knowledge production.

Throughout the twentieth century the production of medical knowledge seeped out of the laboratory and was generated in a range of more diffuse settings within the community. The collation of data on the health and illness of populations by way of epidemiological studies, surveys and so on formed part of what Armstrong (2002) has termed *surveillance medicine* (see chapter 5). Within this context epidemiologists figured prominently in the production of clinical knowledge, which largely focused on risks to health. It has been suggested more recently – albeit tentatively – that a new medical cosmology is being forged, one which I (Nettleton, 2004) call 'e-scaped medicine'. I argue that there is an affinity between the socio-technological changes and this new medical cosmology. This contention is informed by the work of the philosopher De Mul (1999), who argues that the advent of new information and communication technologies (ICTs) not only alters the material reality of what is possible in medical science, but also alters our perception and interpretation of reality – our world-view. The dominant metaphor of the body in the twentieth century was the 'machine', but this is now being replaced by a metaphor of 'information' (Fox Keller, 1995; Martin, 1994; Birke, 1999). These five medical cosmologies are summarized in table 2.1. We revisit the idea that medicine is being 'informaticized' in more detail in chapter 10.

Jewson's thesis, published in 1976, was pivotal in that it challenged the idea that medical knowledge is merely a description of disease; instead he proposed that medical knowledge constructs disease. This is because the processes of production of medical knowledge are permeated by social relations between patients, practitioners and other parties who have interests in what counts as medical knowledge (Nicholson, 2009; Prior, 2009). As such, medical knowledge and practices may be used to reproduce and reinforce existing social structures and values. The relationship between social relations and disease works in two ways: social relations contribute to the creation of diseases, and the language of disease, which is presumed to be 'natural', serves to conceal the nature of social relations – a process of reification (Taussig, 1980).

The application of technical knowledge

A fourth strand of the social-constructionist debate extends Freidson's (1970a) arguments about the application of medical knowledge and techniques. One variant of this approach is that the medical profession achieved its dominant position within the health care division of labour not because of its inherently superior expertise, but because it has managed to create and maintain the control over certain technological procedures and practices. The demarcation of medical tasks in relation to those of other health workers has been set by the dominant profession (Willis, 1990). This is perhaps nowhere more evident than in the history of midwifery. Donnison (1977), for example, has shown how the development of forceps was crucial to the medical profession gaining the upper hand. Forceps, introduced around the 1720s, could

Table 2.1 *Medical cosmologies: an extension of Jewson's (1976) diagram*

Cosmology	*Patron*	*Occupational role of investigator*	*Source of Patronage*	*Perception of 'sick man' (sic)*	*Task of medical investigator*	*Conceptualization of illness*
Bedside	Patient	Practitioner	Private fees	Person	Prognosis and therapy	Total psycho-somatic disturbance
Hospital	State-Hospital	Clinician	Professional career	Case	Diagnosis and classification	Organic lesion
Laboratory	State-Academy	Scientist	Scientific career structure	Cell complex	Analysis and explanation	Biochemical process
Surveillance	State-Academy	Epidemiologist	Professional career structure	Risk assemblage	Convert epidemiological risk to clinical risk	Latent, deviation from norm
E-scaped	State-Academy, Consumer	Information scientists	Professional career structure Commerce	Expert patient Health seekers	Assessment and communication of risks; and assessment of research evidence	Communications breakdown, interaction of systems

Source: Nettleton (2004: 675).

be used only by medically trained male practitioners. Thus, if deliveries presented problems, the medical profession came to insist that midwives should seek out a medically trained practitioner, who, with the aid of technology, could take responsibility for the birth. This set the agenda for things to come, and it is argued by some that doctors control the medical technology that surrounds childbirth in hospital, which in turn ensures that they can limit the role of the midwife (Versluysen, 1981; Garcia et al., 1990). Thus medical technology is imbued with, and cannot stand outside, social relations.

An alternative and more nuanced analysis of the application of technical knowledge presumes that medical technologies do not stand separate to medical work but are embedded in medical practice. This is vividly illustrated in an article by the German sociologist Schubert (2011) who adopts a 'micro-sociological approach for studying the interrelations of bodies, tools and knowledge in medical diagnosis' (p. 856). Informed by the pragmatism and phenomenology developed by the social philosophers Dewey and Heidegger respectively, Schubert conceptualizes clinical diagnosis - core medical work - as a series of ongoing practical judgements that combine technological and interpretive processes. By this he means that diagnostic instruments mesh with doctor's 'perceptual habits' and in effect become embodied. From this perspective, diagnostic tools do not replace clinical judgement or doctors' skills, but instead they become incorporated into medical work giving rise to new contingencies, skills and knowledge. Thus instruments are neither neutral nor autonomous but are transformative agents of change.

Take the invention of the stethoscope, for example. There is a received view in sociology (after Jewson, 1976; see above) that its use served to undermine the doctor–patient relationship, because doctors attended to their patients' bodies looking for objective signs to the relative neglect of patients' accounts of their subjective symptoms. 'Typically, this story is as one of a growing distance between physician and patient, with the stethoscope effectively creating a barrier between the two' (p. 853). Schubert, however, maintains that the use or application of the stethoscope fused the 'bodies of the physician and the patient into a new diagnostic ensemble' (p. 853). Rather than displacing the doctor's sensory skills, the stethoscope requires a 'trained ear' and an ability to interpret the sounds heard within the body. Auscultation also generates the need for a shared terminology in order to describe and classify rales heard in the lungs. Thus diagnostic instruments and technological devices are generative of new embodied skills and forms of knowledge which are invariably open to interpretation and are accompanied by ambiguity and uncertainty and so certainty is an ongoing activity created through practices of 'making sure' (p. 853).

Schubert goes on to demonstrate this fusion between technologies, bodies and knowledge in relation to the contemporary use of mechanical ventilation, used by anaesthetists to control breathing and relax muscles during surgical operations. Mechanical ventilation can be achieved by either manual or automatic devices, with the former always being used at the beginning and end of operations. But Schubert also shows that there is variation in the use of manual and automatic devices between practitioners and places. Drawing on data from an extensive ethnography of anaesthetists undertaken in Germany and Australia, he finds that more experienced anaesthetists, working in smaller, rural hospitals prefer to use manual devices (where the air is controlled by hand), whereas their more junior colleagues and those working in urban teaching hospitals prefer to rely more on automatic instruments. More 'experienced doctors seem to prefer direct observation and rely on their embodied skills to a greater extent than novices' (p. 855). Thus medical knowledge is a continual ongoing accomplishment that is produced through the interplay between technical procedures and those who apply, use and interpret them. The device may produce a knowledge of the body of the patient but it is only meaningful when read by those trained to understand them. We explore this issue of technology in practice in more detail in chapter 9. Medical success is not determined by technological advances, but rather is the outcome of the socio-political struggles that surround technology and its application. The controversial nature of the application of medicine is further debated by the proponents of the medicalization thesis.

Medicalization

The medicalization thesis is perhaps related only indirectly to social constructionism, in that it does not question the basis of medical knowledge as such, but challenges its application. The drivers of medicalization have shifted in the last fifty years. The early proponents of this thesis were keen to draw attention to the ways in which medicine operated as a powerful institution of social control. It does so by claiming expertise about areas of life which had previously not been regarded as medical matters, areas such as ageing, childbirth, alcohol consumption and childhood behaviour (Conrad and Schneider, 1980; Conrad, 1997). Thus it constructs, or redefines, aspects of normal life as medical problems. As Zola (1972: 487) put it, 'medicine is becoming a major institution of social control, nudging aside, if not incorporating, the more traditional institutions of religion and the law'. He relates the medicalization process to wider changes, in particular to 'our increasingly complex and bureaucratic system' (1972: 500) which encourages an ever greater reliance on experts. This dependence upon medical expertise strips ordinary people of their abilities to cope with their own problems (Illich, 1976).

Medicalization combines phenomenological and Marxist approaches to health and illness (Conrad and Schneider, 1980), in that it considers definitions of illness to be products of social interactions or negotiations which are inherently unequal. In other words, people do not have equal power and influence when it comes to the social construction of reality. Professionals are invariably more able than lay people to define what counts as sickness. This means that the scope for social regulation is considerable, because if matters come to be defined as medical concerns, health professionals have the authority to monitor, intervene and pass judgements upon them.

It is in relation to childbirth that the concept of medicalization has been most fully developed (see Kent, 2000 and chapter 6 of this text). Indeed, as we have already seen, the control of pregnancy and childbirth has been taken over by a predominantly male medical profession. Childbirth is surrounded by a whole array of medical technologies, and women are closely monitored from the acknowledgement of conception until after the baby is born. Because childbirth is defined as a 'medical problem', it becomes conceptualized in terms of clinical safety, and women are encouraged to have their babies in hospital. There is a dissonance between women's experiences and the culture of the medical system which defines the meaning of childbirth.

However, the evidence now suggests that in many instances women would have been safer giving birth at home. There they would have been less susceptible to infection and technological interference (Oakley, 1984; Tew, 1990). Thus the medicalization thesis argues that professionals tend to offer biomedical or technical solutions to what are inherently 'normal' aspects of everyday life or social problems. However, there is a paradox here, because while the thesis suggests that the wider socio-psychological context of illness must be taken into account by health professionals, if the latter do take them into account, they are then accused of medicalizing more aspects of social life (Doyal with Pennel, 1979). Thus a more humane medicine may, at the same time, be one which involves more extensive social regulation.

Conrad, one of the initial proponents of this thesis, has argued that the drivers of medicalization have changed (Conrad, 2007). It is not so much the medical profession that determines what counts as disease, but pharmaceutical and biotechnology industries whose international markets and global scale mean that they are able to wield considerable economic and political power. Writing with Barker, Conrad summarizes his position thus:

> the engines of medicalization have expanded beyond medical professionals, social movements, and organizations to biotechnology, consumers, and the insurance industry. There is increasing evidence that commercial aspects of medicine, especially the pharmaceutical industry, are increasingly important in the shaping and disseminating of medical knowledge to promote their products. (Conrad and Barker, 2010: S74)

The pharmaceutical industries develop drugs for common conditions, undertake research to explore the prevalence of symptoms and conditions, develop products and generate 'needs' and wants. Although critics and activists have drawn attention to the way profits may be prioritized over patients – there are few signs of any effective resistance. Busfield (2010) has argued that this may be because doctors, patients and the public tend to be complicit in these processes. Doctors invariably want to be able to treat their patients and so all too readily prescribe medicines, and patients invariably seek treatments to help them get better. Governments and insurance companies, by contrast, have an interest in limiting the use of drugs not least because of the drain on budgets. There are statutory regulations in most countries with which the industry must comply, but the situation is politically complex. Pharmaceutical industries are also major employers, who generate profits, pay taxes and contribute to a nation's GDP. Thus Busfield (2010) points out there are very few 'countervailing powers' that could challenge the activities of what is sometimes referred to as 'big pharma'. A consequence is that global corporations have successfully encouraged people to see their socio-psychological difficulties in biomedical terms. Shyness (Scott, 2006), lack of sexual desire (Hartley, 2006), sleep (Williams, 2011) and sadness (Horwitz and Wakefield, 2007) are just a few of the aspects of ordinary everyday life that have been reconceptualized as medical problems for which pharmaceutical treatments have been developed. This is what Moynihan and Cassels (2005) refer to as 'disease mongering', the way drug companies work to identify symptoms that come to be labelled as disease or illness. Socio-political processes are implicated in the creation and consolidation of medical diagnosis.

Sociology of diagnosis

At the heart of medical work is the act determining what is wrong with the patient and giving symptoms a label - a diagnosis. Thus a diagnosis is both a category and a process and is 'central to the practice of medicine' (Blaxter, 1978: 10). Within the context of Western biomedicine, a diagnosis: validates what counts as disease, offers explanations and coheres patients' symptoms, legitimates illness enabling patients to access the sick role, provides a means to access resources and facilitates their allocation, and forms the foundation of medical authority. Such is the importance of medical diagnosis to medical knowledge a number of authors (Brown, 1995; Jutel, 2009, 2011; Jutel and Nettleton, 2011) have argued that a sociology of diagnosis should exist as a separate field of study in and of itself alongside the sociology of health and illness. A sociology of diagnosis would involve the examination of the social basis of diagnostic categories and diseases, the process of diagnosing and the consequences for both practitioners and patients of applying a diagnosis (Jutel and Nettleton, 2011). All three dimensions - category, process and consequence - are permeated by social, political, technological, cultural and economic factors. A diagnosis is therefore a social creation and a disease category is a classification which has to be agreed upon. Western medicine has many classification schemas for illness, disability and disease, but two internationally established documents that index diseases have dominated medical work for over a century. These are the International Statistical Classification of Diseases and Related Health Problems (ICD), published by the World Health Organization, and the Diagnostic and Statistical Manual of Mental Disorders (DSM). The sociologists Bowker and Star (1999) took the ICD as one of a number of illustrative examples to demonstrate the social functioning and political origins of formal classifications and 'information infrastructures'. It was used as a means of collating, monitoring and managing epidemics and health of populations within and between states. Although contested in some countries and settings, these schema are authoritative and form the basis of the collation of morbidity and mortality statistics, medical training, diagnostic practice and so on. Having gone through many revisions throughout the twentieth century, they are still regularly updated. This reminds us of the fluidity and variability of medical categories - diseases and medical diagnoses come and go. For example, fifty years ago AIDS did not exist, during the 1970s and 1980s there was much negotiation as to the existence, cause and prevalence of the condition, but today it is accepted as an acquired immune deficiency resulting from the human immunodeficiency virus (HIV); an interesting case of a condition that came to be identified as a result of negotiations between, amongst others, political agitators, epidemiologists and immunologists (Berridge, 1996).

Criticisms of social constructionism

Social constructionism is diametrically opposed to the empiricism which forms the basis of medical science (Taylor and Ashworth, 1987), in that whilst constructionists maintain that it is through our ideas and paradigms that we come to understand reality, empiricists (and most medical scientists) maintain that we look at real objects and then develop our descriptions of them. For constructionists to understand what constitutes a specific disease, they have to examine the discourses that surround it, whereas an empiricist, and indeed a medical practitioner, would want to observe the biological manifestations of the disease itself. However, as we can see from our discussion of the various strands of constructionism within the sociology of health and illness, there are some accounts which accept the existence of external realities and others which do not. Thus constructionism is not a unified perspective, and there are differences within the general approach. For example, what we might call 'radical constructionism' denies the pre-existence of a biological base; this is the position taken by Armstrong (1983a: 2), who suggests that: 'The fact that the body became legible does not imply that some invariate biological reality was finally revealed to medical enquiry. The body was only legible in that there existed in the new clinical techniques a language by which it could be read.' Most sociologists, however, prefer to presume the existence of an external reality, and argue that there are variable accounts of it. This position is summed up by Lock (1988: 7), who seeks to

> demonstrate . . . the social and cultural character of *all* medical knowledge, but . . . there is, of course, a biological reality, but the moment that efforts are made to explain, order, and manipulate that reality, then a process of contextualization takes place in which the dynamic relationship of biology with cultural values and the social order has to be considered.

This latter position is more closely akin to *realism* (Bhaskar, 1979; Taylor and Ashworth, 1987; Sayer, 1992). However, a realist approach would draw attention to the limitations of constructionism, in that the latter fails to acknowledge the real or concrete effects of biological, social and physical mechanisms. Realists point out that there is a valid distinction between the real world and descriptions of it. They argue, further, that there are explanations which have varying degrees of adequacy, and that those that are the most adequate are those which have clearly recognizable effects. For example, the notion that humans cannot walk on water is an adequate explanation because its effects are obvious. The realist charge against constructionism has further implications for political debates about health and illness. For example, data gathered on class and health status suggest that there is a relationship between the two, and the adequacy of the explanation is evident from the real effects that class location has on people's bodies (see chapter 7). It is therefore argued that constructionists who would see these effects merely as artefacts of epidemiological techniques undermine the validity of people's experiences as well as attempts to challenge the political circumstances which reinforce inequalities.

Most students reading this chapter will probably have already noted that there is a further predicament inherent in the logic of social constructionism. This relates to the fact that the approach argues that all knowledge is socially relative. This of course has implications for the approach itself. If *all* knowledge, and not just medical knowledge, is contingent, then how can the constructionist view have any validity? This is referred to as the problem of *relativism*. Bury (1986: 151–2) argues that this is an insurmountable problem, and suggests that, because of the 'denial of an independent court of appeal to rationality or scientific method', social constructionists face the irretrievable danger of falling into the 'abyss of relativism'. Gabbay (1982) also acknowledges this difficulty, and through his study of the social construction of asthma, which demonstrates that knowledge of the disease is linked to social and political circumstances, finds that it is impossible to 'disprove' the traditional view of medicine, which, he notes, maintains that the application of rigorous scientific principles will yield a timeless, objective and factual knowledge. Thus the dilemma is not resolved, and so Gabbay (1982: 43) suggests:

> We are faced with the choice between either abandoning our insights because we cannot prove them, or suspending the requirement of proof as inappropriate and scientistic. Our choice will clearly depend on our initial prejudice: those who adhere to the traditional view of medicine will as an article of faith . . . mistrust the unprovable. Those who are prepared to allow the unprovable any validity at all, must be increasingly compelled by it to examine the traditional view.

The argument that all knowledge is socially contingent is not the same as the statement that all knowledge is worthless; rather, it attempts to gain an alternative understanding as to how knowledge is created.

A further, not unrelated criticism of social constructionism is that it undermines the possibility of progress and crucially may not contribute to the advancement of human health. If there are no clear-cut criteria by which developments in medical science or health care interventions can be assessed, then how can we make judgements about the relative merits of therapeutic interventions? If we refuse to accept the validity of any measures of health improvement or engage with the realities of disease, then as sociologists we cannot make any kind of contribution to quality of life or the improvement of human health. Critiques of the constructionist perspectives also point to medicine's achievements, such as the eradication of smallpox, and argue that these are surely sufficient evidence to confirm the validity of scientific knowledge and practice. This is a persuasive and important criticism. Timmermans and Haas (2008) eloquently argue that the sociology of health and illness should expand to include a 'sociology of disease'. Critical of the way in which sociologists 'tirelessly denounce the "construction" of factual knowledges' and marginalize disease, they propose that sociologists integrate biological and physiological dimensions with the social. For example, in order to explore how social life impacts upon the body, sociological studies could usefully incorporate health outcomes and biomarkers and clinical measures. They even go so far as to suggest that training in medical sociology might usefully include developing knowledge of and expertise in physiology and anatomy. Social constructionism has led to scepticism and critique, to such an extent that sociologists of health and illness fail to recognize the contributions that medicine can and does make to human health (Timmermans and Haas, 2008).

Finally, critics suggest that processes of medicalization have been exaggerated and have taken exception to its conspiratorial overtones (Bury, 1986). For example, empirical studies have found that claims that women have been duped by the medical profession into becoming dependent upon medical technology are not borne out in practice (Riessmann, 1983; Calnan, 1984a). Studies of tranquillizer use also demonstrate that not all doctors think and act in ways which perpetuate the dominant ideology, and that women and working-class patients do not accept all that doctors tell them (Gabe and Calnan, 1989). Thus it is suggested that claims of medicalization underestimate people's, especially women's, ability to resist medical ideas and still rely on their own knowledge and experiences.

Whilst it is overly simplistic to suggest that people passively accept the translation of aspects of their lives into medical problems, it is nevertheless also the case that more and more facets of life are conceptualized in relation to health and illness. For example, our lifestyles – what we eat and drink, the amount we exercise, our levels of stress – are increasingly thought of in these terms (see chapter 3). This, however, may be as much to do with the commercialization and commodification of health as with the dominance of the medical profession.

Implications for medical practice and health care

Thus far in this chapter we have seen that medical knowledge is socially created, and that some authors have argued that what are presumed to be pre-existent realities are inextricably bound to social and discursive contexts. These debates have therefore challenged some of our cherished assumptions about medicine, professions and health care. The basis of the medical profession's power is questioned, the importance of biomedical treatments in relation to other forms of healing within Western health care systems may be doubted, and critical appraisals of the social consequences of medicine's contribution to social regulation are encouraged.

The power and status of the professions are linked to claims of expert knowledge. Professional registers (for example, the medical register established with the Medical Act of 1858) are used to ensure that only those people with professionally recognized training are able to practise. The constructionist approach, through its assessment of the legitimacy of knowledge claims, therefore questions the basis of professional boundaries, which are revealed to be the products of socio-political struggles. Wright (1979), for example, in a study of the relative fates of medicine and astrology in the eighteenth century, found that medicine succeeded where astrology failed, because the ideological assumptions and practices on which medicine was founded were congruent with the emerging ideologies of capitalism, whereas those of astrology were not.

Biomedical innovation and the establishment of the medical profession occurred in parallel, and traditional historiography 'has assumed a more intimate relationship, arguing that new science and increased competence brought professional recognition and status' (Shortt, 1983: 54). Thus Shortt argues that what is of importance is the manner in which medicine is used, rather than its content. Doctors presented themselves as exemplars of science, and this helped their profession:

> If medicine's science produced few cures, it did suggest satisfying explanations which, in their apparent objectivity, transcended time, place, and class. When, as in the case of medical attitudes towards birth control, these explanations confirmed traditional social values, their popular appeal was assured. It was within the context of this pervasive paradigm of natural knowledge that biomedical innovation contributed to the professionalization of medicine. (Shortt, 1983: 68)

Science was therefore a resource which the medical profession was able to mobilize in order to convince the public and the state that they were the only occupation capable of providing safe and effective ways of healing. That they were capable of being so convincing was not a function of the content of medical science itself but an effect of the socio-political strategies which they employed to achieve state recognition (see chapter 8).

It is not that an increasingly scientific knowledge of natural objects leads to the acceptance of a profession, but rather that the activities of an occupational group are able to confirm the 'reality' of their objects. As Arney (1982: 19) has shown, the profession of obstetrics 'did not result from technological imperatives or the accumulation of scientific advances', but was 'a strategic success'. Once obstetrics had achieved its strong position in relation to midwives, it was able to extend its scope and practice through the techniques of monitoring and surveillance. Whilst in the nineteenth century obstetricians were concerned only with 'problem' births, increasingly throughout the twentieth century, all births were reconceptualized as *potentially* problematic. They were thus established through the use of monitoring procedures (such as electronic foetal monitors). As Arney (1982: 100) explains:

> Monitoring allows the profession to extend the obstetrical project out into the community and into every aspect of every woman's life. Power and control are magnified by making the object of control more visible and accessible, more 'known' through multiple monitoring schemes. After the monitoring concept was in place, obstetrics did not need to confine itself to the abnormal or potentially pathological birth; every birth became subject to its gaze.

Similarly, a study of dentistry (Nettleton, 1992) demonstrates how the dental profession established its object - teeth which had the potential for decay - through its alliance with public health, which, in turn, helped it to justify the need for the monitoring of people's mouths to ensure the prevention of infectious diseases. The dental examination, which involved the assessment and comparison of mouths, served to establish the 'normal' mouth, with which all others could be compared. Thus it was these extensive prevention routines that confirmed the dental object and thereby the emergence of the dental profession rather than it simply developing as a specialist sub-branch of surgery.

The social-constructionist literature resonates with wider critiques of medicine (see chapter 1), in that it questions the foundations and credibility of medical science and so elevates the relative status of other forms of knowledge. For example, knowledge derived from personal experiences of health and illness may gain a wider validity. It also has pragmatic consequences for the activities of health care professionals, whose practices have been subject to ever closer evaluations and assessments over the last decade. Furthermore, if these constructionist ideas are taken at all seriously, there may be consequences for professional identities. Indeed, among professionals themselves a lack of confidence in biomedicine is increasingly being acknowledged. Thus the constructionist debate is both fuelled by, and contributes to, the wider social context of health and health care. That is a social context which is increasingly being defined as postmodern.

Conclusion: social constructionism and postmodernism

It could be argued that the need, or search for, absolute truths has become a spurious exercise within a postmodern society. Indeed, the search for truth which was grounded in rational science is a fundamentally modernist project. Whilst there is an abundance of literature which attempts to set out the parameters of postmodernism (Featherstone, 1991a; Smart, 1992), it may be useful to conclude this chapter by introducing some of its key characteristics, and briefly examining the extent to which social constructionism can be viewed as a component of it.

First, postmodernism represents a break with modernism, denying any single truth or reality and emphasizing the coexistence of multiple realities. Second, there is a loss of faith in a single, coherent, unified, linear and progressive account of the past. Instead of a legitimate 'history', there are many histories, which, in turn, tend to focus less on significant events and more on the mundane aspects of everyday life. There is a demise of the meta-narrative (for example, Weber's account of rationalization) and an emphasis on particularity, discontinuity and difference. Third, there is a breakdown of hierarchies of knowledge, with the effect that the status of the 'expert' is undermined and the ideas and outcomes of the non-expert are treated as having equal validity. Distinctions between elite and mass cultures, between intellectual figures and figures in popular culture, between medical experts and ordinary people, thereby become less clear-cut.

It follows that social constructionism can be characterized as postmodernist for at least three reasons. First, it denies the existence of truth and the possibility of finding a single valid account of disease and the body. Second, it takes issue with traditional histories of medicine, which have told a story of progress which has led to an increasingly valid knowledge of disease. Social constructionism, on the other hand, takes an eclectic approach: it presents a series of specific and discontinuous arguments, and does not attempt to offer a single unified account of knowledge. Third, this has implications for relationships between presumed medical 'experts' and lay people. All accounts and types of knowledge, whether based on experiential knowledge or on rational science, have a validity. It is to the accounts of lay people, for so long treated as 'inferior' to medical professionals, that we now turn.

FURTHER READING

Armstrong, D. (1983), *Political Anatomy of the Body: Medical Knowledge in Britain in the Twentieth Century*, Cambridge: Cambridge University Press. A Foucauldian inspired account of the construction of medical knowledge in the UK.

Bowker, G. C. and Starr, S. L. (1999), *Sorting Things Out: Classification and its Consequences*, Cambridge, MA: MIT Press. This has become an influential book - it is a sociology of classification and many of the illustrative examples relate to disease and diagnostic categories.

Bury, M. R. (1986), 'Social Constructionism and the Development of Medical Sociology', *Sociology of Health and Illness*, 8: 137–69. An overview of the differing approaches within social constructionism and the theoretical dilemmas associated with them.

Jewson, N. (1976), 'The Disappearance of the Sick Man from Medical Cosmology 1770–1870', *Sociology*, 10: 225–44. A classic paper on the social production of medical knowledge.

Jutel, A. (2011), *Putting a Name to It: Diagnosis in Contemporary Society*, Baltimore, MD: Johns Hopkins University Press.

Porter, R. (1999), *The Greatest Benefit to Mankind: A Medical History of Humanity*, London: Fontana Press. This more conventional yet highly informative text provides further historical details.

Wright, P. and Treacher, A. (eds) (1982), *The Problem of Medical Knowledge: Examining the Social Construction of Medicine*, Edinburgh: Edinburgh University Press. Although published over three decades ago, this remains an excellent collection of papers on the social construction of medical knowledge.

3 Lay Health Beliefs, Lifestyles and Risk

Introduction

Whilst sociologists have long studied aspects of illness, it is only in recent decades that they have turned their attention to the development of a sociology of *health* (Lawton, 2003; Radley et al., 2006). This may have to do with the fact that health is rather more enigmatic than illness and disease. Indeed, as Gadamer (1996) in his book entitled *The Enigma of Health*, points out: 'We need only reflect that it is quite meaningful to ask someone "Do you feel ill?", but that it would border on the absurd to ask someone "Do you feel healthy?" Health is not a condition that one introspectively feels in oneself' (p. 113).

But this was written nearly three decades ago. Today, to ask someone if they feel healthy may not seem so out of place, not least because an imperative for 'healthy' living is increasingly evident in many areas of our lives. For example, sport and exercise are deemed to be 'healthy pursuits', food is marketed in terms of its 'healthiness', and household products are presented as being 'green', so that they may contribute to the maintenance of a healthy environment. Further, a growing range of activities seems to be conceptualized in relation to health: for example, walking, riding a bicycle, eating ice-cream, relaxing, taking a holiday, and a myriad of other aspects of living are treated as being 'health related'. Associated with this increasingly *healthist* society is the commercialization, commodification and consumption of health and healthy *lifestyles*. An indicator of this might be the ever-expanding range of magazines with titles such as *Health and Fitness, Healthy, Here's Health, Men's Health, Natural Health* and *Positive Health Online UK* – not to mention the burgeoning selection of popular health books and web-based resources that may be found in bookshops and on the Internet.

Sociologists' interest in health emerged in part in reaction to the biomedical model, which focused primarily on disease (see chapter 1). A more holistic approach to health and healing, sociologists argued, must also encompass the idea of positive health and well-being. The concept of health itself needs to be explored, and such exploration must take *lay perspectives* (that is, non-professional/expert views) into account. A holistic, or socio-environmental, model of health also emphasizes the need to prevent disease, and as such requires an understanding of how people maintain their health; in other words, it examines their *lifestyles*. Lifestyle is a concept which has come to refer to people's styles of living, which, in turn, are shaped by their patterns of consumption. In relation to health, this refers to eating, the use of legal and non-legal drugs, smoking, leisure and sporting activities, sexual activity and aspects of body maintenance. These activities are thought to be significant, because they are regarded as potential *risk* factors which are associated with health status.

This chapter will therefore examine three key issues in the sociology of health: lay health beliefs, lifestyles and risk. It argues that beliefs about health are rooted in wider socio-cultural contexts, and that lifestyles are inseparable from the socio-economic structures in which individuals live out their lives. Indeed, through the study of lay health perspectives - that is, people's understanding and interpretation of health and actions that pertain to health - sociologists have come to appreciate the extent to which such ideas, beliefs and practices are socially embedded. Lay health beliefs are not simply diluted versions of medical knowledge; rather, they are shaped by people's wider milieux, such as their structural location, cultural context, personal biography and social identity.

The appreciation that understandings of health are context-bound has pragmatic consequences. During recent decades, health has come to be regarded more as a product of social and behavioural factors than as a purely biological phenomenon, and thus public policy encourages people to modify their lifestyles and adopt healthier ways of living. However, to emphasize these lifestyle factors in isolation from their social context is, given what we know about lay health beliefs, somewhat artificial (Korp, 2010). Behaviours which may affect health almost invariably carry social meanings other than those which pertain to health. For example, sexual practices have significant social, personal and cultural meanings which may have little to do with health (Crawford, 2006).

The idea of *risk* has emerged as an important concept in this field for a number of reasons. First, it is used in the form of aggregate probabilities by epidemiologists to identify lifestyle factors, such as smoking, which are associated with ill health (Skolbekken, 1995). However, as we shall see from studies of lay health beliefs, such aggregate-level notions of risk are not necessarily appropriate to the meanings and understandings which structure the lives of individuals. A second reason why risk is relevant is that there is a growing number of phenomena, such as nuclear power and warfare, that carry the threat of unimaginable and incalculable consequences. These types of risk are human-made, and yet they surpass the 'know-how' of the 'experts' who created them. Some argue that whilst modernity was characterized by progress and control, we are moving into an era characterized by uncertainty and unease (Beck, 1992a; Giddens, 1990). Third, heightened perceptions of risk have consequences for people's reactions to, and tolerance of, health dangers. Heightened sensitivities to risk are, for example, apparent in relation to childhood immunization, which involves an assessment of the risks associated with the vaccination and those associated with the possible contraction of diseases. The controversies generated by the measles, mumps and rubella (MMR) vaccination programme throw into sharp relief the changing relationship between lay and expert notions of risk. By contrast, rather more routine aspects of everyday life, such as food and eating, are now fraught with risks and anxieties about food safety. Notions of risk, identity and lifestyle are inherently interlinked, and this is especially evident in the case of AIDS. It is characterized as a 'lifestyle condition', in that the adoption of certain behaviours will increase a person's risk of contracting HIV. Furthermore societal responses to HIV and AIDS provide further insight into the ways in which risks are socially constructed, in that they are bound up with people's concerns about dangers, difference and a menacing 'other'. This chapter therefore takes these three issues (the MMR debate, food and HIV/AIDS), in order to tease out some of the contemporary conceptualization of health and risks. Before we turn to these, let us first consider how lay people view health.

Lay health beliefs

The sociology of lay heath beliefs is of value to health care practice in a number of ways. First, the findings can contribute to an understanding of professional–patient interactions, in that it can provide an insight into lay conceptualizations which might otherwise be treated as simply 'incorrect' knowledge by professionals (see chapter 6). Second, an understanding of people's ideas about health maintenance and disease prevention is crucial to the effectiveness of health promotion programmes (see chapter 10). For example, education campaigns which aim to encourage people to take greater responsibility for their own health may well be ineffective if people hold fatalistic views of disease causation, and do not believe that they can effect change (Keeley et al., 2009). Lay ideas about health are complex and nuanced and belief in them may act as powerful mediators of official health education messages, which, in turn, tend to rely on biomedical explanations of disease causation. Third, the study of health beliefs may contribute to our knowledge of *informal* health care. As Strong (1979a: 605) points out: 'since human action is embodied the care and maintenance of our body is a precondition for all human action. We are obliged to be doctors to ourselves and to others and as such we acquire and refine a variety of medical theories, diagnostic procedures and treatment practices.' Moreover, most health care work is carried out by lay people either in the form of self-care or caring for relatives and friends. As Stacey (1988) notes, we are all health workers. The contribution that ordinary people make to health work is today both officially acknowledged and capitalized upon (Department of Health, 2001).

Tracing the development of this body of work, Prior (2003) observes how the lexicon around lay views has changed. Lay 'beliefs' have metamorphosed into lay 'knowledge', and lay 'experience' into lay 'expertise'. Such changes in vocabulary reflect more fundamental transformations associated with the democratization and consumer focus of health and welfare services. Prior's observation raises some intriguing questions about the nature of 'lay beliefs' and 'expert knowledge'. Can they really be the same? Are they as legitimate as each other? Prior thinks not. He suggests that the term 'lay expert', which appeared in the 1990s, is an oxymoron. While 'lay' by definition refers to a 'non-expert', 'expert' refers to a person who has specialized training in particular skills, practices and academic disciplines. Lay people undoubtedly have information and knowledge of, for example, their own bodies, medications, technical medical procedures used by themselves or those close to them, and the circumstances in which they live (Popay et al., 1998; Monaghan, 1999; Atkin and Amad, 2002; Emslie et al., 2002). But they do not, Prior argues, have expertise that involves understanding of the technical complexities of disease, disease causation, clinical procedures and so on. Thus, while some sociologists are keen to argue that 'lay beliefs' might be better characterized as 'lay knowledge' and 'expertise', others prefer to stay with the concept of belief, which 'has a far less sturdy status than the concept of knowledge' (Prior, 2003: 44).

We return to the changing nature of the relationship between 'experts' and 'non-experts' below, in relation to our discussions of immunization and food, but first let us consider how sociologists have made sense of health beliefs and health behaviour, definitions of health, lay explanations of health, the ideological basis of health beliefs, and the relationship between health maintenance and disease prevention.

Health beliefs and health behaviour

Studies which investigate lay views have produced rich data, which reveal that people hold complex and sophisticated theories about the maintenance of health and the causation of disease. From the 1950s to the 1970s, research carried out by medical sociologists was predominantly influenced by the concerns of health professionals. They were interested in topics such as the under-utilization of health services, in that morbidity surveys revealed that significant numbers of people who experienced symptoms did not seek medical help - in fact there was an *iceberg* of illness within the community (Hannay, 1979); the over-utilization of services, in that many people were presenting trivial complaints to general practitioners (Cartwright and Anderson, 1981); and the fact that patients often did not comply with medical advice and instructions. These early studies found that people's responses to symptoms were contingent upon their cultural context (Zborowski, 1952; Zola, 1966), and that decisions to seek professional help were mediated by social factors (Zola, 1973). Emerging from these studies were the concepts of *illness behaviour* (Young, 2004), activities followed in response to symptoms, and *health behaviour*, activities followed in relation to the maintenance of health (Kasl and Cobb, 1966).

Whilst the early studies on lay beliefs were influenced by concerns about help-seeking behaviour and compliance, more recent studies have been preoccupied with health-related behaviours. This shift is the result of a growing recognition that disease is related to social and behavioural factors. People are encouraged by professionals to participate in both *health procedures*, such as screening, check-ups and immunizations, and *health practices*, such as eating healthily and exercising. How to get people to adopt healthy procedures and practices therefore yielded an extensive research literature. Two early influential theoretical socio-psychological approaches were referred to as *health as a locus of control* (Lau and Ware, 1981) and the *health belief model* (Rosenstock, 1974; Becker, 1974). The locus of control theory suggests that people tend to believe either that they have, or do not have, some control over their lives. Those who hold a fatalistic view are categorized as 'externals', whilst those who consider that their behaviour can influence their health are labelled 'internals'. Within this view, when people are identified as externals from the information they provide in interviews, health education can try to transform them into internals.

The health belief model also investigates people's beliefs, in order to try to identify the extent to which they are motivated to change their health behaviour. Indicators of levels of motivation include perceptions of susceptibility to illness, perceptions of the possible effects of illness, and perceptions of the costs and benefits associated with health-related behaviours. These socio-psychological models of health behaviour were, however, challenged empirically, and it was found that they did not, as they claimed, predict behavioural change (Calnan, 1984b). Views expressed in response to the interviews devised by social psychologists are unlikely to be accurate accounts of future actions. They have also been challenged theoretically, in that they fail to incorporate the socio-structural basis upon which social action takes place (Bunton et al., 1991).

Researchers shifted their focus from behaviour to social action, and their work became more theoretically informed. It addressed questions such as: What constitutes health? How do people make sense of the onset of disease? How do lay people maintain health? It recognized that lay people's beliefs about health, illness and disease have their own logic and validity, and are worth studying in their own right (Lawton, 2002a). Studies draw predominantly on the interpretative sociological tradition, and in particular phenomenology, which seeks to study everyday life to reveal its underlying assumptions (Turner, 1995: 4). Its merits are summarized by Calnan (1987: 8):

> The value of adopting the interpretive approach . . . is that emphasis is placed on understanding lay people's actions in terms of the meaning that they place on these actions. The meaning is itself derived from their own complex body of knowledge and beliefs, which is closely linked with the social context in which they live their daily lives. Thus, rather than treating beliefs about health as idiosyncratic, this approach emphasizes their logic and integrity.

Empirical research reveals the way in which ideas about health and illness are influenced by prevailing ideologies and are mediated by socio-structural circumstances and demonstrates the problematic relationship between knowledge, attitude and behaviours. Thus this research involves the examination of meanings and interpretations which people apply to their daily routines, and in this respect contributes to one of the central aims of the sociological enterprise (Bauman, 1990: 10).

Defining health

It is customary to distinguish between both *negative* and *positive* definitions of health and *functional* and *experiential* definitions (Blaxter, 2010). The medical view of health – the absence of disease – is clearly negative. By contrast, an example of a positive definition is that offered by the World Health Organization (WHO): 'a state of complete physical, mental and social well-being'. A functional definition implies the ability to participate in normal social roles (Parsons, 1979), and this may be contrasted with an experiential definition which takes sense of self into account (Kelman, 1975). Another approach to defining health is via the examination of people's perceptions of the concept. Herzlich's (1973) classic study comprising interviews with eighty middle-class people living in Paris and rural Normandy identified three conceptualizations of health: 'health in a vacuum' – which implies an absence of disease; 'reserve of health' – a biological capacity to resist or cope with illness, which increases or decreases over time; and 'equilibrium' – which is normal health, rarely attained.

These lay conceptualizations of health, Herzlich argues, are related to broader social and cultural contexts; thus the views held by the participants interviewed were at once individual and social – both personal and public. Her approach is explicitly Durkheimian, in that she treats concepts of health as 'social representations'. Flick (2000) builds on this analysis to examine concepts of health articulated by nurses and clerks in contrasting socio-political contexts of West and East Germany and Portugal. Perhaps capturing a temporal as well as a geographical difference, Flick adds a fourth category to Herzlich's threefold classification: that of 'health as lifestyle' – which captures references to fitness, nutrition and so on. As well as overlaps between the concepts of health found in these countries, differences were also discerned, which Flick in turn traces to historical differences in both health care systems and political regimes. Amongst Portuguese women, Flick (2000) found less 'health awareness' than amongst West German women, who in turn expressed the feeling of being 'forced to health'. Whilst the former were generally aware of health issues, they did not feel obliged to take actions to actively promote their own health; by contrast, the latter felt socially and morally obliged to do so. Flick attributes these variations to prevailing political discourses associated with notions of autonomy and responsibility and differential historical experiences of political oppression. We see, then, that ideas about health are socially mediated and vary over time and place.

The ways in which gender mediates conceptualizations of health and accounts of health practices is also evident from studies of men. Dolan's (2011) study of groups of working-class men resident in two contrasting locations in England found that although notions of masculinity and health were shared by all the study participants, there were differences when it came to discussing health-related behaviours. Take the contrast between the following two accounts of the health-related behaviours associated with alcohol consumption. Patrick is in full-time skilled employment, whereas Chris is long-term unemployed; Patrick lives in a 'better-off' area and Chris in a more deprived location:

> Tonight's [Friday] my night to relax . . . I meet the lads and we go out . . . get merry . . . have a laugh. We've got no work tomorrow . . . I've got mates on the dole they go out get pissed every night of the week . . . I wouldn't be able to do that and get up for work (Patrick, 37, less deprived area).

This contrasts with:

> When I go for a drink, I don't really feel like it's enjoyment . . . I feel it's a need to get pissed, a need to get stoned . . . You kind of feel shit that you've got no job . . . no money, so you try to look for an escape from that and then because it costs you money to do that so you end up on this downward spiral . . . People say you drink and smoke and take drugs . . . because you like to have fun, but it is not about that at all . . . It is a form of escapism if you like . . . You numb your brain with certain chemicals and things and that is the escapist aspect of it (Chris, 28, deprived area).

The merit of this study is the way it locates cultural notions of health in a structural location – masculinity is rooted in the social ecology of place. Ideas of gender and class on men's health practices are complex and appear to be contingent on the particular sets of wider socio-economic circumstances. Clearly, then, definitions of health are related to culture, gender, class and structure that permeate people's everyday lives.

Whilst the relationship between beliefs and structural location should not be overstated, ideas about health do seem to map on to social differences and divisions. Blaxter's (1990) quantitative study based upon a large and representative sample found that, with the exception of young men, the absence of disease was the most common definition of health used by respondents when commenting about someone else. Yet she also found that definitions of health varied throughout the life-course and in relation to gender. For example, younger men were more likely to view health in terms of physical strength and fitness, whilst younger women stressed energy, vitality and the ability to cope. A secondary analysis of Blaxter's data to examine the comparative health beliefs of Asian, Afro-Caribbean and White groups (Howlett et al., 1992) found that, compared to White respondents, Asians were more likely to define health in functional terms, and Afro-Caribbeans were more likely to describe health in terms of energy and physical strength. They were also more likely to attribute illness to bad luck. Howlett et al. (1992: 286) point out: 'If this is taken as a dimension of (lack of) power, then this may offer a possible explanation for the apparently "fatalistic" attitudes towards health and illness. Indeed racism is a pervasive force in black people's lives and is seen to be closely related to health and illness.'

We see, therefore, that definitions and conceptualizations of health vary between social, geographical and cultural contexts, not least because within these varying circumstances repertoires of language, values, beliefs and theories are differentially available. A study of two Cantonese-speaking communities in the UK, for example, revealed how the Chinese participants drew upon a diverse range of 'objects', explanations and information when discussing health and illness (Prior et al., 2002). Traditional Chinese medicine, spirits, demons, food, weather and the environment were amongst the 'objects' recruited as factors which could be implicated in health and illness. A striking finding in this study was that health amongst this group was fundamentally related to happiness and inner contentment. To be happy was both equated to, and a prerequisite of, being healthy.

Explaining health

Conceptualizations of health may be found to vary systematically among social groups, but it is likely that different accounts are variously drawn according to social circumstances, and that people's ideas will change over time. People are less likely to work with unified theories or explanations which transcend time and place, and are more likely to have views which are adjusted according to the concerns of the individual. Further, these ideas are 'syncretic in origin' (Fitzpatrick, 1984: 18), in that they are derived from disparate and distinct sources. As Stainton-Rogers (1991) has pointed out, to look for explanations is a modernist project, and she acknowledges that one of the merits of postmodernism (see chapter 2) is that it encourages us to accept that a multiplicity of views and realities can coexist. She argues that people do not construct realities, but are 'clever weavers of stories, whose supreme competence is that they can and do create order out of chaos, and moment to moment make sense of their world amid the cacophony' (Stainton-Rogers, 1991: 9–10).

From interviews with seventy participants, Stainton-Rogers (1991) identifies eight 'alternative accounts' which prevail in contemporary society. These are 'body as a machine', which presumes that illness is naturally occurring and real; 'body under siege', where the body is under attack from germs and/or the stress of modern living; 'inequality of access', which presumes the benefits of modern medicine but is concerned about their distribution; 'cultural critique of medicine', which focuses on the negative consequences of biomedicine as the dominant tradition; 'health promotion', which presumes that health is related to lifestyles; 'robust individualism', which stresses the individual's right to a satisfying life; 'God's power', which regards health as a product of 'right living' and spiritual well-being; and 'will-power', wherein the individual has a responsibility to maintain good health. She further argues that actions will be related to people's accounts. However, this is not a straightforward matter, as people's accounts will of course vary over time, and therefore listening to a person on one occasion does not imply that one can predict their action on another. We must therefore be careful when making inferences on the basis of people's accounts, which are invariably retrospective rationalizations constructed for the purpose of the interview.

From her extensive studies of both lay and medical discourses on health, the anthropologist Emily Martin documents how conceptualizations and explanations of health change over time (Martin, 1989, 1994, 2000). The dominant conceptualizations of health, disease and the body throughout the nineteenth and most of the twentieth century were replete with mechanical metaphors, and were preoccupied with ideas about hygiene, contagion, germs and so on. By the end of the twentieth century, the central motif of health was that of immunity. Her analysis of data generated by participant observation within medical schools, laboratories and patient support groups, and over 200 interviews with a diverse range of people living in the USA, reveals that the immune system is 'at the centre stage of the way ordinary people think of health'.

> Whether you look in the direction of nutrition, exercise, environmental toxins, stress, cancer or AIDS, these days the health arena is saturated with talk about the immune system. The immune system has begun to function culturally as the key guarantor of health and the key mark of differential survival for the twenty-first century. In our neighbourhood interviews, for example, general discussions of health quickly led people (who were not scientists by profession) to name the immune system as the central player. (Martin, 2000: 125)

Ideally, an immune system, which is inherent to a 'body', be it one's personal body or the metaphorical body of an organization, a corporation or whatever, should be 'flexible'. Indeed, flexibility is now a desirable commodity by which individuals and social groups may be judged.

> A conception of a new elite may be forged that finds desirable qualities of flexibility and adaptability to change in certain and superior individuals of *any* ethnic, racial, gender, sexual identity or age group in the nation. The 'currency' in which these desirable qualities will be figured is health, especially the health of one's immune system. (Martin, 1994: xvii)

We can see from the preceding discussion that definitions and explanations of health are inextricably interwoven with socio-economic and cultural contexts. Our ideas about health are shaped by, and therefore reveal much about, prevailing culture and ideologies.

Ideology and 'accounts' of health

Beliefs about health and illness are at once individual *and* social (Herzlich, 1973: 1), and as such are influenced by prevailing social and medical ideologies. Conceptualizations about health and illness in contemporary Western societies reflect the values of capitalism and individualism, in that they are imbued with notions of self-discipline, self-denial, self-control and will-power (Crawford, 1984, 2000,

2006). Notions of dependency are regarded as negative, and having the strength to overcome problems reflects more general social norms and values found in industrialized capitalist societies. Given that our ideas about health are ideologically and socially imbued, it is suggested that it may be more accurate to portray people's descriptions of health as 'accounts' rather than health beliefs (Radley and Billig, 1996; Prior et al., 2002). The term 'belief' conjures up the idea that sociologists are accessing people's subjective interpretations and revealing what people inwardly 'know' and 'believe'. However, in practice, sociologists are capturing people's views that are publicly available and verifiable and, perhaps more importantly, are permeated by public discourses and thereby inherently ideological.

Cornwell (1984), who explored the views of working-class families living in the East End of London, found parallels between her informants' views on health and illness and their ideas about work. Whilst they were aware that they had little control over either their health or their working lives, they took it upon themselves to work hard and make the most of their lot and to 'take seriously the idea that having the "right attitude" is the passport, if not to good health, at least to a life that is tolerable. The moral prescription for a healthy life is in fact a kind of cheerful stoicism, evident in the refusal to worry, or to complain, or to be morbid' (Cornwell, 1984: 129).

In contrast with much contemporary sociological thinking, Blaxter (1997) found that the working-class women rejected the idea that poverty caused ill health. As one woman put it, '"No, I couldn't think it makes any difference myself. I mean, it's like people with money, they get the same illnesses as we get. So I shouldn't think that would make any difference whether you are skilled or unskilled"' (Blaxter, 1997: 751). Puzzled by this, Blaxter (1993, 1997) examined transcripts of interview data in more detail, to try to make sense of why those who are most likely to be vulnerable to the social and material environment tend to blame themselves and deny its impact. Blaxter reasons that these women saw health as the individual's responsibility not simply in terms of leading healthy lives, but because health and illness were bound up with their personal biographies and said something about their own identities. To be ill carries negative connotations with which they would not want to be associated. Another reason why they did not dwell on inequalities was that they were acutely aware of the perils in the environment which had existed in the past and which, by contrast, today seemed relatively innocuous. Popay and her colleagues (2003) have undertaken further research into this issue, and have endorsed the finding that people who live in areas of material deprivation are uneasy with the associations that are made between poverty and ill health because of the 'moral connotations'. One woman, when presented with evidence that people who live in disadvantaged areas die younger than those who do not said: '"I think you'd have to look into it and think again. Yes there's pollution but other than that it's attitudes . . . they are making out that it's all like scum and they're all dying"' (cited in Popay et al., 2003: 13). This same study, however, also found that when people were asked to provide narratives about their own personal experiences of health and illness, these 'same people provided vivid accounts of the way in which inequalities and material circumstances have an adverse impact on their health' (p. 1). It seems that when talking about deprivation and health in *abstract* terms, those people who live in relatively deprived areas resist the suggestion of a link between poverty and health because it introduces yet another negative image of their lives and their locality. In contrast, when talking about their *concrete experiences*, poor housing, pollution, lack of play space, transport and so on were in fact implicated.

These differences between abstract and personalized accounts resonate with a distinction identified by Cornwell (1984) between 'public' and 'private' accounts. Public accounts are those given during initial interviews and present normative views on health and illness. Private accounts emerge after participants have been interviewed on a number of occasions and evoke people's actual experiences of illness, and invariably moral concerns are not expressed. People were keen to present themselves as being healthy, and often initial statements on health status bore no relation to their medical histories. For example, one woman described herself as healthy and lucky in that she had good health, and yet 'Kathleen's medical history included having such bad eyesight as a child that she was expected to be blind by the age of twenty, lung disease including tuberculosis in her late teens, a miscarriage, a thyroid deficiency which requires permanent medication, and six years prior to interviews, a hysterectomy' (Cornwell, 1984: 124). As well as an insistence on good health and a scorn of hypochondriacs and malingerers, the analysis of public accounts revealed a necessity to be able to prove the 'otherness' of illness as a separate thing that happened to the person and was not something for which they could be held responsible. Thus, at a normative level people are concerned to express views that are congruent with medical ideas and the underlying values of capitalism. Disease is seen as a 'thing' from which the person may become alienated (Taussig, 1980).

It is important to point out that lay people do not passively accept medical ideas, and where these ideas do not fit into people's schema, they may be ignored or rejected. It is also evident that medical beliefs do not only filter down to lay people; often the reverse is the case, and lay ideas come to shape medical knowledge and practice (Helman, 1978).

Health maintenance and disease prevention

Studies have found that there is a clear distinction within lay logic between health and disease, and that the two are not mutually exclusive. Although, as we have seen, health is sometimes regarded as the absence of disease, empirical research finds that people may still refer to someone as healthy even though serious disease is present. Relatedly, ideas about the maintenance of health are separated in lay logic from ideas about the prevention of disease. Calnan (1987: 12) states that health and disease are not direct opposites:

> lay ideas about health maintenance were more coherent than . . . ideas about disease prevention. This suggested that people, irrespective of their social class, operate with a range of definitions of health that are not simply connected. Thus promoting health and preventing disease are not direct opposites, that is, positives and negatives, and while women had clear recipes about how to maintain health, they did not necessarily feel they were applicable to disease prevention.

The fact that a large proportion of deaths in post-industrial societies are from diseases that are preventable has promoted extensive research into lay ideas about the aetiology of disease. It appears that there are diseases to which certain types of people are presumed to be more susceptible than others. Heart disease provides a classic example. Men with certain temperaments, who are overweight or who are obsessively active, are considered as being most likely to be susceptible to 'heart attacks'. Thus people are able to identify heart disease 'candidates' based on information given by health educators: namely, men who eat saturated fats, do not do any exercise, and who are hyperactive (Emslie et al., 2002).

However, as Davison et al. (1991) point out, people collectively develop a 'lay epidemiology' which recognizes that not all candidates have heart attacks and some non-candidates do, and that this must therefore be a question of luck. For example, the 'lazy slob' who gorges large quantities of fatty food and smokes is considered to be at greater risk of a heart attack. But the researchers found that people have a proverbial 'Uncle Norman': that is, a person who 'should' be a coronary candidate because he follows unhealthy practices but seems to outlive his relatives. Health promoters, keen to present unequivocal, simplified and straightforward messages, fail to address these anomalies, and so underestimate the sophistication of lay thinking. They conclude that it 'is ironic that such evidently fatalistic cultural concepts should be given more rather than less explanatory power by the activities of modern health education, whose stated goals lie in the opposite direction' (Davison et al., 1991: 16). They may also serve to reinforce the gendered assumptions which are found to be ingrained in people's views on heart disease (Emslie et al., 2002). Davison and colleagues thus found lay notions of personal destiny to be prevalent, perhaps best captured in the phrase 'if it's gonna happen, it's gonna happen'. This concept of luck stands in opposition to the notion of risk. Whilst the latter conjures up notions of mathematical probability, rationality and controllability, the former implies that which is uncontrollable, random and therefore irrational. Thus Davison and colleagues argue that the claims of health promoters based on 'predictability, regularity and certainty' are likely to be counter-productive, as they do not fit with beliefs found in popular culture, or with lay observations that some 'fat smokers' really do live till advanced old age, and some svelte joggers really do 'fall down dead' (Davison et al., 1992: 683).

To reiterate, social action relating to health and social action relating to disease are not necessarily the same thing, in that they may be logically separate and based on distinct forms of reasoning. Ideas about the causation of disease are therefore not the same as ideas about the maintenance of health, as might previously have been supposed.

Lifestyles and consumer culture

The current emphasis on lifestyles in relation to health reflects broader social changes, and is seen to be inextricably interlinked to the rise of *consumer culture*, which is an inherent part of contemporary society. Influenced by Bourdieu's (1984) *Distinction*, Featherstone (1991a: 84) argues that the new petite bourgeoisie produce and disseminate cultural imagery and information which aim to expand and legitimate their own particular dispositions and lifestyles. In relation to the legitimation of 'healthy' lifestyles, the medical profession, health promoters, pharmaceutical companies, and those working within the media promulgate these. They are in a sense cultural entrepreneurs. There is a commercialization of health, in that people are constructed as health consumers who may consume healthy lifestyles.

Central to this is an emphasis on body maintenance (Featherstone, 1991b). Whilst in pre-modern societies disciplined body management was evident in the form of harsh ascetic regimes which would result in higher spiritual ends (for example, the wearing of hair shirts and the eating of simple foods), by contrast, in modern societies body maintenance is concerned with outer appearances and is more akin to hedonism than temperance. This has been encouraged by commercial interests and consumer goods in the twentieth century which relate to two main areas of life: the maintenance of the home (for example, washing machines, vacuum cleaners and dishwashers) and the maintenance of the body (for example, cosmetics, clothes and food). Within consumer culture the body becomes both a site of pleasure and a representation of happiness and success. The appearance of the body reflects the inner self: 'to look good is to *feel* good'. Health education reflects the commercialization of body maintenance. Common to the popular media treatment of body maintenance and health education 'is the encouragement of self-surveillance of bodily health and appearance as well as the incentive of lifestyle benefits' (Featherstone, 1991b: 184). Featherstone also draws attention to the 'transvaluation' of activities such as slimming and jogging; that is, the value of such actions is transformed into something over and above their original use value. For example, 'The notion of running for running's sake, purposiveness without a purpose, a sensuous experience in harmony with embodied and physical nature, is completely submerged amidst the welter of benefits called up by market and health experts' (1991b: 185–6).

To get one's body into shape can be a route to the enhancement of the self, and a fit body can enhance an efficient mind. It is also a sign of competence, self-control and self-discipline, as Bordo (1990: 94) puts it: '[I]ncreasingly, the size and shape of the body has come to operate as a marker of personal, internal order (or disorder) – as a symbol for the state of the soul.' She argues that it is permissible to have a bulky body as long as it is tightly managed (Bordo, 1990: 90). Thus one's outer appearance can affect one's inner mental health. Monaghan's (2001a, 2001b) ethnography of men's body building similarly endorses the suggestion that appearance may be privileged over health. Body building, on the one hand, forms part of a health-promoting lifestyle, yet, on the other hand, involves an engagement with health-damaging behaviours such as the use of illicit drugs. The use of steroids can help to enhance both the sensations experienced during exercise and the appearance of the body. In this respect '"risky" body work' (2001b: 349) is both health enhancing and damaging.

The fitness industry is a prime example of the commercialization of healthy lifestyles. Exercise machines, home videos, stylish exercise clothes and the like are sold for the pursuit of fitness. Glassner (1989) argues that the contemporary craze for fitness also has characteristics which resemble other activities that have been described as postmodernist. Exercise bikes and rowing machines are 'simulations' of the real thing, and home videotapes comprise 'pastiches' of dance, music, and nostalgic and futuristic images. The fitness craze may also be characterized as postmodernist, he argues, in that it blurs some of the dualisms inherent in modernism, such as the self versus the body, inside versus outside, male versus female, and work versus leisure. Finally, a work–leisure dichotomy is blurred as gyms and fitness centres are increasingly found in the workplace, where employees can 'work out'. Thus fitness activities take on the characteristics of work, and leisure pursuits are encouraged within the workplace.

Such health-related activities embody the contradictions between production and consumption that are inherent in advanced capitalist societies. Writing in a North American context, Crawford (2000) argues that 'health promotion' can be conceived of as a professionally mediated and popular 'ritual' that provides 'repertoires' for dealing with the tensions and dilemmas which transcend our experiences of both health and the economy. He suggests that there is a 'metaphorical homology' between economic experience and health experience, 'a parallel set of symbolic oppositions with similar moral and ideological connotations' (2000: 224). Capitalism functions only if people are both producers (workers) *and* consumers, but the behaviours, 'personality structures' and 'ethics' of the two are different. Self-denial, self-control, rationality, self-discipline and will-power are needed in the workplace, but irrationality, release, indulgence and pleasure seeking are compatible with greater consumption. Such co-presence is evident in relation to 'health' practices such as smoking, eating, exercise, drinking alcohol and so on.

Bunton and Crawshaw (2002) illustrate these contradictions in their analysis of men's lifestyle magazines in the UK. The magazines are full of advice on fitness and food, smoking and sexual health. The readers are positioned as consumers of health information. But the information is double-edged; on the one hand, men are encouraged to eat well, exercise and so on; on the other hand, they are encouraged to be indulgent and pleasure seeking. Bunton and Crawshaw find that '[h]ealth risk activities are simultaneously celebrated and pilloried' (2002: 201). The ideological imperative within capitalist societies is that one is free to choose between restraint and pleasure. But as Crawford astutely points out, 'each choice is infused with moral significance; one must exercise freedom "responsibly" [. . .] Instances of loss of control raise a moral question and are carefully evaluated by self and others' (2000: 229). It is not surprising, therefore, that accounts of health are replete with moral values and contradictory positions. One focus group study undertaken in England identified three 'positions' on health: namely, 'positive mental attitude', 'genes and luck', and 'resistance'. Whilst the participants espoused the view that people should have the right attitude, take responsibility for health, and live a good life, they were also disparaging about being too 'goody goody', and so condoned resistance and rebellion - albeit to a limited degree (M. L. Crossley, 2002). Thus, being healthy involves balancing precariously on a moral tightrope. Such moral evaluations certainly surface in the media when topics such as obesity, smoking, health and HIV/AIDS are debated.

Lifestyles and social context

Central to the literature on lifestyles and health is the notion of *risk*. Health can be promoted, and disease can be prevented, by the identification and control of risk factors. To this end, epidemiologists strive to correlate risk factors with disease outcomes; for example, smoking increases the risk of lung cancer, and 'unsafe' sex increases the risk of HIV/AIDS. In turn, these lifestyles become politicized, in that they need to be regulated or controlled. Thus another concept central to discussion on lifestyle is that of *control*. There is a debate on the extent to which individuals are able to control their risk of disease through the modification of their lifestyles.

Sociologists of health argue that the individual's potential for such control is limited in two main ways: first, because although behavioural habits are related to health, they have less impact than the circumstances in which they are embedded (Blaxter, 1990: 202). In her study on health and lifestyles, Blaxter found that harmful behavioural habits have the greatest impact on those who are least vulnerable environmentally. The implication of this is that only 'in the more favourable circumstances is there "room" for considerable damage or improvement by the adoption of voluntary health-related habits' (Blaxter, 1990: 233). It is therefore likely that a concentration on the promotion of health by way of emphasizing health behaviours may contribute to a widening of health inequalities.

The second reason for the limited potential for individuals to shape their lifestyles in ways which are presumed to be desirable is that all social actions are grounded in and constrained by social circumstances. The debate about women and smoking illustrates this well. While there has been an overall decline in the numbers of people smoking over the last decade, the decrease in the number of women smoking has been relatively small. The gap between middle-class and working-class women's smoking patterns has widened although the gap between men and women has decreased. Prevalence rates in 2009 among men and women were 22 and 20 per cent, respectively. This compares with 42 per cent of men and 36 per cent of women in 1980. Twenty-six per cent of mothers in the UK smoked during pregnancy in 2009 (of which 54 per cent gave up at some point before the birth) compared to 33 per cent of women who smoked while pregnant in 2005 (The NHS Information Centre, 2011). Furthermore, young people's smoking is gendered, with 29 per cent of young women aged between 16 and 19 smoking cigarettes, compared with 22 per cent of men in the same age group (ONS, 2005). Smoking in pregnancy has also long been considered to be a significant public health issue (Oakley, 1989). Although it has declined by a third over the last fifteen years, it remains socially patterned. In 2000, 4 per cent of women labelled as 'professional class' smoked, and 26 per cent of those labelled 'manual class' did so (ONS, 2005). Graham et al. (2009) found that measures of disadvantage (e.g., poor childhood socio-economic class, educational disadvantage, young motherhood, poor adult socio-economic class) throughout women's life-course explains the higher rates of smoking just prior to pregnancy amongst this group with measures of life advantage contributing to higher rates of quitting during pregnancy.

The conventional response to this 'problem' has been to educate women about the dangers of smoking, both to themselves and to their babies, in the hope that this knowledge will persuade them to give up. However, this fails to take into account the socially structured aspects of women's lives which are represented in the statistics. Studies have found that women's smoking can be an important coping strategy in the face of the multiple demands that are placed upon them. This is especially so for women with children. Over half of lone parents felt that they had little social support, nearly twice as many as two-parent households (ONS, 2005). Smoking is also associated with material deprivation. Graham has shown, through her qualitative investigations into women's smoking, that it forms a fundamental part of women's daily routines; it is a way of coping with caring in poverty. Further, 'smoking acts as both a luxury and a necessity when material and human resources are stretched . . . In a lifestyle stripped of new clothes, make-up, hairdressing, travel by bus and evenings out, smoking can become an important symbol of one's participation in an adult consumer culture' (Graham, 1987: 55). Thus, whilst affecting women's physical health, smoking may facilitate their mental well-being. Similarly, consumption of food cannot be separated from socio-economic circumstances and the internal structures of the household, such as gender relations and the division of labour. Charles and Kerr's (1988) extensive study of food practices found that they reproduced patriarchal structures within the household. Women took disproportionate responsibility for buying, cooking and preparing food within families. However, this was not matched by their authority to determine what food should be eaten. The women tended to subordinate their own preferences to those of their partners and their children. This echoes Lupton's (1996) observation that cultural assumptions presume that cooking and preparing food are inherently feminine, and bound up with notions of self-sacrifice.

Central to the notion of voluntaristic lifestyles in relation to health is the idea that people are able to make health choices. Graham (1984: 187) suggests that it is more realistic to speak of *healthy compromises*, in that the consumption of food or cigarettes is influenced by the socially structured context in which people live out their lives. In her discussion of health in families, she points out that:

> Health choices are shaped by material as well as mental structures. The barriers to change are represented by the limits of time, energy and income available to parents. In such circumstances, health choices are more accurately seen as health compromises, which, repeated day after day, become the routines which keep the family going.

Graham (1992) has shown that such routines are increasingly exacerbated for many people as the economic circumstances of poor families have worsened during the last decade. This has compounded the delicate task which many women face, of devising budgeting strategies which can be reconciled with health needs. Graham (1992: 220) describes how women constantly search 'for ways of meeting health needs while cutting back on health resources'. This work helps us appreciate why actions which are deemed to be injurious to health remain structurally patterned. It is also evident that even amongst young people, who may not necessarily have obvious constraints, such as dependants, health-related actions are related to the socio-economic circumstances (Pavis et al., 2002).

Lifestyle and risk

As we have seen, the modification of lifestyles is associated with ideas about what constitute threats and dangers to health. As Douglas (1992) has pointed out, risk in the modern context is taken to be synonymous with danger or hazards. Contemporary discourses on citizenship are replete with notions of rights and responsibilities, which in relation to health often translate as the avoidance of risky (in other words, dangerous) behaviours (Petersen and Lupton, 1996; Nettleton, 1997). An investigation into lay people's understandings of risk in England and Australia found that Douglas appears to be right; the participants in the study do conceptualize risk in terms of uncertainty, potential danger, loss of control and so on (Lupton and Tulloch, 2002). However, risk taking was also perceived more positively, in that 'voluntary risk-taking is often pursued for the sake of facing and conquering fear, displaying courage, seeking excitement and thrills and achieving self-actualization and a sense of personal agency' (2002: 115). Taking risks involves dangers, to be sure; but facing (and overcoming) dangers can be exciting, invigorating, lead to 'self-improvement', and may enhance 'emotional intensity'. Risky actions may therefore be pleasurable *precisely* because they are dangerous. Embodied risk taking can therefore enhance embodied pleasures. Just as we saw earlier in this chapter, there is a contradiction between the production and consumption of health, so too there is ambiguity when it comes to embracing and avoiding risks.

Ironically, perhaps, whilst some 'experts' are keen to draw attention to the risks of eating lots of chips, drinking lots of beer, etc., others are denying the risks associated with industrial pollution, the storage of nuclear waste, environmental hazards and nuclear power stations (Potts, 2004). Perceptions of risk are being heightened, but the responses to them are politically circumscribed. As Giddens (1990: 130–1), commenting on environmental risk, notes:

> Widespread lay knowledge of modern risk environments leads to an awareness of the limits of expertise and forms one of the 'public relations' problems that has to be faced by those who seek to sustain lay trust in expert systems . . . [R]ealization of the areas of ignorance which confront the experts themselves, as individual practitioners and in terms of overall field of knowledge, may weaken or undermine that faith on the part of lay individuals.

It is possible to identify two qualitatively different types of risk: those that are calculable and those that are incalculable. The former imply an epidemiological or propensity model of risk based on aggregate level data, whereas the latter are based upon knowledge of the potential causal powers of some phenomenon such as nuclear energy. Some authors have suggested that in a society marked by such risks, the body becomes a concrete site of control, and the pursuit of body maintenance projects represents one of the only arenas of stability and solidity in late modernity (Shilling, 2003; see also chapter 5).

The body and the risk society

Threats to social order are mirrored in ideas about bodily order – if society is endangered, so too is the body within. Mary Douglas (1966) in her treatise on *purity* and *danger* discusses the symbolic and ritual ways in which the world is classified. 'Dirt' and 'pollution' are all those things that are 'matter out of place'; that is, they transgress socially accepted boundaries or classifications, for example, bathroom equipment in the dining room or shoes on the kitchen table. Thus, by definition, 'dirt' is that which cannot be classified or is not on the right side of a socially accepted boundary. Anything that does transcend boundaries is polluting, and carries a considerable symbolic load:

> The whole universe is harnessed to men's [*sic*] attempts to force one another into good citizenship. Thus we find that certain moral values are upheld and certain social rules defined by beliefs in dangerous contagion . . . as we examine pollution beliefs we find that the kinds of contacts which are thought dangerous also carry a symbolic load . . . some pollutions are used as analogies for expressing a general view of social order. (Douglas, 1966: 3)

Contemporary anxieties about global threats or pollution from which no society is immune are reflected by the immunity, or lack of it, of the body. As Turner (1991a:

24) observes: 'The body has once more become apocalyptic given the threat of chemical warfare, the destruction of the natural habitat, the epidemic of HIV and AIDS, the greying/declining populations of northern Europe and the apparent inability of national governments to control medical technology and medical costs.' It is perhaps HIV and AIDS which, more than any other disease, display analogies between pollution beliefs and social order. They constitute a threat to individuals, and the reactions of social groups suggest that, for some, they are perceived as a threat to social order.

Risk in contemporary society

Interest in the area of risk is not confined to the sociology of health and illness. A number of authors (Douglas, 1986; Giddens, 1990; Beck, 1992a; Lupton, 1999) have pointed to the fact that we are living in a society that is characterized by a 'politics of anxiety' (Turner, 1991a: 24). As Douglas (1986: 59) notes, risks 'clamour for attention; probable dangers crowd from all sides, in every mouthful and at every step'. Indeed, in his influential study, Beck (1992a) has described contemporary society as a *risk society*.

Whilst misfortunes in pre-industrial societies were attributable to fate, God(s) or natural disasters, modern risks are increasingly created by the social and economic processes associated with industrialization. Beck argues that modernity both creates risks by our ways of living – working conditions, means of transport, pollution and the like – and compensates for them by means of calculation and political regulation. Further, accidents and illnesses which appear to be, at first sight, highly personal in their consequences are at the same time 'systematically caused, statistically describable and in that sense "predictable" types of events'. This means that everyone is subject to 'political rules of recognition, compensation and avoidance' (Beck, 1992b: 99).

However, as we have already noted, the calculations of risk are becoming increasingly difficult, if not impossible, because of the emergence of phenomena which have unimaginable consequences – 'nuclear, chemical, genetic and ecological mega-hazards abolish the . . . calculus of risks' (Beck, 1992b: 101–2). They are global in scope; there is no satisfactory after-care following their activation; and there are no statistical bases for their calculation. This growing sensitivity to risk also results in a heightened level of anxiety, which, as we have already noted, is further exacerbated by a decline in the faith in 'experts' (Giddens, 1990: 130; Beck, 1992b).

Dangers lurk everywhere: there is pollution in the air, acid in the rain, and radiation in the soil. Contemporary risks such as nuclear waste and acid rain are particularly dangerous, as, not being containable and being ever present, they constitute a constant threat to the body. According to Beck and Giddens, the risks of modern-day living are the product of social organization and decision making. Armstrong (1993) also makes this point, and contrasts the health risks of today with the health risks present in the nineteenth century. Whilst in the nineteenth century health risks were associated with the 'natural' environment, and dangers lurked within water, soil, air, food and climate, today the environmental factors that impinge on health, such as acid rain and radiation, are the consequence of human actions. Of course, not all contemporary health risks are human products – AIDS, for example, is the consequence of a virus. Nevertheless, the disease has come to be *conceptualized* within a social matrix; it exists within a wider context of social activities, and is envisaged in terms of complex social interactions between gay men, intravenous drug-users (IVDUs), and those requiring and administering blood transfusions. In this respect it has increasingly become articulated in the same terms as humanly created risks.

A puzzling feature of contemporary 'risk' is the apparent lack of fit between the scale of risk and the degree of public and media concern about particular issues. As Bellaby (2003) has pointed out, road traffic accidents result in thousands of casualties every year (in 2002 in the UK, 4,596 people received serious injuries or were killed), yet the matter receives little public concern (see also Hunt, 1989). By contrast, insignificant risks of autism reputed to be associated with the MMR vaccine, and a real, but relatively small risk of variant Creutzfeldt-Jakob disease (vCJD) from eating beef, were matters that were debated widely within the media. They also resulted in changes in people's behaviour, with a significant number of parents opting not to have their children vaccinated and an accelerated decline in the consumption of beef. 'Road transport crashes are perceptible risks, the low risk of vCJD is an expert assessment, and the link between autism and MMR is, if anything, virtual. Parents seem to neglect the easily perceptible risk, to reject the expert assessment, and to amplify the virtual risk' (Bellaby, 2003: 726). Thus, on the face of it, people, or in this case parents, do not appear to have a rational response to risk: the greater the quantitative danger, the qualitatively less the concern. However, explorations into subjective perceptions of risk reveal that parents may in fact be making understandable assessments, their priority being to protect their children within a given context. For example, taking a child to school in the car may contribute to health hazards in general, but parents perceive that they are protecting their children from other road-users or abduction by strangers. It is to subjective perceptions of risk and the factors that shape such perceptions that we now turn – in particular, to the topics of 'food safety' and the 'MMR vaccine', which have both been highly controversial issues at the turn of the twenty-first century.

Perceptions of everyday risk: 'food scares' and 'food safety'

'Food defect could make thousands mentally ill' reads a leader in the *Observer* newspaper on 27 June 2004. The article reports on anxieties that significant numbers of people will suffer from mental illness because of intensive agricultural practices that have led to a shortage of omega 3 and omega 6 in our diets. '"We are facing a health crisis more serious and more dangerous than that posed by obesity in the West," said Professor Michael Crawford of the University of North London' (McKie, 2004). Eating more fish could help. It contains omega 3, and is also known to reduce the risk of heart disease. And yet, on Friday, 25 June, a leader in the *Guardian* ran 'Food watchdog's safety limits on eating fish' and reported that the UK Food Standards Agency had 'set safety limits for consumption of fish for the first time yesterday, while advising that most people should eat more fish for health' (Lawrence, 2004). Consumers face a delicate dilemma: eat more fish to improve mental health and avoid heart disease, but make sure not to eat too much because industrial chemicals such as dioxins, PCBs (polychlorinated biphenyls) and methylmercury that accumulate in the fat of fish are associated with cancer or nerve damage. This is all complicated further by the fact that varying levels of fish consumption are recommended for different social groups: girls under 16 should eat two portions a week, boys should eat four; women who are not intending to become pregnant four portions, those who are should eat two. Further guidance is given on various types of fish. These 'news stories' are emblematic of contemporary health risks, and highlight the extent to which the media, government agencies, scientists and the public are interlinked. Precariousness, presentation and perceptions are all critical here. The risks are human-made and uncertain; the presentation of them is mediated by cultural intermediaries such as journalists; and people's perceptions of them are, as we explore below, bound up with broader social and cultural views.

Over the last few decades there have been a whole series of 'food safety' issues, such as salmonella in eggs and listeria from soft cheese in the 1980s, and BSE in cattle and its association with vCJD in the 1990s. Complex and nuanced scientific arguments tend to be presented in overly simplistic, overly exaggerated ways. Seale (2002) suggests that this is further exacerbated by the fact that the media tend to juxtapose 'the innocent familiarity of routinely available substances essential for life' (such as food) with 'hidden dangers lurking in these same substances' (2002: 75).

Green et al. (2003) suggest that the issue of food safety constitutes an 'archetypal illustration' of the types of risk we currently choose to face: first, because the risks associated with food are 'hidden'. Second, and relatedly, they are identifiable only through expert analysis; we cannot actually see, smell or taste the residue from pesticides, the dioxins, PCBs, toxins from fertilizers and so on. Third, the food safety issue is not one of scarcity and hunger, but more one of abundance; food dangers lurk everywhere. Fourth, the dangers are 'human-made', the result of the 'scientization' of risk (Beck 1992a: 170) – for example, GM crops and pesticides. Finally, individuals are propelled to make 'complex assessments' of a wide range of risks and to balance these against the benefits. But how do people actually make these complex assessments? After all, we consume food every day, and so such decisions must become part of our everyday lives.

From their qualitative investigation into people's accounts of their food choices, Green and her colleagues (2003) identified a number of what they call 'short cuts to safety' and 'rules of thumb' that are used to inform decision making. Issues of risk and safety, it emerges, do figure as highly in people's decision making as in the minds of sociological theorists, and rather than being overwhelmed by contemporary debates on food risks, people appear to be adept at creating strategies of confidence in food. Food choices were informed by a wide range of considerations, such as taste, nutritional value, ethical concerns or what you fancy, as well as safety. Interestingly, a series of dualisms were invoked when considering the relative risks of food: for example, home-cooked versus prepared, fresh versus frozen, organic versus non-organic, cheap versus expensive, home-grown versus mass-produced, and locally produced versus foreign or imported. The language of safety was used as a more socially neutral way of communicating what was felt to be more acceptable food. Degrees of 'safety' were expressed in terms not only of damage to food due to transportation, but also 'expressions of symbolic identity versus "otherness"' (Draper and Green, 2002): for instance, the reinforcement of one's national identity by denigrating 'other' nationalities. One American participant in the study said that her husband would not eat English meat, another participant reported that her Swedish grandmother would only buy Swedish meat because she considered it to be 'safer' than English. The rhetoric of safety also served to construct social boundaries and notions of difference: for example, around 'ethnicity', in that dangers invariably resided in social groups that were 'different (from the participants') ethnicity' (Green et al., 2003: 40). The language of 'safety' and 'health risks' could be used by some to make racist comments appear more palatable: for example, 'There is that Indian at the top isn't there, you might just as well have your coffin at the bottom of them stairs if you go to that Indian' (group participant in Green et al., 2003: 40).

In tandem with the increased awareness of human-made risks associated with food, there has been a shift in the governance of such risks, from one of protection of a relatively ignorant public from unscrupulous or negligent food producers to one of informing consumers who are encouraged to choose appropriate foods (Draper and Green, 2002). Similarly, in an analysis of the provision of school meals, Gustafsson (2004) reveals how the rationale and content of policies on school meals were transformed throughout the twentieth century. Concerns to prevent malnutrition in the early 1900s were displaced by a preoccupation with national standardization of provision during the post-war years. By the end of the last century, the emphasis shifted from provision to consumption, and policies aimed to encourage children to make healthy choices. However, inherent in this example of the privatization of risk, whereby children are being governed through more subtle techniques, are concerns 'about a "dangerous" child, posing a danger to a future healthy self' (Gustafsson, 2004: 63). On the one hand, shifts towards democratization and individualization privilege the rights and responsibilities of consumers and active citizens, while on the other hand, such forms of self-governance present problems for politicians, policy makers and practitioners alike, when citizens do not make the 'right' choices. This is especially evident in our second illustration of health and risk, to which we now turn.

Challenging the 'experts': the MMR debate

Mass childhood immunization has long formed a central pillar of preventive medicine on a global scale. It is favoured by governments, health professionals and international organizations such as the World Health Organization, UNICEF and the World Bank. Vaccination programmes for diseases such as polio, whooping cough, hepatitis B, measles and mumps are associated with significant reductions in prevalence. Immunization against smallpox is invariably hailed as *the* great achievement. But acceptance of mass immunization is not inevitable, and there have always been dissenters, as the history of immunization programmes testifies (Wolfe and Sharpe, 2002). The nature and extent of resistance to such programmes is, however, contextually specific, and may vary between developing and industrial countries, amongst religious communities and different historical periods (Streefland, 2001). Within late modern advanced capitalist societies the resistance appears to revolve around notions of trust, or lack of it, in what Giddens (1990) calls 'expert systems'. The controversy associated with the MMR vaccine in the UK illustrates this well.

In the 1990s the uptake of the MMR vaccine in the UK was 95 per cent; by 2000 it had fallen to an average of 86 per cent, with some areas reporting uptake levels of below 80 per cent (Petts and Niemeyer, 2004). The decline is often attributed to the controversy triggered by the publication of, and media interest in, the work of a gastroenterologist and his colleagues, who published a paper in *The Lancet*

(Wakefield et al., 1998) suggesting that behavioural symptoms might be associated with the MMR vaccine. In a subsequent paper they suggested that the hypothesis that the MMR vaccine is associated with autism might be worthy of further investigation (Wakefield and Montgomery, 2000). The conclusions of these papers are tentative and suggestive, but the media coverage was extensive.

MacIntyre et al. (1998: 236–7) identify five 'news values' that provide us with clues as to why this particular health topic gained such extensive news coverage. The first news value, 'scientific advances', may be significant, because although the Wakefield papers were only suggestive, they did raise the possibility of a new development which would have had far-reaching implications. Second, 'divisions amongst experts' is a 'news value' that is especially pertinent in this case, as Wakefield's views are highly contentious and resulted in criticism from many quarters of the medical profession and other medical scientists. Third, the news value 'matters of state' is especially apposite here, as immunization is provided and promoted by the state, and has long been recognized as a source of tension between state control and individual freedom. Fourth, the value 'division in government' is less evident here, although some medical practitioners expressed concern about questioning adherence to the MMR vaccine. Fifth, there was a whiff of 'government suppression' especially in relation to the fact that the MMR is a 'triple vaccine', which can be administered as three separate vaccines. Debates around the merits and de-merits of single versus triple vaccines added fuel to the controversy, and in particular put in to sharp relief the extent to which parents should have the 'right to choose'. Only the triple vaccine was available on the NHS.

The media hype around this issue and the decline in MMR uptake are not, however, as straightforward as might appear. As noted above, vaccination programmes have never been universally accepted, and there is a range of reasons why parents do not have their children immunized. Concerns about the adverse effects of vaccines may outweigh worries about the consequences of contracting the disease. Beliefs and knowledge rooted in alternative explanatory health systems, such as homoeopathy, for example, are at odds with biomedical notions of immunity. Indeed, for some, immunization can reduce rather than enhance immunity (Martin, 2000). It is not simply that people misunderstand or miscalculate the risk, as the so-called 'deficit model' of the public understanding of science implies, but rather that assumptions about health and disease may be at odds with biomedical interpretations (Hobson-West, 2003: 281).

Furthermore, amongst those parents who are positively disposed to immunization, the high-profile coverage in the media tends to challenge 'embedded understandings of the value of immunization' rather than result in outright rejection (Petts and Niemeyer, 2004). Petts and Niemeyer suggest that it encourages 'critical trust': that is, a reliance on formal institutions for knowledge and information in concert with a healthy scepticism as to whether the information given is impartial and unbiased. Thus, while the acceptance of immunization could be challenged, it can, or in some instances cannot be, repaired by way of information gathering – what some sociologists now call 'reflexivity'.

> A focus on the media is to over-simplify the complex interactions between direct and mediated experiences that underpin public perceptions of, and responses to risk.

> The media are an integral part of collective processes of 'making sense' of the world in different social contexts and localities . . . As dynamic mediators . . . the media are active interpreters who seek to resonate with social preferences and concerns. (Petts and Niemeyer, 2004: 18)

The anxieties associated with the triple vaccine are intensified because the presumed risks are profound; they concern children; the adverse effects of autism are feared; and they raise ethical issues of state control (Petts and Niemeyer, 2004). Parental responses are also increasingly influenced by other forms of media – the Internet – by 'networks of parents resisting specific vaccinations' (Streefland, 2001). In the face of such uncertainties, diverse sources of knowledge, information and experience are shared amongst virtual communities, and are interpreted by parents in relation to their own experiences.

Risks and 'lifestyles': the example of AIDS

Perhaps more than any other condition in recent history, Acquired Immune Deficiency Syndrome (AIDS) has generated the most extreme and extensive responses. Since the first case was reported in the USA at the Centre for Disease Control in 1981, the amount of literature produced on the subject has been phenomenal. Journals specifically devoted to AIDS; immunologists and virologists have reported their findings; and epidemiologists mapped the incidence of AIDS and identified the characteristics of those who become infected by Human Immunodeficiency Virus (HIV). In the early decades of the epidemic the media incessantly reported, misreported and moralized on the subject. During the 1980s and 1990s social scientists turned their attention to the behaviours, practices and cultures of what had hitherto been relatively neglected social groups: gay men, prostitutes and injecting drug-users (IDUs). Emerging from this literature is a growing consensus that the risk of contracting HIV/AIDS is shaped by socio-economic and political circumstances, and is profoundly linked to poverty. So too is the prognosis. In those countries where most people have access to health care and treatments, HIV/AIDS is now experienced as a chronic illness that like many others has to be managed. People live with HIV and AIDs (PLWHA). By contrast, throughout much of the world there are those who are less fortunate. HIV/AIDS provides an important historical illustration of notions of health, risk and lifestyle and crucially societal responses to a condition that is transmitted most commonly through human behaviours.

What is AIDS?

It is not possible to give an unequivocal answer to this question. What counts as AIDS and knowledge pertaining to it have invariably changed over the last decades and will undoubtedly continue to do so. Nevertheless, and somewhat crudely, AIDS is currently taken to refer to a deficient cell-mediated immunity as a result of infection by HIV. In particular, HIV penetrates cells within the body which are essential to maintain our immunity. As these cells, known as CD4 cells, are depleted, the virus becomes prevalent, and immunity to diseases is reduced. Diseases characteristic of AIDS include Kaposi's Sarcoma (KS) and a type of pneumonia, Pneumocystis carinii pneumonia. Some authors (Strang and Stimpson, 1990: 8) prefer to substitute the term 'HIV disease' for AIDS because, as they point out, the clinical definitions of AIDS fail to describe the range of health problems which occur once a person has been infected. It is believed that the main ways in which HIV is transmitted are via blood, semen, cervical and vaginal secretions.

Although there is still no cure, the prognosis for some people who are HIV-positive has improved since the development and use of highly active antiretroviral therapy (HAART) in 1996 (referred to in shorthand as antiretroviral treatment (ART)) and many men and women live relatively healthy lives. This represents something of a watershed in both the medical and sociological studies of HIV/AIDS with the earlier period referred to as pre-ART by comparison to the present where treatments are widely available. Overall prevalence rates are in the right direction with a slowing down of rates of infection, reduction of mortality and morbidity. Nevertheless the picture is a complex and changing one. An estimated 33.3 million people were living with HIV at the end of 2009 compared with 26.2 million in 1999; however, despite this increase, the annual number of new HIV infections is declining and has done so since the early 1990s (United Nations, 2010). While this overall trend is encouraging for sub-Saharan African countries, it is less so for some Asian and Eastern European nations where rates are accelerating (United Nations, 2010). Scrutiny of regular reports produced by UNAIDS, the WHO and various non-governmental organizations (NGOs) reveal a fluid picture with not only rates of newly acquired infection changing, but also the variability of modes of transmission. In some contexts HIV is transmitted from mother to baby, in others through sexual intercourse, others still through sharing of needles from injecting drugs. The important point to note is that the incidence, prevalence and spread of HIV/AIDS is variable and is rapidly changing. This is because the rates are a function of social, cultural, political and economic factors which are global in their nature. For example, in the UK the largest proportion of cases of heterosexual HIV is amongst people of African origin, who contracted the virus prior to entering the country. Tomorrow this could be different. The changing epidemiology is related to population flows, which in turn are the result of poverty, conflict and political transformations (Collins and Lee, 2003). This means that those who are living with HIV already face intolerable pressures; there is also the risk that these trends reinforce prejudice and representations of 'others' played out in the media.

AIDS and the risk society

When HIV/AIDS appeared and prompted scrutiny from social and medical scientists, the epidemic seemed emblematic of the non-calculable risks discussed by Giddens and Beck. Politicians and policy makers appeared anxious and media responses to the condition carried all the characteristics of moral panic. Young people were becoming ill and dying but it was not understood why. The story of AIDS provides a fascinating case history of modern/postmodern societal responses to illness and disease. As Sontag (1988: 86–7), who commented on the early responses to AIDS, observed: 'To the death of oceans and lakes and forests, the unchecked growth of populations in the poor parts of the world, nuclear accidents like Chernobyl, the puncturing and depletion of the ozone layer . . . to all these, now add AIDS . . . The taste for worst-case scenarios reflects the need to master fear of what is felt to be uncontrollable.' The uncertainty and disagreements about the cause of the syndrome fractured beliefs in medico-scientific progress. The enduring uncertainty about the scale and the consequences of the epidemic induced anxieties about the possible social and economic consequences. In the early 1980s, experts were flummoxed, and arguments raged about whether the HIV virus actually was the causal agent of AIDS. AIDS was regarded as a 'disease' of lifestyle, and commentators were quick to moralize about the actions of particular social groups. Thus, before the identification of the virus, some scientists thought that lifestyle variables might actually be the *cause* of AIDS. For example, it was suggested that immune overload could have been brought about by 'fast lane' gay lifestyles (Lacey and Waugh, 1983; Hsai et al., 1984); however, such theories have long since been discredited. In the USA in the early 1980s, where the syndrome appeared to be most prevalent amongst gay men, it was even labelled GRID - Gay Related Immune Deficiency - by some.

In the USA, and later in Europe, consumer activism developed within the chasm created by the confused scientific community and governments who were reluctant to take action against the growing numbers of people being diagnosed with - and at that time relatively quickly dying of - AIDS. HIV/AIDs, perhaps more than any other disease in the twentieth century, became politicized, an example of what Giddens (1994) calls 'life politics'. In place of more traditional institutionalized politics, 'life politics' is more personalized, in that people pursue issues which are salient to their own lives, and are not prepared to accept unquestioningly the pronouncements of those in authority. But although such politics are highly personal, they are also global, and indeed AIDS activism certainly saw alliances being forged between groups on the global stage.

The first decade of the epidemic was matched by an 'epidemic of fear and panic'. Strong (1990) refers to this as an 'epidemic psychology'; that is, societies become caught up in an emotional maelstrom which seems to those within it to be getting out of control. Writing in the early years of the epidemic, Strong suggested that the appearance of a new kind of disease, which may be transmitted through the most intimate of human contacts, strikes at the heart of individual and social interactions, and thereby reveals the fragility of social order. It was this perceived threat to social order that generated such fervent moralizing. Such moralizing can also be understood in terms of boundaries. As we have learned from Douglas (1966), points of contact and pollution (such as being infected by a virus) involve the crossing of a body boundary and therefore carry a symbolic load. Body boundaries, in turn, Douglas argues, are found to be represented metaphorically as social boundaries. If the body is under threat from a dangerous 'other', then so is society.

Flowers (2001) constructs an analytic framework of the changes in the management of risk in relation to British gay men. He refers to the early 1980s as a 'confused' period. A second, 'somatic' period of risk management - from the mid-1980s to the 1990s - came about with the understanding that the HIV virus was associated with AIDS, and the management of 'bodies' came to the fore. Health promotion programmes emphasized the need for individuals to act responsibly and rationally. 'Other' discrete bodies - those that had been tested as HIV-positive or perhaps had not been tested but might be participating in 'risky behaviours' - were to be avoided. The turn of the century saw a third, 'technological' period, wherein the advent of new drug treatments and test technologies to monitor viral activity added further dimensions to risk management. Such medical technologies have increasingly placed the risk management of HIV/AIDS in the hands of medical practitioners, which may have the effect of fracturing the community, volunteer support-based systems that characterized the confused period. Flowers suggests that these technological 'advances' contribute to a greater plurality and diversity of 'types of people with HIV': 'gay men can be divided by sexual behaviour (somatic risk), by HIV antibody status, by treatment status, by treatment compliance or concordance, by measures of viral load, by viral genotype, by viral phenotype, by viral resistance to some or potentially all available treatments' (Flowers, 2001: 67–8). Such dividing practices, he points out, exacerbate processes of 'othering' whereby those deemed to be the source of risk need to be subjected to closer scrutiny and surveillance.

The threat of AIDS: a menacing 'other'

Kroker and Kroker (1988), writing in the USA, drew parallels between the fear of AIDS and a generalized fear of the breakdown of immunological systems. For example, they noted that there is a striking resemblance between the medical rhetoric surrounding AIDS and military rhetoric. Indeed, the prevailing metaphors within the AIDS discourse have a military ring to them; they were of 'invasion', 'pollution' and 'alien takeover' (Sontag, 1988; Washer, 2004), and the conceptualization of AIDS as a form of systems breakdown was evident in Emily Martin's (1994) work discussed earlier in this chapter. Certainly during the 1980s the source of the HIV always seemed to be elsewhere: either in different countries or in 'different', and often presumed to be 'deviant', social groups. There were many stories about the origins of AIDS, but the dominant one was summarized by Sontag (1988: 51–2) as follows: 'AIDS is thought to have started in the "dark continent", then spread to Haiti, then to the United States and to Europe, then . . . It is understood as a tropical disease: another manifestation from the so-called Third World.' There are parallels between this story of HIV/AIDS and other infectious diseases such as 'Hong Kong Flu' and 'Spanish Influenza', and SARS, wherein, according to Washer (2004: 2571), 'we lay blame for the new threat on those outside one's own community, "the other"'.

The idea that AIDS originated, and is now widespread, in Africa fits neatly with Western conceptions of a wasting continent where poverty, illness and famine are rife (Treichler, 1999; Marshall, 2005). Traces of this discourse are still evident within the media's reporting of 'African AIDS' (Marshall, 2005). Marshall (2005) argues that these discourses are real in their effects, because they tend to elide with biomedical activities and solutions. For example, if HIV/AIDS is interpreted as being a primarily biological phenomenon, then the solutions will be sought in vaccines and efforts to change the actions of individual bodies. However, if it is understood as a sociocultural and political economic problem, then the solutions will involve challenging global power relations. From her analysis of recent news media in the USA, she finds that 'images of "Africa" that suspend it in a static realm of primitivity' (p. 2521) are still invoked. She also maintains that these disourses provide justification for scientific studies to be undertaken within populations in African countries, which are assessed on different ethical criteria than those in North America.

AIDS-related research has two main strands. Crudely, there is medico-scientific work which aims to yield vaccinations, cures and treatments, and social-scientific research which has focused predominantly on understanding health-related risk behaviours.

Towards a sociology of HIV and risk behaviour

Hart and Carter (2000) propose that an adequate sociology of HIV risk behaviour requires analyses to be undertaken at three levels: what they refer to as the macro-, micro- and meso-social levels. This provides a particularly useful approach to the sociology of health, risk and lifestyles more generally. 'Macro-social analyses' of risk refer to societal level explorations. They identify two main strands of work: first, that of Beck (1992a) and other accounts of the risk society. Here the fracturing of faith in expert systems is highlighted and in particular the ways in which patients, users, consumers, lay people - call them what you will - reappropriate knowledge about their body and related concerns. As we noted above, responses to HIV/AIDS and AIDS activism are paradigmatic illustrations of such social movements. Indeed, there is a fairly substantial research literature on the development of expertise and circulation of knowledge (Rosengarten, 2004). However, as Hart and Carter also point out, such strides towards 'therapeutic "choice", "empowerment" or "reflexivity" is severely limited' (2000: 242) for most people who live with HIV/AIDS, as they are disproportionately poor, socially disadvantaged and politically marginalized.

The political economy strand of macro-social analyses is therefore more instructive in terms of making sense of HIV/AIDS risk. As Hart and Carter put it: 'sexuality and drug consumption are in fact subject to social and economic forces beyond the immediate control of individual, local communities, and, often nation states' (2000: 243). An example of this perspective is the 'migrant labour thesis', which serves to explain why eastern, central and southern African countries have such high levels of HIV/AIDS (Kalipeni et al., 2004). As we noted above, the prime mode of transmission in these regions is unsafe heterosexual sex. Processes of colonization of these regions resulted in the establishment of large plantations and mines, which drew male labour from the surrounding hinterlands. Consequently, men were away from their homes and families for long periods of time. This had detrimental consequences for small-scale agricultural economies, which became unsustainable. Where there is chronic lack of food, women have to look to alternative means for survival. The situation both contributes to, and compounds levels of, prostitution and domestic instability (Craddock, 2004). From this perspective, therefore, we can see that 'Socio-economic conditions conducive to HIV transmission were largely created during colonial administrations that, though highly differentiated in form and function according to region, were nevertheless virtually universal in disrupting economic livelihoods, social practices, and community cohesion' (Kalipeni et al., 2004: 13). This political economy perspective also casts light on the extent to which issues of migration brought about by war, poverty, and economic and political instabilities exacerbate circumstances which facilitate 'risk' behaviours which lead to increased levels of HIV.

The concept 'risk environment' is used to capture social-structural production of risk. In a discussion on HIV risk and IDUs, Rhodes et al. define 'HIV risk environment' as 'the space - whether social or physical - in which a variety of factors exogenous to the individual interact to increase the chances of HIV transmissions' (2005: 1027).

Environmental factors which can be both barriers to, and facilitators of, individuals' risk behaviour are many and varied, and include factors such as 'trade and population movement', 'neighbourhood disadvantage and transition', 'prisons and criminal justice systems and law enforcement systems', 'social norms and networks', 'social capital' and 'armed conflict'. Rhodes and his colleagues make an important distinction between 'structural HIV prevention', with orientation towards changing social systems and institutions, and risk reduction strategies, which are orientated towards community level change. Thus the former involves social intervention, which is 'extra-individual', the unit of analysis being the social system, and change may include policies such as national debt relief, immigration regulations, trade relations, legislation and so on. 'Community HIV prevention', by contrast, is oriented towards social groups or networks within given geographical areas.

Community level prevention comprises what Hart and Carter refer to as meso-social change. Meso-social considerations refer to organizational issues, be they formal organizations of education (e.g., schools), religion (e.g., churches), health care (e.g., health centres, hospitals) or informal organizations such as socio-political groupings and activist groups. Hart and Carter argue that interventions at this meso level can be particularly effective in providing a buffer between structural and individual risks. They cite the example of needle exchange schemes. These take the form of local, community-based centres, where IDUs can access free clean needles, thus reducing their dependence on sharing used needles. Again at this meso level, schemes such as the licensing and HIV testing of sex workers in Senegal and the '100 per cent condom use' programme in Thailand have met with significant success (Davey and Hart, 2002).

Micro-social analyses explore the social meanings of behaviours that are deemed to be risky. Analyses which focus on the meanings and interpretations of risk provide clues as to the prevailing social and cultural norms which shape people's views, beliefs and actions. Kaler's (2004) anthropological study of men's 'AIDS-talk in everyday life' reveals how men living in Malawi (where rates of HIV/AIDS are high) assess risks associated with unprotected sexual intercourse with women. From numerous informal conversations with men in a wide variety of situations, she identified two main perspectives on AIDS risk: the 'agency perspective' and the 'inevitability perspective'. The former presumes that it is possible to lower one's risk to AIDS; the latter holds that actions to avert risk are pointless, because AIDS is so common that one will get it anyway, or, for others, it is simply God's will. In terms of agency, when taking action to avoid risk, many men spoke in terms of 'risk groups', in that they felt able to distinguish between women who they deemed to be at relatively low and high risk. Social status, financial independence, self-control, village or urban dwellers were criteria used to assess women's likely HIV status, and in turn to influence their decision to use a condom. This analysis therefore throws light on the men's 'risk landscapes' (Davison et al., 1992), which in turn are influenced by social and cultural norms.

Ongoing awareness of perceptions of risks is important for the development and implementation of health promotion and disease prevention strategies. Since the turn of the millennium, rates of risk practices have increased in Europe, North America and Australia (Elford and Hart, 2005) leading to the view that there is a 'hyper-individualization' of sexual activity and a concomitant loss of the sexual community that was evident in the early days of HIV/AIDS. Davis's (2008) study of gay men's accounts of sexual practice, however, provides empirical material that challenges this thesis and provides evidence of a 'continued salience of community for sexual practice' (p. 182). His analysis focuses on barebacking - intentional sex without the use of condoms - because this practice has come to be seen by some to epitomize the individualized, *caveat emptor* approach to risky sex. However the men's accounts reveal a more nuanced picture and the practice tends to be negotiated and based on shared decision making. Unprotected sex between partners is a joint decision revealing a kind of 'sexual citizenship' with presumed rights and obligations. The moral ambiguities that surround sexual activity are negotiated and renegotiated on a day-to-day basis. Thus promotional literature that advises gay men to 'assume nothing' about sexual partners who may be HIV positive is read by them to be patronizing and critical. Davis found that gay men do not resist the idea of undertaking safe sex practices; what they do resist is the moralizing tone of the international literature that implies individuals are not cognizant of the risks involved.

Attention to meanings is important in that it helps us appreciate that the epidemiological view of risk is a partial one. Two perspectives on risk behaviour have emerged from such micro-level studies: namely, 'situated rationality theories' and 'social action theories'. The former claims that an individual's assessment of risk is 'situation dependent' (T. Rhodes, 1997: 213). For example, a study in London of the social meanings and social processes of illicit drug use found that whilst HIV infection was a concern for users, it was relatively low down on the hierarchy of 'risk priorities' (T. Rhodes, 1997). 'Social action theories' contend that risk assessment is contingent not only on a person's prioritization of risk, but also on the social dynamics of situations, recognizing therefore the extent to which risk behaviours are contingent upon and produced by social interaction, negotiation and prevailing social norms and values. Rhodes and Cusick (2000) illustrate this in their study of relationships between HIV-positive people and their sexual partners, where they find a balance has to be struck between 'relationship safety' and 'viral danger' within the emotional context of their relationships. Love and intimacy may therefore form part of their social action.

Living with HIV/AIDS

In those areas where HIV-positive people are able to access HAART (also referred to as just ART), HIV has been transformed from a life-threatening disease to a chronic illness which can be managed through strict adherence to complex medications. The transformation of HIV from terminal illness to chronic condition is undoubtedly a major achievement, but living with HIV is still associated with uncertainties, which in turn are highly context-specific. The experiences of a middle-class, white, gay man born in the UK are very different from those of a black man born in Africa who has come to the UK as a result of political persecution, has uncertain citizenship status, and is living in poverty (Green and Smith, 2004). A study of black women and men who had migrated from a number of African countries to the UK reveals further diversity in what might at first sight appear to be a homogeneous group (Doyal and Anderson, 2005; Doyal et al., 2009). But their life histories are diverse, reflecting not least the different places they had come from, their reasons for migrating to the UK, and their legal status. All experienced degrees of poverty, discrimination, felt and actual stigma, and feelings of 'otherness'. Doyal and colleagues found that for many the diagnosis of HIV was but one element in a turbulent life: 'Thus, an HIV diagnosis may have a very different texture when it represents not a huge disruption in a largely predictable narrative but yet another trauma laid on top of forced migration, sexual violence and the death of partners and children' (2005: 1734). The women devised their own distinctive way of coping and responding to their circumstances. However, this sample of women has one thing in common: namely, that because they are in the UK, they have access to medical care and medication. If they were to leave and to return to their 'homes' (with which they strongly identify) and in some cases to their children, they would risk losing access to treatment, and therefore ultimately their lives. Paraphrasing Karl Marx, Doyal and Anderson (2005) state that these women are 'working hard to survive HIV but not necessarily in circumstances of their own choosing'; a paradox that will continue if female migration to wealthy countries increases, and was one felt by the men too who found their experiences compounded by the way they have to negotiate new lives in the context of diaspora (Doyal et al., 2009).

The transformation of HIV from a route to a terminal disease to one of chronic illness as a result of ART generates a further series of tensions (Rosengarten et al., 2004). Whilst the medication prolongs life, there are also a number of iatrogenic side-effects, such as nausea and diarrhoea, rash, anaemia, pancreatitis, diabetes, heart disease, lipoatrophy (fat loss) and lipodystrophy (fat redistribution) (Moyle and Boffito, 2004). Lipoatrophy, which may result in a thin and withdrawn appearance, and lipodystrophy, wherein the stomach may become distended and the back and breasts become enlarged, clearly impact upon body image, and in turn on self-identity. From her analysis of accounts given by users of ART, Persson (2004) highlights a series of ambivalences towards the drugs. Whilst the therapy may be successfully suppressing the virus and improving levels of immunity, as indicated by viral load tests, it may also be contributing to morphological changes in the body which act as a marker of being ill. Thus, as Persson puts it, 'The virus which might no longer be technologically detectable in the hidden *interior* of a person's blood paradoxically becomes detectable on the *surface* of their body' (2004: 52). In addition, embarking on ART creates a further degree of responsibility, in that the viral load test is a technology of surveillance, which monitors the patient's ability to keep their viral loads down (Rosengarten et al., 2004). Thus, for those living with HIV, there is a whole series of obligations and responsibilities associated with the management of their condition.

These obligations are intensified where there is regular monitoring of the immune status through tests for CD4 counts and viral load. A study of 95 men and 8 women in Taiwan (Lew-Ting and Chen, 2008) reveals how these clinical markers are interpreted and deployed by lay people to manage their immune status. All the participants were aware that greater CD4 counts and lower viral load were preferable but did not see the results of tests as definitive, not least because there is often a disjuncture between the test scores and their subjective health status. Lew-Ting and Chen identified contrastive responses to test results. A minority (N = 11) were 'preocuppied' by their counts and 'demonstrated an unremitting attentiveness to virtually any changes in bodily state' (p. 1045). This relatively disadvantaged socio-economic group contrasted to the majority of respondents who took a 'pragmatic' stance, questioning the reliability of the counts and were of the view that what constitutes a good CD4 count can vary between individuals. Furthermore, some felt that having a number of greater CD4 cells was less important than maintaining a stable count. This analysis of 'lay immunology' reveals that quantitative measures were not simply accepted as accurate markers of bodily or health status. Participants relied on multiple sources of information to assess and monitor their immune status and deployed a variety of strategies to manage their condition. The test is more than an observational device distinct from the body; rather there is a dynamic relation between the two, conceptualized by Rosengarten (2009) as a 'coextensive relation between information and flesh: that is, processes through which what initially seems to be "information" turns out to transform that which we know as "flesh" or, conversely, flesh turns out to have informational effects' (p. 5). Clinical data, practices and procedures read and render the body intelligible and how the body responds refracts on the data, practices and procedures. Those living with HIV are not simply monitored or treated but their bodies inform biomedicine. Interpretations are in flux, not least as we have seen amongst the men and women with HIV in Taiwan whose perceptions and reinterpretations of markers refract destabilizing understandings of body with HIV. Thus lay immunology, lay epidemiology and lay health beliefs are not distinct from medical knowledge; rather there is a dialectic between them.

The example of HIV/AIDs is indicative of a further significant change in the experience and management of illness and this is what Aronowitz (2009) explores in his paper 'Converged experience of risk and disease'. Chronic conditions such as diabetes, heart disease, cancers and rheumatoid arthritis require perpetual management that is directed at reducing anticipated developments. Diseases themselves harbour risk factors of other diseases so not only must people manage symptoms but they must be vigilant to the possible pathological effects associated with their conditions. The management of health risks thus becomes more problematic and subject to scrutiny for those who experience illness, which in turn is the focus of our next chapter.

Conclusion

This chapter has attempted to explore various aspects of the relationship between health, lay beliefs about health, lifestyles and risk. We have seen that discourses around health have emerged as an important feature of contemporary societies. However, understandings and beliefs about health clearly vary among different groups. This variation is largely accounted for by the social, cultural, biographical and economic context within which individuals are located. Central to the emergence of these discourses about health has been the concept of lifestyle. This notion often refers to those aspects of social life over which individuals appear to have some choice – and as such, has tended to emphasize differential patterns of consumption, such as exercise and smoking. However, we have seen that this interpretation is a rather naïve one, as people's lifestyles, like their beliefs, are, to a significant extent, socially embedded and socially structured. We have also seen how the concept of risk has emerged of late, as a central articulating principle of health and lifestyle discourses. This is especially evident in discussions of AIDS and HIV. The chapter therefore concluded by critically examining the concepts of risk and lifestyle associated with HIV/AIDS.

FURTHER READING

Aronowitz, R. A. (2009), 'Converged Experience of Risk and Disease', *The Milbank Quarterly*, 87, 2: 417–22.

Blaxter, M. (2010), *Health*, 2nd edn, Cambridge: Polity. This provides a comprehensive account of conceptualizations and theorizations of health.

Crawford, R. (2004), 'Risk Ritual and the Management of Control and Anxiety in Medical Culture', *Health*, 8, 4: 505–28. A considered analysis of the consequences of attempts to control health risks.

Green, J. (1997), *Risk and Misfortune: The Social Construction of Accidents*, London: UCL Press. A neat, thought-provoking example of contemporary risk is examined in relation to the construction and conceptualization of accidents.

Hart, G. and Carter, S. (2000), 'A Sociology of Risk Behaviour', in S. J. Williams, J. Gabe and M. Calnan (eds), *Health Medicine and Society: Key Theories, Future Agendas*, London: Routledge. This study examines the sociology of risk in terms of macro, meso and micro perspectives, and provides a useful structure for analysing any number of substantive issues of health and risk.

Nettleton, S. and Gustaffson, U. (eds) (2002), *The Sociology of Health and Illness Reader*, Cambridge: Polity. The chapters in Part II, 'Health and Risk', contain a mix of conceptual and empirical accounts of health and risk.

Rosengarten, M. (2009), *HIV Interventions: Biomedicine and the Traffic between Information and Flesh*, London: University of Washington Press.

The data presented in relation to HIV/AIDS are constantly changing; for updated information, see www.unaids.org

4 The Experience of Chronic Illness and Disability

Introduction

Virtually everyone has been ill at some point in his or her life. The onset of an illness often means that everyday routines such as going to work, attending lectures or cooking a meal are disrupted. It also means that the sufferer is likely to feel both mentally and physically unwell for a period of time. In our society perhaps one of the most common types of illness is a bad cold, and when it occurs, we may feel tempted to stay at home rather than go to work, take some aspirin, and expect those around us to be sympathetic to our condition. Being well aware that the symptoms will be short-lived, we can look forward to feeling better within a matter of days. However, this is not the case if the illness is a chronic one. Chronic illnesses, such as heart disease, types of cancer, asthma, multiple sclerosis, AIDS, rheumatoid arthritis, diabetes, Parkinson's disease, epilepsy, psoriasis, ulcerative colitis and senile dementia are, by definition, long-term. Thus the impact upon the sufferers' lives and those around them is inevitably more profound.

In Western industrialized societies chronic conditions are becoming increasingly common, so much so that most of us will know someone who suffers from some kind of chronic illness and will be aware that the implications of such conditions extend well beyond biophysical changes. For example, if a member of a family experiences senile dementia, it is likely that this will have an impact on the rest of the family in terms of the decisions which have to be made about caring responsibilities and the financial implications of having a relative who can no longer look after him- or herself. This in turn can impose a severe strain on the relationships between kin.

It is clear, therefore, that biophysical changes have significant social consequences. Illness reminds us that the 'normal' functioning of our minds and bodies is central to social action and interaction. In this respect the study of illness throws light on the nature of the interaction between the body, the individual and society. If we cannot rely on our bodies to function 'normally', then our interaction with the social world becomes perilous; our dependence on others may become exacerbated, and in turn our sense of self may be challenged. For example, the onset of rheumatoid arthritis can result in severe restriction of bodily movements, which may mean that the individual becomes dependent upon others to perform tasks previously carried out by him- or herself. This, especially within a culture which emphasizes independence and self-reliance, can be threatening to the sufferer's self-esteem. It can also make social interactions, which in our society are for the most part based on notions of reciprocity, particularly precarious. As Freidson (1970a: 235) puts it, a 'chronically ill person who "expects too much" or "makes too many demands" is likely to be rejected by others'. This means that the person who is ill has constantly to make judgements about the appropriateness of his or her demands on others.

Essentially, then, chronic illness can impact upon individuals' daily living, their social relationships, their identity (the view that others hold of them) and their sense of self (their private view of themselves). It is on these *experiences of illness* that sociologists have focused their attention. It has emerged from the literature that responses to illness are not simply determined by either the nature of biophysical symptoms or individual motivations, but rather are shaped and imbued by the social, cultural and ideological context of a person's biography. Thus illness is at once both a very personal *and* a very public phenomenon.

This chapter will introduce two perspectives which have dominated the sociology of illness; these are the functional and interpretative approaches. The first highlights the extent to which the onset of illness can involve the adoption of an appropriate social role - the *sick role*. The second approach, by contrast, focuses on how the person who is ill and those around him or her make sense of the illness, and how these interpretations affect action. To a significant extent the interpretative approach to illness was formulated through critiques of the functionalist approach, and so it seems logical to take the two in turn. In this chapter we will also discuss some of the key concepts and findings which have emerged from research into the experience of illness. These include notions of self and identity, the management of symptoms to maintain the appearance of normality, uncertainty, stigma and coping strategies. It will become apparent that people who experience long-term illness are often creative in the ways in which they react to their physical conditions.

The sick role

Illness is often related to capacity to work and/or fulfil social obligations. However, the presence of illness must be sanctioned by the medical profession. This forms the central premise of Parsons' (1951) concept of the *sick role*. Parsons makes a distinction between the biological basis of illness and its social basis, and argues that to be sick is a socially as well as a biologically altered state. What constitutes illness in any given culture will therefore be related to the norms and values that prevail (Parsons, 1979). Although, as we will see throughout this chapter, experiences of illness change over time and as norms and values alter in relation to broader social transformations, Shilling (2002) argues that the 'deep cultural values underpinning' the rights and obligations associated with the sick role endure - not least the cultural expectations that we should look after our own bodies and equip ourselves with the knowledge and skills to manage our own illnesses.

Sickness is a form of deviance, an 'unconscious motivation' to break with the learned capacities of adulthood. However, the sick person is not culpable, and is therefore granted certain rights and privileges. Thus the sick role prescribes a set of rights and obligations. A person who is sick cannot be expected to fulfil normal social obligations, and is not held responsible for their illness. In turn, however, the sick role assumes that the sick person should want to get well and, to this end, must seek and co-operate with technically competent medical help. It appears that this 'role' is acknowledged within the lay discourse of Western societies, as can be seen by the comments made in interviews cited by Herzlich and Pierret (1987: 194): 'When one is sick, one obviously tries to get better as soon as possible. Personally, I do everything I can, I try to do my utmost to be cured as quickly as possible . . . I would be a good patient, come to think of it.' And another said: 'It is a moral duty to recover one's health, the first duty to oneself and everyone else . . . seeking help from those who can restore one's health, that is to say, the doctors.' The sick role thus indicates that the person who makes an effort to get well will be granted a social status, as Herzlich and Pierret (1987: 53) again explain:

> To be *sick* in today's society has ceased to designate a purely biological state and come to define a status, or even a group identity. It is becoming more and more evident that we perceive the reality of illness in these terms, for we tend to identify our neighbour as 'a diabetic', almost in the same manner as we identify him [*sic*] as 'a professor', or 'a mason'. To be 'sick' henceforth constitutes one of the central categories of social perception.

Thus illness may become part of the identity of the sufferer, and this is especially significant, as we shall see, for those with long-term illnesses.

The changed identity of the sick person is contingent upon the reaction of others, and how people respond depends on the nature of the disease itself. For example, people will react differently to someone with an illness which is considered to be very serious and life-threatening than to someone who has a more minor condition. With this in mind, Freidson (1970a), drawing on 'societal reaction' (or 'labelling') theory, further elaborated Parsons' concept. The extent to which a person is granted the rights and privileges of the sick role, Freidson argues, turns on the seriousness of the imputed disease and its legitimacy. He postulates three types of legitimacy: first, there are those cases where it is feasible for a person to get well, in that their disease can be treated, and so the legitimacy of their access to the sick role is *conditional*; second, in the case of incurable illness, the access to the sick role must be *unconditionally legitimate*, because the person cannot act to 'get well'; and third, where the illness is stigmatized by others, the person's access to the sick role may be treated as *illegitimate*, and the rights and privileges of the sick role are unlikely to be granted. It is important to appreciate that these societal reactions are historically specific, and in fact Freidson's descriptions refer to white American middle-class society of over three decades ago. This is shown in table 4.1. Parsons' original formulation of the sick role is to be found in cell 5. This typology is important, because, first, it draws attention to the extent to which the experience of illness is bound up with the wider social context, and, second, because it makes clear that the meanings imputed to illness can impact upon the experience and the identity of the sufferer.

The concept of the sick role as described by Parsons is an ideal type and therefore, as he himself observes, does not necessarily correspond with empirical reality. Indeed, a moment's reflection on one's own experience is likely to bring to mind circumstances where the sick role did not apply. For example, we might have symptoms but refuse to seek professional help, or we might feel ill but carry on with activities which may make our condition worse. Nevertheless, in relation to the study of the experience of illness, one of the principal merits of the concept of the sick role is that it provides us with a heuristic device against which actual illness behaviours and experiences can be assessed. Studies such as these reveal the range and complexity of illness behaviours.

Table 4.1 *Types of deviance for which the individual is not held responsible by imputed legitimacy and seriousness*

Imputed seriousness	Illegitimate (stigmatized)	Conditionally legitimate	Unconditionally legitimate
	Cell 1	Cell 2	Cell 3
	Stammer	A cold	Pockmarks
Minor deviation	Partial suspension of ordinary obligations; few or no new privileges; adoption of a few new obligations	Temporary suspension of a few ordinary obligations; temporary enhancement of ordinary privileges. Obligations to get well	No special change in obligations or privileges
	Cell 4	Cell 5	Cell 6
	Epilepsy	Pneumonia	Cancer
Serious deviation	Suspension of some ordinary obligations; adoption of new obligations; few or no new privileges	Temporary release from ordinary obligations; addition to ordinary privileges. Obligation to co-operate and seek help in treatment	Permanent suspension of many ordinary obligations; marked additions to privileges

Source: Freidson (1970a).

Access to the sick role

As we have seen, from a functionalist perspective, people who feel sick have an obligation to get well, and this first requires that they seek medical advice. However, most people, most of the time, do not go to the doctor when they are ill. Indeed, prevalence studies have revealed that most symptoms are never seen by practitioners (Hannay, 1979): there is a *symptom iceberg*. Certainly most of the time, if we have a cold, a bad back or a bout of hay fever, we probably would not want to bother the doctor. Conversely, if we did, general practitioners would get rather irritated, as one of the main sources of exasperation with their work is patients who present with trivia (Charles-Jones et al., 2003). However, it is not only trivial symptoms that fail to reach health professionals; studies have also found that people suffering from extreme pain or even experiencing a heart attack (Pattenden et al., 2002) do not necessarily seek help.

There appears to be a moral dimension to seeking help, and people do appear to be concerned not to be, or to be seen to be, 'time-wasters', but are keen to use services responsibly. For example, Goode et al. (2004) in a study of callers to NHS Direct (a 24-hour telephone helpline) reveal how users *perceived* that they are less likely to be seen as a nuisance or as a 'time-waster' by nurse advisers than they are by doctors. This is in part due to the organizational form of the service, which is regarded by the callers as being less resource hungry than a face-to-face consultation. The service may also serve to confirm the caller's need for a visit to a medical practitioner, and so confer their legitimate access to the patient role. Ironically, the service was established in order to divert demand from doctors, but in fact it reinforces the patient's pathway to the doctor's surgery. Thus this service, and of course the vast array of health information sites on the Internet (Hardey, 1999), extend the sources of advice that people can make use of when assessing whether or not they should seek formal professional advice. Thus symptoms may be self-medicated or advice may be sought from friends, relatives, websites and so on. Indeed, prior to the availability of on-line information, a study by Scambler et al. (1981), in which women kept health diaries for six weeks, found that on average 11 lay consultations were noted for every one medical consultation. Of a total of 547 lay consultations, 50 per cent were with husbands, 25 per cent were with female friends, 10 per cent with mothers, 8 per cent with female relatives, and 7 per cent with various others, including boyfriends and fathers. Of course, the advice of those consulted may be to visit a practitioner.

Freidson refers to this as the *lay referral system* - a system that is now much more varied and complex than it was when Freidson coined the term. This is due not least to the Internet - which for most students reading this text will form a key part of their everyday lives. Gray et al.'s (2005) study of adolescents in the UK and the USA found that they regularly use the Internet, and are keen to be active participants in their own health care. As this woman states:

> I think that patients - they just want to be more clued up nowadays, and know what's going on for themselves instead of like just going to a doctor and him telling them that 'This is wrong with you, and you're going to have to do this'. They want to be able to do things for themselves, help themselves, and not be totally reliant on seeing doctors and things, and not making out that they're just completely stupid. (UK female, 17–18 years)

However, the authors also find that the participants are keen to trust in and depend on health professionals: Parsons' image of the sick role still prevails.

> You're not going to go on the internet if you have cancer. . . . If you've got a big tumour or something, you're not going to go online to fix it! . . . But if you have like - problems like - I don't know, your cuticles are cracking - like 'I'll go online - I'll see if they have remedies for bad cuticles' or something. (US female, 16–18 years)

Thus there is a distinction between symptoms which warrant specialized interventions and those that do not. This observation about cancer, however, is an interesting one, because studies of people who are diagnosed with cancer find that they do use on-line resources to seek out information about the merits and de-merits of treatments and to gain support from others who share their illness experiences (Ziebland, 2004).

The decision to consult may be due to a range of factors other than the presence or severity of symptoms. Zola (1973) identified five factors, or 'triggers', which contribute to the decision to seek help. First is the occurrence of an interpersonal crisis: for example, going through a divorce or losing a job might lead someone to reflect on their symptoms which have been ongoing for some time. A second trigger might be the perceived interference of illness with social or personal relations. A painful knee might prevent someone taking part in the activities of a walking club, or poor breathing might hinder someone from visiting the pub to be with their mates. The third trigger is 'sanctioning', that is, another person might legitimize the need for, or in fact insist on, a visit to the GP. Fourth is the perceived interference with vocational or physical activity. For example, someone might feel that they can no longer do their job properly because of their symptoms and so feel bound to seek help. Finally, the 'temporalizing of symptomatology' refers to the common practice of saying, if my rash has not cleared up by next Friday, then I will go to the doctor. The significance of these triggers is that they demonstrate that seeking help is an ongoing social process, rather than a straightforward response to physical symptoms.

People do not respond to the biophysical aspects of symptoms, but rather to the *meaning* of those symptoms. Many 'common' ailments – for example, stomach pains, headaches or a stiff neck – may be 'explained away' or 'normalized'. They may be attributed to circumstances such as working late at night, eating too much strong cheese or sitting in a draught. If these ailments do turn out to be manifestations of a more serious illness, it may take some time for this to be recognized. Pattenden et al. (2002) found that patients who were admitted to hospital following their second, third or fourth acute myocardial infarction (heart attack) delayed seeking help. Reasons for delay included explaining away symptoms, finding the symptoms were very different from their previous experiences, not wanting to believe that they were actually having another heart attack, and not wanting to make a fuss. The pathway to a consultation with a health professional is more varied than it was when Zola was writing in the 1970s – not least because of the profusion of sources of information and advice. But having analysed the findings of empirical studies of lay usage of the Internet and NHS Direct, Hanlon and I (Nettleton and Hanlon, 2006) suggest that Zola's triggers still have a validity. We conclude that:

> On the one hand there is a growing diversity of health care provision and use, and yet on the other hand the norms and values that underpin notions of health care use are concurrently contributing to a reinforcement of caution and conventionality. Whilst health care users may be engaging with an increasingly complex patchwork of services their conceptualizations of what it means being a good patient guides their help seeking practices.

Thus accessing the sick role can be a complex process. The interpretation of symptoms will invariably be culturally specific, and bound up with normative conceptions of the body. As Kleinman (1988: 13) explains:

> To understand how symptoms and illnesses have meaning, therefore, we must first understand normative conceptions of the body in relation to the self and the world. These integral aspects of local social systems inform how we feel, how we perceive mundane bodily processes, and how we interpret those feelings and processes.

Because the interpretation of symptoms is context-dependent, Kleinman suggests that it is imperative that health practitioners are aware of the cultural as well as the biological basis of symptoms.

The variable interpretation of ailments is not restricted to lay people, and when presented with symptoms, doctors are bound to draw on the same 'common-sense' interpretations as the rest of us. In his study of people who have been diagnosed as having multiple sclerosis (MS), Robinson (1988a) found that this was often the case. However, when the doctor makes an assessment of the situation or a diagnosis, the consequences may be more far-reaching, as one study participant explains:

> I became ill in 1975–6 with difficult to identify symptoms, some of which seem now clearly to be MS. At the time I was working in the evening, as well as the day, and doing up a house as well . . . I saw the doctor and was treated for depression, *after which I did become depressed.* In a way I felt this was partly because I lost credence – people didn't believe in me any more so I took the opportunity to let go of the reins and let others take over. Anyway I felt and I still do that I was able to sustain the pace and that wasn't why I was so weak and 'ill feeling' . . . However, I took the treatment and the label. (Robinson, 1988a: 20, my emphasis)

We can see, therefore, that even after someone has sought professional help, access to the sick role is not necessarily all that straightforward and a considerable tenacity is sometimes required on the part of the sufferer to gain legitimate status as sick. Not securing a diagnosis means that people may be living in diagnostic limbo, and this in turn may impede access to social and practical support.

Lay legitimation of the sick role

Access to, and legitimation of, the sick role is also mediated by structural variables such as age, gender, class and ethnicity. The response of practitioners to their patients, for example, has been found to vary according to the social background of the latter (see chapter 6). Likewise, in other situations the extent to which a person is permitted to enter the sick role will be mediated by the perceptions of others. This became evident in an ethnographic study of a primary school, which describes the social processes of accomplishing sick role status (Prout, 1986). Some children were more readily granted the status by the school staff than others. Their success was predicated on where the children were located on a hierarchy of 'wetness'. Wet children, Prout (1986: 120) explains, were those who 'were unable or unwilling to face up to the assumed rigours of an instrumental, demanding or competitive world'. The extent to which the staff came to view children as 'wet' was related to their perception of the children's parents (invariably mothers), age and gender. For example, Tina, who was often allowed by her mother to stay 'off school', was known as a 'wet' child, and thus when she complained of pains in her neck, nothing was done about it. Alan, by contrast, who was a fairly tough boy, was allowed to go almost immediately to the school secretary when he felt ill.

Thus legitimacy of access to the sick role can also be influenced by moral evaluations. This may even occur when someone has received confirmation of sick role status from a health professional. For example, the credibility of a medical diagnosis may well be undermined for those who are only mildly affected by a disease or who have remissions. As Joy, a respondent in Robinson's (1988b: 58) study of MS, articulates:

> Some people can't understand why I'm in a wheelchair sometimes and not other times . . . with some as long as I look cheerful and say I'm feeling fine they can cope with me but if I say I don't feel well they ignore the remark, or say I *look* well! I feel that some of them think I'm being lazy or giving up if I'm in a wheelchair, and they are inclined to talk right over my head to my pusher. (emphasis in original)

Conditions such as chronic pain, which do not fit any medical category and are idiopathic (that is, they have no identifiable cause) are especially problematic.

We have seen that entering the sick role is more complex than the original concept suggests, as meanings and perceptions interfere with the process. Finally, it is noteworthy that there are also pragmatic considerations which prevent the straightforward acquisition of sick status. For example, it may be impossible to be relieved of normal social duties if these involve caring for others and/or the general running of a household. As Graham points out:

> [W]hile a mother is quick to identify and respond to symptoms of illness and disability in others, she appears less assiduous in monitoring her own health. Her role in caring for others appears to blunt her sensitivity to her own needs. Being ill makes it difficult for individuals to maintain their normal social roles and responsibilities: since the mother's roles and responsibilities are particularly indispensable, mothers are reluctant to be ill. (Graham, 1984: 159)

Imputation of responsibility

Freidson's typology of sickness recognizes that those who acquire sick role status do not necessarily escape blame, and may still be construed as culpable. This is especially significant at a time when there is a growing range of so-called lifestyle diseases (see chapter 3). For example, smokers who suffer from lung cancer may be held responsible for their illness, and in some cases doctors may refuse to treat them. During recent decades the scientific literature has tended to locate the causes of disease in features of people's personalities. If the personality is the source of illness, for example, if the stressed or anxious person is more likely to get coronary heart disease or cancer, then this can have significant implications for the sufferer's sense of self, the reactions of others, and the sufferer's ability to overcome the illness (Pollock, 1993). Whilst, as we shall see, the presence of illness can impact upon a person's sense of self, to imply that a person's 'self' is the cause of a disease, or at least its prognosis, can have profound socio-psychological consequences. The sick role context in contemporary post-industrial societies is more diffuse and responsibilities for responding to symptoms and managing illness potentially more onerous. Even in those circumstances where people are not blamed for the onset of a condition, there is an expectation that people should do what they can to get better. A positive personality and creative response to disease is triumphed. This is evident in the blurring of commercial and charitable organizations who seek to raise funds, undertake research and offer support for conditions once stigmatized such as cancer or heart disease.

The ubiquity of the pink/red ribbon culture demonstrates this. Red ribbons for AIDS and pink for breast cancer are the symbols of the cause-related marketing activities of what have become international charitable organizations. Gayle Sulik's

(2010) book *Pink Ribbon Blues: How Breast Cancer Culture Undermines Women's Health* traces the rise of this phenomenon, detailing how organizations such as the charity 'Susan G. Komen Race for the Cure' have forged alliances with businesses such as KFC (Kentucky Fried Chicken) to generate funds to invest in diagnostic technologies and pharmaceutical treatments. Significantly, they recruit those who have been diagnosed or their families to become proactively and positively involved in the race. This leaves little scope for those who do not or cannot participate. It becomes difficult to challenge the seemingly laudable aspiration to search for a cure or take positive action in the face or illness. But there is a more sinister consequence, because to opt out either because one cannot or will not participate can be read as an abrogation of responsibility. The sick role becomes extended not only to getting well, but to being positive, creative and seeking to manage not only one's own health but that of others.

In sum, within this section we have seen that the sick role constitutes a culturally specific ideal-typical response to illness. The reality of everyday life, however, is more complex than the concept itself suggests. The interpretation of symptoms, the decision to seek help, and the conferring of rights and expectations on the sick person are mediated by the social and cultural environment. A key dimension of the sick role is that it is incumbent on the sick person to make every effort to get well. Clearly this may be inappropriate to people who are chronically ill. As Bury (1988: 113) points out, 'No simple "role prescription" exists in our society for the chronically ill, or even those with whom they have contact, to guide social interaction.' It is to the experience of chronic illness more specifically that I will now turn, but this first necessitates that we reflect on the meaning of illness itself.

The meaning of illness

In order to highlight the social basis of illness, some authors distinguish between disease and illness. Kleinman (1988: 3) suggests that disease is a biophysical event and the prime concern of medical practitioners, whereas illness 'refers to how the sick person and members of the family or wider social network perceive, live with and respond to symptoms and disability'. Dingwall (1976: 26) also argues that there is no such thing as 'essential illness'; rather, illness is construed through the meanings and interpretations that are accorded to certain categories of experience, and 'there is no necessary relationship to any biological happening'. Advocating the need for a negotiated approach, Dingwall (1976: 121) states: 'Illness action is the outcome of continuing efforts on the part of the sick person, and those with whom he [*sic*] associates, to make sense of what is going on in the light of the knowledge, resources and motivations available to them.' Thus, rather than simply observing illness behaviour, sociologists must endeavour to understand illness action. The former refers to the way people behave given the presence of symptoms, whilst the latter focuses on how people make sense of and interpret their illness experience and, crucially, what it means to them. When people have the opportunity to give voice to their experiences of illness, it becomes evident that their accounts are woven into their biographies.

Illness narratives

The experience of illness reflects the person's experience of life. Kleinman (1988: 49) refers to this as an 'illness narrative':

> a story the patient tells, and significant others retell, to give coherence to the distinctive events and long-term course of suffering. The plot lines, core metaphors, and rhetorical devices that structure the illness narrative are drawn from cultural and personal models for arranging experiences in meaningful ways and for effectively communicating those meanings . . . The personal narrative does not merely reflect illness experience, but rather contributes to the experience of symptoms and suffering.

Given that the interpretation of illness contributes to how it is experienced, Kleinman argues that it is crucial that practitioners understand and take heed of the lay person's story.

When G. Williams (1984), for instance, asked people suffering from arthritis what they thought caused it, he found that they interpreted this as a question relating to their biography, and answered accordingly. This serves to illustrate that beliefs about the cause of illness need to be understood as part of a larger interpretative process which Williams calls *narrative reconstruction* – that is, the routine way in which we make sense of events in our lives. How people make sense of their illness is within the context of their personal biographies, and in turn this must invariably be influenced by, and meshed with, the cultural values of the society in which they live. Sociologists have therefore produced descriptions of the everyday situations of particular chronic diseases, and in so doing have highlighted the biographical and cultural context in which illness emerges (Radley, 1993: 1).

Illness narratives contribute to an understanding of the experience of illness (Hyden, 1997; Bury, 2001). They are particularly instructive in contributing to an understanding of how people experience, make sense of, and incorporate their illness into their identity. Hyden (1997: 55) identifies five such uses of illness narratives:

> 1. [T]o transform illness events and construct a world of illness; 2. to reconstruct one's life history in the event of chronic illness; 3. to explain and understand the illness; 4. as a form of strategic interaction in order to assert or project one's identity; and lastly 5. to transform illness from an individual to a collective phenomenon.

Hyden is referring here primarily to narratives elicited in the context of research interviews. Of course, all narratives are context-dependent, and so stories we present to doctors, nurses, family, friends and so on will vary and may complement or even at times appear to contradict each other. Illness narratives not only provide insights into the experiences and views of the narrator, such as the practical consequences of living with symptoms and how illness influences social relationships, but more than this, they also afford insights into the cultural and social factors that shape, or give rise to, people's experiences. The narrator invariably draws upon the language, beliefs, ideologies, metaphors and representations that are available to them (Radley and Billig, 1996; Bury, 2001). In sum, the story reveals as much about the culturally available discourses as it does about the minutiae of the teller's life.

Frank (1995) identifies three 'types' of illness narratives, which vary in terms of their general storyline or plot. He calls these the 'restitution', 'quest' and 'chaos' narratives. The *restitution narrative* is typified by the Parsonian sick role; a person is ill, finds out what is wrong, seeks help and/or uses medication, and gets better. As Frank points out, the empirical adequacy of this narrative is less salient than is its force as a 'master narrative'. It fits social expectations, and is dominant in popular culture. It is the narrative that we are most comfortable with, and the one medicine can most comfortably hear.

The *quest narrative* is 'defined by the ill person's belief that something is to be gained through the experience' (1995: 115). The illness may become a metaphorical journey from which the ill person may gain self-awareness, or the ability to help others. Public illustrations of the growing salience of this type of narrative are the growing numbers of people who recount their stories within the public domain. For example, one journalist published a piece in the *Guardian* listing '21 things I would never have known if I hadn't had cancer'. Before listing each lesson learned, she writes:

> In the aftermath of diagnosis, I found myself on edges and in abysses I have never been to before. But terrible as it was it was never boring. It became a project, a journey, a new way of understanding myself, others and the world around me. There are things I would never have known or experienced if I had not had breast cancer. (McFadyean, 2005: 15)

Narratives may also be written in virtual space. Hardey (2002), for example, reviewed personal home pages constructed to tell stories of illness and identified three elements to such accounts. There were stories of 'explanation' of illness, stories of 'advice' on conditions, and stories offering 'solutions'. In addition, some Internet sites offered products and services which people claimed to have benefited from and wanted to share with others. Experiential knowledge is therefore shared and exchanged within a growing diversity of media sources. From her analysis of cancer patients' engagement with the Internet, Ziebland (2004) maintains that not only do they gain information, but their interaction with others in the virtual environment typifies the 'quest narrative'.

The *chaos narrative* is the antithesis of the restitution narrative - in that there is no clear beginning and no actual or imagined end. There is no narrative 'structure' as such; no 'plot', no clear 'route map', and no 'metaphorical journey'. Consequently, chaos narratives are difficult to 'listen' to, and they are also difficult to 'hear', because they may invoke anxiety in that the very existence of an illness that cannot be 'cured' reminds the listener of their own vulnerability. Furthermore, chaos narratives remind practitioners of their limitations. 'In these stories the modernist bulwark of remedy, progress, and professionalism cracks to reveal vulnerability, futility and impotence' (Frank, 1995: 97). It is also the most embodied form of story:

> the body telling chaos stories defines itself as being swept along, without control, by life's fundamental *contingency*. Efforts to reassert predictability have failed repeatedly, and each failure has had its costs. Contingency is not exactly accepted; rather, it is taken as inevitable.

Narratives of medically unexplained symptoms

The distinction between illness and disease alluded to above arose in the context of the emergence of the biomedical model with its associated dualisms. That disease can be located within the anatomical frame forms the basis of the biomedical model and the clinical method that have their roots in the pathological anatomy developed in the eighteenth century (Foucault, 1976) (see chapters 1 and 2). The idea that the origins of disease are located within the interior space of the body continues to dominate both medical and popular discourse. 'As a result', Aronowitz (2001: 803) suggests, 'many patients lost their symptom-based and clinically based diagnoses and became "medical orphans".' This is intensified by the deployment of increasingly sophisticated technologies, such as positron emission tomography (PET) and magnetic resonance imaging (MRI), which mean that practitioners believe that they can determine the site of disease with greater and greater confidence (Dumit, 2000). This serves to fabricate 'genuine disease' as opposed to the 'experience of illness', but it also means that people whose symptoms are unexplained may become more 'at sea'.

As we have noted above, some clinically unexplained syndromes may secure labels such as myalgic encephalomyelitis (ME) (L. Cooper, 2002) or repetitive strain injury (RSI) (Arksey, 1998; Turner, 1995), but the 'diagnoses' invariably remain contested. However, the label itself may provide some recourse (however precarious) to some form of categorical identity and access to a support group or a specialist clinic for support. By contrast, those who live with 'unnamed' unexplained illness have no coherent sense of what their seemingly disparate symptoms may amount to.

Nettleton et al. (2004, 2005) carried out a study of men and women who had attended a neurology clinic with symptoms which remained clinically unexplained. A significant proportion of neurology patients (between 20 and 40 per cent) fall into this category. We suggested that patients' accounts were reminiscent of Frank's (1995) *chaos narratives*. They were characterized by confusion and uncertainty; there was an absence of a clear-cut problem which could lend itself to treatments (as would be the case for the restitution narrative), and so there is no clear beginning or end. There were 'no route maps' for that 'metaphorical journey'. Indeed, they lacked any sense of an illness trajectory. The following questions remained unanswered: 'Will my condition deteriorate?', 'Will it improve?', 'What is the cause of my symptoms?', 'Will it stabilize?' Most participants in the study had endured symptoms for many years, and found it difficult to remember the chronology of their visits to clinics or specialists, or the wide variety of investigations they had endured and the endless 'negative' results. Their accounts tended to be more a 'merry-go-round' of hope and despair than providing any sense of a definitive progression. As Frank (1995) argues, there is a socio-cultural emphasis on being 'successfully ill'; this involves finding solutions, treatments and therapies; 'fighting' one's symptoms, and even gaining insight into one's sense of self. Not surprisingly, therefore, unresolved illness experiences make significant others feel uneasy, and 'solutions' such as special diets or alternative therapies are invariably offered. We tend to feel more comfortable with the *restitution narrative*, and so seem to feel compelled to provide answers and hope. This in turn can be dispiriting for those who have lived with their illness for decades; as one woman put it, 'I just want permission to be ill'.

Ulcerative colitis – an example of a chronic condition

Before turning to the more general findings of studies of chronic illness, it may be useful first to consider in some detail the impact of one particular disease upon people's lives. I will discuss the example of ulcerative colitis (hereafter referred to just as colitis) by drawing on a study carried out by Kelly (1992), who explored the experience of this illness in some depth with forty-five colitis sufferers.

Colitis 'is a non-specific inflammatory condition of the mucous membrane of the large bowel and rectum' (Kelly, 1992: 1). The main symptoms of the disease are diarrhoea, blood in the stool, abdominal pain, raised temperature, and loss of weight and energy. Its onset is most common in early adulthood. The symptoms are unpredictable, and are likely to involve periods of greater severity punctuated by periods of remission. The unpredictability of symptoms, especially of diarrhoea, can interfere with social functioning. For example, rushing away to the toilet during conversations or meals can be disruptive and embarrassing, and such apparently odd social behaviour has to be accounted for. The proximity of toilets becomes essential, and this can present logistical problems in the case of travel arrangements or work environments. There are also socio-psychological consequences, as the symptoms, especially the loss of control over defecation, can affect a person's identity, which in turn may impact upon the sense of self. As Kelly (1992: 38) explains:

> Adult men and women, whatever their social class, whatever their social roles, are obviously adults who, in Western culture, do not defecate uncontrollably in public. It is one of the basic distinguishing features of adulthood, as against infancy, early childhood and old age that control of the anal sphincter is a taken-for-granted accomplishment. The loss of that control is not only at odds with being an adult, it also suggests flawed moral character.

Thus colitis is a condition wherein a person loses control over some aspects of his or her physical body, in a way that has profound social consequences. In this respect it draws attention to the centrality of the body for 'normal' social interaction.

Most colitis sufferers pass through a series of stages, or transition phases, throughout the course of their disease. First, initial symptoms are experienced, and have to be made sense of; second, actions are taken to try and deal with the symptoms, and help is sought; third, the disease is diagnosed; fourth, the person has to learn to live with the diagnosis and symptoms; fifth, in some cases surgery is carried out which involves the removal of the large bowel, and an ileostomy is constructed which means that the ileostomist does not defecate in the same way as other people, and so enters a sixth phase of having to learn to use and live with the stoma appliance. At all these stages, people living with colitis have to learn to cope. Coping is multifaceted, and for all the respondents at all the stages of their illness careers, coping with emotional, social and practical threats is necessary.

Initial symptoms such as diarrhoea and abdominal pain were invariably 'explained away' by respondents in 'common-sense terms' as being due to factors such as tiredness, piles, stress, period pains, bugs, nerves or over-indulgence – all perfectly 'normal'. However, as the symptoms persisted, people were 'triggered' into action, which usually took the form of a visit to their doctor. The doctor, however, did not invariably diagnose the condition immediately, and drew on the same types of explanation as the lay respondents. Despite the unpleasant technical procedures used for the diagnosis of colitis, most people were relieved to find out what was actually wrong with them. However, this does not diminish the fact that the consequences of the diagnosis itself have to be coped with, more especially the chronic or long-term nature of the condition.

Learning to live with the symptoms involves the routine adoption of further *coping strategies*. A key problem is *uncertainty*. Colitis symptoms tend to be cyclical, but periods of remission and exacerbation are unpredictable. There is also uncertainty in that loss of control of bowel movements can occur at any time. In attempts to deal with this problem, people tried to monitor and control their diet; they would also scan the environment to ensure that they had toilets close to hand; and they might even avoid certain social situations, especially those which involved eating and drinking in public. One important goal of these coping strategies is to be able to live life as 'normally' as possible and to maintain a 'normal' identity. This, however, is not necessarily without problems, as Kelly (1992: 37) explains: 'The difficulty for the person with colitis is that his or her attempt to present a relatively normal self to others is continually being threatened, because of the inherently unstable nature of the condition. This means that impression management is always precarious.' The presentation of a semblance of normality usually required the co-operation of relatives and/or partners who were able to collude and offer support in the venture. However, as Kelly suggests, not disclosing the illness can be precarious, and not everyone is willing to act as an ally in the maintenance of normality, as Gloria, who worked in a hospital, found out:

> 'I was talking to somebody and went into the sluice for something, and that was it. It just came from me. It was torture. And sister took one look at me, and my uniform was saturated: it was very embarrassing for me. She told me to go home. But I said I would just change and get on with my work. But she sent me home anyway. I was back the next day, but I was caught out.' (Kelly, 1992: 42)

However, actually disclosing information about the disease can also be risky, as another respondent found out. When he informed his prospective employers of his illness, they rescinded their job offer.

Being faced with the decision as to whether or not to have an operation which will get rid of the disease but will mean having an altered body and a stoma appliance presents the colitis sufferer with a further set of concerns which have to be addressed. There are the emotional consequences of learning to live with a changed body, and there are the practical consequences of having to learn how to use a stoma appliance. The respondents in Kelly's study devised a whole array of further coping strategies for dealing with their altered status. On the whole, the practical skills of changing the appliance were acquired relatively quickly, and problems, such as leakage, were overcome with experience and trial and error. As Gwen explains:

> 'I've no bother with keeping bags on. I find it quite easy. With my appliance there is a face and a wafer thing to start with, then the bag itself. With the other one I used, you needed a wafer, a karaya ring and then a bag, and then you had to put the clip on the bag and it didn't take long. I usually change it every three days, but I could actually go longer than that, I could. I could go four or five. The thing I find awkward is disposing of the bags when you are away from home, y'know it's a bit awkward, you don't like to dump them in somebody's bin.' (Kelly, 1992: 77)

Dealing with sexual and social relationships, however, is often more complex, and can affect a person's self-confidence. For those people in long-term relationships, sexual relations did not constitute a problem, but for those who were not, the situation was more threatening. As Rhona put it, 'I am eighteen years old. Who's goona love me with this?' (Kelly, 1992: 86). Respondents who anticipated sexual relationships drew on a range of coping strategies, such as 'being frank or honest, by trying to find the right moment, or by simply withdrawing' (Kelly, 1992: 87).

The findings of this study of colitis are important, not only from the standpoint of understanding this particular disease but also because they have much in common with other studies which have examined different chronic conditions. As Kelly (1992: 48) observes:

> The striking thing about many such studies is that while the symptoms of rheumatoid arthritis, Parkinson's disease, or diabetes, for example, are clearly different from those of colitis, in many ways the problems posed by such illnesses have a quality which cuts across particular medical diagnosis and is common to them all.

What we learn from Kelly's study, which reflects the findings of others, is the extent to which this chronic illness is woven into the fabric of people's lives, and the fact that it impacts upon a person's self and identity. It is characterized by uncertainty, which begins prior to the initial diagnosis of the disease and continues throughout the person's illness career. It also involves a considerable amount of work to develop strategies for coping with the emotional and practical consequences of the disease. Perhaps most crucially, it reminds us of the extent to which we rely on our body and its significance in social interaction. As Kleinman (1988: 45) succinctly notes, the 'fidelity of our bodies is so basic that we never think of it – it is the certain grounds of our daily experience. Chronic illness is a betrayal of that fundamental trust.'

The 'key problems' associated with chronic illness are identified by A. L. Strauss (1975: 7–8): medical crises and their management; the control of symptoms; carrying out prescribed regimens and the management of problems attendant upon these regimens; prevention of, or living with, social isolation caused by lessened contact with others; adjustment to changes in the course of the disease such as exacerbations or remissions; attempts at normalizing both interaction with others and styles of life; and funding to pay for treatments and to survive despite partial or complete loss of employment. Clearly, researchers have identified a whole series of problems associated with chronic conditions. They have also begun to understand the ways in which people cope and respond to such problems, and it is clear that such responses are mediated by the social environment in which they reside.

Chronic illness and disability

Associated with many chronic illnesses are physical disabilities. For example, the latter are often the outcome of impairments which result from musculo-skeletal complaints such as arthritis or diseases of the nervous system such as Parkinson's, multiple sclerosis and strokes. The relationship between impairment and disability is, however, contentious and socially contingent, and is reflected in debates which hinge on the social or medical bases of disability both within academia and beyond. Such tensions are reflected in the attempts to devise classificatory tools. In 1980 the WHO devised an *International Classification of Impairments, Disabilities and Handicaps* (ICIDH). It defined *impairment* as the loss or abnormality of physiological or anatomical structure or function; *disability* as restriction or lack (resulting from impairment) of ability to perform an activity in a manner or within a range considered normal; and *handicap* as a disadvantage for a given individual with a disability as a result of the social, economic and political circumstances in which he or she lives. Defined thus, primacy is given to the biological and individual dimensions of disability which emphasize people's limitations, rather than to social barriers. In 2001, therefore, the ICIDH was replaced by the *International Classification of Functioning, Disability and Health* (ICF), which 'seeks to locate an understanding of disability at the intersection between the biological body and social and institutional structures' (Imrie, 2004: 291). The rationale was to incorporate both the biomedical and the social models of disability.

The biomedical model presumes that biological impairment is the key determinant of disability, and consequently emphasizes the merits of rehabilitation or interventions (such as adaptations) to facilitate what is – within this perspective – considered to be 'normal' functioning. Evaluation tends to be orientated towards what individuals 'need' so that they may 'fit' into and readily 'function' in wider society. The social model, by contrast, maintains that disabilities themselves are a function of a society which fails to take account of people who have physical impairments. Disabilities are a consequence of a society in which disabling attitudes and disabling environments prevail. There is a tendency to presume that people who have 'functional impairments' such as blindness, deafness or restricted mobility have 'special needs'. But these needs become 'special' only within a context which excludes, marginalizes or fails to take them into account in the first place. Thus disability is not a function of the physical incapacities of an individual, but is socially created. Evaluations of physical and social environments are necessary in order to overcome disabling societies.

Disabling environments are therefore both physical and social. For the most part, the built environment is intended to cater to those people who have no physical impairments, and designs invariably presume that people can climb stairs, see obstacles such as posts on pavements, and take extended steps on to buses. The social environment may also in itself be disabling – for example, there is a tendency to view people with disabilities as either tragic figures or heroes who have the strength of character to overcome what are regarded as their own individual disadvantages. Even health promotion campaigns can contribute towards the reinforcement of negative images. Wang (1992), writing in the USA, notes how injury prevention campaigns unwittingly promote the stigmatization of people with disabilities as they contend that the risk of becoming disabled is an unacceptable one in our society. One poster used to promote the use of seat-belts reads: 'If you think seat belts are confining, think about a wheelchair.' Thus attempts to encourage people to take fewer risks both draw upon and reinforce the stigma of being disabled. There is an assumption that to have some kind of impairment is to be a lesser person.

To speak of 'the disabled' is problematic in many respects, as it places a diverse group of people within a single category. However, it can also be viewed more positively, in that it draws attention to the minority status of people who have disabilities, and as such contributes to the creation of a sense of solidarity and resistance and highlights the political nature of disability. Tensions between the social and medical models of disability have resulted in productive sociological theorizations that transcend the physical body *and* the social context. As Williams and Busby (2000: 182) put it: 'the ontological reality of the impaired body is central to the development of any social theory of disability'.

Edwards and Imrie (2003) argue that Bourdieu's theorizations of the body may be instructive here, and in particular his concepts of 'habitus' and 'symbolic violence'. 'Habitus' refers to 'internalised, "embodied" social structures' (Bourdieu, 1984: 468) which are acquired or unconsciously learned through living in one's social world. Thus one's habitus – one's way of being – is both collective and individual. Embodied practices in turn are implicated in social inequalities, and certain bodily comportments (such as accent, dress, gait) are ascribed differential social values, and thereby accrue physical capital within differential 'social fields'. Medicine is one such social field, and the assumptions inherent in the biomedical model surface in other contexts. For example, Edwards and Imrie (2003) found that employers'

> attitudes reinforce biomedical conceptions of disability as reducible to (bodily) impairment, or as one interviewee, a manager of a property firm, commented: 'nobody wants to be prejudiced against the disabled but there are certain things they cannot do . . .' [. . .] These statements de-value disabled people, and their bodily capabilities, as 'less than able', and reflect Bourdieu's [. . .] comments that 'elementary acts of bodily gymnastics . . . are highly charged with social meaning and values'. (p. 247)

Thus medical discourse, they argue, is central to many prevailing definitions of disability and incorporates values which emphasize the need to 'correct or normalise the disabled body' (p. 248). The images, language, actions, meanings and practices inherent to medicine and beyond may serve to violate people with disabilities and indeed some other illnesses. Bourdieu captures this process neatly with the notion of 'symbolic violence'.

Such 'symbolic violence' is evident in Lonsdale's (1990) study of women and disability. For example, she found that women were often denied their womanhood. There was a common assumption that women with disabilities are asexual. This has advantages and disadvantages. Some women noted that at least they were to some degree spared the relentless sexual harassment to which women who do not have disabilities are subject. If sexuality was acknowledged, they were, as is the case with women in general, presumed to be heterosexual. Women who do not have disabilities are encouraged to have children, but those who do tend to be discouraged. Many people, including some health professionals, tend to assume that women with disabilities are unable to cope with motherhood, they are asexual, that children of parents with disabilities will suffer, that the disability can be inherited, and that child rearing requires physical mobility and dexterity (Lonsdale, 1990: 76). This is evident from the experience of one woman who now has an 8-year-old daughter:

> 'The first thing the doctor said to me was, "Have this pregnancy terminated." I said I didn't want to. Then he said, "After the pregnancy you can get sterilized." I said I didn't want to get sterilized. He sent me away for a thinking period. When I went back, he said had I thought about it, and I said I hadn't because I'd already made up my mind. He was very good after that. I found the hospital quite difficult. They didn't know how I was going to deliver the baby with muscular dystrophy. They came up with all sorts of frightening and bewildering ways of how I would deliver it. I thought, no, I don't think so, that doesn't sound like me. They were suggesting suction devices. They said I wouldn't have the muscle to push. Then my doctor said he wasn't sure how I was going to carry out the pregnancy. He said if at six or seven months they thought it would be too difficult for me, they would take the baby then. I

> thought, they are planning my life for me. I told them that no way would they take the baby when I was six or seven months. And when I went back to the ante-natal, they told me I was to come in about three weeks before time. So they said they would start me off. So I said no. And then I went into labour quite naturally and normally. After that, the specialist who looks after my muscular dystrophy said that it was amazing, he had never heard of anyone with muscular dystrophy having a baby.' (Lonsdale, 1990: 76)

Assumptions that people with disabilities are less able, or other than 'normal', can compound the business of mothering. Thomas (1997) found that when faced with these views, mothers felt under pressure to 'present themselves and their children as managing normally' and avoided asking for any help which might only reinforce prejudices of others that they were unable to cope. These ambivalences invariably impact upon a person's sense of self and identity.

Self, identity and illness

Bury (1988, 1991) has distinguished between two aspects of the impact of chronic illness in suggesting that there are two types of meaning. First, there is 'meaning as consequence', that is, the effects on the practical aspects of everyday life following the onset of symptoms, such as disruption to work and domestic routines, the management of symptoms, and so on. Second, there is 'meaning as significance', which refers to the connotations and imagery associated with given conditions. It is the meaning as significance which affects individuals' sense of self and the reactions of others around them (Charmaz, 2000). The meaning as significance will of course vary according to the socio-cultural context in which the illness occurs. It may also vary across the life-course; for example, Sanders et al.'s (2002) study of people experiencing osteoarthritis found that older people portrayed their symptoms as integral to processes of ageing, and thereby played down the meaning as significance; it was part of 'normal ageing'. However, the disruption to their day-to-day lives – the meaning as consequence – was very evident.

We saw from the study of people's experiences of colitis that chronic illness can affect a person's self and identity. To a great extent this was the consequence of both the actual or the imagined reaction of others to a person who is ill and of the cultural context in which people live. These factors mean that social interaction becomes more difficult, as taken-for-granted assumptions and shared 'definitions of the situation' cannot be relied upon. Bury (1988, 1991) refers to this as 'meanings at risk': that is, people who are chronically ill and/or have disabilities constantly have to risk the fact that their interpretations of a situation might not be shared by others. For example, calls for sympathy may be rejected, or, on the other hand, attempts to 'carry on as normal' may be regarded by significant others as inappropriate in the light of a deterioration of symptoms. Thus relationships may be scrutinized more closely.

Taking a symbolic interactionist perspective (which sees identity as a product of the interaction between the self and significant others), Charmaz (1983) examined the impact that social interaction had on the 'selves' of people who had physical disabilities. From her study it became apparent that the informants were concerned about the person they see themselves becoming and about valued self-images from the past which they feel they have lost. Charmaz refers to this process as 'loss of self', and observes four dilemmas which emerge from it. First, individuals scrutinize interactions with others for any signs of discreditation. Second, sufferers are inclined to foster dependence on others to achieve self-definition, although this tends to strain relationships. Third, as illness increases, sufferers find that they need more intimate contact to preserve their crumbling self-images, although at the same time they are often becoming less capable of maintaining relationships. As Charmaz (1983: 191) explains, if 'they openly reveal their suffering, show self-pity, guilt, anger or other emotions conventionally believed to be negative, they are likely to further estrange those who still take an interest in them'. The fourth dilemma concerns the impact of cultural values, in that in a society where 'doing' is privileged over 'being', those who cannot perform conventional tasks tend to lose the very means needed to sustain a meaningful social life. However, this 'loss of self' is not necessarily a permanent feature, and Charmaz (1987) also illustrates ways in which people move beyond this state and are able to create new 'reconstituted identities'. Of the people she studied, she found that 'they participated actively in creating their lives and, moreover, *themselves*' (Charmaz, 1987: 318, emphasis original). Thus, sense of self and personal identity will vary over time and with the various stages of the illness career.

In Western cultures self-image, the internal conception of oneself, is often related to body image, and the image portrayed is shaped to a great extent by the diet, advertising and fashion industries (Lonsdale, 1990). Consequently, those conditions which impact upon the physicality of the body can lead to negative self-image. Clearly this is not invariably the case; nevertheless, there are four factors which make it more likely (Lonsdale, 1990: 66–7): first, if there are negative reactions from the outside world, statements such as 'She was so pretty before her accident'; second, where there is lack of control over bodily functioning, which is not normally associated with adulthood; third, if cold, hard and metallic appliances are used; and fourth, if there is a fear of sexual or social rejection.

Illness as 'biographical disruption' and 'biographical reinforcement'

We have seen that when people try to make sense of the onset of their illness, they locate it within the wider context of their past lives. In this sense chronic illness can be understood as a *biographical disruption* (Bury, 1982), in that it disturbs not only one's physical body, but the trajectory of one's whole life at a number of levels.

> First, there is the disruption of taken-for-granted assumptions and behaviours. Second, there are more profound disruptions in explanatory systems normally used by people such that a fundamental rethinking of a person's biography and self concept is involved. Third, there is a response to disruption involving the mobilization of resources in facing an altered situation. (Bury 1982: 169)

Because the onset of chronic illness may involve the disruption of a person's biography, the reassessment of one's life is to some extent inevitable. As we have seen, this can involve a process of loss of self; it can also serve as a turning-point in life, which can involve a changed identity.

Bury's concept of biographical disruption has been revised in the light of empirical studies which place the onset of illness in the context of other events which take place in people's lives. As S. Williams (2000) points out, a feature of contemporary life is what Giddens (1991) calls 'reflexivity', the 'never-ending cycle of biographical appraisals, revisions and improvements, health related or otherwise' (S. Williams, 2000: 61). Pound et al.'s (1998) study of older people who had suffered strokes found that the experience was not considered to be so much a major disruption of their lives as a continuation of their biographies through which they had endured many other harsh and difficult events and situations. This finding was further supported by Larsson and Grassman (2012) whose study of older people found that repeated disruptions shaped the lives of men and women who experienced various chronic conditions, but significantly the disruption was still salient to them even in those cases where they had lived with chronic conditions for many years. Change, it seems, characterizes the lives of people with chronic conditions since their early years rather than continuity, and it remains difficult to navigate both for those living with the conditions and their carers.

Some people find that the biographical disruption can also have positive consequences. It can initiate a rethinking about the direction of a person's life; it can mean that the sufferer may become a more insightful person; and it may result in new opportunities never before imagined. A 50-year-old woman who suffers from diabetes is cited by Herzlich and Pierret (1987: 211) as saying: 'one is a better person than before, one is more courageous, in fact *one knows oneself*... This is definitely an enrichment, it's a kind of philosophy ... not the burnt-child philosophy of one who is beaten, no, but a constructive philosophy.' There is, however, a danger that this view can give rise to a new tyranny that moralizes about a pious fulfilment in the face of suffering. Thus the onset of chronic illness which may result in changes in the physical functioning of one's body can have both negative and positive consequences for one's sense of self and identity. While not denying the extent of suffering that people endure, we may also acknowledge the positive outcomes of both illness and disabilities.

The political context of the self

We can see, then, that the self, identity and social milieux are intimately related. Strategies for maintaining a sense of self in the face of illness can, in this respect, be seen as an extension of those strategies with which we all routinely engage. This is because how we are able to present ourselves to the outside world – our identity – is likely to impact upon our private self. This in turn is mediated by our social and political context. However, in the face of illness, the whole process comes under threat and closer scrutiny. G. Williams (1993) refers to this process as the 'pursuit of virtue', the attempt to remain virtuous in the face of adversity. He illustrates this notion by describing the strategies, or 'moral accompaniments', that Mrs Field, a 62-year-old woman who has suffered from rheumatoid arthritis for eight years, uses to maintain her semblance of self. The three strategies she adopts tell us as much about her perception of the socio-political context in which she resides as they do about the illness itself. The three issues which are of particular salience to her are maintaining her independence and not having to make demands on other people, keeping her house clean, and never owing any money. Of course, these are more difficult to sustain when experiencing pain from arthritis; yet at the same time they take on a greater significance, because to fail in any of these respects implies that the disease has got the better of her. In other words, 'ways of being well and bearing illness are instances and embodiments of ideological and social practice' (Radley, 1993: 4).

Stigma

Goffman's work on stigma and the management of self has been influential in the study of the experience of chronic illness and disability. More recently the view that people who live with chronic conditions experience stigma and are stigmatized is being challenged (Green, 2009), and we will expand upon these debates below. Nevertheless, it remains a useful and viable concept which it is important to appreciate. Goffman's definition of stigma is based on a distinction between 'virtual social identity' – that is, the stereotyped imputations we make in everyday life – and 'actual social identity' – that is, those attributes which an individual does actually possess. Stigma occurs when there is a discrepancy between virtual and actual social identity. Stigma, according to Goffman, 'is really a special kind of relationship between attribute and stereotype' (Goffman, 1968: 14). It is the process by which the reaction of others 'spoils' normal identity.

The likelihood of stigmatization will, according to Goffman (1968), vary according to the following factors: first, visibility, the extent to which the signs or symptoms of a condition are recognized by others. Psoriasis is an example of a continually evident condition, as Jobling (1988: 226) has described:

> those who develop psoriasis are potentially challenged by semipermanent disfigurement, which is damaging to social attractiveness and self-esteem in the many circumstances where their lesions may be revealed to the world. Moreover the constant shedding of an unusual, unaesthetic body product, namely waste skin, which is difficult to manage, makes self-presentation and a normal everyday life all the more difficult . . . Additional to this comes the suspicion of culpability through poor personal hygiene; and the widespread perception of skin conditions as exceptionally infectious or contagious.

Second, and related to this, is 'know-about-ness': the extent to which others are aware of an illness. For example, the fact that a person suffers from epilepsy may not be known to those people with whom he or she works. Third, the degree of obtrusiveness: the extent to which the flow of interaction is impeded. For example, a severe stammer may impede normal codes of communication. Finally, the perceived focus, the perception that others have about an individual's ability to participate fully and normally.

Goffman identifies a further important distinction which helps us appreciate the meaning of illness. This is between the 'discreditable' – that is, attributes which are not visible and therefore are only potentially stigmatizing – and the 'discredited' – that is, attributes which are visible. The problem for the discreditable is to restore their status and identity, while the problem for the discredited is to control the flow of information about these blemished aspects of self.

This orthodox view of stigma, which implies that the public are, in general, ignorant of the true nature of many diseases and are prone to reacting on the basis of stereotypes, has been challenged. A study of people who suffer from epilepsy has suggested that this conventional view relies too much on *enacted* stigma – that is, discrimination against people on the grounds of their perceived inferiority - rather than *felt* stigma - that is, a feeling of shame which is associated with their fear of enacted stigma (Scambler and Hopkins, 1986; Scambler, 1989). Enacted stigma was found to be less prevalent than the orthodox view of stigma might lead us to believe, and, in fact, it was people's felt stigma that caused the most anxiety. Once diagnosed, people felt bound to, or were encouraged by those close to them, to conceal their condition, and were consequently at risk of being 'found out'. Stigma-bearers share the value system of those around them, and thus experience a sense of shame. Accordingly, they tend to employ strategies to overcome their shame and try to present themselves as 'normal'. Scambler refers to this as the 'hidden distress model' of stigma.

However, Scambler (2004) also cautions that the 'hidden distress model' needs to be deployed with care. There is a danger that it reinforces the authority of biomedicine and presumes that disease labels are unquestioningly accepted rather than negotiated. It may also serve to reinforce the idea that disease is a personal tragedy. Relatedly, it can imply that the ill person is something of a victim who internalizes their fate. For this reason it is crucial to acknowledge that stigma is not an attribute of individuals, but is rather a thoroughly social concept which is generated, sustained and reproduced in the context of social inequalities. As Parker and Aggleton (2003) point out, processes of stigmatization are part and parcel of processes of power, domination and discrimination; what becomes stigmatized is bound up with prevailing norms and values. It is a socialized concept, a culturally relative concept that cannot be adequately understood individualized.

Given stigma is historically and culturally situated, it is likely to shift in significance over time. In her book *The End of Stigma? Changes in the Social Experience of Long-term Illness*, Gill Green (2009) explores the thesis that societal transformations have served to reduce the degree of stigma that people living with chronic illness and disability are likely to face. Drawing upon both her own personal experience of, and research into, multiple sclerosis in concert with her research into the lives of people living the HIV, mental health problems and with substance users, she develops a nuanced account of the social changes that are weakening the potency of stigma. Her argument is an important one because it reveals the way in which macro social change intertwines with personal experiences. Fukuyama's (1989) 'end of history' thesis, which points to the demise of battles between ideologies and how this has be matched by the grip of economic and political liberalism that gives primacy to consumer culture, choice, and individualism, is her point of departure. A number of characteristics associated with this mode of neo-liberalism potentially undermine stigma; these are discussed under three headings: organizational, personal and technological. In terms of organizational matters, she discerns a form of 'anti-stigma action' that can be seen in the identity politics that have displaced ideological battlegrounds. Mental health, disability and HIV/AIDS are examples of the multiplicity of health-related pressure groups that populate the political landscape. As we have discussed elsewhere throughout this book, such pressure groups promote positive images to counter assumptions about illness, help to shape anti-discrimination legislation, provide support networks and have been effective in the promotion of the social model of illness. The articulation of illness narratives by people who have experienced illness through various forms of social media have also helped to craft more positive images of illness and given space to proud, positive self-identities, enabling the person rather than the illness to figure prominently. Technological innovations have meant that conditions that only decades ago would have been terminal can now be managed to such an extent that living with a chronic condition can for some interfere to a lesser extent with day-to-day lives. HIV, for example, although still not curable, is manageable through the use of antiretroviral drugs, as are forms of cancers and heart conditions. Altogether, these developments give rise to a mosaic of identities with the consequence that categories of those who are stigmatized are less clear-cut. Diversity means that the identification of deviance and difference is complex. Green concludes that the 'three challenges do not of course operate in isolation. Each is informed by and drives the others. Operating as a whole, they provide effective resistance to stigma and minimize the power and impact of stigma upon the people living with a range of long-term conditions' (Green 2009: 124). Although stigma associated with illness and disability cannot 'be consigned to the history books', Green notes the signs are hopeful that its effects could be diluted.

Coping strategies

Balancing

We saw in the example of colitis how fundamental are coping strategies to people who have chronic conditions. The coping strategies which people adopt to maintain their 'maximum relative normality in the face of incapacitation or stigmatization' (Gerhardt, 1989: 139) have also been described for a range of other illnesses (Kelleher, 1988; Pinder, 1988). To some extent, such strategies are common to everyone, as all of us are continually weighing up the pros and cons of taking certain actions, making choices and decisions about how best to accomplish tasks and to achieve goals. Pinder (1988) refers to this process as 'balancing', and has shown in her study of Parkinson's disease that this process is more precarious in the face of a chronic illness which is characterized by uncertainty and unpredictability. For example, sufferers often have to weigh up the costs and benefits of taking drugs which might both alleviate symptoms and result in unpleasant side-effects. It is difficult to balance the two in the face of uncertainty about the possible onset of symptoms themselves, which often come and go for no apparent reason. There are also decisions to be made about carrying on as normal and not telling others about one's illness, and risking the possibility that it may become evident. This has to be balanced against the consequences of disclosing to others that one has Parkinson's disease or avoiding situations where people might find out, which may result in social isolation.

Coping, strategy and style

Commenting on the literature which describes how people adapt to chronic illness, Bury (1991) distinguishes between the concepts of 'coping', 'strategy' and 'style'. Whilst in practice the applicability of these terms will invariably overlap, analytically they are distinct. *Coping* refers to 'the cognitive processes whereby the individual learns *how* to tolerate or *put up* with the effects of illness . . . [which] involves maintaining a sense of value and meaning in life' (Bury, 1991: 460–1). By contrast, *strategy* alludes to 'the actions people take, or *what people do* in the face of illness' (Bury, 1991: 461). Finally, *style* incorporates the cultural circumstances and connotations of an illness, and refers to '*the way* people respond to, and present, important features of their illnesses or treatment regimens' (Bury, 1991: 462). The perception and presentation of illness vary according to the socio-cultural context of the sufferer. For example, Radley (1989) has shown how such differences in style are embedded in interpretations of the body and the self. As suggested above, coping, strategy and style are interrelated, and what is common to them all is that they are compounded by uncertainty and unpredictability.

Work and resources

The experience of chronic illness can very often mean a severe reduction in resources in terms of energy, skill, strength, time, money, friends and so on. Consequently, sufferers adopt strategies to overcome these restrictions. These have been conceptualized as forms of work. Corbin and Strauss (1985) understand chronic illness in terms of three types of work: *illness work*, which consists of regimen work, crisis prevention and management, symptom management and diagnostic-related work; *everyday life work*, which refers to the daily round of tasks that keep a household going, such as housekeeping, occupational work, child rearing, sentimental work and activities such as eating; and *biographical work*, which involves the reconstruction of the ill person's biography.

Managing medical regimens can be arduous. Writing about psoriasis, Jobling (1988) notes that 'psoriasis-as-treated' can be hard work. Sufferers find that they are caught in the 'Sisyphus syndrome'. In Greek mythology, Sisyphus was condemned by the gods for his misdemeanours to roll a huge boulder to the top of a mountain; as he approached the summit, the boulder would always slip and fall to the bottom, and he would be forced to begin again. So too with patients; they work hard with various treatment regimens, only to find that their condition has changed very little. As with other areas of work, with time people may store up considerable amounts of knowledge and experience, and develop quite sophisticated skills. This knowledge and skill may lead people to question the traditional roles assigned to doctors and patients. The following, for example, is an extract from an account by a 36-year-old man of a haemodialysis session:

> 'One really has one's life in one's hands, when it comes to asepsis, to the rinsing of the blood disks, or the treatment itself . . . the machine is very advanced, it has an alarm system that keeps track at all times of the different constants one must watch, but one has to pay attention, one is really responsible for one's life . . . everyone has it . . . but not to this degree . . . three times a week, if I make a mistake, that can be the end of me . . . you yourself *become responsible even though it is not necessarily your job* . . . I have never studied medicine, I have never studied nursing, but practically I have the same responsibility for myself'. (Herzlich and Pierret, 1987: 216, emphasis in original)

Thus the patient becomes to a significant extent independent of health professionals, and as a key health care provider is able to make decisions and pursue treatment regimens that fit in with what Herzlich and Pierret (1987) refer to as a 'social logic' as well as a 'medical logic'. Whilst a medical logic would imply a strict adherence to a therapy best suited to a patient's physiological condition, a social logic implies therapies or treatments that fit in with the other demands of daily living.

Atkin and Ahmad's (2002) study of young people's experiences of thalassaemia major illustrates this well. Thalassaemia major is a recessive genetic condition wherein the body is unable to make sufficient haemoglobin. As part of their treatment, people who have the condition have to inject drugs using a battery-operated infusion pump for 8 to 12 hours a day for 5 to 7 nights a week. Non-use of the infusion pump can be fatal. The study found, however, that although teenagers were aware of the consequences, they resisted using the pump, and adherence to the treatment became a source of tension between them and their parents. In particular, during their mid-teens it became an issue that was symbolic of their struggle for independence, part of the negotiation of their own identity – an experience common to many households with teenagers. During these years the 'social logic' demanded as part of 'the wider process in which they make sense of the relationship between the body, self and illness, and maintain relationships' (2002: 232) took precedence over the 'medical logic' required for health and longevity.

Self-help groups and social movements

It has become evident throughout this chapter that patients are not simply passive recipients of care but, together with their relatives and friends, are also providers of that care (Stacey, 1988). Thus lay people develop considerable expertise and knowledge, which may even surpass that of the so-called experts within the medical profession. This knowledge and experience may be shared among those people who suffer from the same illness. Self-help groups have been set up, sometimes at the instigation of, and sometimes in opposition to, the medical profession, to provide informal support for those people with certain conditions, to educate people more generally about a particular disease, to support relevant research, and to lobby for changes. Herzlich and Pierret (1987: 225) suggest that self-help groups concerned with illness form 'part of the larger protest movement' that is becoming evident in contemporary Western societies and constitute a form of social movement (Brown and Zavestoski, 2004).

Self-help groups provide support on both individual and collective levels. For their individual members, they may offer emotional support and may be invaluable during the early stages of a person's illness career to overcome social isolation and loneliness. As many members have expertise in the provision of care, practical assistance may also be available. The ability to provide this level of support may contribute to the positive identity of people who are sick. This is also facilitated by a sense of solidarity which can be achieved among those who share a common problem.

At the collective level, the establishment of solidarity amongst a self-help group may result in the pursuit of change at a political level. It can result in the mobilization of those concerned to become more active consumers of care and to engage in activities which are aimed at overcoming prejudice and discrimination. This is especially evident for conditions such as HIV/AIDS. For example, Gillett (2003) illustrates how Internet sites provide a forum for people living with HIV/AIDS 'to raise the private troubles' as 'public issues', and enable people to exchange experiences, knowledge and views which fail to get represented in more traditional forms of media. Thus new alliances and allegiances may be fostered.

As G. Williams (1989) has pointed out, modern self-help groups are the descendants of an uneasy relationship between the two ideologies of individualism and collectivism, where individualism is the dominant partner. Self-help groups exalt the freedom of the individual, in that they encourage independence from others and a sense of autonomy. Yet, at the same time, they try to foster a notion of solidarity and attempt to demand support and resources from the state and/or other sources.

Despite the tensions that are inherent within self-help groups, it is apparent that the sick person today is 'rarely totally passive' (Herzlich and Pierret, 1987: 229). From their historical study of the sick in society, Herzlich and Pierret have found that the sick person has changed in conjunction with the socio-cultural and political context:

> From the anonymous victim of epidemics as collective scourges, from the traditional image of the alienated and passive 'patient' to the 'self-provider of medical care' as a new cultural figure, to the 'healthcare user' as a collective actor in the public-health system, and finally to the militant for whom the body is the basis of a new political action. (Herzlich and Pierret, 1987: 229)

This reformulation of the patient in relation to the social context is neatly illustrated by Klawiter's (2004) analysis of one woman's experiences of breast cancer in North America. Clara Larson (a pseudonym) was diagnosed with breast cancer in 1979 and again in 1997. The same disease was experienced very differently, however, within these two historical contexts. Klawiter uses the concept *disease regime* to capture the ways in which structural circumstances shape individual experiences. Disease regimes comprise 'the institutionalised practices, authoritative discourses, social relations, collective identities, emotional vocabularies, visual images, public policies and regulatory actions though which diseases are socially constituted and experienced' (p. 851). Such regimes are altered in part as a result of activities of 'health social movements' – 'collective challenges' to health and medical and related practices (Brown and Zavestoski, 2004). In the late 1970s – the first disease regime – Clara's story had been one of disempowerment, relative isolation and involvement with surgeons who had little interest in her views and certainly did not acknowledge her sexuality, her 'self' or her embodiment.

> In the first regime, her experience of breast cancer was relentlessly individualised. She looked for a sisterhood of survivors but never found one. She engaged in acts of civil disobedience but remained isolated. Surgeons were the undisputed sovereigns within the medical setting, and structurally speaking, the only role available to women with breast cancer was that of the duly compliant patient. (Klawiter, 2004: 865)

However, by 1997 a new regime had been forged – at least in the San Francisco Bay area where Clara lives. Here

> Clara was treated in a feminist and lesbian-friendly cancer centre. She decided between medical alternatives, attended patient-education workshops, participated in her treatment as a member of the 'health care team' that consisted in a range of healthcare professionals – both regular and alternative [. . .]. Support groups, medical information and practical resources for women with breast cancer were freely

> available. Women with breast cancer had become a visible presence in the public domain and breast cancer survivors were now heralded as heroes rather than pitied as victims. Breast cancer had been politicised. (Klawiter, 2004: 866)

Klawiter's study locates women's experiences of breast cancer at the intersection of two socio-historical trends that represent a shift in the presumed authority of the medical profession and solidification of patient empowerment. This intersection forms a key theme in Fair's (2010) analysis of the contested illness Morgellons.

Fair (2010) provides a compelling account of the way in which a North American woman Mary Leito orchestrated support from lay and scientific communities to help to make sense of her son's dermatological condition and in so doing gained legitimacy for the disease label Morgellons. Her son's symptoms - open skin lesions, infections and tiny fluorescent fibres protruding from under his skin - were diagnosed as delusional parasitosis (DP). Leito questioned the diagnosis and was then herself diagnosed as having Munchausen by proxy. Not content with these psychiatric labels, she drew upon her own scientific training to research the symptoms and discovered a medieval French skin disease called Morgellons that appeared to match the pattern of her son's illness. She established a research fund and a website which, to her surprise, garnered much interest from people suffering the same symptoms. Some years later a research scientist and a paediatrician happened upon her website and offered to investigate further. The research scientist using a dermatoscope (a microscope for examining skin) confirmed the presence of fluorescent fibres embedded under the skin. The visualization of the fibres in concert with an increasingly vociferous patient group led to a larger research project led by the US Centers for Disease Control and Prevention (CDC). The status of the condition shifted, it began to be acknowledged by the medical community and diagnostic protocols were developed for use by clinicians in practice when dealing with patients who presented with the symptoms. As Fair notes, the formation of this novel disease category demonstrates how 'the internet can empower and politicise a contested illness community' and how 'the internet impacts on clinical practice' (p. 607). Conscious that their patients may have read about the disease, clinicians deploy the language of Morgellons because it is mutually acceptable; it makes the patients feel that their symptoms have legitimacy and their condition is an accepted one. In this instance the patient constituency were keen to medicalize the condition and have it explained in biomedical terms; to replace what they perceived to be an outmoded and dismissive label, namely delusional parasitosis. Fair suggests that this case neatly captures a tussle between two ideologies; patient empowerment and medical authority resulting in a 'doctor–patient compromise' (p. 597). Thus once again we see a fracturing of clear-cut ideologies and a complex play of power relations between patients, carers and professionals when it comes to understanding and caring for the body.

Conclusion

This chapter began by describing the concept of the sick role, and then went on to demonstrate how it fails to capture the full complexities of the experience of illness. To fully appreciate such experiences required that we examine both the meanings and the interpretations of illness for both sufferers and other people. We saw that these meanings and interpretations are shaped by the wider socio-political context. Illness, I argued, is both inherently individual *and* social.

Implicit in much of the discussion has been the importance of the body. This was especially evident in the case of chronic illness, wherein the relationship between the body and self is seriously disrupted. Ordinarily we do not reflect on our bodies; we take for granted the fact that they can function as we require them to. However, for the sick person, the body, as Toombs (1992) suggests, undergoes a metamorphosis and becomes a 'diseased body' which is separated and alienated from the self. When describing her own experience of MS, Toombs reveals how, when living with a chronic illness, 'one feels inescapably embodied' (Toombs, 1992: 134). Sociologists, in their attempts to transcend the individual, and to espouse an approach which looks beyond the body, have tended to neglect the latter. However, more recently the body itself has become a significant site of sociological scrutiny, and it is to this literature that we turn in the next chapter.

FURTHER READING

Frank, A. (1995), *The Wounded Storyteller: Body, Illness and Ethics*, Chicago, IL: University of Chicago Press. An insightful exploration of illness narratives.

Goffman, E. (1968), *Stigma: Notes on the Management of a Spoiled Identity*, Harmondsworth: Penguin. A classic and influential analysis worth revisiting.

Green, G. (2009), *The End of Stigma?: Changes in the Social Experience of Long-term Illness*. Abingdon: Routledge.

Herzlich, C. and Pierret, J. (1987), *Illness and Self in Society*, Baltimore, MD: Johns Hopkins University Press. Although written a few decades ago, this book, which conceptualizes illness as a social representation, provides an illuminating insight into the way in which experiences of illness are at once personal and social.

Nettleton, S. and Gustaffson, U. (eds) (2002), *The Sociology of Health and Illness Reader*, Cambridge: Polity. The chapters in Part III, 'Experiencing Illness', include a number of empirical studies of people's experiences of living with chronic illnesses.

Thomas, C. (2007), *Sociologies of Disability and Illness: Contested Ideas in Disability Studies and Medical Sociology*, Basingstoke: Palgrave Macmillan.

5 The Sociology of the Body

Introduction

The importance of the body to the sociology of health and illness is in many ways obvious. As we saw in the previous chapter, illness can limit the normal functioning of the body, and this can have profound psychological, social and political consequences. Moreover, health is increasingly conceptualized in terms of body maintenance activities such as exercise, diet and the avoidance of unhealthy products like cigarettes and alcohol (Crawford, 2006). Such health-related activities form a key aspect of our contemporary consumer-oriented society. A further reason why the body is central to the sociology of health and illness is that medical science has devised the means to alter the boundaries of our physical body. For example, it can reconstruct parts of our bodies through plastic surgery; it can move internal organs from one body to another; it can assist in reproduction; and it can interfere with the genetic structures of the unborn. Thus the constraints and limits of the physical body today are different from what they were only a few decades ago (C. Williams et al., 2003). However, as Shilling (2003) has pointed out, there is a degree of irony here: the more we know about bodies and the more we are able to control, intervene and alter them, the more uncertain we become as to what the body actually is. The boundaries between the physical body and society are becoming increasingly blurred.

In many respects we have intriguing relationships with our bodies. It is the only thing that each and every one of us is permanently 'with'; yet when it comes to the inner workings of our own body, many of us actually have relatively scant knowledge of it. Our complex relationships with physical bodies are neatly captured in Tony Walter's (2004) ethnographic study of visitors' reactions to the *Body Worlds* exhibition of plastinated anatomical specimens which, for a number of years, toured many countries and has now been seen by millions of people. The plastination process, invented by the creator of the exhibition, an anatomist Gunther von Hagens, enables bodies to be preserved, and displayed vertically with their interiors - organs, sinews, veins - made visible. The audiences' responses captured in Walter's analysis are of interest here because, as we reflect upon them, they also serve to highlight a number of themes which transcend the literature on the sociology of the body and which are explored in this chapter.

As you might imagine, the exhibition itself is highly controversial, with many commentators condemning the very idea of it. This reminds us that how we regulate, manage, dispose of, display, work and look upon bodies is replete with controversy, as debates associated with developments in relation to new reproductive technologies (NRTs), organ donation and stem cell research testify. Second, the exhibition itself comprises a commercial venture; technologies of the body are created for various consumers, be they patients, health practitioners, or the public, and patented technologies yield significant profits for biomedical industries. Furthermore, this also reminds us of the ways in which bodies are commodified - for example, with the buying and selling of body parts and organs. Third, the visualization of the anatomy's interior in this setting is paralleled by the development of imaging and visualization techniques such as ultrasound, MRI, PET and, most spectacularly, the visible human project (see below) which extends the medical gaze and enables it to 'see' inner reaches of the body that have hitherto been opaque. Fourth, some visitors to the exhibition found the poses of the bodies to be disconcerting; some of the whole-body plastinates were constructed in such a way that they were evidently 'doing' an activity such as basketball, chess or swimming. It seemed that the juxtaposition of the doing/living and the dead/inert body generates troubling thoughts about the distinction between life and death, between 'a person' and 'a body', and between the 'real' and 'unreal'. As Walter (2004: 473) recorded in his field notes, 'At the chess player, a seven-year-old girl, looks, frowns, and asks "Is it real mummy?" Pause. "It was once." ' This in turn relates to the theme, that the 'performance' of a body is central to ideas about self and identity, and is one that runs through the literature on the sociology of the body (and the experience of illness discussed in chapter 4). A further concern expressed by visitors and commentators was that there were so few female bodies in the exhibition, and with only one exception, the female body plastinates revealed aspects of reproduction 'implicitly defining the female as a reproductive machine' (Walter, 2004: 483). Such marginalization of women and preoccupation with their reproductive capacities touches on one of the most enduring debates within the sociology of the body, and we return to this topic in some depth at the end of this chapter.

However, we will first outline the reasons why medical sociologists became interested in the body, and then set out the main perspectives on the topic: the naturalistic, the social-constructionist and the phenomenological. We will then discuss some recent theoretical developments which have striven to develop a synthesis between these approaches. This work has been significantly influenced by the writings of Foucault, Elias and Bourdieu, and so relevant ideas from their work will also be outlined.

Whilst these male social theorists have been influential in the sociology of the body, feminist sociologists were the first to recognize and make explicit the significance of the body for social theory. Feminist analyses of women's bodies have revealed the extent to which medical and scientific descriptions of the biological basis of bodies are socially constructed, and may be used for ideological purposes such as maintaining gender inequalities. They have also contributed to an appreciation of the ways in which women's bodies have long been regulated by a male-dominated medical profession. Today this regulation and control are perhaps nowhere more evident than in developments in the field of the new reproductive technologies (NRTs). The chapter therefore concludes with a consideration of this literature.

Why are medical sociologists interested in the body?

It is only since the mid-1980s that we have been able to talk about a 'sociology of the body'. However, sociology has long been implicitly concerned with bodies and their actions and intentions; their language and gestures; the impact of material circumstances on their health status; and the impact that disabling illnesses may have on social interaction, self and identity. In fact, Shilling (2003) alludes to the body's *absent presence* in sociology.

Nevertheless, there are a number of wider societal changes which contributed to an explicit concern with the body. The most important of these are women's attempts to reclaim control over their own bodies from a male-dominated medical profession. This is evident from the success of a book produced by the Boston Women's Health Book Collective (1998) (first published in 1970 with the ninth edition published in 2011), *Our Bodies, Ourselves.* Feminist writers have also drawn attention to the political status of the physical body, and have demonstrated how it is a medium through which women have been exploited by men.

A second and related reason is the development of technological innovations such as those associated with human reproduction. These have highlighted the variable nature of the boundary between the natural and the social body. They have generated ethical debates about the status of the foetus and when human life actually begins and ends (Heitman, 2002). The pace of change with such technologies has accelerated in recent decades as a result of developments in the '"new biologies", transspecies transplantation, transgenics and cloning' (Brown and Webster, 2004: 2; Webster, 2008) and, for example, in what Raz (2009) refers to as 'reprogenetics'.

Third, the cult of the body in consumer culture increasingly forms an important dimension in postmodern societies (Featherstone, 1991a, 1991b, 2010). There is both a commercial and a cosmetic interest in the body: in keeping fit, keeping slim and keeping young. Writers on postmodernism in particular have drawn attention to the shift from bodies as producers of things to bodies as consumers of things, such as aerobics, health foods and exercise videos – in short, the 'fitness industry'. In addition, the growth of the cosmetic surgery industry is recognized to form part of these broader social trends of consumerism, commercialization and the pursuit of the 'perfect body' (Davies, 1995; Gilman, 1999; Shilling, 2003).

Fourth, demographic factors, such as the 'greying of populations', have highlighted the changing nature of human bodies. These changes have also raised new issues associated with longevity. Furthermore, the variable meanings of ageing have come to the fore as a result of studies which have examined the embodied experiences of ageing within a variety of contexts, and are critical for an adequate understanding of the life-course (Hockey and James, 2003, 2007). The greying of populations has generated questions pertaining to the ownership of bodies, as is evident in debates on euthanasia. In our secularized society, the taking of one's own life, or that of a friend or relative who requests it, is not so much a sin as a crime against the state.

A further reason for the growing concern with the body during the 1980s was the appearance of HIV/AIDS (see chapter 3). In an era characterized by an ageing population, it came as a shock to come to terms with the death of young people; AIDS highlighted the limitations of medical technology. Further, and in some respects echoing the activities of the women's movement, throughout the 1980s and 1990s people with AIDS (PWA) came together to take charge of their destinies and ensure that they retain some independence from medical control. The case of HIV/AIDs provides a neat historical example of the politicization of the body and the way in which activism shaped medical research (Davis and Squire, 2010).

A final reason for an interest in the body is a growing concern with ethical issues which pertain to it. Debates about the ethics of research on embryos and about the denial of treatment to people who 'abuse' their bodies by smoking have received considerable media attention. Questions such as the following are being asked: Who should have a say over the destiny of our bodies? What are the boundaries between life and death? Is it appropriate that matters such as these should be decided by the medical profession? Indeed, there is a growing sense of uncertainty about the body which strikes at the very heart of our lives. As a character in a Tom Stoppard play says: 'The only beginning is birth and the only end is death. If you can't count on that, what can you count on?' Today, however, with developments in medical technology, we are not quite sure when life does, or should be said to, begin and, on occasion, when it should end. Not surprisingly, perhaps, issues associated with the body have come to the fore in contemporary popular and political debates.

Debating embryonic stem cell research

The controversies surrounding developments in embryonic stem cell research serve as a pertinent illustration of these debates. Stem cells are 'those cells that form very early in an embryo's development and from which "stem" our different organs and tissues' (Brown and Webster, 2004: 72) – essentially cells that can renew tissue. The stem cells used in embryonic stem cell research may be created from those embryos donated by people who have undergone IVF treatment, or from embryos created purely for research purposes through a process called cell nuclear replacement, also known as therapeutic cloning. The UK government has supported the development of this research, but is also sensitive to public concerns, and undertook a public consultation before passing the Human Fertilization and Embryology (Research Purposes) Regulations in 2001. The consultation and ensuing debates are polarized, in part as a result of the way the media structures debates, but also, as Clare Williams et al. (2003) point out, because the discussions struggle with definitions 'of human life itself'. This, Williams and her colleagues suggest, 'adds a new twist' to the long-standing controversy surrounding anti-abortion campaigns: 'To the question "when does life begin?" it adds the question: when does life *end* and how do we define death?'

Legally, all embryos used for research have to be destroyed after fourteen days. Williams and her colleagues compared the 'rhetorical strategies' used by the proponents and opponents of stem cell research and found that whilst the former repeatedly highlighted the fourteen-day time limit, the latter group ignored or refused to acknowledge the significance of the rule – but instead emphasized the 'human potential' of all embryos. The proponents of the research emphasized the 'microscopic' size of the pre-fourteen-day-old embryo and referred to 'indeterminate cells', which are merely 'biological fragments'. By contrast, the opponents invariably talked about *human* embryos and emphasized notions of personhood, vulnerable beings which had rights of protection. The debate is captured elsewhere by Waldby (2002: 313):

> [W]e can discern two conflicting ideas about the life of the embryo, and about the idea of 'life' more generally. For opponents of stem cell research, the life of the

> embryo is biographical, the beginning point of a human narrative that should be allowed to run its social course. For advocates of stem cell research the life of the embryo is a form of raw biological vitality. From this point of view the embryo is not killed. Rather its vitality is technically diverted and reorganized.

A somatic society

Most sociologists would agree that recent decades have seen a transformation in the type of society in which we live. This new societal form has been variously described as postmodern, late modern, post-Fordist and so on. Turner (1992), however, suggests that we are moving towards what he refers to as a 'somatic society'; that is, a social system in which the body constitutes the central field of political and cultural activity. The major concerns of society are becoming less to do with increasing production, as was the case in industrial capitalism, and more to do with the regulation of bodies. Indeed, the debate discussed above provides a salient illustration of this claim. Turner writes:

> our major political preoccupations are how to regulate the spaces between bodies, to monitor the interfaces between bodies, societies and cultures . . . We want to close up bodies by promoting safe sex, sex education, free condoms and clean needles. We are concerned about whether the human population of the world can survive global pollution. The somatic society is thus crucially, perhaps critically structured around regulating bodies. (1992: 12–13)

The concerns of the somatic society are also evidenced by the concerns of contemporary political movements such as feminist groupings, pro- and anti-abortion campaigns, debates about fertility and infertility, the Green movement, and so on.

In sum, we can see that there are social as well as purely academic reasons for the growing interest in the body. However, the more we know about the body, the more elusive it appears to become. As Turner (1996: 42) comments in *The Body and Society*, 'In writing this study of the body, I have become increasingly less sure of what the body is.' In fact what the body 'is' will be determined in part by the perspective that we bring to bear on it.

Perspectives on the body

There are two polarized perspectives on the body, the naturalistic and the social-constructionist positions (Shilling, 2003), and phenomenology comprises a third perspective, which is often used as a bridge between the two extremes (Turner, 1996). The naturalistic approach assumes that the body is a real biological entity, which exists as a universal phenomenon irrespective of the social context in which it resides. The social-constructionist approach, by contrast, argues that the body is socially created, or invented, and as such is contingent on its social and historical context (see chapter 2). The reality of the body at any given time is simply an effect of how it is seen and examined. Finally, the phenomenological approach suggests that the key to understanding the human body is the mind and, more especially, the notion of 'lived experience', which suggests that people interpret and thereby create their worlds in meaningful ways.

The naturalistic perspective

The naturalistic approach emerged during the eighteenth century, and has dominated Western discourse ever since. This view maintains that all human behaviours and social relations can be explained in terms of their biological basis. Sociobiology is a discipline which falls within this perspective. It offers theories that maintain that all human behaviours and social relationships are biologically, genetically and evolutionally determined. It explains human actions and social differences in terms of their biological predispositions. For example, personality traits such as aggression, intellect and, more recently, sexual orientation are accounted for in terms of genetic predispositions.

It is argued by some that theories about the biological bases of difference are developed at times of political change and struggle. Bleier (1984), for example, has illustrated how Wilsonian sociobiology came to the fore in the mid-1970s to counter the views of second-wave feminists. Indeed, it is also noteworthy how attempts to identify a homosexual gene are not only being vociferously pursued by some, but are also receiving much media attention, at a time when popular anxieties about gay lifestyles are being articulated in the press (Radford, 1993).

The ideas that the biological basis of the body determines all forms of human and social life, and that the nature of the physical body is not impinged upon by social context, are both invariably rejected by almost all sociologists. These ideas are criticized for being reductionist, overly deterministic and scientifically flawed (Bleier, 1984). Nevertheless, the ways in which this supposedly real and natural entity, 'the body', have been understood are of significant sociological interest. Biological, physiological and anatomical theories of the body tell us as much about prevailing political ideologies as they do about the body itself. Indeed, as Scott and Morgan (1993: 6), following Armstrong (1983a), point out, '*Gray's Anatomy* needs to be understood as a cultural artefact . . . as a topic to be studied rather than straightforwardly as a resource.'

The reality of the body has long been used to account for, and justify, inequalities between men and women. It is argued, within the naturalistic perspective, that because men and women are physically so different, it is 'natural' that they should lead very different lives and be capable of distinct types of activity. However, Laqueur (1990) has documented in some detail how this idea of *difference* emerged only after the 1800s. Prior to this, men and women were assumed to be of the same sex but of different genders. Female reproductive organs were understood to be the same as male ones, only they were 'inside out'. They had the same names: what we now refer to as the ovaries were the female testicles; the uterus was the scrotum; and the vagina the penis. The male was assumed to be the norm, and the female an inferior version of it. Men had more 'heat' than women, and this accounted for their reproductive organs being on the outside. Women, being cooler, were closer to animals, which were cooler again than humans. Thus, working within a hierarchical thought system, although men and women were structurally similar, the male body was regarded as the perfect form of the species.

However, by the end of the seventeenth century men and women came to be regarded as distinct, and physiological and anatomical differences began to be emphasized (Oudshoorn and Van Den Wijngaard, 1991). Martin (1989) cites the work of the nineteenth-century biologist Patrick Geddes who described two opposite processes which functioned throughout the bodies of men and women. These were 'upbuilding, constructive, synthetic processes', which he called anabolism, and a 'disruptive, descending series of chemical changes', which he called katabolism. These processes occurred throughout the body, permeating at the level of both entire organisms and cells. Females were principally anabolic, and males katabolic:

> It is generally true that the males are more active, energetic, eager, passionate, and variable; the females more passive, conservative, sluggish, and stable . . . The more active males, with a consequently wider range of experience, may have bigger brains and more intelligence; but the females, especially as mothers, have indubitably a larger more habitual share of the altruistic emotions. The males being usually stronger, have greater independence and courage; the females excel in constancy of affection and in sympathy. (Geddes writing in 1890, quoted in Martin, 1989: 33)

We can see, therefore, how accounts of the biological basis of the body have both drawn upon and contributed to the cultural assumptions that dominate about men and women.

Working in the USA, Lawrence and Bendixen (1992) used medical anatomical textbooks published between 1890 and 1989 as a 'cultural resource' to examine the way in which men's and women's anatomies were presented. They found that in illustrations, vocabulary and syntax, the texts depict the male anatomy as the norm. Thus the male anatomy forms the basic model of 'the' human body. For example, when discussing male anatomical structures, texts referred to them as 'the', whereas female structures were always labelled as such. Through a detailed numerical and textual analysis, they found that despite public debates about gender representation, there has been very little change over the period studied. The female anatomy is therefore always presented as deviant from the norm – it constitutes the 'other'.

How medical students are trained to conceptualize the body is important, as in contemporary society the medical view of the body is often treated as the most accurate interpretation. Indeed, as Frank (1990: 135–6) notes, 'Medicine does . . . occupy a paramount place among those institutional practices by which the body is conceptualized, represented and responded to. At present our capacity to experience the body directly, or theorize it indirectly, is inextricably medicalized.' The alternative perspectives on the body are to some extent an attempt to offer different conceptualizations from that of medicine. Medicine's view of the body, whilst the most influential in Western societies, is not the only one.

Concurrent developments within schools of thought within the disciplines of biology and sociology have led some commentators to argue for a more constructive dialogue between these subjects (S. Williams et al., 2003; Birke, 1999, 2003). The proponents of this view suggest that there is a danger in simply castigating biological explanations as reductionist and/or determinist, and instead argue that it is necessary to challenge the assumptions inherent in the dominant biological discourses, with a view to establishing a non-reductionist biology, and thereby develop a more appropriate biological analysis of the body. Birke, both a feminist and a biologist, suggests that it is not biology *per se* that is the problem, but the 'simplistic assumptions' that tend to underpin it, and its recent 'obsession with genes and molecules' (2003: 44). She argues that the inner workings of the body – its physiological processes – are neglected by sociologists at their peril. 'What goes on inside the biological body remains a mystery, to be explained (if at all) only in the esoteric language of biomedicine' (Birke, 1999: 2). Rather like the *Body Worlds* exhibition (discussed above), this is a controversial and, in many ways, an exciting view, in that it invites social scientists to engage with discourses about the inner reaches of the body, rather than limiting themselves to analyses of it surfaces, it actions and its regulation.

The naturalistic perspective thereby takes a new turn, and a number of implications emerge from these debates. First, there is a blurring of the boundaries between the biological and social sciences. Working in a political economy perspective, Dickens (2001), for example, argues that the social organization of capitalism permeates and, over time, disproportionately alters the physicality of bodies according to their relative location within the system. Capitalism may be 'modifying human biology in its own image' (2001: 93) (see chapter 7). Second, with a new conceptualization of the biological body as one which is more flexible, transformative and 'self organizing' (Birke, 1999), old ideas of the biological as immutable are challenged.

An example of this is the challenge to the long-standing distinction between 'sex' (as biological) and 'gender' (as social). The problem with this, Fausto-Sterling argues, is that 'sex is often – albeit incorrectly – seen as immutable, while gender is often, albeit incorrectly, seen as malleable' (2003: 143). Fausto-Sterling (2000, 2003) proposes a Developmental Systems Theory (DST), an approach which explores the interaction of biological processes in concert with social circumstances. In her book *Sexing the Body*, Fausto-Sterling (2000) takes a number of examples to illustrate how different biological features of men's and women's bodies can be explained by their different social experiences. A third, more pragmatic implication of this work is that it points to the need for a new relationship between health activists – most particularly feminists – and scientists. As Birke (2003: 43) explains,

> While feminist theory tends to eschew the biological, biology does enter the debate in some areas of feminist activism, such as environmentalism and health. But that engagement is often ambivalent, moving uneasily between outright rejection and a need to take on board what science says. However much we may, at times, need science, we can also recognise that the stories science tells are limited, that they recreate the passive body and hard-wired organisms that we want to disavow.

Finally, and perhaps most radically, these theorists are arguing for a paradigm shift: a move from making sense of the world in linear terms of cause and effect, to working within what has become known as the 'new science' of complexity and emergence. This view argues that an empiricism, which rests on the assumptions of reductionism, has had its day (S. Johnson, 2001). Within this paradigm, an adequate analysis of the biological body must be one which locates and sees the organism as 'deeply embedded in, and part of multiple environments'; it does not exist in a 'vacuum' (Birke, 2003: 43). In some ways the transformations of the naturalistic perspective have occurred because of the insights of the social-constructionist perspective on the body, and it is to these that we now turn.

The social-constructionist perspective

As we saw in chapter 2, there is a range of approaches to social constructionism. There are those who argue that the body and diseases are effects of the discourses which describe them (Armstrong, 1983a); that is, they are an effect of what Foucault (1976) calls the 'gaze' (we discuss Foucault's ideas in more detail below). Others, by contrast, argue that the body has a material base, which is shaped and altered by social practices and its social context (Connell, 1987; Shilling, 2003). For example, the bodies of males tend to be stronger in Western societies than those of females. This, they argue, is because men are encouraged from a very young age to participate in certain types of sports and games which are likely to develop their muscles. Thus, as we also discussed in the previous section, social expectations may have a very 'real' effect on bodily structures (Connell, 1987). Whilst men may, on average, be able to carry heavier loads than women in the UK, this is not the case elsewhere. For example, in the High Atlas Mountains of Morocco, it is the Berber *women*, rather than the men, who invariably carry extremely heavy loads on their backs over long distances, loads which most people brought up in the UK would find, quite literally, back-breaking. The shape and potentiality of the body vary, therefore, according to social environment.

Another variant of this perspective is that developed by the anthropologist Mary Douglas. She argues that the *perception* of the physical body is mediated by the social body. The body provides a basis for classification, and in turn the organization of the social system reflects how the body is perceived.

> The social body constrains the way the physical body is perceived. The physical experience of the body, always modified by the social categories through which it is known, sustains a particular view of society. There is a continual exchange of meanings between the two kinds of bodily experience so that each reinforces the categories of the other. As a result of this interaction the body itself is a highly restricted medium of expression. (Douglas, 1970: xiii)

Thus, according to Douglas, the body forms a central component of any classificatory system (Douglas, 1966, 1970).

Following in the Durkheimian tradition, she maintains that all societies have elements of both the sacred and the profane, and that the demarcation between the two is fundamental to the functioning of social systems. Thus societies respond to disorder by developing classificatory systems which can designate certain phenomena as 'matter out of place'. 'Where there is dirt there is system . . . This idea of dirt takes us straight into the field of symbolism and promises a link-up with more obviously symbolic systems of purity' (Douglas, 1966: 35). Anything which transcends social, or bodily, boundaries will be regarded as pollution. Ideas, therefore, about bodily hygiene tell us as much about our cultural assumptions as they do about the 'real' body and our medical knowledge of it.

The phenomenological perspective

The third approach to the body is rooted in the phenomenological sociology developed by theorists such as Merleau-Ponty in his text *Phenomenology of Perception* (1962). Contemporary authors have taken from Merleau-Ponty the idea that all human perception is embodied; we cannot perceive anything, and our senses cannot function, independently of our bodies. This does not imply that they are somehow 'glued' together, as the Cartesian notion of the body might suggest, but rather that there is an oscillation between the two. This forms the basis of the key concept here: namely, *embodiment*. Human beings, their perception and their consciousness are invariably embedded within the body; humans are 'embodied' social agents (Nettleton and Watson, 1998). The self and the body are not separate, and experience, whether conscious or not, is embodied. The concept of *embodiment* emerged from within this perspective, and is highly influential in sociological analysis of the body, to such an extent that some sociologists prefer to aspire to an 'embodied sociology' rather than a 'sociology of the body'. These ideas contribute to the idea of the 'lived body', which emphasizes the merits of analysing bodies within the world from the point of view of bodies themselves, rather than theorizing abstractly 'about' bodies in a 'disembodied' way (Williams and Bendelow, 1998). This perspective has given rise to empirical analyses of bodily experiences such as pain, which is of course central to the experience of health and illness (Bendelow, 2000).

The core characteristic of the 'lived body' is intentionality. Leder (1992: 27), who espouses this view, explains that 'the body is not simply a thing in the world, but an intentional entity which gives rise to a world'. He argues that biomedicine has focused on the 'body-as-machine', concentrating only on the physical aspects of the body, to the neglect of the mind and the person. This approach has been developed most usefully in the sociology of the experience of illness, where it offers the possibility of a sensitive analysis of the relationship between the self, identity and the body (see chapter 4). When 'normal' bodily functions are restricted, it becomes difficult to live with one's body unreflectively. Conversely, when our bodies function as we intend them to, we tend to take them for granted. If we plan to get up in the morning and go to work, for the most part we rarely reflect upon how we will transport our bodies. Thus there has been a tendency within sociology to ignore the embodiment of human agency. This is one of the main issues which sociologists of the body have tried to address. In doing so, they have attempted to develop some kind of synthesis between these three perspectives.

Conceptual resources and analytic tools

We have seen that the prime focus of the naturalistic perspective is the biological basis of the body, the main analytic concern of social constructionism is society, and phenomenology highlights the importance of the intentionality of the actor. Combing these approaches, sociologists (Turner, 1992, 1996; Shilling, 2003; N. Crossley, 2001, 2006) have attempted to forge a sociology of the body and in so doing developed useful conceptual resources that can be deployed for empirical studies of the body.

Body techniques

In 1934 the anthropologist Marcel Mauss published an article with the title 'Techniques of the Body', which for many decades was relatively neglected by sociologists. But its value has now been realized and it has been influential for sociologists of the body. In the paper he points to 'the ways in which from society to society men [*sic*] know how to use their bodies' (1973 [1934]: 70). What may appear to be natural bodily functions and actions are in fact shaped by the social contexts in which our bodies reside.

> Walking or swimming, for example, and all sorts of things of the same type, are specific to determinate societies; that the Polynesians do not swim as we do, that my generation did not swim as the present generation does.

He draws our attention to the fact that there are cultural, historical and geographical variations between how we walk, swim, sleep, run, even how we hold a spade. Reflecting on his experiences in the trenches in World War I, Mauss recalls how the English troops did not know how to use French spades, and so they were forced to change 8,000 spades per division when the English relieved a French division and vice versa. Again reflecting on the war years, he recalls how this taught him to sleep in any location and in any position.

Thinking about sleep as a social rather than a biological process represents a fascinating example of the intersection between the social, physical and biological body (Williams, 2011). And indeed over the last decade the sociology of sleep has emerged as an exciting subfield of study. What this literature on sleep has revealed is the extent to which how, where, when and who we sleep with is variable between time, place and throughout the life-course. Sleep throws up interesting questions associated with one of the core debates in sociology around agency and structure. Much as we may want to, we cannot make ourselves sleep as Williams and Crossley (2008: 4) point out: 'The transition to sleep lies beyond [our] voluntary control.' We can, however, develop what Hislop and Arber (2003) would call 'personalised sleep strategies', which might include nightly rituals to try and foster sleep. What happens in our daily lives can impact upon our ability to sleep and our chances of having a good night's rest are associated with our position on the social hierarchy (Arber et al., 2009). For example, it is gendered, with women in middle age more likely to experience problems sleeping than men of all ages. Hislop and Arber (2003) found this to be due to the fact that women's multiple caring responsibilities from the day extend throughout the night with women doing emotional and physical labour caring for children, supporting partners, worrying about their families and so on. Schwartz (1970) notes that 'temporal and spatial sleep patterns may be employed as an index of lifestyle' (p. 496). Sleep as an index of lifestyle is perhaps nowhere more starkly demonstrated than amongst homeless drugs users who are marginalized in terms of their physical as well as socio-political environments (Nettleton et al., 2012). A study of recovering heroin users found that learning how to cultivate sleep as a body technique without recourse to drugs was a major hurdle and formed an important aspect of their recovery process (Nettleton et al., 2011a, 2011b). Their embodied sleep biographies of drug use, sleeping practices that were at odds with conventional temporal sleeping patterns, emotional troubles associated with their often troubled lives and the physical discomfort associated with detoxification all conspired to make the sleeping in the transition from drug use to potential abstinence difficult. This highlights the fundamentally embodied nature of sleep which is a personally and politically negotiated process (Meadows, 2005). Sleep as a body technique is influenced by social norms about where and when it is appropriate to sleep. To deviate from such norms is to defy what Williams refers to as the social etiquette of sleeping. How much sleep a person actually has may be constrained by pragmatic considerations such as working hours, caring responsibilities and so on. This in turn might determine whether we experience sleep of sufficient quality in order to function, which in turn is contingent upon what our biological body requires.

Body techniques then refers to our bodily practices and habits that we often take to be natural processes and practices, to such an extent they tend to be neglected within sociological inquiry. Sleep serves as a good illustration of such a technique and, like many other body techniques, brings together the biological, phenomenological and constructed aspects of embodiment. The body in this regard can be worked upon and may even become a project.

Body projects

In *The Body and Social Theory*, Shilling (2003) has argued that the body may be best conceptualized as an *unfinished* biological and social phenomenon, which is transformed, within changing limits, as a result of its participation in society. For example, styles of walking, talking and gestures are influenced by our upbringing. Shilling's theorization of the body owes much to the work of Bourdieu (1984), who argues that bodies are used as markers of distinction, and that in contemporary society the self and identity are significantly tied to the body. Shilling also derives much from the work of Elias (1978), who has documented in immense detail the way in which our bodily actions and natural functions have altered over time in accordance with social sensibilities.

From the idea that the body is continually in a state of *unfinishedness*, Shilling develops the notion of the *body as a project*. That is, the body is 'seen as an entity which is in the process of becoming; a *project* which should be worked at and accomplished as part of an *individual's* 'self/identity' (Shilling, 2003: 5). Creating and maintaining a healthy and fit body is an example of an increasingly common type of body project.

Shilling's (2003) notion of a body project is based on two propositions: first, that we have the technological knowledge and ability to intervene and substantially alter the body; second, that growing numbers of people are increasingly aware of the body as an unfinished entity which is shaped partly as a result of lifestyle choices. Following Giddens (1990, 1991), Shilling argues that in a society which is dominated by risk and uncertainty, the body has come to form a secure site over which individuals are able to exert control:

> Investing in the body provides people with a means of self expression and a way of potentially feeling good and increasing the control they have over their bodies. If one feels unable to exert control over an increasingly complex society, at least one can have some effect on the size, shape and appearance of one's body. (2003: 6)

In this context, death takes on a new meaning. Given that self and identity are increasingly tied to the control of the body, death represents the ultimate end to that control. In this respect, Shilling argues, death and society's response to it must form a key aspect of the sociology of the body. Death clearly highlights the convergence of forms of institutional control or regulation over bodies: namely, medicine, religion and the law.

Regulating bodies

The central problem addressed by Turner (1992) in *Regulating Bodies* is how to reconcile those arguments which postulate that the body is a social construction with those that adhere to the value of studying the nature of the lived body. He suggests that, in fact, these two perspectives have different concerns, and that the perspective adopted depends on one's level of analysis. For example, the social-constructionist may be concerned with the social representation of the body in medical textbooks, whereas the phenomenologist may be more interested in the experience of chronic illness.

An adequate sociology of the body, he argues, is hindered if we remain stuck in dualisms about the body's ontological status (that is, whether it is real or not) and its epistemological status (whether our knowledge of it is valid). Thus he advocates what he calls 'epistemological' and/or 'methodological pragmatism', which accepts that the body is both 'concurrently socially constructed and organically founded' (Turner, 1992: 17). He argues that the German distinction between the body as *Körper* (the objective instrumental body) and as *Leib* (the subjective animate body) is particularly instructive. Thus the body is an object that one can both observe, and at the same time makes observation possible (Turner, 2003: 281). Society's reaction to the physical body impacts upon the lived body, and, in turn, the actions of the latter affect the former. These concepts provide an analytical handle to understanding the body as a thing and the body as it is lived. He sums up his strategy thus: 'There appear to be strong reasons for regarding the body as simultaneously both discursive and animated, both *Körper* and *Leib*, both socially constructed and objective. The emphasis which we give to any or all of these dichotomies will depend on what type of research we want to undertake' (Turner, 1992: 57). The body as a physical entity and the body as lived refer to the bodies of individuals, but Turner is also concerned with the regulation of populations of bodies.

Turner therefore examines the ways in which bodies are controlled within society, and finds that it is the institutions of law, religion and medicine that are most preoccupied with such regulation. The role of these institutions is especially evident at the birth and death of bodies. Whilst the control of bodies by the Church has gone into decline, the control of bodies by the medical profession is in the ascendant. He argues, echoing the earlier writings of Zola (1972) and Conrad and Schneider (1980), that as society has become more secularized, it has also become more medicalized, with medicine now serving a moral as well as a clinical function:

> Medical practice in our time clearly does have a moral function, especially in response to AIDS and IVF programmes for unmarried, single women, but these moral functions are typically disguised and they are ultimately legitimized by an appeal to scientific rather than religious authority . . . medicine occupies the space left by the erosion of religion. (Turner, 1992: 23)

Developing an analytical framework which works at two levels – the bodies of individuals and the bodies of populations – Turner identifies four basic social tasks which are central to social order. We might refer to these as the four 'r's. First, reproduction, which refers to the creation of institutions which govern populations over time to ensure the satisfaction of physical needs – for example, the control of sexuality.

Second, the need for the regulation of bodies, particularly medical surveillance and the control of crime. Third, restraint, which refers to the inner self and inducements to control desire and passion in the interests of social organization. Fourth, the representation of the body, which refers to its physical presentation on the world stage.

Turner's conceptualization of these four 'r's owes a great deal to the ideas of Foucault, especially his writings on normalization and surveillance. These draw attention to the ways in which bodies are monitored, assessed and corrected within modern institutions. Indeed, as Turner himself suggests, the growing number of recent publications on the body 'are a testimony to the profound impact of Michel Foucault on modern developments in medical history and medical sociology' (Turner, 1991b: 272). Because the work of Foucault has been so influential on the sociology of the body and of health and illness, it is worth considering in some detail (see chapter 2).

Foucault and the body

A central theme which runs through Foucault's work is that the shift from pre-modern to modern forms of society involved the displacement of what he terms *sovereign power*, wherein power resided in the body of the monarch, by *disciplinary power*, wherein power is invested in the bodies of the wider population. Disciplinary power refers to the way in which bodies are regulated, trained, maintained and understood, and is most evident in social institutions such as schools, prisons and hospitals. Foucault argues that it is within such institutions that knowledge of bodies is produced. For example, the observation of bodies in prisons yielded a corpus of knowledge which we now know as criminology, and the observation of bodies in hospitals contributed to medical science. Foucault refers to this process as *power/knowledge.*

Power/knowledge

Disciplinary power works at two levels. First, individual bodies are trained and observed. Foucault refers to this as the 'anatomopolitics' of the human body. Second, and concurrently, populations are monitored. He refers to this process as 'regulatory controls: a bio-politics of the population' (Foucault, 1981: 139). It is these two levels – the individual and the population – which form the basis of Turner's arguments about regulating bodies which we have discussed above.

The basis for this transformation of power, Foucault claims, was the 'demographic upswing' in the eighteenth century (Foucault, 1980b: 171), which led to a need to regulate the population. A technology of the population involved a whole series of assessments and estimations, and so statistics came to be a crucial discipline. 'Within this set of problems, the "body" – the body of individuals and the body of populations – appears as the bearer of new variables' (Foucault, 1980b: 172). Indeed, within a whole series of institutional settings – schools, hospitals, prisons, health centres – bodies are examined, and information is processed about them. This is a process that is unique to modern societies. The details of human bodies are perpetually subject to scrutiny, and the knowledge of bodies, in aggregate, contributes to the development of social policies, which in turn are aimed at the alteration of bodies. For example, babies are repeatedly weighed, standard weights are deemed appropriate, and those who deviate from them are considered to be in need of dietary controls.

Perhaps the easiest way to grasp this relation between power and knowledge is to consider what Foucault refers to as the three main instruments of disciplinary power. The first is *hierarchical observation*. This refers to those sites where individuals can be observed, such as schools and prisons. The design of these buildings is such that they facilitate observation. Foucault's famous illustrative example was a prison designed in the form of a panopticon. This design was such that the officials could have the possibility of seeing all the criminals. The source of power lay in the fact that the prison warders had, if they so wished, total surveillance and, because of this, the prisoners were induced to watch over themselves. They had to behave correctly, or else they might be seen. The panopticon has a further function, in that it serves as a laboratory of humans; information can be collected and collated about all those who are contained within it. There is a link between technology, power and knowledge. It captures the disciplinary nature of our society wherein information is gathered about individuals and bodies, and they are induced to watch over their own behaviour. It requires 'Just a gaze. An inspecting gaze, a gaze which each individual under its weight will end by interiorizing to the point that he [*sic*] is his own overseer, each individual thus exercising this surveillance over, and against, himself. A superb formula: power exercised continuously and for what turns out to be a minimal cost' (Foucault, 1980a: 155).

The second instrument of power is *normalizing judgement*, which refers to the fact that the actions or attributes of each individual are compared with the actions of others. Individuals are assessed and measured, which permits a norm to be established. The judges of normality, for Foucault, are everywhere - teachers, doctors, social workers, health promoters, and so on (Foucault, 1979: 304).

The third instrument of disciplinary power combines the normalizing judgement and the hierarchical observation: it is the *examination*. Here the individual subject can be both assessed and corrected. Dentistry is an example of this (Nettleton, 1992). Since the mid-nineteenth century the goal of dentistry has been to ensure maximum surveillance of mouths and teeth. The profession emerged within the context of preventive health programmes, which operated in schools, health and welfare clinics, and the home. In particular, mothers and children were encouraged to attend, their mouths were inspected, and epidemiological data were kept, which in turn provided standards by which each individual could be assessed. Activities associated with dentistry also illustrate how bodily routines were learned within certain sites and then internalized. Toothbrush drills carried out in schools in the early part of the twentieth century taught children how to clean their teeth and how to hold a toothbrush; further, they were instructed at what times they should carry out this routine when at home. Today, although tooth-brushing skills are still taught, the style of pedagogy is less regimented and more diffuse (Nettleton, 1992).

Foucault noted that since the 1960s the nature of disciplinary power has changed somewhat. From the eighteenth until the early twentieth century it was believed that 'power had to be heavy, ponderous, meticulous and constant', hence the formidable regimes in hospitals, barracks, factories and families. Since then, however, it has been recognized that 'industrial societies could content themselves with much looser forms of power over the body' (Foucault, 1980c: 58). Studies of power in health care have borne this out. Arney and Bergen (1984), for example, have argued that a 'medical revolution' took place after the Second World War, wherein the more limited anatomical approach to medicine was superseded by a more socio-ecological approach. Medicine, they argue, is now practised not just on physical bodies but on thinking people. Indeed, as sociology has begun to incorporate the body, so medicine has, at one and the same time, begun to incorporate the social.

Whilst the panopticon might provide an appropriate model of medical practice in the nineteenth century, Armstrong (1983a) suggested that an alternative representation was required to capture the essence of medical practice in the twentieth century. He suggested that it was the Dispensary (with a capital D to differentiate it from the building) that provides the most appropriate symbol. The Dispensary was a place from which drugs were dispensed and where the sick from the local community could be attended to. The Dispensary, like the panopticon, was a building, and like the panopticon exemplified 'a new perceptual structure - a new way of seeing illness' (Armstrong, 1983a: 8). 'Where Panopticism had in effect offered to the observing eye that which was an enclosed space, the school, the hospital or the prison, the Dispensary through its juxtaposition of observation and community replaced enclosed physical space with an open social domain' (Armstrong, 1983a: 16). Whilst the clinical gaze within the Panoptic structure explored localized pathology, the Dispensary regime permitted the observation of social relationships and networks; symptoms passed through a social, rather than simply a physical, space. Thus there has been a shift from the biological anatomy of the body to its political anatomy. With this change in the structures of medical institutions, the dichotomies between health and disease, sane and insane, young and old, normal and abnormal, have become blurred. Instead of being placed on either side of these binary divides, bodies are placed on a continuum. In recent decades the structures of medical institutions and technologies which scrutinize the body are being transformed again within the context of the 'Information Age' (Nettleton, 2004), wherein the biological and information sciences have come together to analyse, scrutinize, visualize, represent, make sense of and understand bodies in radically new ways. A high-profile example of this is the *Visible Human Project*.

From biopower to biovalue: the Visible Human Project

In 1994 the US National Library of Medicine placed the digitized image of a man's dead body on the web – the bodily interior being made visible to anyone who cares to access it on their computer screens. A year later the body of a woman was also digitally preserved and presented. As the authors of the website explain:

> The two bodies acquired through donations met bioethical standards of informed consent: a 39-year-old convict executed in Texas by lethal injection; and a 59-year-old Maryland housewife who died of cardiovascular disease. Scientists scanned the cadavers, using CT (computerized tomography) and MRI (magnetic resonance imaging). The corpses, deep-frozen in blue gelatin, were then shaved to remove thin cross-sections of tissue, from head to toe. As each layer was removed, the exposed surface was digitally photographed, creating data that computer software could reassemble, navigate and manipulate. (<www.nih.gov/exhibition/dreamanatomy/da_visible_vishumhtml>)

This is known as the Visible Human Project (VHP), and in some ways represents a further example of those technologies which are used to 'see' the inner reaches of the body.

From the x-ray to magnetic resonance imaging (MRI), positron emission tomography (PET) and computed tomography (CT) scans, the 'clinical gaze' is becoming more sophisticated, and the images of the body's interior more vivid. But there are differences. The images on the website are accessible to a much wider audience, and so extend well beyond the confines of traditional medical institutions. In addition, there is a blurring of boundaries between the real and the unreal, the private and the public, the dead and the living; the real body becomes a 'digital substance' (Waldby, 2000: 6) which permeates the virtual and the real.

In her book *The Visible Human Project*, Catherine Waldby (2000) argues that the whole exercise represents a further extension of Foucault's notion of biopower. The VHP is at once a means of both examining and experimenting on the body, and therefore it is also a means by which knowledges of bodies are generated and circulated. The VHP involves the formation of a unique archive of two bodies in the form of data files; it comprises a 'reserve' that may be drawn upon by those engaging in biomedical projects (p. 34). Not only does this generate knowledge; it also produces 'surplus value', in that there are significant commercial interests involved in the production of medical technologies, be they equipment, drugs or whatever. This is what Waldby calls *biovalue* - the 'surplus value' that is yielded by this and indeed other biotechnologies of the body (e.g., stem cell research, discussed above). *Biovalue* 'refers to the yield of vitality produced by the biotechnological reformulation of living processes' (Waldby, 2002: 310).

There are two motivations for generating *biovalue*: first, the hope that biotechnologies will result in a better understanding and, thereby treatment, of disease; second, the pursuit of exchange value of biomedical commodities - be they patents or pills - that are the yield of the interventions. Indeed, *biovalue* is 'increasingly assimilated into capital value, and configured according to the demands of commercial economies' (Waldby, 2000: 34). The counterpart to the VHP, observes Waldby, is the Human Genome Project (HGP), in that both projects are means by which the body comes to form a database, an archive, and so a source of bio-information.

> While understanding the human body as a database or information archive may be metaphorical at one level, at another this mode of understanding produces material practices that work the body as database. The instrumentation specific to the VHP and the HGP address the body so that it acts as an archive, laying it open as a source of bio-information. The VHP cuts up the body so that it can act as a visual and morphological archive, while the HGP has a large repertoire of molecular practices (polymerase chain reaction, automated DNA fluorescence sequencing, pulse field gel electophoresis) that make the body's sequences of DNA intelligible and mappable. (Waldby, 2000: 39–40)

These represent the most recent examples of power/knowledge, of observing and generating knowledges of bodies and human subjects. According to Foucault, humans are both 'objects' and 'subjects' of power, but the mechanisms and technologies of power change between social and historical contexts.

That people's actions and behaviours are modified in relation to the wider social context, and are connected to changing relations of power, is a theme that is also explored by Norbert Elias, another 'social theorist' whose work has had a significant impact on the sociology of the body. Although in most respects very different from Foucault in his form of analysis, he is also interested in the way in which bodily behaviours are shaped and, like Foucault, in how they have come to be increasingly individuated. Furthermore, both authors draw attention to matters which were long regarded as trivial and peripheral to sociology.

Civilizing the body

The work of Elias is concerned with the link between the state and state formations and the behaviours and manners of the individual. He offers a 'figurational sociology'; this means that he works at the level of social configurations, rather than societies. In fact, for Elias, societies are the outcome of the interactions of individuals. In his studies in the first volume of *The Civilizing Process* (first published in 1939 in German), Elias (1978) examines in detail changes in manners, etiquette, codes of conduct, ways of dressing, ways of sleeping, ways of eating and changing ideas about shame and decency associated with bodies.

According to Elias, the civilizing process began in the Middle Ages within court societies, where social mobility became more fluid and people's futures could be determined not only by their birthrights, as had been the case under the feudal system, but also by the extent to which they found favour with the sovereign or his or her advisers. In short, people were more inclined to be on their 'best behaviour'.

Early medieval personalities were characteristically unpredictable and emotional; they were inclined to be indulgent; and there were virtually no codes surrounding bodily functions. However, within court societies codes of body management were developed, and copious manuals were written on how and where to sleep and with whom, how to behave at table, appropriate locations for defecation, and so on. Changes in behaviour affected social relations, and as social relationships were transformed, so the compulsions exerted over the self and others became internalized. This process, according to Elias, accelerated in the sixteenth century. People came to have greater self-control over behaviours associated with the body and a heightened sense of shame and decency: 'The individual is compelled to regulate his [*sic*] conduct in an increasingly differentiated, more even and more stable manner . . . The more complex and stable control of conduct is increasingly instilled in the individual from his earliest years as an automatism, a self compulsion that he cannot resist' (Elias, 1982: 232–3). This civilizing process involves three key progressive processes (Shilling, 2003: 164–7): socialization, rationalization and individualization.

Socialization refers to the way in which people are encouraged to hide away their natural functions. Thus the body comes to be regarded more in social than in natural terms. In fact, we find many natural functions offensive or distasteful – for example, if someone sitting next to us on a bus vomits over our clothes, or if someone wilfully urinates in an 'inappropriate' part of our house. Rationalization implies that we have become more rational, as opposed to emotional, and are able to control our feelings. Finally, individualization highlights the extent to which we have come to see our bodies as encasing ourselves as separate from others. It is important, therefore, that we maintain a socially acceptable distance between ourselves and others. These processes, which have resulted in the so-called civilized body, can present problems for those who actually have to work with bodies and violate those conventions normally adhered to in Western societies. This is perhaps nowhere more evident than in the nursing care of the body.

Nursing care and the body

A problem for the health care of the body is that it may conflict with our sensibilities which have emerged with the civilizing process. From the 1500s to the 1900s an 'invisible wall of affects' arose between bodies,

> which is often perceptible today at the mere approach of something that has been in contact with the mouth or hands of someone else, and which manifests itself as an embarrassment at the mere sight of many bodily functions of others, and often at the mere mention, or as a feeling of shame when one's own functions are exposed to the gaze of others. (Elias, 1978: 69–70)

Julia Lawton (2000, 2002b) draws upon Elias's insight to explain why some patients with terminal illnesses remain in hospices, whilst others are more likely to be discharged and sent home to die. While undertaking an ethnography of a hospice, she observed that those patients whose bodies became 'unbounded' remained within the formal care setting. Unbounded bodies were those which experienced 'incontinence of urine and faeces, uncontrolled vomiting (including faecal vomit), fungating tumours (the rotting away of a tumour site on the surface of the skin) and weeping limbs which resulted from the development of gross oedema in the patient's legs or arms' (Lawton, 2002b: 98). That which transcends an unbounded body constitutes 'matter out of place' (Douglas, 1966; see above) and therefore offends against order. Furthermore, in a context of civilized bodies which are increasingly individualized and private, the 'natural' functions of the body are removed from public view and offend against our sensibilities. Such theorizations also help to explain Lawton's further observation that those patients whose bodies were 'unbounded' appeared to become more withdrawn and disengaged from those around them. They 'exhibited behaviour which suggests a loss of sense of self' (Lawton, 2002b: 101), which is perhaps not surprising if we concur with the contention that in a late modern context, personhood – self and identity – is dependent upon 'the possession of a physically bounded body' (2002b: 101).

Nursing care more generally invariably involves assistance with basic body care such as sleeping, eating, grooming and defecating. All those activities that have become 'civilized', and thus 'privatized', are dealt with publicly by the nurse. This aspect of nurses' work has long gone unnoticed, but has recently been described in Lawler's (1991) excellent study, *Behind the Screens: Nursing, Somology and the Problem of the Body*.

Quintessentially, the work of nurses is about caring for bodies. This is a problem, in that they must directly attend to those bodily functions which have, in a 'civilized' society, become taboo. Consequently, nurses skilfully negotiate social boundaries and create new contexts so that both patient and nurse can avoid feelings of shame and embarrassment. Nurses have to negotiate the socially delicate territory of invading another person's space in intricate ways by using specific methods. The methods that Lawler identified were the creation of a new *system of rules* and a set of *specific contextors*. Significantly, these are learned through personal experience, and are not formally taught.

The four basic rules are: the 'compliance rule', the 'dependency rule', the 'modesty rule' and the 'protection rule'. Patients are expected to 'comply' with the instructions of the nurse, because they are 'dependent' upon him or her. These two rules are fairly straightforward when patients are sedated or very ill; however, more skilful negotiation over assistance with body care is required when patients are in the recovery stage. The 'modesty' rule is particularly fragile, and most often broken. Here the patient is expected to be neither too modest nor too embarrassed when body-care routines are being carried out. Finally, the 'protection' rule, whereby the nurse must acknowledge the potential for embarrassment and ensure the patient's privacy, contributes to the maintenance of socially acceptable body care.

To ensure effective adherence to these rules, the nurses sought to ensure five 'specific contextors' which 'define the situation': wearing a uniform, acting in an appropriate manner, 'minifisms', asking relatives to leave before carrying out body care, and discourse privatizations. Nurses involved in the study believed that the wearing of a uniform was essential to making their acts permissible. So too was acting in an appropriate manner: the nurses spoke of being 'professional', 'matter-of-fact', and 'in control'. The nurses also commented about how they used 'minifisms' – that is, they would understate or underplay situations. For example, if a patient vomited all over her or his bed, the nurse would, in front of the patient at least, underplay its significance. Fourth, and to ensure adherence to the protection rule, nurses would ask relatives to leave before carrying out body care. Finally, nurses used 'discourse privatizations': that is, 'the nurse uses a form of discourse with the patient which ensures that certain body functions and aspects of patient care are discussed as a private matter between the nurse and the patient' (Lawler, 1991: 166).

By far the most problematic areas of the body for the nurse (and potentially for the patient) are those associated with sexuality and genitalia: 'The body and sexuality are intimately interrelated but there are important differences between the sexes which are reflective of patriarchy and a culture which is not comfortable with issues relating to sexuality and the body' (Lawler, 1991: 112). Consequently, it is in the area of sexuality that the rules are most likely to be either broken or stretched to their limits. This is especially so where male patients are concerned (Lawler, 1991: 86). First, most nurses are women, and the nurse–patient encounter is a social event where gender needs to be managed. Second, masculinity and the power of men over women are very often enacted through the body. Third, nursing activities very often involve a level of intimacy that is not usual outside a sexual encounter. Fourth, nurses experience sexual harassment from patients just as women do in society generally. Consequently, body care carried out for men is often found to be the most precarious. When faced with carrying out their first 'sponge' (wash) on a real person, most nurses prefer that their patient be a woman. As one nurse recalls, 'I can remember the very first day on the ward . . . *begging* that they let me do a female one [sponge] first because I couldn't bear the thought of pulling down a pair of man's trousers' (Lawler, 1991: 121, emphasis original).

The context of the nursing care can be disrupted when the patient and nurse define the situation differently. For example, the patient may define the situation as a sexual encounter and the nurse as a nurse–patient encounter. As another nurse informed Lawler (1991: 151), 'The ones that make it really hard for you are the . . . types . . . [who] like to show they can get erections and all sorts of things while you are sponging them . . . They're the ones that make it difficult.' Thus, through violations of socially acceptable bodily behaviour, men try to assert an alternative definition of the situation, a sexual rather than a nursing encounter. The social negotiation required for invading another person's bodily space is a particularly delicate exercise, and relies on the extent to which appropriate social contexts can be created and sustained.

What both Lawton and Lawler's studies have in common is that they describe work on bodies by bodies who in turn are employed to undertake this labour. Such activity has been conceptualized by Twigg and her colleagues (2011) as 'body work', that is 'work that focuses directly on the bodies of others: assessing, diagnosing, handling, treating, manipulating, and monitoring of bodies, that thus become the object of the worker's labour' (p. 1). The concept is a valuable one because it highlights not only the ambivalences associated with work on the body that inclines to transgressing body boundaries as we have explored above but it also highlights the lack of fit of body work with procedures, policies and regulations that characterize formal work settings. For example, body time does not always correspond with clock time and so the boundaries of shifts and working hours may be out of sync with the needs of those bodies that are being cared for. Attempts to increase productivity, speed up or rationalize care work are difficult where the attention is given to bodily needs and rhythms which in turn are variable and unpredictable. Body work requires a co-presence, workers and bodies they work upon must be in the same place at the same time and this has implications for staffing levels and workers' mobilities. Even within the context of virtual worlds and health care at a distance – body work remains hands on and proximate. As care becomes privatized and demographic trends reveal a growing ageing population, the mundane, messy realities of body work are especially salient. Body work thus represents a transportable concept and can be studied across health care regimes in order to:

> trace the tangible effects of changes in the organisation of services, funding, and other 'external' constraints on how body work is structured, measured, monitored and experienced. The concept of body work is especially useful in capturing the variability and timeliness of human needs for care and the costs for patients and workers of failing to allow for this, and therefore the contradictions inherent in the provision of care guided by measures of efficiency and standardised protocols (Twigg et al., 2011: 12).

A further issue that is evident from studies on body work is the performative aspect of bodies – how they are presented to others and how this in turn can both reflect and reinforce power relations and social inequalities. The way bodies are trained and socialized may contribute to their shape, size and posture, which in turn can be cited as markers of social difference. Connell (1987) has suggested that because the biological differences between men and women are not in fact that great, there is a tendency to exaggerate them. Indeed, ethnomethodological studies have shown that men and women have constantly to work at, or accomplish, gender differences (Garfinkel, 1967). Gender differences, Connell (1987: 85) argues, come to take on the appearance of being natural:

> The social definition of men as holders of power is translated . . . into muscle tensions, posture, the feel and texture of the body. This is one of the main ways in which the power of men becomes 'naturalized', that is, seen as part of the order of nature. It is very important in allowing belief in the superiority of men, and the oppressive practices that flow from it, to be sustained by men who in other respects have very little power.

Dimensions of the body, therefore, can actually contribute towards the reproduction of social inequalities. In this respect bodies may differ in terms of what Bourdieu calls physical capital.

Bourdieu and physical capital

It has long been recognized that position in the social structure impacts upon the body in terms of health status (see chapter 7). That is, morbidity and mortality rates are greatly influenced by class, 'race', gender, etc. Bourdieu (1984), however, has suggested that the body can influence social location.

Bourdieu analysed social inequalities in terms of four different forms of capital. Location in the social hierarchy involves varying amounts of economic capital (money, wealth, property); cultural capital (education, knowledge of arts and high culture); symbolic capital (presentation of self, demeanour); and physical capital (body shape, talk, gait, speech). In his discussion on taste, and in particular food choices, Bourdieu (1984: 190) writes:

> the body is the most indisputable materialization of class taste, which it manifests in several ways. It does this first in the seemingly most natural features of the body, the different dimensions (volume, height, weight) and shapes (round or square, stiff or supple, straight or curved) of its visible forms, which express in countless ways a whole relation to the body, i.e., a way of treating it, caring for it, feeding it, maintaining it . . . It is in fact through preferences with regard to food which may be perpetuated beyond their social conditions of production (as, in other areas, an accent, a walk, etc.) and also, of course, through the uses of the body in work and leisure which are bound up with them, that the class distribution of bodily properties are determined.

Shilling (1991, 2003) has developed this idea and argued that the physical body can contribute to the reproduction of social inequalities. Working-class people, he argues, have a more 'instrumental' orientation to their bodies; for example, they are likely to have a more functional view of illness, and thus the body is treated as a 'means to an end'. Participation in sport and exercise maps on to occupational class with those in higher ranking positions and who have post school qualifications more frequently engaging in physical activity for the purpose of body maintenance, a finding that is more pronounced for women than it is for men. Sixty-nine per cent of women in routine occupations never do any exercise and yet this is the case for only 26 per cent of women in managerial or professional occupations (Bennett et al., 2009: 160).

The *conversion* of physical capital refers to the translation of such bodily activities into other forms of capital, be they social, economic or cultural. An example of the conversion of physical capital into economic capital for working-class men would be through sport; for example, they may become footballers or boxers. This process is precarious, however, due to the high risk of injury or the short-term nature of such careers, and is in any case extremely rare. This approach incorporates both the lived body and the physical body. It also incorporates ideas about the representation of the body. How bodies, in various social and cultural settings, are represented will in turn significantly affect our perception of them.

Feminism and bodies: perceptions and assumptions about women's bodies

The way in which cultural assumptions underlie our perception of the body is the main theme of Emily Martin's (1989) study, *The Woman in the Body*. As she says, 'I try to get at what *else* ordinary people or medical specialists are talking about when they describe hormones, the uterus, or menstrual flow. What cultural assumptions are they making about the nature of women, of men, of the purpose of existence?' (Martin, 1989: 13). As we have already seen, social metaphors are prevalent in medical texts and journals. In her book Martin graphically illustrates how bodies are described in nineteenth-century medical texts in ways that reflect the social and economic system, in that the body formed the model of industrial society.

The body resembled factories and communication systems, and certain parts carried specialized functions. In the twentieth century the development of molecular biology drew on metaphors from information science and management, the co-ordinating centre of which is the central nervous system. The dominant image of the female reproductive system is that of a signalling system which functions in a manner analogous to a radio transmitter. Martin (1989: 40) cites a textbook written by Lein in 1979:

> Whereas the nervous system has characteristics in common with a telephone network, the endocrine glands perform in a manner somewhat analogous to radio transmission. A radio transmitter may blanket an entire region with its signal, but a response occurs only if a radio receiver is turned on and tuned to the proper frequency . . . the radio receiver in biological systems is a tissue whose cells possess active receptor sites for a particular hormone or hormones.

The 'female brain–hormone–ovary system' is described in terms of a hierarchy whereby directions and orders are given, and as such relates to the dominant form of organization in Western capitalist societies.

A consequence of this is that 'normal' biological processes come to be defined in negative terms. For example, the menopause is defined in terms of a breakdown in a system of authority, and menstruation is defined as a production system that has failed to produce. Women's bodies come to be seen as 'another kind of horror . . . the disused factory, the failed business, the idle machine' (Martin, 1989: 45). The metaphors used reinforce the traditional roles assigned to women; they presume that if a woman menstruates, then once again she has failed to produce a baby, and the menopause renders her as unproductive and superfluous to society's requirements.

The images that the 165 women Martin interviewed had of their bodies reflected those of the doctors. This is not surprising, as the language which ordinary women use to construct themselves is influenced by prevailing medical, social, economic and political discourses. The central tenet that the women used was 'your self is separate from your body'. Associated with this were five further conceptualizations. First, 'your body is something that your self has to adjust to or cope with'. Many of the women felt at odds with their bodies, and 'unpleasant' biological functions were something that had to be 'coped' with. Second, 'your body needs to be controlled by your self'. Many women spoke of differing degrees of control over their bodies, which could potentially become beyond their self-control. Third, 'your body sends you signals'. Again, the women articulated how their 'separate' physical body could transmit messages to the self, and when these messages were received, they tried to act upon them. Fourth, 'menstruation, menopause, labour, birthing and their component stages are states that you go through or things that happen to you (not actions you do)'. The women felt that it was something that happened to them and did not express it as an experience that unified their physical and lived body. Finally, 'menstruation, menopause and birth contractions are separate from the self. They are "*the* contractions", "*the* hot flushes" (not *mine*); they "come on"; women "get them". The women felt that things happen to their bodies, which are, again, removed from the self' (Martin, 1989: 77–8).

The women, however, were not simply swamped by the medical discourse, because they simultaneously drew on alternative discourses. This was especially true of working-class women. Whilst the middle-class women may have articulated a dissatisfaction with the medical model, at the same time the language of medicine was more evident in their interview data. Working-class women were less likely to use the medical metaphors of failed production, and were more likely to see menopause, menstruation and childbirth as part of life. The working-class women especially draw upon a phenomenological as well as a medical model.

Martin suggests that women have a view of the world that is different from that which currently dominates. This is as a consequence of the way in which women experience their bodies. Their bodily processes go with them everywhere, and so they invariably transcend those dichotomies constructed within capitalist societies, such as home versus work, nature versus culture, women versus men, private versus public.

> Because their bodily processes go with them everywhere, forcing them to juxtapose biology and culture, women glimpse every day a conception of another sort of social order. At the very least because they do not fit into the ideal division of things (private bodily processes begin at home), they are likely to see that the dominant ideology is partial: it does not capture their experience . . . When women derive their view of experience from their bodily processes as they occur in society, they are not saying 'back to nature' in any way. They are saying on to another kind of culture, one in which our rigid separations as oppositions are not present. (Martin, 1989: 200)

Martin's analysis integrates the biological and the social, and so overcomes the sex versus gender or the biology versus social dichotomy.

In this respect Martin's study fits neatly into the contemporary theoretical literature on the sociology of the body in that it combines naturalistic, constructionist and phenomenological perspectives. Furthermore, it highlights the significance of embodied social action. Like the study by Lawler, discussed above, it also emphasizes the extent to which women's experience of bodies can contribute to our understanding, and theoretical developments, of the body. It is through empirical studies such as these that we are most able to appreciate the relationship between the body, health and illness.

It was, of course, the feminist literature which first drew attention to the importance of the body for sociological analysis. This occurred as a result not only of academic debate but also of women's experience. Women's bodies have been increasingly medicalized, and one of the key aims of second-wave feminism was to reclaim control over the female body. This is not easy, however, as innovations in medical technology permit more and diverse forms of control over women's lives and bodies. One particularly overt example of this is in the area of the new reproductive technologies.

Reproductive technologies

The regulation of bodies and the control of reproduction are central issues within the sociology of the body. This is closely bound to the control of female sexuality which has, in different forms, existed in both religious and secular Western patriarchal societies (Turner, 1996). Reproductive technology has been used both to regulate populations and to enable some women (depending on their social, economic and religious contexts) to have control over their reproduction. The presence of such technology has altered our preconceived notions of the boundaries between the social and the physical body. However, it is not the presence of the technologies *per se* that determines their impact on people's lives, but the social and political context within which they are located and from which they derive their meaning (Faulkner and Arnold, 1985). Technological innovations in themselves do not shape people's lives. Rather, it is the *application* of them which is inherently social (Freidson, 1970a; McNeill et al., 1990). This view is demonstrated empirically by an ethnography carried out in a town in the north of England. Whilst most people's lives had not been directly affected by new reproductive technologies (NRT), the researcher found their very existence to have social and cultural resonances, in that NRTs provide a 'window' into people's implicit notions of kinship and relatedness (Edwards, 2000). There is a dialectic between NRTs and issues of kinship and identities, which in turn are imbued by morals, values and ethics. It is hardly surprising, therefore, that debates about reproduction and regulation are so heated.

Stanworth (1987) has grouped those technologies which aim to intervene in the process of reproduction into four categories: first, fertility control technologies such as the pill, diaphragms, intra-uterine devices and the condom; second, those which are designed to manage labour and childbirth such as foetal monitoring, episiotomies, Caesarean sections and forceps; third, screening techniques, such as ultrasound and amniocentesis, which monitor the foetus for any 'defects'; and finally, conceptive technologies which are designed to overcome infertility and are referred to as assisted or new reproductive technologies. These include artificial insemination by donor (AID) and fertility drugs, *in vitro* fertilization, egg donation, embryo donation, and the low-temperature storage of gametes and embryos. But only two decades later, another category can be added to this list, and that is technologies associated with embryonic stem cell research (see above). These are 'clearly reproductive in a biological sense of depending on cell division, but how they reproduce and for what purpose is far removed from the specific arena of the reproduction of children' (Brown and Webster, 2004: 73). Innovations in relation to technologies of reproduction are being transformed in association with developments in molecular biology - in particular, genetics and the use of DNA-based technologies - for the management and supervision of the reproductive process referred to by Ettorre (2002: 65) as 'reproductive genetics'.

We can thus see that reproductive technologies require varying degrees of technological equipment and sophistication. AID, which has been used in Britain since the 1930s (Pfeffer, 1987), can be carried out by anyone at home. There is no need for medical intervention. Similarly, surrogacy with self-insemination can be negotiated informally. In the UK a Feminist Self-Insemination Group advised and helped women to use this low-tech method for the promotion of pregnancy (R. D. Klein, 1984). Such activities are not deemed acceptable, however, by those who prefer reproduction to be subject to medical and legal regulation. The Warnock Committee (1984), which was set up in 1982 to look into the ethics of technologies of human reproduction, was adamant that all forms of 'artificial' modes of reproduction must take place only under medical supervision. Regulation of reproductive technologies has become increasingly formalized; in the UK, for example, the Human Fertility and Embryology Authority (HFEA) established in 1991 is the body which constantly reviews and issues guidelines and codes of practice for assisted conception and embryo research.

It is clear that there is a prevailing belief that pregnancy and childbirth must be monitored both medically and legally. Zipper and Sevenhuijsen (1987) have pointed out that the desire to regulate surrogacy is reflected in other reports produced throughout Western Europe, and that this is the outcome of suspicions about the credibility and validity of women's actions. There is a perception that if ordinary people were to make their own arrangements, this could threaten the social order. This is evident in the HFEA's reports, which repeatedly allude to the need to allay the public's fears associated with new forms of conception and with research carried out on embryos.

Nevertheless, people have always devised their own ways of organizing procreation, and it is likely that they always will. *In vitro* fertilization is a more complex technique. It involves removing an egg from a woman, then fertilizing and returning it to the woman's womb or to the womb of another, 'surrogate' mother. The first child to be born by this means in the UK was Louise Brown, in 1978, hailed as the first 'test-tube baby'. Then, as now, men and women who use NRTs find themselves caught up in a maelstrom of media attention. Although IVF and AID are now considered to be routine procedures, those instances where their use is seen to challenge dominant social norms and conventions generate vociferous debate. For example, in the USA, the case of a lesbian couple who have two children using sperm donated by a gay couple with whom they are friends, has received much media attention. The women are the children's legal parents (Dillon, 2004). Right-wing groups are uncomfortable with this, and are keen to restrict reproduction.

On the other side of the globe, a similar, highly emotive debate took place in Australia at the turn of this century (J. L. Smith, 2003). The right-wing government set out to restrict lesbian and single women's access to NRTs. In 2000, as a result of the so-called McBain case, the Federal Court ruled that as a result of the Sex Discrimination

Act of 1984, all women should have equal access to assisted reproductive technologies. The then Prime Minister said that 'the issue primarily involves the fundamental right of a child within our society to have the reasonable expectation, other things being equal, of the care and affection of both a mother and a father' (Howard, 2000, cited in J. L. Smith, 2003: 72). Those keen to restrict access invariably highlight the presumed rights and needs of the unborn child, whereas the concerns, feelings and needs of the mother are at best marginalized or at worse pilloried (J. L. Smith, 2003). We can see that reproductive techniques raise legal and ethical issues, and highlight the differential status of women's bodies within Western societies. Responses to the dilemmas created by the NRTs reinforce existing beliefs about the social organization of sexuality and reproduction. The ideology of motherhood is reinforced, and patriarchal family life is privileged.

This relates to a second issue raised by the context in which NRTs are applied, and this is the status of pregnancy. Women's bodies are rendered superfluous to the creation of life. Oakley (1987) notes that the delivery of babies by Caesarean section to brain-dead women has contributed to this vision. 'It has now become technologically possible to ignore the status of pregnant women as human beings' (Oakley, 1987: 39). The mother and the foetus have increasingly come to be seen as two separate bodies rather than one, and this has significant implications for the care of women in childbirth. Although in the USA and in the UK the foetus is not a 'person' with legal rights, Weaver (2002) documents how obstetricians appeal to the courts to enforce Caesarean births in the best 'interests' of the foetus. She found that within the 'mother–foetal conflict', the mother tends to be presented as selfish or irrational while the foetus is a helpless, vulnerable victim. This championing of the unborn is a theme which runs through contemporary debates on NRTs, as we noted above. Terms such as 'artificial', 'surrogacy' and 'test-tubes' have led to 'the eclipsing of the pregnant women's part in childbearing' (Stanworth, 1987: 26).

As with most issues, there is no feminist orthodoxy on NRT, but rather a range of responses. For some, the creation of NRTs is seen as an end-stage in men's desire to control women, and men's aspirations to appropriate reproductive power have been realized (Corea, 1985; Hanmer, 1985; Rowland, 1985). Biological mothers will be reduced to 'mother machines' (Corea, 1985). Others, however, have argued that it is not the technologies themselves which are problematic, but the social context within which they are developed and applied. Rather than advocating a return to natural motherhood, women must participate in the development and evaluation of these technologies which hitherto have been left to 'malestream' science and medicine, and so make sure that these technologies come to be within the control of women (Stanworth, 1987; McNeill et al., 1990). Thus it is recognized that technologies can be at once liberating and controlling.

Certainly the notion that NRTs empower women and enable them to make reproductive choices is accepted by most as simplistic. Sociologists have long asserted that the idea of choice is circumscribed, and is invariably compromised by prevailing social norms and values, as well as by people's social, economic and cultural resources. The imperative of biological parenting is, for example, shaped by sociocultural ideas about natural and normal parenting. The availability of technologies which can permit this serve to both capitalize on and reinforce such norms. 'Choice', as Brown and Webster (2004: 62) succinctly put it, 'is not an innocent term.'

The complexities pertaining to 'choice' are explored in Rapp's (2000) ethnographic exploration of women's experiences of prenatal diagnostic technologies (such as amniocentesis and pre-implantation genetic diagnostics (PGD)) in the USA. The study arose from her own experience of her foetus being 'diagnosed' with Down's syndrome, her termination, and her subsequent reflections on the complexity of the dilemmas involved. From her extensive interviews with women from diverse social backgrounds, observations in health care settings, and conversations with health care providers, she concluded that women who are offered such technologies become 'moral pioneers'; 'they are forced to judge the quality of their own foetuses, making concrete and embodied decisions about the standards for entry into the human community' (Rapp, 2000: 3). When making a decision to undergo prenatal testing, women 'were participating in an impromptu and large-scale social experiment'. Rapp recalls a conversation with one health worker, 'an African-American non-profit education administrator', who was quick to refute Rapp when she referred to women's choices. For this health worker, 'decisions' was a more appropriate word. 'She was insisting that the intersections at which pregnant women act are not so much "chosen" as constructed by forces much larger than women themselves' (2000: 313).

Abortion of a foetus because of an 'abnormality' brings us into the realms of eugenics. Within the medical profession, most doctors are keen to distance themselves from the 'negative eugenics model', and work instead with a 'therapeutic', or 'positive eugenics model', claiming that women are offered screening so that they can make 'informed' decisions. Ettorre's (2002) study of the views of clinicians throughout Europe reveals that there is an assumption that information about abnormality is valuable to mothers so that they can abort the foetus. Such findings throw into sharp relief questions about the value we place on certain bodies – those that are considered to be less than 'normal' and may be classified as having disabilities. In this way eugenics may be presented in a more liberal, positive form, but for many it may be no less disturbing (Kerr, 2004).

Foucault, feminism and NRTs

A further view of NRTs is that taken by Foucauldian feminists such as Sawicki (1991). Whilst Sawicki acknowledges the importance of the work of feminist challenges to NRTs, she interprets the struggle between challenges made by women to 'malestream' technology in a more positive way. She distinguishes, following Foucault, between the 'repressive model of power', which emphasizes the way in which women are repressed and oppressed by men, with the 'disciplinary model of power', which focuses on the struggles and resistances between men and women. Male domination, she argues, is not homogeneous and static, but rather changes in response to the resistances of women. As we have seen above, Foucault argued that disciplinary power was essential to the development of modernity: 'in so far as it made possible a "controlled insertion of bodies into the machinery of production", then it must also have been indispensable to patriarchal power as it provided instruments for the insertion of women's bodies into the machinery of reproduction' (Sawicki, 1991: 68).

Disciplinary power works not by force or violence, but through the creation of new norms – in other words, normalization, the creation of new objects and subjects of knowledge. Herein lies its effectiveness and the means by which it gains and secures its hold over bodies. NRTs, Sawicki (1991: 83) argues, are disciplinary techniques that 'represent one of a series of types of body management that have emerged over the past two decades rendering women's bodies more mobilizable in the service of changing utilities of dominant agencies'. Whilst these techniques render women's bodies useful to the agencies that regulate, study and control them, they are also creative. The adoption and use of NRTs by certain groups have created new subjects: fit mothers, unfit mothers, infertile women, surrogate mothers, carry mothers and so on. A corollary to this is that they create new sites of resistance; for example, lesbian and single women have resisted the restrictions placed on access to services by resourcefully negotiating other avenues of reproduction such as clinical (within the context of formal health care) or non-clinical (self-arranged) donor conception (Nordqvist, 2011).

We can see, therefore, that the recognition of the body as a site of political struggle has been a major force in the women's health movement. Knowledge of women's bodies which had been usurped by men is being regained by women. The implications of this for health and health care are significant. Individuals can no longer be treated as passive, inert objects who have no say in how they want their bodies acted upon. Bodies form a key site of political struggle, and their presence forms a key dimension of the interactions between health carers and those who are being cared for.

Conclusion

This chapter has discussed developments in the sociology of the body which are of particular significance to the sociology of health and illness, because they are about the relationship between the physical body, healthy or otherwise, and social interactions. Recent developments have involved attempts to bring together the salient aspects of three main perspectives on the body: the naturalistic, the social-constructionist and the phenomenological. From this work two key concepts have emerged. First is the *body as a project*, which draws attention to the fact that the body is always in a state of becoming (Shilling, 2003). It is constantly acted upon and altered, and so is in a state of unfinishedness. Thus bodies are changed and shaped by their actions (e.g., exercise), by physical interventions (e.g., surgery), cultural expectations (e.g., the cultivation of a certain gait), and socio-biological processes (e.g., ageing). Second is the *regulation of bodies*, which draws attention to the political dimensions of the control and maintenance of bodies (Turner, 1996). Bodies form key sites of political struggles, and this is perhaps nowhere more evident than in the area of health and medical care.

We have also seen that political struggles and social inequalities are inherently embodied. For example, the body may be a source of physical capital which may be converted into other forms of cultural or economic capital by way of training, education and other forms of socialization. Moreover, the means of regulating bodies and their reproduction can serve both to maintain and to reinforce patriarchal structures. Power may be exercised through the application of technologies and medical practices which act upon bodies.

FURTHER READING

Brown, N. and Webster, A. (2004), *New Medical Technologies and Society: Reordering Life*, Cambridge: Polity. Informed and accessible analysis of the salience of new medical technologies for health, illness and the body.

Hockey, J. and James, A. (2007), *Embodying Health Identities*, Basingstoke: Palgrave Macmillan.

Howson, A. (2012), *The Body in Society: An Introduction*, 2nd edn, Cambridge: Polity. A clear and very accessible introduction to the sociology of the body.

Nettleton, S. and Gustaffson, U. (eds) (2002), *The Sociology of Health and Illness Reader*, Cambridge: Polity. The chapters in Part I, 'Bodies', include both conceptual and empirical chapters on issues such as genetics, organ donation, dying and the construction of medical knowledge of the body.

Shilling, C. (2012), *The Body and Social Theory*, 3rd edn, London: Sage.

Turner, B. S. (2008), *The Body and Society: Explorations in Social Theory*, 3rd edn, London: Sage.

Twigg, J., Wolkowitz, C., Cohen, R. and Nettleton, S. (2011), *Body Work: Critical Themes, New Agendas*, Oxford: Wiley-Blackwell.

Webster, A. (2008) *Health, Technology and Society: A Sociological Critique*, Basingstoke: Palgrave Macmillan.

6 The Sociology of Lay–Professional Interactions

Introduction

The aim of this chapter is to explore the nature of encounters between lay people and health professionals. Lay people and patients meet with health professionals in many different settings and for many different reasons. These may range from interactions with a district nurse within the home, a consultant surgeon in a hospital, a dentist in a dental surgery, a pharmacist in the local pharmacy, or a general medical practitioner at a health centre. Despite the diversity of health care encounters, the sociology of health and illness has for the most part focused on those between doctors and patients. Nevertheless, a number of emergent themes and issues transcend this literature, being of relevance to professional–patient encounters more generally.

Issues which have emerged from this literature are as follows. First, lay–professional relationships both reflect and reinforce wider social relations and structural inequalities, especially those of gender, 'race' and class. Second, and related to this, such relationships, and the values perpetuated within them, form key dimensions of social control and regulation. Third, health professionals have often neglected to take the patient's view seriously, and this is being addressed as a serious limitation of contemporary formal health care. This is important because, as we have seen in chapters 3 and 4, most people are able to develop sophisticated accounts about health and illness. The social science literature has revealed that lay people want to, can and do play an important part in interactions with trained health care workers. Fourth, the quality of interaction affects the outcomes of health care. Such outcomes include the extent to which a patient recovers from an illness for which he or she has been treated, or the level of satisfaction with the health care provided.

Sociological analyses of professional–patient interactions can be categorized into two main types: first, *macro* approaches, such as structural-functionalist and structural-conflict perspectives, and second, *micro* approaches, which focus on the characteristics of interactions themselves, such as those deriving from interactionism and ethnomethodology. This chapter will discuss each of these perspectives.

The chapter will argue that the nature of relationships between lay people and experts changed towards the end of the last century. The professional–patient relationship, once characterized as a meeting between the knowledgeable expert and the ignorant lay person, is now more appropriately, and more accurately, described as a 'meeting between experts' (Tuckett et al., 1985). A number of factors have contributed to this transformation. First is the changing disease burden, which has involved a rise in chronic conditions which cannot be cured. This means that medical practitioners have had to come to terms with their own limitations and recognize the importance of care and social support. Second is the fact that people are encouraged to take responsibility for their own health and are more knowledgeable about factors which influence their health status. Many illnesses today are associated with social and behavioural factors, and these are matters which are becoming 'common knowledge'. Consultations are increasingly likely to include discussions about lifestyle choices, and not just focus on writing prescriptions for specific pathological conditions. Third, health care 'users' are being encouraged to exercise their choice and act as discriminating 'consumers' (see chapter 10). Today patients can access vast amounts of information. Should you want to seek out information about virtually any illness or disease that you can think of, you can do so by surfing the Internet.

The changing context of lay-professional interactions

The medical knowledge which for so long was presumed to be accessible to qualified practitioners only is now – theoretically at least – available to everyone. Not surprisingly, the medical profession is concerned about this, and some are suggesting that changes to medical practices are necessary in order to adapt to these new circumstances. For example, Richard Horton wrote in the *The Lancet*:

> The fundamental change between past and present medicine is access to information. There used to be a steep inequality between doctor and patient. No longer. As people understand the risks as well as the benefits of modern medicine, we increasingly desire more information before we are willing to rely on trust to see us through. This need to be transparent about what doctors know (and what they do not), to engage in a consultation on closer to equal terms with patients, has changed the way medicine is practiced. (2003: 40)

R. Smith (2003), also a doctor, conceptualizes these changes as a move from what he calls 'industrial age medicine' to 'information age health care'. Within the context of the latter, old working practices give way to new ones. Smith argues that doctors have to recognize that their patients may be 'smarter' than they are, work in networked organizations rather than hierarchical ones, acknowledge that their clinical knowledge can be patchy, and make use of information tools and systematic reviews of evidence, rather than just relying on their clinical experience (see chapter 10). In the older 'industrial age medicine', it was presumed that people would be cared for most effectively by health professionals. For policy makers, the prime issue was one of encouraging people to recognize when they were ill and to seek advice from experts. By contrast, in the context of 'information age health care', lay people themselves are presumed to have knowledge and skills and can be recruited to care for themselves.

Such transformations are likely to lead to – albeit subtle – changes in the relationships between professionals and patients, between medical institutions and the state, and between medicine and sociology. Writing in a North American context, Potter and McKinlay (2005) argue that one such change is that doctor–patient interactions are now more accurately portrayed as 'encounters' rather than relationships – not least because the meetings between patients and professionals tend to be one-off, fleeting, impersonal interactions which are increasingly pervaded by commercial considerations. 'Compared to the twentieth century where the doctor–patient could be characterized by depth and history, the 21st-century relationship between doctor and patient can increasingly be characterized by superficiality and focussed on the here and now' (Potter and McKinlay, 2005: 476). This observation is qualified, in that the empirical basis of this transition may vary between medical conditions, with some chronic long-term illnesses resulting in more enduring relationships. Nevertheless conceptually and empirically their point is an important one. The Parsonian paradigm tradition that still dominates research in this field does tend to draw our attention to the one-to-one relationship and in so doing eclipse the organizational context in which it takes place. May (2007) urges sociologists to contextualize the meeting between professionals and patients, not treating it as a one-off event between individuals. As he points out:

> the clinical encounter itself is only one part of an assemblage of complex organizational, institutional and disciplinary resources and practices, in which units of analysis are to be found at diverse organizational interfaces – and where subjectivities are constructed and worked out in multiple and diverse ways in relation to new managerial technologies. (2007: 41)

It is instructive to acknowledge and include structure and context into the analysis of relations, which in turn will enhance a sensitivity to social, technological and political changes. Such alterations are likely to be gradual, and may in fact result in a greater diversification of encounters rather than generalized shifts. Certainly the 'cultural values' which underpin relationships between professionals and patients remain remarkably enduring within the context of medical encounters (Shilling, 2002).

Professional–patient relationships: norms and expectations

Parsons (1951) used the doctor–patient relationship to illustrate his notion of a social system. His analysis has been an influential one in the sociology of health and illness, and many contemporary debates about professional–patient interactions are swayed by it. For Parsons, society comprises actors who perform a range of social roles (e.g., mothers, teachers, doctors and patients) which facilitate the smooth functioning of society. In this respect doctors and patients perform and fulfil certain role obligations: the doctor treats ill people, and a person who is ill enters the 'sick role' (see chapter 4) and makes an effort to get well. According to this theory, the doctor needs the patient, and the patient needs the doctor. It is for this reason that Parsons views the doctor–patient relationship as a reciprocal one.

Doctors and patients, according to Parsons, have certain rights and obligations. When patients are ill, on his definition, they are in a 'socially deviant state', and so they must want to get well. Doctors are obliged to help them regain their health. They are obliged to apply a high degree of knowledge and skill when administering treatment, to be altruistic and to forgo self-interest, to be objective and emotionally detached, and to be guided by a professional code of ethics. If they fulfil these obligations, society will, in return, grant them three rights: the right to examine patients physically and emotionally, the right of autonomy in their professional practice, and the right to occupy a position of authority in relation to the patient.

We can see, therefore, that although the relationship is reciprocal, it is not equal. Whilst professionals are granted power, status and prestige, patients are not. From a functionalist perspective, this has a number of positive consequences. It ensures that those who have formalized knowledge and technical ability will gain rewards and therefore want to apply their skills. This is necessary to maintain a healthy society. It also means that patients will trust trained health professionals.

For Parsons, the asymmetry of the relationship is not problematic. This is because the rights and duties of the physician are underpinned by three social norms or values: universalism, collective orientation and affective neutrality. Essentially this means that everyone should be treated equally, that the collective interests of patients are more important than the professionals' self-interest, and that value judgements do not colour clinical decisions. In sum, anyone - irrespective of their age, gender, race or class - will be granted legitimation to enter the sick role and will be given help, support and treatment. The sick patient, Parsons argues, who presents with a specific problem must be dealt with on 'objective, scientifically justifiable terms' (Parsons, 1951: 435).

This is of course an ideal type, and as in the case of the sick role, everyday realities depart from this ideal (see chapter 4). The idea that this asymmetrical doctor–patient relationship invariably has positive consequences has been challenged. For example, patients may have more knowledge about their condition than medical practitioners. People often accumulate expertise about their own bodies and come to have a special knowledge of their experience of health and illness. It is thus frustrating if the practitioner does not want to acknowledge the patient's view. One woman, describing the difficulties she had in making the doctor listen to her, put it thus: 'I've lived with this body for seventy odd years. If I don't know when it's not working properly I don't know who does' (Sidell, 1992).

The underlying assumptions on which this type of 'functional' relationship is based are also questionable. Value judgements do enter into medical encounters. Diagnoses and treatments have been found to vary according to the patient's class, gender and race. Studies of psychiatrists have found that in relation to 'black' patients, they are more likely to give drugs and diagnose schizophrenia (Elster et al., 2003). Doctors have also been found to vary the amount of information they give according to the patient's education, income, gender (Lutfey et al., 2008), personal characteristics and communicative style (Street, 1991). They also find certain patients and certain types of illness more troublesome than others (Stimpson, 1976; H. Roberts, 1985; Shaw, 2004).

At a time when behavioural factors are increasingly being recognized as the antecedents of many illnesses, value judgements may be made as to the patient's culpability for their illness. This can result in patients feeling guilty about their symptoms. Value judgements may also be made about the suitability of treatment. For example, in the summer of 1993, much controversy was generated in the media as a result of a decision taken by some medical consultants not to administer tests and carry out coronary bypass surgery on people who continue to smoke. This decision, based on the argument that resources should not be spent on people if they smoke, as they have little chance of recovery (Underwood and Bailey, 1993), has been contested by those within and beyond the medical profession (Dean, 1993). Such decisions are considered by many to be value judgements rather than purely clinical decisions. The debate, which focused on the need to ration resources and direct them to those cases which will benefit most, highlights the extent to which responses to individual patients are likely to vary according to the economic and political context in which they are made.

There is therefore a discrepancy between the institutionalized norms and expectations of the professional and the norms and expectations of everyday clinical practice. Freidson (1970a), who argues this point, also maintains that the doctor–patient relationship is perhaps more accurately characterized by *conflict* than by consensus. He sees the relationship between professionals and patients as a particularly precarious one, and maintains that this is because certain conflicts are endemic within it. He writes of a 'clash of perspectives'; 'the separate worlds of experience and of reference of the layman [*sic*] and the professional worker are always in potential conflict with each other' (Freidson, 1975: 286).

Professional–patient relationships: conflicts and challenges

Bloor and Horobin (1975) further elaborate on this potential for conflict. They suggest that its source lies in two basic assumptions held by doctors about how patients should behave. On the one hand, patients should use their own judgement to decide when it is appropriate to seek medical advice; yet, once this advice is sought, they must defer to the doctors' judgements and interpretations. Thus the patient is placed in a 'double bind'. Deciding when it is appropriate to seek medical advice is a matter which many people find difficult. This is especially so when people are caring for dependants.

Studies of Accident and Emergency (A&E) departments have found that medical and nursing staff regard many of the cases presented as 'rubbish'; that is, people who present with symptoms which are considered to be inappropriate and/or trivial (Jeffrey, 1979; Dingwall and Murray, 1983; H. Roberts, 1992). H. Roberts (1992: 114–15), who carried out fieldwork in an A&E department, found that health providers had a tendency to make comments such as:

> Casualty Officer 1: 'About 70 per cent is rubbish. We get sent a lot of rubbish.'
> Casualty Officer 2: 'There's a lot that shouldn't be here. More than half.'

Mothers who turn up at A&E with young children are especially problematic; they are viewed as being over-anxious, which results, it is claimed, in their propensity to overreact. As one doctor commented to Roberts (1992: 119), 'Anxious mothers, I sometimes think that they haven't got the sense that they were born with.' However, Roberts also points out that in spite of the obvious conflict between the lay and professional perspectives, there is also a significant degree of common ground between them. Parents often bring their children to the A&E when they are unsure about symptoms, 'to be on the safe side'. Doctors also have a tendency to take actions to err on the safe side in the face of uncertainty. Both parents and doctors feel liable for the consequences of their actions. This is not surprising, given that both doctors and parents are key health workers; they are both providing health care for the child. When given the opportunity to elaborate on the rationale for, and the context within which actions have been taken, it most often becomes evident that the mothers have acted appropriately. Thus much of the conflict that has been inherent in lay-professional relationships has resulted from the lack of attention paid by providers to the patients' views.

Edwards et al. (2004) probed beyond the fact that surveys consistently record high levels of patient satisfaction with health care services. Employing both phenomenological and structural perspectives in their analysis of interviews with patients at varying stages of their health care, they identified three 'psycho-social pressures' which mitigate against patients acting on their criticisms of health care. These are 'the relative dependency of patients within the health care system; their need to maintain constructive working relationships with those providing their care; and their general preference for holding a positive outlook' (2004: 159). Edwards and colleagues argue that these factors lead people to downplay their complaints or negative experiences, and in fact the psychological cost of pursuing them can be significant in itself. The act of complaining may violate their sense of 'self'. As they point out:

> If a patient has waited a long time for surgery and has invested much effort in coping with it psychologically and physically, they may prefer to hold onto the notion that it all went well [. . .] it is possible that reinterpretation of health care experiences in a more positive light may have a therapeutic effect. (Edwards et al., 2004: 177)

Among those people who do complain about primary health care practitioners, two concerns are particularly prevalent: first, the manner of practitioners, and, second, difficulties in convincing them of the seriousness of a patient's condition for whom a visit is being requested (Nettleton and Harding, 1994). The ability to be supportive and empathetic to patients is also recognized by lay people to be an essential quality. For example, one complainant wrote in her letter to a health authority: 'It would seem that Dr X lacks some of the qualities that will give his patients feelings of trust and understanding, qualities *which I feel are essential* for a good GP' (Nettleton and Harding, 1994: 54).

The enduring theme of both the consensus and the conflict perspectives is that the doctor–patient relationship is asymmetric. Despite their differences, Parsons and Freidson agree that the medical profession is in a dominant position. The professionals derive power from legitimized status and presumed technical expertise. This, in turn, enables them to function as mediators of social control, and, as such, they are in an ideal position to contribute to the perpetuation of dominant value systems. Their routine activities and practices can, potentially at least, serve to reinforce dominant ideologies.

The ideological bases of doctor–patient consultations

Marxist analyses of health care have argued that doctor–patient encounters are sites where the dominant ideologies of wider society are reproduced (Mishler, 1984; Waitzkin, 2000). Thus the profession of medicine serves as a powerful agency of social control.

> From a position of relative dominance, doctors can make ideologic statements that convey the symbolic trappings of science. These messages reinforce the hegemonic ideology that emanates from other institutions – the family, educational system, mass media and so forth – and that pervade our society. The same messages tend to direct client's behaviour into safe, acceptable, and non-disruptive channels; this is the essence of social control in medicine. (Waitzkin, 2000: 124)

It is argued that within medical encounters doctors reinforce the economic relations of production, in that they define health as the ability to work and convey the message that work is preferable to idleness (Waitzkin, 1984). Further, socio-emotional problems are medicalized; that is, they are converted into technical ones. 'Symbolically, scientific medicine shifts the focus to the physical realm, depoliticizes the social structural issues involved, and mutes the potential for action by the patient to change the conditions that trouble him [*sic*]' (Waitzkin, 1984: 352).

The problem with this perspective, however, is that medical practitioners cannot win. If they take the wider social circumstances of the patient into account, they are accused of medicalization, and yet if they do not, they are accused of ignoring the social bases of illness. Thus there are a number of theoretical and empirical problems with this quasi-Marxist perspective. Blaxter (1983: 1143), in a discussion of the contribution of health services against the consequences of poverty, captures this dilemma when she writes:

> To meddle with matters which are social, economic and political is medical imperialism. On the other hand, given that health systems are a major institution of advanced societies, it can be argued that this counsel of despair, is a weak refusal to accept responsibility, and an excuse for giving up the most intractable problems as the business of somebody else.

A reconceptualization of the professional role from one that simply offers treatment and therapy to one that is political would alter the limited scope of the professional-patient relationship (Blaxter, 1983).

A further problem with this perspective lies in the empirical validity of the thesis that medicine serves the interests of capital and that it serves to act as an institution which ensures 'people's adherence to norms of appropriate behaviour' (Waitzkin, 1989: 225). As we have already seen, patients do not necessarily accept medical interpretations or follow medical advice, and are not therefore as easy to manipulate as this social control thesis implies. Moreover, practitioners are becoming increasingly aware of the limits of biomedical 'solutions' for many problems. For example, in a study of general practitioners and their propensity to prescribe tranquillizers to women who experienced symptoms of depression, Gabe and Lipshitz-Phillips (1984) found that GPs were reluctant in many cases to prescribe them, because they were aware that the factors that caused depression were often social in origin, and were also aware of the limitations and adverse effects of the drugs themselves. Nevertheless, it is undoubtedly the case that the control of women by medical practitioners has a long history, and is perhaps manifest most overtly in the doctor-patient consultation.

The extent to which a practitioner should assert his or her authority is problematic. If they believe they have greater knowledge about what is 'best' for the patient, should they insist that the patient complies with their instructions, or should they defer to the patient's wishes? This dilemma is highlighted by Fisher (1986) in a discussion which centres on an analysis of encounters between doctors and patients where the need for cervical smears is at issue. She suggests that doctors are in a 'double bind': if they tell patients that they have to have a smear, they may be accused of paternalism; yet, if they do not insist that a woman has a smear, they may be abrogating their responsibility to serve the patient's best interests. In fact, Fisher found that in those cases where women were not keen to have a cervical smear, the doctor invariably went along with this and avoided taking one. She argues that for the well-being of the patient, doctors should use their authority. However, she fails to acknowledge that some lay people may have sound, rational and sometimes clinical reasons for not wanting to pursue the 'apparently' healthy option. Unless the lay person is given the opportunity within a consultation to elaborate on their explanations for their choice, the final decision made within the context of the consultation cannot, by definition, be a rational one, as it would be based on only partial information.

Women, medical practitioners and ideology

Other variants of the conflict perspective are those approaches which emphasize the gendered nature of power within medical interactions. Writers from a variety of feminist perspectives have pointed to the sexist ideologies which underpin medical science and medical practice (Ehrenreich and English, 2011). For example, some student doctors have reported that they have found the culture of medical education to be sexist (Hinze, 2004). Some medical practitioners have been reported to find 'women's problems' particularly troublesome (Stimpson, 1976; H. Roberts, 1985). Further, it has been argued that many medical textbooks present women as inferior to men; they highlight their sexual passivity, reinforce the normality of heterosexuality, and use demeaning images (Martin, 1989).

Feminist responses to these issues fall, as they do within many areas of sociology and social policy (F. Williams, 1989), into two main approaches: radical and reformist. Radical feminists regard modern medicine as inherently patriarchal and oppressive, and this is demonstrated by the way in which men have seized control over women's bodies. This approach argues that satisfactory professional–patient relationships will be achieved only when health care is provided by women for women within environments which are non-sexist, non-racist and non-heterosexist. Reformist responses, on the other hand, argue that it is necessary to change the existing system from within: for example, by recruiting more women as doctors and health managers, making professionals more accountable to their patients, and making them more aware of issues of power and structural disadvantage.

The radical response to such reformist views is that simply recruiting more women can have only a limited effect, as they are unlikely radically to transform the system of care, and that it is unrealistic to expect most women to be very different from their male colleagues. The radicals point towards the pockets of feminist practice already existing in both the NHS and self-help groups which challenge conventional forms of health care and give women more control over their own bodies (Foster, 1995) as possible models for future development. Such health care rooted in feminist philosophy would invariably effect a transformation in relationships between professionals and patients. In practice, attempts to develop health care which reflects feminist rather than paternalistic values have been found to be fraught with difficulties (Craddock and Reid, 1993). Ironically perhaps, advances made by the women's health movement in the 1980s and the then right-wing British government shared a common concern in this respect, in that they both wanted to make services user- rather than provider-driven. Craddock and Reid (1993: 75), who developed a Well Woman Clinic, observe wryly, 'the end results coincide with the motives of the Government to encourage consumer choice and representation and increased professional accountability'. But the consequences of these debates and social movements should not be underestimated or forgotten. The nature, content and ideological basis of contemporary health practices have been altered as a result of feminist challenges, and indeed both men and women are recognizing the merits of more gender-sensitive health care (Bendelow et al., 2002; Doyal, 1998).

Although the social theorist Habermas (1970) was more preoccupied with class than with gender, the views inherent in many feminisms resonate with his critical theory. For Habermas, ideology and domination are evident both at the macro level of politics and the micro level of face-to-face interactions. Medical science is ideological, and is all the more sinister because it has the appearance of objectivity. Within doctor–patient consultations ideological messages are communicated under the guise of medical science. Critical theory maintains that such domination makes for 'distorted communication' – that is, the effective communication and exchange of true, rather than ideological, information can take place only in a context where both parties are equal. If one group is oppressed by another – for example, women by sexist doctors – we can never be sure that the information conveyed is reliable and untainted by ideological messages. In theory, egalitarian, non-hierarchical organizational structures of health centres provided for, and by, women offer the potential for the exchange of undistorted knowledge and information, and thereby provide a genuine alternative to an institution which has contributed significantly to the subordination of women. Thus, the political problem for some feminists is how to devise strategies which engender conditions and structures which will facilitate such communication. More recently, and not least as a result of feminist challenges to health care, this has become the political problem for policy makers, who seek to promote more symmetrical clinical encounters characterized by *concordance* rather than *compliance*, and which ultimately ensure that patients pursue the most effective ways to get well.

From 'compliance' to 'concordance'

The medical profession, keen to ensure that patients follow their clinical advice, have recruited sociologists to help in this enterprise. Indeed, much of the work which illuminates patients' responses to, and experiences of, medical regimens emerges as a result of these engagements with medical practice. Since the second half of the twentieth century, one of the prime concerns of medical practitioners has been how to ensure that patients take their medicines. Two clinical categories have dominated the ensuing debates: *patient compliance* and *patient concordance*. Although, as we shall see, sociological studies contribute to their formulation, what is perhaps more sociologically intriguing is the historical contingency of the concepts in and of themselves.

Through his analysis of medical literatures, Greene (2004) provides an illuminating account of the proliferation of the term 'patient compliance'. Definitively defined in 1974 as 'the extent to which the patient's behaviour (in terms of taking medications, following diets, or executing other lifestyle changes) coincides with clinical prescription', the use of the label exploded throughout the medical literature. What was it, Greene asks, that led to such a veritable and rapid increase in the use of this 'novel clinical category'? He answers this question by offering three possible explanations, which are likely to be complementary rather than competing.

A *materialist* account maintains that the notion of patient compliance came to the fore as a result of epidemiological transformations (the relative rise of chronic and the decline of acute disease) in concert with a shift from in-patient to community care. The list of medications for chronic conditions grew, and being at home, patients had to ensure that they took them. In order to check that patients were indeed complying with their doctors' orders, a growing range of sophisticated surveillance techniques was devised. Aware that patients might lie about their medicine taking, practitioners could use 'tracer techniques', blood tests and so on to assess the truthfulness of their stories.

An alternative explanation argues that there is an affinity between the preoccupation with compliance and a profession under siege. This *ideology of control* thesis draws attention to the fact that during the 1970s the authority and credibility of the profession were being challenged by a range of academics, feminists, consumer movements and so on. Such challenges highlighted the lack of patient autonomy and the ineffectiveness of medicine. The idea of non-compliance therefore provided an ideal solution: if patients did not comply, this could help to 'exculpate physicians when bad outcomes resulted' (Greene, 2004: 336). Thus,

> compliance research became an arena in which medicine could deal with its increasing number of critics and failings by subsuming and pathologizing them. Documenting the extent of noncompliance was simultaneously exculpatory and activist. It not only relocated blame from the physician to the patient but it also constructed research methodologies and policy recommendations regarding which sites could be targeted for intervention. (2004: 338)

As we will see below, this nexus between physicians, policy makers and practice is evident in relation to concordance – the modern-day version of compliance.

But first, let us consider Greene's third explanation, which he refers to as the *niche of self-critique*. This suggests that the concern with compliance arose as a result of critics who were emerging from *within* medicine itself. In sum, young, proactive physicians highlighted the limitations of medical practice, and brought their epidemiological tools to bear on the problem. New alliances where forged between clinical epidemiologists, medical sociologists, pharmacists and nurses, who revealed that the cause of non-compliance lay not only with recalcitrant patients but also with poor medical practice. If doctors were better communicators, the problem of non-compliance might be alleviated.

As noted above, today the term 'non-compliance', with its connotations of blame and moral disapproval, is no longer regarded as acceptable, such negative features having been highlighted by sociologists. For example, in the mid-1980s Conrad (1985), in his paper 'The Meaning of Medication: Another Look at Compliance', examined the use of medications by people living with epilepsy, and concluded that non-compliance might actually 'be a form of asserting control over one's disorder'. Over half the participants in the study experimented with their own medication regimes, rather than simply complying with the doctor's advice, a proportion which is reflected in studies of other conditions (e.g. Benson and Britten, 2002).

Thus the term 'compliance' has been replaced by terms such as 'non-adherence' and 'concordance', which are considered to be more humane and less authoritarian, no doubt in part in association with broader societal changes associated with the risk society and the information age (Stevenson and Scambler, 2005). But fundamentally, they address the same concern. 'Concordance' has been defined as 'an open exchange of beliefs about medicine about which prescribing and medicine decisions may then be based' (Marinker et al., 1997). Patients and doctors ought to work together, share and exchange views about treatment options, and come to joint decisions about treatment. This represents a shift from the doctor-centred to the 'patient-centred approach' in medical care (Mead and Bower, 2000). As with compliance, clinicians, sociologists, pharmacists and epidemiologists work together fastidiously to refine the processes of communication and to point to the structural constraints that prevent patients implementing their agreed goals in practice (Stevenson et al., 2000; Barry et al., 2001; Bissell et al., 2004). Surveys reveal that patients do indeed want to participate in their care, and at times the clinical decision making (Coulter, 2002; Coulter and Magee, 2003), but concurrently they want to be able to trust and depend on their doctors (Lupton, 2002).

In some respects these developments in themselves create a new degree of uncertainty and precariousness, which needs to be negotiated within professional–patient interactions. In particular, the presumed erosion of trust in professionals led Stevenson and Scambler (2005) to venture that the aspirations to achieve concordance might in fact result in what Habermas (see above) would refer to as 'systematically distorted communication', which they explain thus:

> The movement towards mutuality and reciprocity, which reflects more general changes in society, means that open strategic action has become less acceptable. It may have been replaced by concealed strategic action. Concealed strategic action incorporates not only conscious deception or manipulation but also unconscious deception or systematically distorted communication. (2005: 15)

Communicating risk in consultations

The shift towards shared decision making is bound up with changes in the content of consultations, which today very often involve informing patients about risks rather than simply providing definitive diagnoses or treatments. To this end researchers are developing communication tools with a view to assisting practitioners in this aspect of their work. Factors that contribute to increased communication of 'risk' in consultations include the rise of surveillance medicine, wherein epidemiological analyses reveal numerous lifestyle clinical 'risk factors' (Skolbekken, 1995; Olin Lauritzen and Sachs, 2001). In addition, there is a move towards 'evidence-based medicine', wherein practitioners are encouraged to use interventions for which there is (usually statistical) evidence of the effectiveness (see chapter 10). Such information can be shared with patients to enhance 'evidence-based patient choice'. Technological developments, most notably in genetic testing and other screening technologies, also enable practitioners to determine a patient's (or perhaps more accurately) a 'potential' patient's risk of disease.

Quintessentially clinical consultations pertaining to epidemiologically derived risk factors involve applying findings derived from probabilistic data to individuals. In her analysis of women who had found a lump in their breast, which, although benign, can be considered to increase the risk of breast cancer, Gifford (2002) usefully delineates the 'meanings' of such lumps in relation to three types of risk: epidemiological risk (which is derived from population level data), lay risk (which relates to individuals' experiences of risk), and lived clinical risk (which captures the work of the clinician who has to mediate between the other two). Thus clinicians have to translate their knowledge of statistical risk and apply it to the women before them. In the case of benign lumps, Gifford found that clinicians have a tendency to treat the 'risk' as if it is an undesirable condition that needs to be treated. However, a significant degree of uncertainty remains, and the 'lived clinical risk' involves the 'clinician's own experience of being wrong'. As a result, clinicians tend to err on the side of caution and intervene to treat the benign lumps. In this context the women find themselves in a 'grey zone' between health and disease – 'a condition of non-health' (2002: 221).

The dilemmas inherent in communicating risks are also explored by Olin Lauritzen and Sachs (2001) in their study of the ways in which nurses communicate the results of routine health tests to parents of children (e.g., height and weight) and 40-year-old men (e.g., cholesterol levels). Here again the nurses have to draw on risks which are derived from population data, but in the consultation they are a property of the individual patient. As a result they find that 'the encounters between the nurse and the individual resemble a balancing act performed within the context of a clinical conversation. Awareness of risk has to be balanced against undue anxiety, and personal responsibility against the limited possibility of changing existential conditions'. If the results deviate from the norm, the outcome of the assessment itself becomes a 'threat'. In addition, the results raise the possibility of control – in that lifestyle changes can be made to improve the situation. But the balance between encouragement and undue anxiety can in and of itself be a 'risky' one.

Within the context of clinical genetics, where people may be referred for screening as a result of their family history, in order to determine their genetic risk of cancer, Scott et al. (2005) found that people who are considered to be at 'low risk' of cancer articulated greater levels of anxiety than those found to be at higher risk. This seemingly perverse finding makes more sense when the reasonings of the patients themselves are taken into account. Those patient-clients deemed to be at low risk are unlikely to be referred to clinical geneticists, whereas those at 'moderate' or 'high risk' are. In addition, the higher risk groups will be regularly monitored within secondary care. As one man who was found to be at low risk of colorectal cancer said:

> 'once they have got involved and said "you should be checked" just be to- [I felt] I won't say fobbed off, but written off with just a note saying, you know . . . Virtually it is saying "don't bother us". That is my opinion . . . I felt a bit unhappy then and even more so when [my brother] was sent for tests, and more so again when they found something. So I have sort of been through three stages of concern between then and now. And as I say, I just felt a bit, sort of pushed to one side I suppose.' (Scott et al., 2005: 1872)

New forms of patient experience and new types of patient: not a patient as such; indeed, Scott and colleagues use the term 'patient-client'. Such a categorization is an indication of a new creature – a patient but not a patient. A person in that blurred 'liminal position betwixt the healthy and the sick' (2005: 1869).

'Being at risk' is not a comfortable position to be in, and no doubt is one of the reasons why genetic screening services provide extensive opportunities for counselling in order to communicate the genetic information to at risk individuals and their families. But this in turn can be fraught with difficulties, and although premissed on the principles of autonomy, informed consent and non-directedness, prevailing norms and values have been found to permeate these consultations just as they do in other professional-patient interactions (Atkin et al., 1998; Pilnick, 2002).

Professional-patient relationships as social interactions

Study of the processes of symbolic communication between social actors provides a complementary approach to the study of professional-patient relationships which we have discussed hitherto. These micro-level analyses reveal the ways in which participants present themselves, how they manage their identities, and how power relations are played out and negotiated. Whilst the structural constraints on action are acknowledged, interactionist studies, with their focus on face-to-face interaction, illustrate the complexities and nuances of relationships between health professionals and patients.

Within the context of general practice, Stimpson and Webb (1975) revealed the importance of strategies – that is, the attempt to direct and control a consultation towards one's own desired ends. The outcome of a consultation therefore depends not only on the nature of the patient's medical complaint but also on the nature of the negotiation. Patient strategies include rehearsing, presenting symptoms only partially, excluding information and ignoring the doctor's advice. Thus, whilst the relationship is still acknowledged to be asymmetrical, the patient is not without alternative sources of power.

In their study, *Politics of Pain Management: Staff-Patient Interaction*, Fagerhaugh and Strauss (1977) observed how organizational settings profoundly affect the character of the interactions between patients who are in pain and staff, and argue that the quality of these interactions is crucial for effective pain management. Improvements in care, and the alleviation of pain, must therefore involve organizational as well as biological, psychological and clinical innovations. Building on the concept of *negotiated order* (A. L. Strauss, 1978), the authors see the hospital as emerging from an ongoing process of negotiation and renegotiation. Things are 'accomplished' through a process of bargaining and balancing. For example, staff may balance more work for themselves versus quicker pain relief, while patients may balance pride in not complaining about pain versus the difficulty of enduring it without the use of drugs (Fagerhaugh and Strauss, 1977: 25). In this respect patient care is conceived of as a political process; 'patients and staff members wheedle, argue, persuade, bargain, negotiate, holler at, shriek at, command, manipulate relevant contingencies, and attempt to deceive' (Fagerhaugh and Strauss, 1977: 8). They also draw attention to the ideological dimension of these processes, in that the hospital setting serves to perpetuate the disease model of care; they state that 'the organization of the hospital ward is astonishingly inadequate to deal with the non-acute (medical or non-medical) aspects of chronicity' (Fagerhaugh and Strauss, 1977: v). The qualitative aspects of social relationships between staff and patients must, therefore, form an integral part of patient care.

What becomes evident from these studies is that although professional-patient relationships are inherently unequal, both participants are able to influence the outcomes of the consultations. Patients are not simply passive recipients of care; they are also active participants in the processes of health care work. The relationship between professionals and patients is likely to be enhanced if practitioners are able to recognize and encourage patients to be involved. Indeed, this is the view that underpins the notion of concordance that we discussed earlier in the chapter.

The ritual and ceremony of medical consultations

In a detailed study of more than 1,000 consultations between doctors and parents with young children in outpatient clinics in Scotland and the USA, Strong found that what he refers to as 'the ceremonial order of the consultations was remarkably invariant' (Strong, 1979b: 38). The notion of ceremony alludes to the social form of the relationships; that is, the set of rules or, to continue the metaphor, rituals that make medical consultations distinct social occasions. Within this conceptualization, a participant's action is not only prescribed by circumstances (as was the case in the functionalist account), but rather serves as a resource. Strong (1979b: 13) prefers to use the notion of 'role format' rather than the concept of social role. Role formats 'are not the structures which totally determine action but are instead routinized, culturally available solutions which members "use" to solve whatever problems they have at hand'. Strong argues that certain rituals are carried out routinely, which allows us to recognize, or be familiar with, doctor–patient consultations. These exist over and above individual interactions, and as such are inextricably interlinked with macro-level structures. Individual actors are therefore both constrained by, and able to draw upon, these structural factors.

From his analysis he identified four types of role format: the *bureaucratic format*, the *charity format*, the *clinical format* and the *private format*. These role formats are more or less evident in various settings, and sometimes the boundaries between them are somewhat blurred.

The *bureaucratic format* is the most common within NHS settings. Within this format both the doctor and parent are polite, courteous and avoid conflict. Doctors operate with an idealized image of motherhood and are never openly critical. The relationship is, however, asymmetrical. Mothers were presumed to be 'technically incompetent'. 'Their idealization as naturally loving and able was thus counterposed by an equivalent idealization of their medical ignorance' (Strong, 1979b: 70). This asymmetry is brought into sharper focus in the *clinical format*. In this instance the clinician's expertise is made especially evident, and interactions are such that the mothers presumed the doctor to be technically authoritative. Mothers rarely agreed with the doctor, as to do so would imply an ability to evaluate the clinical evidence. Whilst in these two formats the competence of the 'expert' is assumed, in the *private format* the competence of the doctor is not presumed; rather, it is 'sold'. Practitioners display their qualifications, and when referring to colleagues, they invoke specific named experts instead of hospital departments, so that parents can judge their credentials. Only in a minority of interactions did doctors try to reveal a mother's inadequacy; Strong terms this the *charity format*. Here doctors carry out 'character work', which takes the form of an interrogation to expose a mother's guilt.

Invariably mothers were treated as being technically incompetent. This can be reinforced by tactics such as interrogation by the doctor and control of the conversation. This is evident in the following example from Strong's (1979b: 43) research, where the presenting problem was nappy rash.

> *Dr S*: What do you wash her nappies in?
> *Mother*: Ivory Snow.
> *Dr S*: Why do you use Ivory Snow?
> *Mother*: Well, it's supposed to make the nappies softer than other washing powders.
> *Dr S*: How do you know Ivory Snow makes nappies softer?
> *Mother:* (shrugs awkwardly): Well, mm . . . (she mumbles something about her mother and advertisements).
> *Dr S*: You don't want to believe everything you see in the adverts. It's a business. That's their business. Your business is your baby.

The doctor then explained that nappy rash was due to ammonia in the urine and that Ivory Snow was too weak. The mother should therefore use ordinary washing powder.

> *Mother*: I do put vinegar in it.
> *Dr S* (in amazed tone): Why do you do that?
> *Mother*: Well, I was told.
> *Dr S*: Who told you?
> *Mother*: Well, my mother did.
> *Dr S*: What difference does it make?
> *Mother*: Well, she said . . . I thought it would . . .
> *Dr S:* It doesn't do any good at all.

The doctor then gave an explanation of the chemistry involved.

The doctor not only asserts his authority and knowledge but also reinforces the idea that only the mother has the best interests of *her* baby at heart. The washing powder industry and the baby's grandmother may try to interfere, but the implication is that only she, the mother, and the doctor should decide what is best for the child.

The enduring feature of all the consultations was the doctor's authority to control the whole event. The 'medical control of the consultation was systematic, all pervasive and almost unquestioned' (Strong, 1979b: 129). This was achieved in a number of ways. For example, doctors would interrupt parents or break off conversations, involve themselves in exclusionary activities such as writing and talking to medical students or other members of staff; speaking to the parent through the child; getting the parents to make sure that the children cooperated with them; and adopting a question-answer sequence, eliciting information but not explaining why such information was needed.

However, mothers and fathers are not always totally passive. If they did attempt to challenge the doctor's authority, they also had to challenge the ritual bases of the interaction; in fact they 'threaten the entire social occasion'. Direct challenges are very rare, and when they do occur, they invariably become very highly charged and emotional exchanges. The following is a discussion which involves an incident where a mother felt that she had been misinformed about the side-effects of a treatment.

> *Mother*: She took a headache on the Friday and then she was sick *all day* on the Saturday and *all day* on the Sunday and she had to stay off school . . .
> *Dr I*: Well, we don't think that it is the fault of the drug.
> *Mother*: Well, Dr Hastings (GP) thought it was.
> *Dr I*: Well, I don't really.

Mother: It all seemed part and parcel of it.
Dr I: Well . . .
Mother: . . . you were giving her, I'd looked out for it . . .
Dr I: Well . . .
Mother: . . . but you told me it was a sedative.
Dr I: Well . . .
Mother: Well, I read the note in the chemist. And it said it *was* a stimulant.
Dr I (with raised voice): I know, and you read that it was given as a stimulant to adults.
Mother: It said it was a stimulant when I read it in the chemist's.
Dr I: It didn't say that at all.
Mother: Well, I called in Dr Hastings and he was very upset . . . There just couldn't have been any other reason for it . . . There's no doubt about it at all . . . And I'm not going through all *that* again . . . Dr Hastings couldn't find any other reason for it.

The doctor regained this situation by reasserting his position through adopting an authoritative, if not to say patronizing, tone. The doctor continued the consultation by making an ironical but heavy appeal to his authority, and the mother began to treat him, conversationally at least, as the 'proper expert':

Dr I: My own feeling, Mrs Logie, for what it's worth, is that this illness is not related to the X [the prescribed drug]. X doesn't produce these effects in children.
Mother: Do they not have fevers or sore throats, then?
Dr I: No.

Only in four out of the 1,000 cases did consultations end in direct conflict. Thus, whilst lay people may challenge, within the setting of the consultation the doctors are able to draw on their resources – status, training, etc. – to maintain their authority. Whilst the source of the doctor's authority is undoubtedly structural, it is maintained and reinforced at the level of the subtleties of social interaction. In this sense, the doctor's authority is what the ethnomethodologists would term 'accomplished'.

Accomplishing 'cases'

A more recent investigation into the accomplishment of 'cases' in child health services finds that conceptualizations of 'good' and 'bad' parents endure, as do moral judgements (S. White, 2002). White provides an insightful analysis of such morality in inter-professional talk which is orientated towards making judgements about 'cases' (in this instance, children) as to whether they are '*medical*', '*psychosocial*' or what she calls '*not just medical*' cases. This latter category is especially interesting, in that it captures those instances where a biomedical problem is identified, but the problem is presumed to be exacerbated by parenting practices and child protection issues. The 'not just medical' cases involve 'particularly complex story telling' as the 'case' of 'Sarah' reveals.

Sarah is a 20-month-old child who has a very rare syndrome which has resulted in a range of complex medical problems. She has undergone surgery for her stomach, has taken antibiotics for her kidney, has asthma and diabetes, and problems with her eyes and ears. Thus far she has been under the care of nine different consultants.

Within the context of a case conference, her consultant paediatrician outlines her circumstances to his colleagues. He produces growth and weight charts to describe her physical development. But the charts, he suggests, reveal that her development during her time at home is not as it ought to be; her weight gain is not sufficient. This provides an opening for the consultant to introduce 'character work' about Sarah's mother, as the following extract shows.

> I have also observed the following. The mother concentrated on the medicalization of all Sarah's care. When she first appeared *she went on about* all the nine consultants she was under, the number of medical problems that she had, that she was very difficult to manage, that no one would be able to manage her medically and *questioned us* as to how many children with [the name of the syndrome] I've managed and that they were totally unpredictable. She appears to have a very negative outlook for Sarah, she wasn't going to grow, she wasn't going to develop, she was going to go to a special school and her husband hadn't really taken any of this on board . . . Her mother also said that if Sarah puts on weight it will put a strain on her heart and she will die of heart strain. *I've reassured her that's not true* and if she doesn't put weight on she won't be able to do lots of other things. *She's convinced that there is more and more wrong with Sarah* and to a certain extent there is something in that. I mean she has developed diabetes and we also know that there is another metabolic problem to do with how she handles protein which might make her prone to sickness episodes, but in reality that doesn't seem to be a problem. (S. White, 2002: 422; emphasis added)

The references to the mother 'going on about', 'questioning' doctors and holding erroneous beliefs, are, White suggests, part of the argumentation aimed at convincing his colleagues that she has symptoms associated with Munchausen Syndrome by Proxy. Her lack of maternal instinct is at the core as the consultant continues:

> I don't personally believe that the *maternal instinct,* or whatever . . . To have a child in the house of Sarah's age, not be able to feed her and not have any feelings of need to feed her. *Most parents would not be able to tolerate that.* They would be force feeding the child, *they would be beside themselves with worry* about her not eating and there's none of that. (S. White, 2002: 423; emphasis added)

The italicized phrases are an example of a 'contrast structure': it sets up an expectation of proper behaviour in order to contrast it with the presumed behaviour of Sarah's mother. Thus the typification of this case is constructed through the organization and the structure of the talk. This linguistic device is routinely deployed in attempts to accomplish poor parenting and to draw attention to potential child protection cases. White suggests that the heightened profile of child protection issues over recent decades 'has made its mark on the ceremonial order of the clinic'. Although most still follow the 'bureaucratic format', those cases which are classified as psychosocial and 'not just medical' are increasingly likely to follow the 'charity format' and be more confrontational. Again, the preciousness of consultations is exacerbated by broader social trends, and clinicians, rather like patients, may find themselves in a double bind.

> Clinicians who raise concerns about parenting may develop reputations for excessive zealotry or unnecessary punitiveness, but those who fail to explore some social dimension to the problem may (retrospectively) risk charges of naïvety or collusion with parents. Obviously, this failure may also very directly expose children to further

> risk and abuse. It is for this reason that the accounts of the 'not just medical' cases often start as 'fragile stories', that is they are defensively designed [. . .] orientated to the need to persuade and to the possibility of challenge. (S. White, 2002: 432)

Once again this reminds us of how the interactions between professionals and patients are based on shared assumptions which are continually being renegotiated and accomplished in the light of prevailing social values and social change.

Accomplishing doctor–patient relationships

The social organization of verbal and non-verbal interaction is the province of a branch of ethnomethodology called conversational analysis (CA). From this perspective, medical consultations are seen as 'interactional accomplishments' created and sustained by all the participants. Both non-verbal and verbal interaction is examined, and it has been found that there is a relationship between the two. Heath (1984) analysed videotapes of patient consultations with GPs and found that bodily movements were related to the nature and quality of the interaction. For example, when the doctor looked at the patient, the latter was more likely to speak; conversely, when the GP turned away, the patient would pause or stop speaking. Addressing the problem of effective communication, Heath (1984) suggests that if only doctors could be aware of their interactions, relations between doctors and patients could be improved.

Whilst Heath focuses only on the organization of the interaction *per se*, C. West (1984) examines it in relation to the social identities of the participants, thereby overcoming the classic rebuke of CA, that it fails to incorporate wider dimensions of power and social structure. West carried out an empirical analysis of doctor–patient interactions focusing on the organization of talk. The social organization of talk appears to vary systematically according to the social status of the speaker. For example, a study of interactions between men and women in natural settings found that 95 per cent of all interruptions were initiated by men (Zimmerman and West, 1976). Similarly, in doctor–patient interactions studied by West (1984), of 188 instances of interruption, doctors initiated 67 per cent, and patients initiated 33 per cent. Furthermore, the likelihood of the doctor interrupting the patient varied according to the age, ethnicity and gender of the patient and the gender of the doctor. It is evident from this study that gender has primacy over professional status, although it is important to note that West was working with a very small sample (fourteen male and four female patients), and so it would be inappropriate to generalize.

A further illustration of the unequal nature of the relationship was the use of questions. Of 773 questions observed in all the interactions, 91 per cent were initiated by doctors. Moreover, those questions which were initiated by patients were 'dispreferred'. 'Dispreferred' is a technical term used by conversation analysts which refers to those utterances which are structurally delayed in turns and sequence. In this sense, the patients themselves through the *organization of their talk* contributed to the asymmetry of the relationship. Indeed, when they did ask questions, they often displayed some form of speech disturbance. 'Put simply, patients displayed considerable difficulty "spitting out" their questions' (West, 1984: 89). Although patients were unlikely to ask overt questions, West illustrates how they were more likely to ask 'conditionally relevant questions' (West, 1984: 99). These were question-like items that did not elicit answers *per se*. For example, they might involve requests for 'repair' or 'confirmation' of prior utterances, or might be markers of 'surprise'. From this point of view, whilst the relationship may be asymmetrical, the asymmetry is created and sustained by both the doctor and the patient. Thus, even at the level of spoken interaction, the patient is not simply passive, but may actively contribute to the accomplishment of an unequal relationship.

Earlier in this chapter we discussed how patients very often face a'double bind' (Bloor and Horobin, 1975), in that they must assess the appropriateness of their symptoms and yet, once in a consultation, there is an expectation that they should defer to their doctor. Heritage and Robinson (2006) conceptualize this as the means by which patients present their medical concern as 'doctorable': that is, they have to present their symptoms in such a way that they are legitimately worthy of clinical attention. Patients deploy a range of strategies to justify their visit. These include: their complaint warranted treatment in the past; other people urged them to visit; their symptoms have been endured for a long while; self medication has not been effective; their symptoms are abnormal and so on. This is evident in the following mundane example (Heritage and Robinson, 2006):

1 *Doc*: What can I *do* for you?
2 *Pat*: It's just - I woudn' normally come with a cold, = but I
3 'ad this: *co* : : ld. (0.4) fer about.hh > m's been < on
4 (Fri:day). = I keep *cough*in' up green all the time?

The patient highlights the significance of this particular cold by claiming that she would not 'normally' visit with a cold, and reinforces her symptoms with the reference to coughing up 'green'.

Such justificatory strategies are also evident in Drew's (2006) analysis of telephone conversations where patients are making calls to doctors 'out of hours'. Within the NHS an 'out of hours service' provides medical care beyond the normal working hours. When people ring for help, the doctor will assess whether he or she needs to visit the patient or should offer telephone advice. Such calls, it seems, are characterized by what Drew calls 'misalignments': that is, a situation wherein the doctors and the callers display a different orientation to the questioning phase of the consultation. The callers are invariably concerned about the seriousness of the symptoms and the need for treatment, and so they tend to respond to the doctor's questions as if he or she is seeking information about the possible seriousness. The doctor, on the other hand, elicits information in order to confirm her initial impression that the case is routine, and not urgent. Drew identifies three 'patterns' of misalignment: callers' 'dramatic detailing' of the patient's symptoms, a 'different sense of the diagnostic significance of certain symptoms', and a contrasting response to the callers' 'diagnostic hypotheses'.

Callers tend to embellish their accounts of symptoms and offer additional symptoms in response to questions about symptoms which are not present. When it is evident that the doctor is about to end the call with suggested advice and reassurance, callers (indicated as Clr below) sometimes offered possible diagnosis.

12 *Doc*: hm:. . hhh ^*h*mm, (.) well it doesn't sou : nd I
13 think- (.) *too* exc*i*:ting but - +

14 *Clr— >no* [: . I don't <think of it maybe> a gr*u*m:blin'
15 *Doc*: [.hhh *mm,*
16 *Clr*:—> ap*pen*:dix or: *som*:ethi : ing. *Y*'know, hh
17 *Doc* mm *ye*:h- well there isn't *re*ally such a th*i*:ing as
18 a grum:bling ap*pen*:di:x

The caller not only presented the diagnostic hypothesis in a qualified manner (see the use of 'maybe' and 'or something'), but also does so in response to the doctor's indication that there is nothing seriously wrong. In the sixty calls that Drew analysed, there was no evidence of overt conflict; but what the findings do suggest is that callers and doctors seem to have 'different perceptions of the "abnormality" and "normality" of symptoms'. Furthermore, the callers and doctors resist 'albeit implicitly, and perhaps passively – the other's apparent assessment of the seriousness or urgency of the ailment/condition which those symptoms may betoken' (Drew, 2006).

Emotional labour and health care work

Hitherto we have concentrated mainly on interactions between doctors and patients in relatively structured medical consultations. If we focus only on these forms of practitioner–patient interactions, we could lose sight of a crucial dimension of formal health work: the considerable amount of caring and emotional labour involved. When people are ill, in pain, in a strange environment, and fearful of what is going to happen to them, they are likely to want support and comfort. Although both are clearly central to health care, it has been found that these aspects of health care work are often carried out by those 'lower down' in the medical hierarchy. The skills and functions associated with emotional labour are often unacknowledged and devalued.

James (1989), drawing on her study of a hospice, shows how a significant part of the work there is emotional labour. This is seen as women's work, and is *in fact* mainly carried out by women. Emotional labour must be flexible, so that it can be responsive to the needs of others. To be effective, she argues, the 'labourer's' skills must include being able to understand and interpret the needs of others, being able to provide a personal response to these needs, being able to juggle the delicate balance of each individual and of that individual within a group, being able to pace work, and taking into account the needs of other individuals. Bolton's (2001) Goffmanesque study suggests that nurses are 'emotional jugglers', in that they are performers having to deftly switch their – often quite intense – emotional performances throughout their work.

Male professionals are often 'emotional managers', and set the parameters, while others do the work. In the hospice, where James did her fieldwork, although the male Medical Director was in charge of co-ordinating 'total care', much of the difficult work of emotional labour – for instance, telling people that they were going to die – fell to a female doctor. More significant, perhaps, was the aftermath of such a disclosure, which may go on over days and weeks, and is largely managed by female nursing staff – in other words, those closest to the patients. Nurses told James how invaluable they found the auxiliaries, especially the older ones, because they were key people in understanding the patients' greatest concerns.

What this study highlights is the fact that caring and emotional aspects of health care are sometimes excluded, or rather devalued, in relation to professional–patient interactions. It appears that caring skills are not as highly valued as technological skills, and they are usually carried out by those who are lower down in the medical hierarchy. This has been recognized to be an important limitation of medical consultations by both academic researchers and lay people. In some cases it has contributed to debates about the appropriateness of medical practitioners' involvement in certain aspects of health care. This is particularly the case in those areas of health which have become unnecessarily medicalized, for example, childbirth (see chapter 2).

Medicalization: childbirth

The perspective of women and obstetricians on the experience and outcomes of childbirth are very different. Women and the medical profession, it has been argued, have a qualitatively different view and experience of childbirth. Graham and Oakley (1986) have described the different *frames of reference* between women and doctors. 'Frame of reference' refers to an ideology – that is, a system of values and attitudes through which mothers and doctors view pregnancy.

Three key aspects of the frame of reference are as follows. First, that the 'doctor knows best' – that is, the idea that reproduction is a specialist subject about which doctors are the experts. This is manifest in discussions between doctors and women. Case notes are routinely taken to be more reliable than women's accounts:

> *Doctor*: How many weeks are you now?
> *Patient*: Twenty-six-and-a-half.
> *Doctor* (looking at case notes): Twenty weeks now.
> *Patient*: No. Twenty-six-and-a-half.
> *Doctor*: You can't be.
> *Patient*: Yes, I am; look at the ultrasound report.
> *Doctor*: When was it done?
> *Patient*: Today.
> *Doctor*: It was done today?
> *Patient*: Yes.
> *Doctor* (reads report): Oh yes, twenty-six-and-a-half weeks, that's right. (Graham and Oakley, 1986: 106–7)

A second aspect of the frame of reference is the process of medicalization, which Oakley argues has occurred despite lack of evidence to support the use of medical procedures. Around 95 per cent of births are normal; yet they are treated like an illness, and mothers as patients. The whole process involves an array of technical procedures used for testing, screening, scanning, monitoring and so on. A further dimension of the frame of reference is that women are typified as patients, and care is referred to as management of labour. The outcomes or 'indices of success' also vary between women and doctors. The key criticisms of maternity care which have emerged from both within and beyond the social science literature are summed up by Oakley (1993) as: that pregnancy and childbirth are not illnesses; that women are human beings; that obstetrics should be scientific; and that happiness is an important outcome of good obstetric care.

The ongoing debate about the merits of home versus hospital delivery is a tangible illustration of these different frames of reference. Although birth is a natural process in the UK, over 95 per cent of babies are born in hospitals (Health Commission, 2008). It is within this organizational context that doctors are better able to wield their control, that women are less able to control their environment, and that care and support are most likely to be interventionist. Whilst the UK and USA are highly medicalized, Scandinavian countries and the Netherlands are less so, and there, where birth is seen as a normal physiological process, rates of clinical interventions such as Caesarean sections are significantly lower (Johanson et al., 2002). A change in the location of care will have implications for the nature of professional–patient interactions. For example, in the case of home births, the midwife will have a greater degree of autonomy, and therefore a greater and more continuous involvement with the women she is supporting. There is now a growing recognition that the patient, or lay person, must be more actively involved in formal health care generally. The training and education of all health professionals have been reformed to encourage this and they are encouraged to see their patients as active participants, rather than clinical, pathological objects. Similarly, sociologists have called for more integrative approaches to the analysis of childbirth in order to overcome polarized and polemic debates (Walsh, 2010).

Medicalization: Depression

Sophisticated marketing techniques, designed to encourage people to reflect on their feelings, encourage individuals to see themselves as having issues that might readily be remedied through a recourse to treatment. Otherwise healthy people can be transformed into 'patients' with symptoms and disease. In so doing lay people quite literately 'buy into' these definitions of illness – shyness becomes social anxiety disorder (SAD), sexual desire becomes sexual dysfunction (Hartley, 2006) and trouble sleeping becomes a sleeping disorder (Williams, 2011). Turn to the Internet and you can find tools to rate your symptoms alongside the promotion of remedies and drugs to cure them (Ebeling, 2011). The Internet is an effect medium for direct-to-consumer advertising and since the turn of the century drug companies have invested heavily to market their products directly to lay people bypassing the health professionals. As curing becomes a commercial rather than caring activity, people are construed as, and may behave like, medical consumers. Symptoms, disease categories and treatments are negotiated through a complex set of alliances between industry, consumer organizations, patient advocacy groups and health professionals. Ambiguous symptoms and health concerns coalesce and are co-constructed in relation to the proposed functions of drug therapies.

Perhaps one of the most ubiquitous examples of this is depression and related mental health problems. David Healy (2006) demonstrates how the boundaries of various forms of clinical depression are fluid. Furthermore, branded drugs are marketed not only to treat depression but significantly to prevent it amongst those people who display characteristics that position them as being 'at risk' of depression. Drugs previously used to treat manic depression are now marketed as 'mood stabilizers' – thus they are promoted not only as treatments but as therapies for those who may in the future suffer from manic depression or bipolar disorder. Healy documents the example of 'bio-polar disorder' to illustrate how this was split into two types. Bipolar I – includes patients who are hospitalized and bipolar II – includes those who report episodes within the community. The prevalence and therefore the market significantly expanded.

Professional-patient relationships and the discourse of the social

We have seen throughout this chapter that patients are not simply passive recipients of health care, but are actively, and often proactively, involved in the process, although very often their influence may remain subtle and covert. That patients should be more involved in medical consultations, and health care more generally, has been the view of both liberal medical reformists (Balint, 1956; Byrne and Long, 1976) and social scientists since the latter decades of the twentieth century. Moreover, it appears that during the last few decades this is increasingly becoming the case and that the content and structure of professional-patient interactions are changing.

The changing basis of professional-patient relationships has been articulated by a number of sociologists whose analytical approach is explicitly Foucauldian (Armstrong, 1979, 1984; Arney and Bergen, 1984; Silverman, 1987). They have argued that the power relations within such relationships can be reconceptualized, in that they are now characterized more by disciplinary than by sovereign power (see chapter 5). In other words, practitioners today are less likely to exert overt, ideological control over their patients, and are also less oppressive in their approach. Rather, they are more likely to try to encourage their patients to voice their opinions and to take responsibility for their health and make decisions about the direction of their treatment regimens.

Arney and Bergen (1984) explored the nature of the medical encounter and concluded that since the 1950s it has changed considerably. They present their argument through the depiction of two images of medicine. First, the anatomy lesson, which portrays the dissection of a corpse and so suggests that medical 'truth' is to be found within the anatomical frame. Disease in this context is a discrete entity, which is located within the realm of the pathological. A second image is superimposed upon this corpse, that of living patients; these 'people' represent the new focus of medicine - that is, life. The origin of medical truth no longer lies in the corpse, where it had been sought by violent intrusion, but in the words of the speaking patient. As Arney and Bergen (1984: 169) argue:

> Medicine is compelled by its own logic to speak *with* the patient and to abandon its arrogant logic of speaking for the patient, who must remain silent. Both doctor and patient are compelled to speak with one another in a common language around which a field of power forms to govern them both.

The two images, however, are still familiar to us. This is because, as Silverman (1987: 201) points out, Arney and Bergen are concerned with 'the *direction* of change rather than a description which is valid for all instances'.

The origins of the importance of the patient's view have been traced to the formulation of two emergent fields of medical discourse (Armstrong, 1984; Silverman, 1987: 200; Nettleton, 1992). These were the discovery of mental and psychosomatic illnesses, which, in turn, elevated the importance within medical discourse of people's emotions and feelings. Further, and at about the same time in the early 1950s, epidemiology began to focus on the social causes of mortality and morbidity, and therefore came to acknowledge the relevance of people's social circumstances to health and illness. Thus the feelings and circumstances of the patient came to form part of his or her illness, its diagnosis and prognosis, and therefore formed a crucial element of the professional–patient interaction. Thus is summed up by Gerhardt (1989: 325) when she writes:

> now the patient comes to matter as one who feels pain, or experiences satisfaction: that is, as the person in his or her entirety of previously clinically irrelevant identity. Through this incorporation of person-related aspects, mirrored in how medical care is received and experienced, the realm of what comes under medical control is broadened considerably.

Studies which have involved interviews with health care practitioners have found this to be the case. May (1992), for example, found that nurses within a hospital setting are keen to know about the social as well as the clinical aspects of their patients, and this may result in their modifying health care routines. May tried to elicit the type of information that nurses would require to develop a satisfactory nurse–patient relationship, and found that they wanted information about their patients' lives at home: who they live with, their daily routines, their family and friends, their fears and worries, and so on. A study of dental practitioners (Nettleton, 1992: 53) found that dentists also required information about their patients' home lives, and that decisions about appropriate advice on prevention and treatment were made in the light of this information. As one dentist put it, today practitioners 'have to consider so many aspects of their lives which are *private* really'.

Medical power in this context is different from the notion of power which is inherent in the quasi-Marxist or structural perspectives which, as we have already noted above, see practitioner–patient interactions as sites of medical domination in that they contribute to the perpetuation of ideological forms. Here power refers to the discourses of health and medicine; that is, the language, the activities and the practices associated with them. It is these activities that fabricate medical objects: at one time, the pathological anatomy of the patient, and now, the active person who resides in a wider social context. Of course, the discourses of the professional, the social scientist and the patient are interrelated. There is a dynamic relationship between them which facilitates the types of change that we have described. Armstrong has captured this by way of an analogy: he considers the apparently unproblematic relationship between the customer and the cashier in the supermarket:

> Both parties have well defined roles, their interaction is usually minimal and neither party expects to have to negotiate differences of meaning or mutual anxieties. Imagine now a large research grant being awarded to investigate the relationship. Both parties would have to start examining their relationship so they could relate their feelings to the research team: the confession of silent thoughts would be encouraged and new problems of misunderstandings would be identified. Gradually a mechanical relationship – virtually between a bag of shopping and a cash till – becomes problematic in that as the customer comes to look for and respond to the personal meanings of the cashier so the cashier becomes more than an extension of the till but a 'whole person' in her [*sic*] own right. (Armstrong, 1983b: 458)

Thus we can see that changes in practice are both captured in, and facilitated by, social research.

A concern about this more 'holistic' approach to professional-patient interactions, one which takes the 'whole person' into account, is that doctors, or health care workers more generally, are legitimately able to encroach on more and more aspects of people's lives. Medical surveillance becomes totalizing. Indeed, I touched on this issue above when I discussed the paradox which is inherent in the critique of medicalization. This was, to reiterate, that if medicine takes the social aspects of health and illness into account, it is accused of medical imperialism; if it does not, it is accused of medical reductionism. Thus humane and holistic medicine is castigated as extending the web of medical power and surveillance. However, the Foucauldian notion of surveillance is different from the concept of medicalization, as it is based on a different conceptualization of power. Whilst in the former, power is a more flexible and productive concept, in the latter, the power of those in authority is repressive and oppressive. In the former, it is not so much held as shared. Thus Foucauldian interpretations of professional-patient interactions draw attention to the fact that as surveillance over lay people's social lives and feelings increases, so too do their opportunities for resistance. Strategies of resistance have been explored empirically by Bloor and McIntosh (1990) in the context of therapeutic communities and health visiting. Clients or patients can choose what information to disclose and not to disclose; they can choose either to follow advice or ignore it; they can present partial information or what the professional 'wants to hear', and so on. As one mother noted in a discussion about her health visitor: 'Ye just agree wi' her and do yer own things 'cause she's no' here every day to check' (1990: 174). Bloor and McIntosh analyse professional-client relationships within a new analytical frame, and thus offer fresh insight. They draw our attention to the fact that resistance cannot be 'considered in isolation: power provokes resistance; indeed, there is a sense in which power creates resistance; "resistance is itself part of a disciplinary relationship"' (Bloor and McIntosh, 1990: 180). This approach draws attention to the fact that strategies and negotiations observed at a micro level can be understood in terms of, and indeed contribute to, broader social transformations observed in wider society, such as the decline in an unquestioning faith in biomedicine, an increasing scepticism about 'expert' knowledge, a proliferation of medical information and knowledge on the Internet, and the formation of a consumer-oriented culture.

It may be that, within the context of the information age and the associated technological transformations, a further image of the patient may come into being: one that quite literally gives primacy to the patient's own image. Forms of telemedicine which incorporate information and communication technologies (ICTs) are being developed. An example of this is the use of ICTs and video-conferencing systems to 'store and forward' digital images for diagnostic purposes. The doctor-patient interaction requires neither spatial nor temporal proximity – the clinical gaze rests on the digitized image of the patient rather than the patient him- or herself (see chapter 5). An ethnography of a teledermatology clinic in the UK reveals some of the potential consequences of 'remote doctors and absent patients' (Mort et al., 2003).

Dermatology patients attended community clinics, where nurses took photographs of their skin conditions and a brief history. These were then forwarded to the consultants in the specialist hospital departments. Herein, Mort et al. (2003) suggest, not only is the patient reduced to an image, but the dermatologist's role is confined 'to diagnostic reasoning against an image on the screen of a personal computer'

(p. 278). The dermatologists were uneasy about their lack of contact with the patient - colour tone, texture, touch and critically the patient's view were absent, and so they did not feel as confident in making their diagnosis. Thus the social and interactional work was carried out by the nurse who took the photograph. She or he in turn became a producer of knowledge, rather than simply an information-gatherer. The nurses, aware of the constraints of the technology, had to decide which types and sources of information they should generate in order that the consultant could make a considered diagnosis. Professional–patient relationships are once again being reconfigured, along with socio-technological transformations. The figure of the doctor depicted at the patient's bedside in Jewson's (1976) cosmology of 'bedside medicine' (see chapter 2) is being redrawn to include a range of other practitioners and a multiplicity of sites and settings.

Conclusion

The contact that patients have with formal health care professionals forms a critical area of study within the sociology of health and illness. For most people such interactions form their main encounters with health care services. An adequate sociology of these meetings must incorporate both macro and micro levels of analysis. The minutiae of day-to-day contacts can only be understood sufficiently in the light of the socio-structural and cultural context in which they are played out. Certain characteristics of professional–client relationships have been identified in the literature: their asymmetrical nature; their ideological potential; and the tendency for participants to adopt mainly covert, and only rarely overt, strategies to determine the outcome of consultations. During the last few decades the contribution that lay people make to the nature of interactions has been acknowledged, and it has been suggested that their participation has increased. The increasingly active role played by the patient or lay person is presumed to be emblematic of wider social transformations, such as the decline of faith in expert and universalistic notions of medical science. Ideological shifts which pronounce the values of choice and consumerism (see chapter 10) have also given credence to the validity of the lay person's view.

FURTHER READING

Heritage, J. and Maynard, D. (eds) (2006), *Communication in Medical Care: Interaction between Physicians and Patients*, Cambridge: Cambridge University Press. Empirical studies of doctor–patient interactions drawing on techniques of conversation analysis.

May, C. (2007), 'The Clinical Encounter and the Problem of Context', *Sociology* 41, 1: 29–45.

Potter, S. J. and McKinlay, J. R. (2005), 'From Relationship to Encounter: An Examination of Longitudinal and Lateral Dimensions in the Doctor–Patient Relationship', *Social Science & Medicine*, 61, 2: 465–79. The extent to which relationships have been shaped by cultural and economic transformations is explored here.

Rapp, R. (2000), *Testing Women: The Social Impact of Amniocentesis in America*, London: Routledge. Rapp's ethnography, discussed in chapter 5 of this volume, highlights the dilemmas associated with prenatal testing that are salient for many other reproductive technologies - so too is her concept of women as 'moral pioneers'.

Strong, P. (2002 [1979]), *The Ceremonial Order of the Clinic: Parents, Doctors and Medical Bureaucracies*, London: Ashgate. Informed by Goffman, this analysis of interactions in US and UK clinics is a classic study and a great read.

7 Social Inequalities and Health Status

Introduction

Social inequalities in health have long been recognized. Reports on the 'labouring classes' produced in the mid-nineteenth century revealed how those who were poor experienced more disease and illness than those who were rich. The twenty-first century is no different: poor people die younger than people who are rich; they are more likely to suffer from most of the major 'killer' diseases; and they are more likely to suffer from chronic long-standing illnesses. During the last century in the UK the overall life expectancy of the population has increased for both men and women, from 45.5 years for men and 49 years for women in 1901, to 75.7 for males and 80.4 for females in 2001 (ONS, 2005). However, this general increase disguises increasing inequalities in mortality rates between rich and poor. It is argued that, taken as a whole, the *absolute* health of the population has increased. However, the gap between the mortality and morbidity rates of those who are poor *relative* to those who are rich has also increased, an increase which has become especially marked since the early 1980s (White et al., 2003). Social epidemiological research undertaken in the UK has provided evidence that by the end of the first decade of the new millennium: 'Inequality in mortality is now greater than at any time since comparable records began' (Thomas et al., 2010).

Evidence of health inequalities is vast and well documented. At the close of the millennium the UK New Labour government commissioned an *Independent Inquiry into Inequalities of Health* (Acheson Report, 1998), which unequivocally reported that there were differences in morbidity and mortality rates across the social spectrum for most major causes of death, including coronary heart disease, lung cancer, respiratory disease, strokes and suicide. At the end of the twentieth century, the life expectancy differences between social class I and social class V was 5.2 years for men and 3.4 years for women (Pantazis and Gordon, 2000). In England, people living in the poorest neighbourhoods on average die 7 years earlier than those living in the richest neighbourhoods. Furthermore, those who live in poorer areas have higher chances of living with disabilities with the average difference of living a disability free life being 17 years (Marmot, 2010). These health inequalities between people residing in different places and social positions persist not only in the UK (Hacking et al., 2011) but throughout the world. As stated in the World Health Organization Report, *Closing the Gap in a Generation: Health Equity through Action on the Social Determinants of Health*:

> A child born in a Glasgow, Scotland suburb can expect a life 28 years shorter than another living only 13 kilometres away. A girl in Lesotho is likely to live 42 years less

> than another in Japan. In Sweden, the risk of a woman dying during pregnancy and childbirth is 1 in 17,400; in Afghanistan, the odds are 1 in 8. Biology does not explain any of this. Instead, the differences between - and within - countries result from the social environment where people are born, live, grow, work and age. (WHO, 2008)

In 2001, whilst 3.4 per 1,000 live births died in the first year of life in Hampshire and the Isle of Wight, 8.6 per 1,000 died within their first year in Birmingham and the Black Country (ONS, 2005). Rates of illness are also socially patterned. In 2001 amongst those people in employment the rates of limiting long-standing illness or disability for people in professional or managerial occupations were half those for people in routine occupations (ONS, 2005). Residents of the most deprived areas of England are more than twice as likely to have one or more disability as those who live in the least deprived areas (Department of Health, 2002a).

Thus the evidence is compelling: there is an association between health and socio-economic circumstances. However, the nature of this link is the subject of much controversy, and indeed constitutes the heart of the 'health inequalities debate'. This debate focuses on two principal concerns: first, technical considerations about how data on health and social circumstances are most appropriately measured and interpreted; second, how the link between health and social circumstances is to be explained. In sum, the debate is both empirical and theoretical. There is a vast literature on this topic, and it is easy to feel overwhelmed by it. One chapter cannot possibly do justice to this whole area of study. My aim is simply to try to highlight some of the key parameters of the sociological debate, which may serve as a guide to further reading and investigation.

Studies of health inequalities have focused on those variables which comprise indicators of people's social circumstances. Social class, gender, 'race' and geographical location all influence a person's access to material and social resources (including housing, education, transport, income and social support), living and working conditions, and their social status. In turn, patterns of health and illness are related to these variables. This is because some of the main determinants of health are social and environmental in origin. As we shall see, this is evidenced by historical studies which have found that improved health has more to do with improved nutrition and wealth than with developments in medical science. In this chapter we will examine the nature of health inequalities in relation to a number of these variables. I will highlight the technical problems of measurement for each, and then consider the varying explanations which try to account for the patterning found in the data.

Measuring health

The *incidence* of deaths or disease refers to the number of cases in a given period. The *prevalence* refers to the total number of cases at a certain point in time. Incidence and prevalence are normally presented as *rates* (for example, the number of cases per 100,000 people) rather than crude numbers, as this makes for more meaningful comparisons. These rates can also be expressed in age- and sex-specific terms, and if the data are available, in terms of other categories such as region, ethnicity or occupational class. This is important, as clearly the frequency of diseases in populations varies according to such factors.

Most studies of health inequalities rely on mortality and morbidity data. Data on mortality in Britain are derived from death certificates, which include information on sex, age, area of residence, occupation or last occupation, and cause of death. Despite the apparent objectivity of such data, studies of the social organization of death certification reveal that this information is likely to be variable (Prior, 1985). For example, middle-class death certificates have been found to have more than one description of cause. This, it has been suggested, is because they are regarded as being in need of more explanation than working-class deaths (Phillimore, 1989).

Data on morbidity can be collected from a number of different sources, such as levels of absenteeism, rates of consultation with GPs, and surveys of self-reported illness. More recently, increasingly sophisticated measures of morbidity have been developed which incorporate subjective well-being. There are now various instruments available to measure perceived health problems, which do not ask directly about symptoms but, through a series of questions about health, identify those people who are in distress or at risk (see Bowling, 2005).

Epidemiology and sociology

The discipline of epidemiology involves the study of the prevalence and incidence of disease and illness. Indeed, the study of health inequalities involves epidemiologists and sociologists working closely together, with the former often providing evidence of those factors which are associated with particular diseases. Perhaps the best-known finding of epidemiological research was the establishment of the relationship between smoking and lung cancer by Doll and Peto in the 1950s. Thus as Gerhardt (1989: 262) explains, 'epidemiology becomes a basic science providing research on which medical sociology relies . . . the individual is seen as an incumbent of multiple roles or statuses each of which carry a certain risk or susceptibility to sickness or premature death.' Although epidemiologists and sociologists work together, they are rooted in different paradigms. Whilst sociologists are fundamentally concerned with social interactions and social processes, epidemiologists are more concerned with the characteristics of *individuals* which, in aggregate, predispose them to certain diseases (Stacey, 1987).

Reformist and materialist epidemiologies and the 'efficacy debate'

The efficacy debate comprises a literature, generated by 'reformist' epidemiologists, which challenges the presumed effectiveness and appropriateness of biomedicine (Dubos, 1959; McKeown, 1976) and questions the efficacy of many aspects of medical intervention (Cochrane, 1972; Oakley, 1993). Proponents of this view argue that conventional medical histories have overplayed the contribution that medical science made to the reduction of mortality in the nineteenth and twentieth centuries. It was the work of the epidemiologist and demographer McKeown (1976) that stimulated this debate in the mid-1970s. He questioned the validity of the biomedical model (see chapter 1) and more especially the idea that human health depends upon medical intervention. He argued that it is the conditions under which humans operate that are essential to the understanding of improvements in health. He substantiated this thesis by carrying out a historical demographic analysis which found that the population growth of England and Wales in the nineteenth and twentieth centuries was due to a reduction of death rates, and especially deaths in childhood. The main reason for the reduction of death rates was a decline in diseases such as cholera, diphtheria and tuberculosis, and this was due to improvements in nutrition, changing reproductive practices and hygiene. The influence of medical interventions such as immunization did not make any significant contribution until the middle of the twentieth century.

The McKeown thesis has, however, been criticized for concentrating on individual and behavioural rather than socio-structural factors (Szreter, 2002). Whilst it may be regarded as radical, in that it challenges conventional medicine, it is argued that politically it is somewhat tame. Whilst most writers accept that the rise of living standards was significant for the improvement of health, there is debate about which components of standards of living are the most important. For example, Blane (1990) examined changes in mortality rates in the period between 1870 and 1914 in relation to the economic cycle and changes in 'real' wages (that is, money wages in relation to the price of commodities). He argued that changes in real income and working conditions for many social groups were more significant for the reduction of mortality than improvements in nutrition and sanitation. Such changes were brought about not only because of public health reforms, but as a result of the collective actions of workers. As Blane (1990: 51) points out: 'Although workers were not primarily motivated by concerns over their health, improved health was the medically predictable consequence of their success.'

This debate reflects the differences between *reformist* and *materialist* histories. The *reformist* perspective identifies a wide range of social and environmental factors such as pollution, lifestyle, income and nutrition, all of which may influence the likelihood of certain diseases. A *materialist* epidemiology, by contrast, examines the forces that shape society, with class relations being regarded as pivotal (Navarro, 2004: 96). A logical outcome of both theses is that we must divert resources towards gaining an understanding of the interactive effects of the multifarious causes of diseases and the identification of those people who are more likely to experience disease and illness. Although the reformists challenge the medical model, they remain within the paradigm of medical epidemiology. Today in industrialized countries, they argue, the main threat to good health is 'personal behaviour', that is, 'in relation to diet, exercise, tobacco, alcohol, drugs, etc.' (McKeown, 1976: 178). In contrast, the materialist perspective emphasizes factors such as poverty, bad housing and structural inequalities, which, for some, are the result of capitalist economic development (Navarro, 1978, 2004; Townsend, 1990).

It is evident from these two perspectives that the issue of responsibility for health is inextricably interlinked with debates on causation. For example, although the reformists incorporate social factors, their emphasis is on diet, behaviour and hygiene, to the relative neglect of socio-economic factors such as the distribution of income and wealth. This, it is argued, leads to the perpetuation of the notion that premature death is an individual rather than a social responsibility (Popay, 2009). This theme, individual versus structural explanations, as we will see, is a perennial one in the health inequalities debate. We will begin our discussion, however, with what might at first sight appear to be a rather unusual example of the social patterning of mortality.

'Heat wave': the case of heat-related deaths

Eric Klinenberg's (2002) book *Heat Wave: A Social Autopsy of Disaster in Chicago* deciphers the reasons for the unequal distribution of heat-related deaths during a heat wave in Chicago in 1995. In many respects the book encapsulates all the various perspectives within the sociology of health inequalities. In particular, the study highlights that what might look like purely physically induced random events are, in fact, fundamentally social in origin.

Klinenberg's study was prompted by his observation that between 14 and 20 July 1995 there were 465 officially recorded 'heat-related deaths' in Chicago. During this period Chicagoans endured temperatures that exceeded 100°F for three consecutive days. This number of deaths is high compared to other high-profile 'disasters'; for example, the Oklahoma City bombing in April 1995 resulted in 168 deaths, and the crash of TWA Flight 800 resulted in 230 deaths. Klinenberg makes the point that more people die in heat waves in the USA than in hurricanes, floods, tornadoes or earthquakes. Receiving much less attention, heat waves are relatively 'silent and invisible killers of silenced and invisible people' (p. 17). The rationale for the study, therefore, was to make visible the largely unseen factors which make heat waves so lethal for some social groups and not others.

A clue to the puzzle of the high death rate is that the deaths did not occur at random. Older people were more likely to die than those who were younger; 73 per cent of the heat-related deaths were people over 65 years old. People living alone were also at risk. Public officials proactively searched for the relatives of 170 heat wave victims, and even today fifty-six bodies remain unclaimed, their possessions still boxed in the county offices. Men (after adjusting for age) were twice as likely to die as women. African Americans had the highest rate of death, with a ratio of 1.5 : 1 compared to other 'ethnoracial' groups; a ratio which rose to 1.8 : 1 amongst 55–64-year-olds and 1.9 : 1 for those over 85 years. By contrast, only 2 per cent of heat deaths were Latino Americans. Deaths were also unevenly spread between districts across the city. Two districts – North and South Lawndale – which are strikingly similar in terms of their demographic characteristics (e.g. age, poverty and income) had significantly different rates of heat deaths. North Lawndale had nineteen deaths (40 per 100,000 residents) and South Lawndale had three deaths (less than 4 per 100,000).

In sum, age, household composition, gender, race and area all influenced the chances of surviving the heat. It is these epidemiological findings that beg explanation. Klinenberg assesses the explanations that were proffered at the time and finds them wanting. These explanations are of interest to us here, because they mirror those put forward to explain inequalities in health. One such 'explanation' revolved around the question: Are the deaths 'really real'? Local politicians questioned the classification of deaths by disputing the criteria used to categorize a death as 'heat-related'. This explanation was amplified as a result of media attention, and 'the legacy of calling the heat wave death figures into question continues to this day' (p. 205).

A further explanation rested on the fact that the deaths were the consequence of a 'unique meteorological event', being a natural and inevitable consequence of extreme heat. Furthermore, older, vulnerable people were surely about to die anyway, and so the figures were misrepresentations; the heat selectively kills those who are more vulnerable, whilst the stronger ones survive.

A third explanation is that the deaths were the result of inappropriate behaviours and responses. Local activists blamed city officials, city officials blamed the utility providers, others blamed the media for inadequate warnings, and yet other officials blamed families for not looking after their own, and blamed individuals for not looking after themselves. Variants of this view are those that sought to explain the differential death rates amongst African American and Latino communities in terms of culture. Suggestions were made that Latino Americans living in South Lawndale were physiologically more suited to hot weather, and that their extended family ties provided support through the crisis. Klinenberg points out (pp. 88–9) that the physiological explanation is rooted in myth, not science, and the extended family argument fails to explain why white elderly Americans were also 'protected' in this district.

A fourth explanation, and the one preferred by Klinenberg, argues 'that place-specific social ecology and its effects on cultural practices account for much of the disparity in the heat wave mortality rates for the two Lawndales' (p. 91). North Lawndale has 'the dangerous ecology of abandoned buildings, open spaces, commercial depletion, violent crime, degraded infrastructure, low population density, and family dispersion [which] undermines the viability of public life and the strength of local support systems, rendering older residents particularly vulnerable to isolation'. However, in South Lawndale 'busy streets, heavy commercial activity, residential concentration, and relatively low crime promotes social contact, collective life, and public engagement in general and provides particular benefits for the elderly, who are more likely to leave home when they are drawn out by nearby amenities'. During the heat wave it was this latter social ecology with 'the possibilities for social contact that helped the vulnerable Chicagoans to survive' (p. 91).

The two districts have their own histories, associated with racism and industrial inertia. In 1950, 87 per cent of the population of North Lawndale was white Caucasian; a decade later 91 per cent was African American. Work in nearby factories was plentiful until the 1970s, when the large electrical companies began to close. The industrial demise was accompanied by rapid outward migration; the population halved between 1970 and 1990, and was accompanied by the abandonment of businesses. Thus transformations associated with exclusion, abandonment and ghettoization resulted in a district which lacked any commercial or social infrastructure, or 'animated public spaces' (p. 98). There were high levels of violent and drug-related crime. By contrast, nearby South Lawndale had, since the 1960s, experienced an inward migration of significant numbers of Mexican Americans. Shops, agencies and other local businesses had been established. Public spaces were busy and vibrant; there were lower levels of crime; and older people were more likely to be seen on the streets. There were places to go. From his sociological investigation he concludes that:

> [E]xtreme exogenous forces such as the climate have become so disastrous partly because the emerging isolation and privatization, the extreme social and economic inequalities, and the concentrated zones of affluence and poverty pervasive in contemporary cities create hazards for vulnerable residents in all seasons. (p. 230)

Thus his explanation points to the salience of the political and economic histories of 'place'. Socio-economic transformations over time help explain why there were differential rates of heat-related deaths in the extremely hot weather. Klinenberg's study is explicitly Durkheimian; the account of the 1995 heat wave, he argues, 'represents an exemplary case of what Marcel Mauss called a *total social fact*, one that integrates and activates a broad set of inner workings of the city' (p. 32).

The 'really real', selection, cultural and social ecology explanations summarized in relation to the heat-related deaths resonate with the explanations put forward in relation to other dimensions of social patterning of health. As we shall see, these are commonly referred to as the 'artefact', 'health selection', 'biological', 'cultural or behavioural', and 'materialist or structural' explanations. We will look at variants of these in turn in relation to class, gender, 'race' and locality differences in mortality and morbidity.

Social class and health

As has already been indicated, there is a clear relationship between patterns of mortality, morbidity and social class, an association that endures with remarkable consistency. If anything, the gap is now more pronounced (White et al., 2003). This might lead one to conclude, as do many Marxist sociologists, that this is because 'class' differences are inherent to capitalist social relations (Navarro, 2004; Muntaner and Navarro, 2004). However, there is also evidence to suggest that social class – as traditionally understood by both Marxist and Weberian analysts – has lost much of its saliency. As Arber and Cooper (2000) point out, since the 1990s the key material divide for children's health is whether their parents are in paid employment, rather than their position in the class structure.

Such findings contribute to the suggestion that we are witnessing the 'death of class', and that social divisions are now increasingly configured around diverse and fractured categories such as employment, locality, identity and consumption patterns (Savage et al., 2005; Scambler and Higgs, 1999). Such debates are complex, not least because they merge conceptual differences about what constitutes a social class with issues concerned with how best to operationalize (or measure) whatever the preferred conceptualization is. There is no doubt that researchers must accurately capture that which they purport to measure, and that it must be made explicit what they are actually measuring (Bartley, 2004). However, there is a sense in which these debates often become so detailed that one may be left with the impression that the technical details of the debate matter more than the issue of inequality itself. There is a danger that such a preoccupation may offer excuses for procrastination (Navarro, 2004: 93). As Carr-Hill (1987: 509) notes, the debates 'will not be resolved by "further research": the time is long overdue for a redistribution of resources to eradicate poverty'. Nevertheless, if we want to be able to make sense of the evidence – some of which we will examine briefly in the next section – it is important that we understand the basic parameters of the debate. So, having looked at some of the evidence, we will then briefly turn to some of the main technical issues of measurement and the competing theories that have been offered to account for social class inequalities in health.

The evidence

There is a huge amount of data on social class inequalities in health and a number of different ways of presenting it. Table 7.1 shows the life expectancy of men and women

Table 7.1 *Life expectancy at birth by gender and social class, 1972-1976, 1987-1991 and 2002-2005*

	1972-6		1987-91		2002-5	
Social class	Males	Females	Males	Females	Males	Females
I	71.9	79.0	76.2	81.1	80.0	85.1
II	71.9	77.1	75.0	80.7	79.4	83.2
IIIN	69.5	78.3	74.4	80.0	78.4	82.4
IIIM	70.0	75.2	72.7	77.9	76.5	80.5
IV	68.3	75.3	70.8	77.4	75.7	79.9
V	66.5	74.2	68.7	76.6	72.7	78.1
Non-manual	*71.2*	*77.7*	*75.0*	*80.4*	*79.2*	*82.9*
Manual	*69.1*	*75.2*	*71.7*	*77.5*	*75.9*	*80.0*
All	**69.3**	**75.3**	**72.6**	**78.3**	**77.0**	**81.1**

Source: ONS (2007).

at birth in 1972-6 compared to the situation fifteen years later in 1987-91, and thirty years later in 2002-5. In 1972-6 the life expectancy for all men was 69.3, whilst that for all women was 75.3. In 1987-91 life expectancy at birth for both men and women had increased by around 3 years (for men to 72.6, and for women to 78.3); in 2002-5 life expectancy at birth for both men and women had again increased, for men to 77.0 (up by a further 5 years) and for women to 81.1 (up by a further 3 years). However, the extent of both life expectancy and improvements in life expectancy varied significantly in relation to social class. At the most crude level - the differences between non-manual and manual social classes - in 1972-6 the difference amongst men was 71.2 compared to 69.1 (2.1 years), whilst in 1987-91 it was 75.0 compared to 71.7 (3.3 years), and in 2002-5, 79.2 compared to 75.9 (3.3 years). For women the difference was 77.7 compared to 75.2 (2.5 years) in 1972-6; 80.4 compared to 77.5 (2.9 years) in 1987-91; and 82.9 compared to 80.0 (2.9 years) in 2002-5. So, not only are differences in life expectancy related to class, but so too are rates of improvement. Life expectancy has been increasing for all social class groups, but the rate of improvement has often been faster for already advantaged groups, thus increasing overall levels of inequality. A recent ONS report summarizes other similar evidence in this area. Table 7.2 presents data in relation to differential death rates rather than life expectancy, varying by NS-SEC - a new measure of social class that we will discuss briefly below (table 7.3) - and gender.

To take one illustrative example, Table 7.2 shows that amongst men in higher managerial and professional occupations, the age-standardized death rate in 2010 was 128 per 100,000 people, whereas amongst men in routine occupations it was 458 - a ratio of 3.6. The comparable figures for women in the same period were 80 and 287 - also a ratio of 3.6. It is worth noting that in 2001 the ratio for men was 3.2, and for women 3.0. So, although death rates for all social class groups declined over the decade, the rate of decline has been significantly faster amongst the highest social classes than amongst the lowest - inequalities have increased over time.

Table 7.2 *Age-standardized mortality rates[a] by seven-class NS-SEC for males and females aged 25–64, 2001, 2005 and 2010*

	Rate per 100,000 people		
	2001	2005	2010
Males			
Higher managerial and professional	178	147	128
Lower managerial and professional	280	249	210
Intermediate	296	287	253
Self-employed	339	307	278
Lower Supervisory	373	339	317
Semi-routine	465	420	399
Routine	564	514	458
Females			
Higher managerial and professional	105	94	80
Lower managerial and professional	145	131	122
Intermediate	155	157	156
Self-employed	180	167	153
Lower Supervisory	205	184	186
Semi-routine	225	244	230
Routine	318	285	287

[a] Data have been directly age-standardized using the European standard population.
Source: ONS (2012).

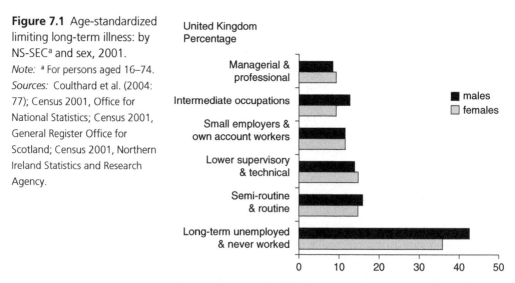

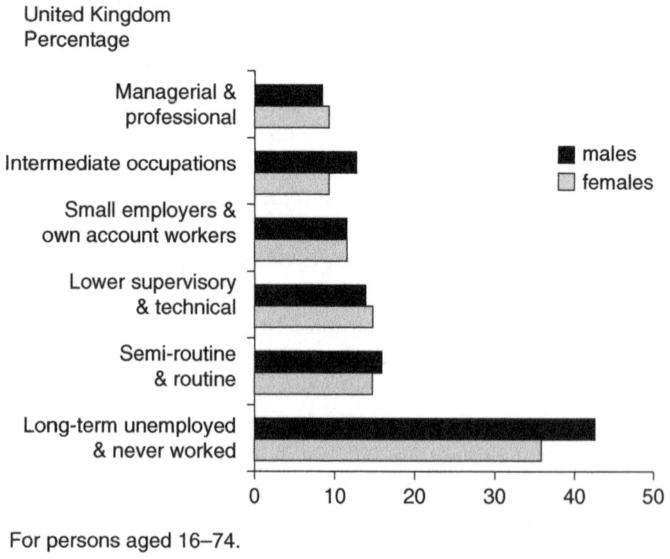

Figure 7.1 Age-standardized limiting long-term illness: by NS-SEC[a] and sex, 2001.
Note: [a] For persons aged 16–74.
Sources: Coulthard et al. (2004: 77); Census 2001, Office for National Statistics; Census 2001, General Register Office for Scotland; Census 2001, Northern Ireland Statistics and Research Agency.

Moving from inequalities in mortality to inequalities in morbidity, figure 7.1 shows how patterns of limiting long-term illness vary by NS-SEC and gender. It shows a clear gradient in the proportions reporting limiting long-term illness even after controlling for age differences between the groupings. Whereas under 10 per cent of people in the managerial and professional group report such a limitation, the figure is closer to 15 per cent amongst those in semi-routine and routine occupations, and over 40 per cent amongst males who are long-term unemployed or who have never worked.

Such 'class variations' are apparent not just in relation to physical health; they also manifest themselves in variations in mental health. Neurotic disorders are reported by a full one-fifth of those in the unskilled manual category, compared to just 9 per cent in the professional group. This means that those in the lowest social class are over twice as likely to suffer from a neurotic disorder as those in the highest social class (Coulthard et al., 2004).

The problems of measurement

As we have seen, the measurement of health is a complex exercise, and this is also true of social class. There is not the space to examine these issues in any great depth here, and those students who require more detail should read Bartley's (2004) *Health Inequality*. Four key issues can be identified: the changing size of social classes, the numerator/denominator problem, the appropriateness or otherwise of different forms of data analysis, and the fact that class is such a global concept.

1. *Social classes are changing in size.* Carr-Hill (1987: 523) has calculated that between 1931 and 1981 social class I increased in size by 217 per cent, from 1.8 per cent of the economically active male population to 5.7 per cent, whilst over the same period the size of social class V decreased by 55 per cent, from 12.9 per cent to 5.8 per cent. Thus it can become difficult to judge whether health inequalities between social classes have changed or whether it is the relative sizes of social classes which have changed. Illsley (1986: 152) is concerned with this issue when he argues that 'valid comparisons involve the comparisons of like with like. If we wished to compare two countries . . . or two regional areas . . . over time, our first step would be to check the boundaries.'

2. *The numerator/denominator problem.* The standardized mortality ratios (SMRs) for social classes are worked out by dividing the number of deaths in the occupations entered on death certificates (numerator) by the number of people in given occupations as recorded in the Census (denominator). However, there is some evidence to suggest that the measurement of occupation in the Census is more subtle, and thus may differ from that recorded on death certificates (Carr-Hill, 1987: 513). As we said above, the problem is further compounded by the social processes involved in death certification. Clearly errors above or below the line will lead to inaccurate estimates of SMRs, with some analysts suggesting this could be as much as 20 per cent either way (Kunst et al., 1998).

3. *Appropriate techniques for analysing the data.* The choice of techniques used to analyse data on health inequalities is determined largely by issues of conceptualization. Some researchers maintain that we should analyse data at an individual level, whilst others argue that we should analyse data at a group (for example, social class) level. At the risk of some over-simplification, those who focus upon individuals, such

as Le Grand (1985; Illsley and Le Grand, 1987), find that inequalities in mortality have narrowed, whilst those using data at a group level come to the opposite conclusion (Pamuk, 1985). Thus we can see that what appears as contradictory evidence may actually reflect the different techniques adopted by those carrying out the research.

4. *Class as a global concept.* The measurement of social class, although based upon an ordinal classification of different occupations, is routinely treated by social scientists as an indicator of material resources. However, although the association between social class and health is well established, the specification of the actual *mechanisms* which link them together often remains unclear. More recently researchers have begun to unravel the relative impact of different dimensions of social class and its various correlates upon health with the aid of various multivariate statistical techniques. Although this approach still does not allow for a full causal analysis of the link, it does allow for a much more subtle set of connections to be established.

These, and other issues, have structured debates about the most appropriate measurement of social class, and have led to the development of a range of alternative operationalizations of the concept. Perhaps the most significant development has been the attempt to improve upon the Registrar General's social class classification based on occupation class which has been in use through various iterations since 1911. Throughout the twentieth century most British studies of social class were based on the Registrar General's Social Class classification. Indeed, some of the data we examined above were presented using this classification. However, in 2001 a new classification was released called the National Statistics Socio-Economic Classification (NS-SEC), and this is now widely used in official statistics. Here socio-economic classifications are based on occupation, in combination with employment status and in some cases size of workplace (Donkin et al., 2002b). As such, they overcome the division between 'manual' and 'non-manual' class groupings and incorporate other dimensions of employment which contribute to employment security, status, opportunities and so on. It is therefore more precise, and less all-encompassing than the old classification. Bartley (2004: 27) lists the principles on which the new schema is based as 'the timing and payment of work (monthly versus weekly, daily or hourly); how much autonomy the worker has in deciding when to start and leave work; promotion opportunities; degree of influence over planning of work; [and] level of influence over designing their own work tasks'. Table 7.3 provides details of the new classification.

Explaining the links between class and health

The observed associations between indicators of social class and health present a puzzle for sociologists. Why is it that we consistently find such relationships? Unfortunately there is no one answer to this question, and a number of explanations have been offered. Each explanation derives from different theoretical interpretations, and each implies a different set of policy implications. Published some decades ago, the so-called Black Report (Townsend and Davidson, 1982) usefully classified these into four main groups: artefact, health selection, cultural and materialist. Since then, these terms have dominated the health inequalities debate and provide a useful summary of the key arguments. However, since the 1990s two further explanations have emerged: namely, the psycho-social and life-course explanations.

Table 7.3 *National Statistics Socio-Economic Classification*

1	Higher managerial and professional occupations, including employers in large firms, higher managers, professionals whether they are employees or self-employed
2	Lower managerial and professional occupations and higher technical occupations
3	Intermediate occupations (clerical, administrative, sales workers with no involvement in general planning or supervision but high levels of job security; some career prospects and some autonomy over their own work schedule)
4	Small employers and self-employed workers
5	Lower technical occupations (with little responsibility for planning own work), lower supervisory occupations (with supervisory responsibility but no overall planning role and less autonomy over own work schedule)
6	Semi-routine occupations (moderate levels of job security; little career prospects; no pay increments; some degree of autonomy over their own work)
7	Routine occupations (low job security; no career prospects; closely supervised routine work)

Source: Bartley (2004: 27).

1. *Artefact explanations.* This explanation sees both class and health as artefacts of the measurement process, and so it follows that any observed relationship must also be an artefact (Townsend and Davidson, 1982: 154). As with the heat-related deaths discussed above, are class-related death rates 'really real'? Following from the ethnomethodological tradition of Garfinkel (1967), it is recognized that diagnostic practices and the identification of the cause of death vary over time and space. Variations in diagnosis, certification, classification and coding processes have been identified as contributing to observed class and health relationships (Bloor et al., 1987). Thus this explanation draws our attention to the social processes that are involved in the production of statistics. To a great extent the inequalities debate accepts that ill health is a biological category, which is differentially reflected in class; in this way it is 'limited to analysing medical thought from the outside, rather than entering into the epistemological domain of medicine' (K. White, 1991: 48). Thus the artefact explanation reminds us that health and disease may also be understood from the social-constructionist perspective (see chapter 2). Another variant of this explanation does not question disease classifications but instead points to the assumptions made in the calculations. It is argued that the enduring and widening health inequalities are a 'mathematical artifact' because as the overall risk of mortality falls, an increase in relative inequalities in health outcomes is inevitable (Scanlan, 2006).

2. *Health selection explanations.* This perspective argues that health status can influence social position. It is suggested that those who are healthy are more likely to be upwardly mobile, and those who are unhealthy are more likely to 'drift' into lower social classes. For example, using data from the 1946 British National Birth Cohort, Wadsworth (1986) has shown that males who had a serious illness in their childhood are more likely to end up in a lower social class. Thirty-six per cent of males of non-manual origin who were seriously ill moved down the social scale, whereas only 23

per cent of those who were not ill had a similar experience. The evidence, however, is mixed. Using data from the Whitehall II study, Chandola et al. (2003) found little evidence to support the thesis that either mental or physical health resulted in changes in employment grade, and the effect of existing healthy status was significantly smaller than the effects of employment position on changes in health. This account of social class differences has a social Darwinist – survival of the fittest – ring to it. But this is not an inherent feature of the approach. For example, P. West (1991) draws attention to the need to understand the social processes involved in health selection. He argues that those people who suffer ill health may well be discriminated against. In terms of social mobility, young adults are particularly vulnerable.

> In focusing on that period between youth and adulthood, it would seem that the processes which are likely to have a major impact on health selection . . . are identifiable within the educational, training and occupational complex. Of specific importance is the way opportunities for individuals with particular attributes are structured by 'gatekeepers' or agents of educational and occupational systems. (West, 1991: 382)

Thus within this explanation we can see a shift from an individualist perspective which implies the 'survival of the fittest' to an account of health selection which offers a more sociological interpretation, in that it highlights the impact of ideology and discrimination within existing social structures.

3. *Cultural or behavioural explanations.* In contrast to the health selection explanation, which treats health as the independent variable, the cultural approach presumes that health is the dependent variable. That is, it assumes that social class differences cause variations in health status, rather than vice versa. One of the explanations proffered for the heat-related deaths in the Chicago heat wave, we may recall, was that people failed to take sufficient precautions; they perhaps did not drink enough water or use their air conditioning. Ways of living are presumed to vary between different social positions; in particular, people in lower social classes indulge in more unhealthy behaviours, such as smoking, drinking alcohol, eating more fat and sugar, and taking less exercise. And indeed many of these activities are significantly related to socio-economic position (Wanless, 2002). At one extreme, these lifestyle factors are seen to be in the control of the individual, and so it is up to the individual to alter his or her behaviour and nurture more healthy attitudes. At the other extreme, such behaviours are treated as being rooted in people's social circumstances, but nevertheless remain, from this perspective, the main cause of social inequalities in health. The behavioural perspective rests comfortably with prevailing medical and political ideologies which give primacy to the individual and are expounded in official documents.

4. *Materialist explanations.* This alternative social causation approach emphasizes the effects of social structure on health. In general, this approach focuses on the impact of factors such as poverty, the distribution of income, unemployment, housing conditions, pollution and working conditions in both the public and the domestic spheres (Blackburn, 1991). For example, when smoking and employment history are held constant, there still appears to be a relationship between poor housing and the presence of respiratory symptoms (Eames et al., 1993) and heart disease (Marmot, 2004).

Some argue that the cultural and material explanations can be conflated, pointing to the interaction between behavioural and structural factors, and suggest that it is more fruitful to try to find the right balance between them (MacIntyre et al., 1989). Others dispute this suggestion. Whilst accepting that it is essential to recognize that behaviours are not autonomous, they point out that to combine the two explanations

> is unhelpful because although it intends to emphasize the social rootedness of lifestyles, such theorizing tends to discount any influence of the social and material environment that is not mediated through behavioural patterns. Thus intervention becomes reduced to developing culturally sensitive methods for encouraging changes in lifestyle and neglects the possibility of change in the environment. (Davey Smith et al., 1990: 376)

Indeed, this comment in many ways anticipates New Labour's response to improving health, which emphasizes the importance of healthy lifestyles, albeit acknowledging the context of social inequalities (Department of Health, 2004b; chapter 10 below).

5. *Psycho-social explanations.* Two empirical observations which suggest that the social patterning of health cannot be fully explained by absolute material poverty prompted the development of this perspective. In his book *Unhealthy Societies: The Afflictions of Inequality*, Wilkinson (1996) presents data which show that national levels of life expectancy do not equate with national levels of wealth. Focusing on advanced capitalist societies, he found that the gross national product (GNP) of a nation is related to life expectancy. However, the central argument here is that it is not simply the case that the more wealthy a country is, the more healthy it is likely to be. Having explored this in relation to a range of health and social outcomes, Wilkinson and Pickett (2009) found that there is a threshold of average per capita income beyond which increased income does not lead to longer life. The key variable is inequality: the more egalitarian a nation is, the healthier its population will be. Inequality is detrimental to the health status not only of the poor, but of the population of the country as a whole. They found an association between income equality and the average life expectancy in a number of selected countries. Those countries which have a relatively equitable distribution of income – for example, the Netherlands, Norway and Japan – have relatively high life expectancies.

However, for a number of reasons we must be cautious when interpreting these data, and the work has been subjected to heated debate (Saunders, 2010). First, only some countries were selected for analysis, and so we cannot be certain that the same results would be found if other countries were included. Second, we cannot be sure that it is equality of income *per se* that affects life expectancy; it might in fact be something else about those countries which affects health (for example, provision and levels of education for the population as a whole). Third, it is possible that life expectancy reflects the past experiences of people living in a given country, rather than its present distribution of income. Nevertheless, other studies which have compared states or districts that varied in terms of income inequalities do lend further support to the findings that degrees of inequality can contribute to mortality (Lynch et al., 1998).

The second set of observations derives from the Whitehall study. It seems that there are 'fine grain' differences in health status between the relatively 'better off' groups of civil servants. Marmot (2004) and his colleagues were puzzled as to why a social class gradient is so evident amongst those who are not poor in an absolute sense. Rates of heart disease were found to be four times greater amongst the junior ranks of the civil service than the most senior grades. The gradient still holds after 'risk' factors such as smoking, blood pressure, cholesterol level and glucose tolerance have been taken into account (Wilkinson, 2000: 6).

These findings have led these authors to conclude that within the world's relatively rich countries, health inequalities can be explained by the psycho-social dimensions of inequalities (Elstad, 2002). This is summed up in the title of Marmot's (2004) book *Status Syndrome: How your Social Standing Directly Affects your Health and your Life Expectancy*. On this view inequality and social status can affect health in two main ways: lack of social cohesion and lack of self-esteem. Unequal societies, it is suggested, are less cohesive, and so are socially divisive. Such lack of cohesion results in people feeling more isolated and lacking social support. In addition, people lower down the social hierarchy feel less able to control their circumstances, a feeling which can be internalized and can reinforce anxiety and stress. Certainly there are numerous studies of the workplace (e.g., Siegrist, 2010; Siegrist and Marmot, 2004) and other circumstances (Nettleton and Burrows, 1998) which lend support to this thesis. Durkheimian in its orientation, this explanation highlights the salience of social integration, cohesion and degrees of what is referred to as 'social capital' (Putnam, 2000).

This focus on cohesion has resonances with the social ecology explanation articulated by Klinenberg in his heat-wave study. But this perspective also highlights the psychological impacts of social structures: 'We feel hurt, angry, belittled, annoyed and sometimes superior as the processes of social distinction and social exclusion thread their way between us' (Wilkinson, 1996: 226). Such psycho-social injuries, it is claimed, affect health *directly* by adversely affecting the cardiovascular system (e.g., blood pressure), the endocrine system (e.g., the secretion of cortisol) and the immune system (e.g., the number of T cells) (Elstad, 2002). They also affect health *indirectly* by inducing people to participate in 'unhealthy' activities. Some authors (S. Williams, 1998) have argued that an embodied approach to inequalities which reveals the interactive qualities of psychological, physiological and social structures may help to provide a way through the impasse of the agency and structure debate which remains a recurrent theme in this literature (see chapter 5).

These studies challenge fundamental assumptions inherent to neo-liberal market economies that presume economic growth is both possible and desirable. They point to a growing body of evidence that indicates that economic growth in the developed world is no longer improving health, happiness or measures of well-being. This thesis has been widely disseminated by Wilkinson and Pickett (2009) in their book *The Spirit Level: Why More Equal Societies Almost Always Do Better*. The title of the book encapsulates their thesis and they provide numerous illustrative examples of health and social issues (e.g., mortality, morbidity, teenage pregnancy, poor educational outcomes, drug use, mental health, obesity, homicide) that score worse in societies which are more unequal. They claim that greater degrees of inequality generate a host of problems associated with social differences, that this in turn gives rise to divisive class prejudices and crucially 'it also weakens community life, reduces trust, and increases violence' (Wilkinson and Pickett, 2009: 45). What is striking is the reception that the book has received. Perhaps in part because it is clearly aligned with an ideological position and for those on the political Left, it provides a valuable source of data and a persuasive argument. Perhaps too because of the vociferous nature of the criticism it has received, largely, though not exclusively from those with opposing political preferences. But much of the debate has centred on the methodologies used and the presentation and interpretation of the data. The sociologist Peter Saunders (2010) published a report with the provocative title *Beware False Prophets: Equality, the Good Society and The Spirit Level.* He claims that only one of the correlations in the book - that between infant mortality and income inequality - holds any validity, and that the other associations are either false or ambiguous. He claims Wilkinson and Pickett are 'alarmingly cavalier' (p. 27) in their use of regression analysis - whether bivariate or multivariate. For example, they are selective in the countries they include in their modelling and they ignore 'outliers', that is extreme cases which can distort the slope of a trend line making the associations appear deceptively clear cut. Another text with a similarly challenging title, *The Spirit Level Delusion: Fact-checking the Left's New Theory of Everything* (Snowdon, 2010) lends weight to Saunders' critique by suggesting the data are at best partial and at worse deceptive.

Thus we see that, like all the other explanations of inequalities in social class and socio-economic position, the psycho-social model of causation has been challenged. First, as we have just noted, the empirical observations themselves have been contested, with some analysts finding less consistent associations between degrees of inequality and mortality (Ross et al., 2000; Saunders, 2010). Second, the focus on the subjective and psychological dimensions of inequality serve to detract from the structural aspects, and so serve to reinforce blame and ultimately result in highly individualized responses to what are seen by many as political and structural issues (Lynch et al., 2000). Although the orientation of this perspective is on inequality *per se,* rather than the attributes and resources of individuals, the interpretation is framed in terms of individual consumption rather than collective production. Navarro (2004), for example, has argued that the health inequalities industry now focuses on individual indicators of class (e.g., income, education, car ownership, occupation) rather than on 'class relations', 'class struggle' and 'class exploitation'. In other words, it has become sanitized and individualized, and fails to incorporate sufficiently the ways in which political and economic processes which shape the distribution of power and resources (e.g., wealth, services and environment) determine health.

6. *Life-course explanation.* How circumstances, events and experiences influence a person's health from before they are born and throughout their whole lives is seen as crucial to understanding health inequalities by those who espouse the life-course approach. It is neatly summed up by Blane (1999: 64) as an approach that sees 'a person's biological status as a marker of their past social position and, through the structured nature of social processes, as liable to selective accumulation of future advantage or disadvantage. A person's past social experiences become written into the physiology and pathology of their body.'

As with the previous psycho-social explanation, it appears to be especially apposite to those countries whose major causes of death are non-infectious diseases, as there is evidence that the cumulative effect of adverse and stressful circumstances can contribute to such diseases. This is a relatively new vein of work, and spans a range of perspectives (Kuh and Ben-Shlomo, 1997, 2002). A 'life-course political economy explanation', for example, argues that these influences will, in turn, be shaped by the political and economic context of a person's life. Other analysts seek to explore how critical times or experiences (such as serious illness) interact with other events with the result that they may have long-term consequences. The empirical basis of the perspective is facilitated by the availability of longitudinal studies and statistical techniques which enable researchers to examine how 'health in adult life may be the result of complex combinations of circumstances taking place over time' (Bartley, 2004: 103). It comprises the mirror image of the health selection argument outlined above. Rather than focusing on how people's health status selectively influences their social status, it claims that people who are already socially disadvantaged often endure an 'accumulation of disadvantage'.

Marsh et al.'s (1999) study of the lifetime effects of housing circumstances is an example of this approach. These authors undertook an analysis of the national child development survey (NCDS), a longitudinal study based on data on all children born in Great Britain between 3 and 9 March 1958. In contrast to cross-sectional studies, it allows investigators to ascertain the extent to which factors have long-term effects. Here they explore the proposition associated with life-course theories that there could be an accumulation of risks associated with housing deprivation throughout the course of life. Whilst their findings are equivocal, they are able to conclude overall that 'housing history matters', as adults who are currently living in good housing circumstances are more likely to be ill if they experienced adverse housing conditions earlier in life. Their overall conclusion is materialist: 'The impact of multiple housing deprivation would appear to be the same order of magnitude as addressing the issue of smoking and the risk to health posed by multiple housing deprivation seems to be, on average, greater than that posed by excessive alcohol consumption' (1999). Whilst this approach has many merits, it is not without problems. For example, a significant proportion of the sample had infectious diseases in childhood, a situation less likely to occur today. In addition, the researchers may be constrained by the questions asked, and measures used decades ago which may be 'out of sync' with contemporary society. For example, the issue of gender was in the main overlooked in analysis of health inequalities until the 1980s. It is to this dimension of inequality that we now turn.

Gender and health

The evidence

Prior to the 1980s men and women were rarely distinguished within analyses of social class and health, and when women's mortality rates have been taken into account, women have tended to be classified by the occupation of their husbands or, if single, by their own occupation. Occupation and occupational classifications were often more relevant to men's work than women's (Arber, 1990: 85). The picture was misleading (H. Roberts, 1990). However, alternative measures more suited to the lives of women were devised (Arber et al., 1986; Barker and Roberts, 1986). In recent decades, work on gender tended to focus on women's health in order to address the disproportionate attention given to men. Whilst women in lower social classes have been found to have worse health than middle-class women, the gradient is not as steep as it is for men. However, when other socio-economic indicators are used, such as composite measures of housing tenure, car ownership and occupation, the relationship between socio-economic status and mortality becomes more significant.

For many decades the research on gender and health was dominated by the orthodoxy that 'men die quicker but that women were sicker'. Today, however, it is widely acknowledged that associations between gender and health are more complex than this dictum implies, and that they vary considerably over time and between places. During the last few decades, life expectancy has increased globally, and women's life expectancy has increased faster than that of men, although there are exceptions, not least in southern African countries where women are increasingly at risk from HIV/AIDS (see chapter 3).

Arber and Thomas (2001: 101–2) identify four patterns of gender inequalities in mortality, which in turn they map on to differential socio-economic and political contexts. First are regions where 'women outlive men by 5–7 years': as noted above, in the UK, where the life expectancy for men is 75.7 and for women 80.4 (ONS, 2005), in the USA, 74 and 80 years, in Japan 78 and 85 years, and so on. Some developing countries also fit this pattern: for example, in Brazil in 2000 male life expectancy was 64 and women's was 73, and Peru it was 67 and 72 years respectively (United Nations, 2004). Arber and Thomas suggest that the gap between men and women is closing, and this may be due to changes in gender roles, 'risky' health behaviours and women's participation in the paid work-force.

Second, countries where 'women outlive men by 2–4 years' tend to be 'transitional societies', where there is a decline in previously high maternal mortality rates and where women are structurally - materially and economically - disadvantaged. Certainly maternal related deaths vary dramatically: whilst in developed regions of the world, there are 20 maternal deaths for 100,000 live births, this rises to 440 deaths per 100,000 live births in developing regions. Whilst in northern Africa there are 130, in sub-Saharan Africa there are 920 maternal related deaths per 100,000 live births (United Nations, 2004).

Third, countries where there is 'no gender difference or men outlive women' are currently countries in which women experience low social status and are disadvantaged in terms of access to nutrition, health care and education. Globally, boys' infant mortality is higher than girls', but this tends to be reversed in countries where gender-based discrimination outweighs biological advantage (United Nations, 2004). In Afghanistan, for example, the life expectancy for both men and women is 43 years. In Bangladesh, women's life expectancy has only very recently exceeded men's, and is now 62 years for women and 61 years for men, with a very similar pattern occurring in India and Pakistan.

Finally, countries where 'women outlive men by 8 or more years' tend to be associated with major socio-economic transformations. For example, countries in the former Soviet Union reveal this pattern: the life expectancy for men and women are 65 and 75 years in the Ukraine, 61 and 73 years in Russia, and 68 and 78 years in Lithuania.

These gendered patterns of mortality indicate that there is no inevitability about the gender differences in life expectancy. They are historically and socially contingent, and may well look very different in coming years and indeed there are indications of changes in wealthy regions. For example, in the UK although women on average outlive men, the gap is decreasing with men's life expectancy gaining more quickly than women's; in 1969 the gap was 6.3 years, by 2007 it had reduced to 4 (Annandale, 2009: 127–8).

Turning to morbidity, there are few differences between men and women for most diseases in most Western nations, and in particular for those which are the major causes of death, such as cancers and heart-related diseases (Bartley, 2004: 139). This is especially so when socio-economic differences are taken into account (Emslie et al., 1999). For example, cancers are the major cause of death for women in the UK, and are second to circulatory diseases for men (ONS, 2005). The differences between men and women who report a long-standing limiting illness and restricted activity in the previous 14 days are of marginal significance. However, the 'healthy life expectancy' for women is 69 years and 67 for men, and so as a result of living longer they will have more years in poor health (ONS, 2005).

It seems, then, that the long-held assumption that women are more ill than men is not so simple. This idea may have arisen because women were more ill in the past, or it may be a function of the type of data cited. For example, if health service data is used as an indicator of morbidity it would appear that women are more unwell than men. For example, in 2002, 13 per cent of men and 19 per cent of women had visited their GP 14 days prior to being interviewed. The gap is greater amongst the 16–44 age-group (9 per cent of men and 18 per cent of women), but narrows in the 45–64 age-group to 15 per cent and 17 per cent respectively (ONS, 2005). Data on stays in hospital also show variations between men and women within different age-groups. One explanation may be that women's excess use of GP services may be more for health reasons (e.g., associated with reproduction) than for illness. Certainly MacFarlane (1990: 44–5) found that when conditions associated with reproduction are excluded, the difference in admissions of men and women between 15 and 44 years virtually disappears. Amongst adults, women are more likely than men to experience neurotic disorders (e.g., depression and anxiety); however, boys are more likely to experience mental health disorders than are girls. Relatedly, suicide rates in England and Wales are much higher for males than females of 15–19 years. In 2000, the suicide rates increased steeply to 8 per 100,000 males and 3 per 100,000 females. These data are of course only illustrative, but the key point is that the picture is a complex and changing one, and data must always be considered in the socio-historical context.

An historical study by Hunt (2002) illustrates this point very well. Using longitudinal data collected as part of the West of Scotland Twenty-07 Study, she compared two generations of women born in the same geographical locality only 20 years apart. There are many differences between women born in the early 1930s and in the early 1950s. First, changes in life expectancy; in the 1930s it was around 58 for men and 62 for women, but by the 1950s the gender gap had increased with life expectancies rising to 68 and 74 years. Second, infant mortality rates had halved in this same period. Third, marriage too changed, with rates of divorce increasing significantly for the later cohort, and this in turn is related to the growing number of lone parents that is a feature of contemporary life. Fourth, the younger 1950s cohort had fewer children. Finally, the socio-economic circumstances of these women born only 20 years apart were very different. The early 1930s was a time of austerity; whereas for those born in the 1950s, much of their lives were in an era when it is was reputed that 'we had never had it so good'. Welfare – education, health care, employment – would benefit the younger group. We can see, therefore, that when we use indicators or measures of concepts such as gender, we may often be tapping into a complex set of historically specific processes. This also has implications for the life-course perspective on health inequalities discussed above.

Explaining the links between gender and health

As we have seen, gender differences in mortality and morbidity are far from straightforward and vary over time and place, which makes the task of explaining what is going on very difficult indeed. Nevertheless, in relation to the gendered variability of mortality rates, Arber and Thomas (2001: 103–4) usefully discern seven explanations, the first three of which they find of limited value. The first, *biological* explanation, which focuses on genetic and physiological differences, they find wanting because it could not explain the wide and shifting mortality gaps between men and women. They find the second, *psycho-social* explanation, which highlights personality differences, to be of marginal significance, although degrees of 'masculinity' and 'femininity' may have some relevance (Hunt, 2002; Emslie et al., 1999). Arber and Thomas find some evidence to support the view that differential *risk behaviours* are likely to contribute to differences. For example, over time the relative rates of men and women drinking alcohol and smoking have altered. In the 1970s men were much more likely to smoke than women were; now there is little difference, and amongst the younger age-groups women are more likely to smoke than men (ONS, 2005). Waldron (2000) proposes the 'gender role modernization thesis' to capture the way in which socio-economic and culture transformations influence these behavioural trends.

The fourth set of explanations relate to *occupational and work-related factors*. Being in paid employment and educational qualifications are increasingly important indicators which differentiate health, especially amongst women (Lahelma et al., 2001). Elderly women have lower personal incomes than do elderly men, and this is associated with the nature of their paid employment over the life-course. They are significantly more likely to suffer from substantial functional disabilities. The combination of these two variables becomes evident from data on gender inequalities in later life. Popay and Bartley (1989) have researched the health consequences of domestic labour. The 'labour conditions' of the home - air pollution, noise, damp, temperature extremes, access to lavatory and access to first-aid facilities - were found to impact upon health status. With the exception of noise, overall, women seem to work in more favourable conditions in the formal labour market than they do in domestic labour settings. This is particularly significant given the findings of a survey of 1,700 households in London, which found that women with children spend on average 64 hours per week on domestic labour if they have a full-time paid job; 75 hours per week if they have a part-time job, and 87 hours a week if they have no paid job. In total, 57 per cent of the women (with or without children) in the sample 'laboured' in the home for at least five hours a day, compared to 14 per cent of men (Popay and Bartley, 1989: 91).

A fifth explanation highlights the differential *social roles and relationships*, which in turn must be understood in the wider social context. You may recall that gender was an important factor in the Chicago heat wave, with men being more vulnerable due to their social isolation and lack of social support. More recently, in a UK context, Perren et al. (2004) found that men living alone were more likely to have frequent conversations with their neighbours. However, they were less likely than women living alone to have relationships which involved providing and receiving favours, a difference which the authors conclude 'may contribute to the elevated risk of social isolation among lone older men' (p. 965).

The unequal distribution of *power and resources within the home* explains the health status of men and women. The intra-household distributions of power, money and labour disadvantage women throughout the world. For throughout the world women do disproportionately most of the labour, yet earn significantly less and have less control over domestic resources (Moss, 2002). Until recent decades, women's economic disadvantage within the home remained invisible. Research into the distribution of resources within households has shown that women fare badly and that money and goods are not distributed evenly (Pahl, 1990). Furthermore, women spend relatively more of their personal income on household goods – especially food – than do men, and are more likely to be responsible for 'maintaining the material and psychosocial environment of the home and well being of those who live there' (Graham, 2002: 248).

For Arber and Thomas (2001), their final explanation, which highlights the *social structural differences within society*, is the most important. There are differences in mortality and morbidity between men and women, and there are also differences among women themselves which show that material circumstances play an important part in determining the health status of women. For example, women are more likely to be lone parents, which in turn is associated with material disadvantage and with poorer health for both mothers and their children (Arber and Cooper, 2000; Graham, 2002). Gender differences are also evident among lone parents. Popay and Jones (1990) found not only that lone parents have poorer health than parents in couples, but also that lone fathers had different health problems from lone mothers. The former were more likely to suffer long-standing illness, probably because they are older and more likely to be widowed. However, on all other indices, lone mothers had worse health than lone fathers, and they were also found to have worse socio-economic circumstances: they were younger; they were less likely to be owner-occupiers; they were less likely to be in employment; and they were much more likely to be in receipt of means-tested state benefits. Arber and Thomas thus conclude: 'Women in most societies are more likely than men to be poor, have less education, and live in disadvantaged material circumstances. The feminization of poverty in the US and UK has been widely acknowledged, and is particularly associated with lone motherhood and older women' (2001: 108). This is why it is crucial, as Hunt (2002) suggests (see above), that any analysis of gender differences is 'explained' in relation to the socio-historical context and is cognizant of socio-economic transformations.

Annandale's (2009) exhaustive account of such transformations in her book *Women's Health and Social Change* represents such an analysis. She also offers a theorization that helps to make sense of recent data on gender and health. As noted above, the gap between life expectancy between men and women in post-industrial societies is narrowing and this she suggests must be understood in terms of the demise of binary sex/gender differences and the advent of not only more diverse gendered patterns but also inherently unstable gendered identities. She refers to patriarchal capitalism of the twentieth century as the 'old single system' with sex differences corresponding to gender, and the lives of men and women being scripted in terms of patterns of working - paid and unpaid - in relation to the capitalist industrial economies. The twenty-first century is characterized by a 'new single system' of patriarchal capitalism, where divisions between men and women are increasingly blurred and fragmented with significant changes in, for example, paid employment with women entering some occupations and professions at the same rates as men and gendered pay gaps decreasing and so on. Women also take part in social participation and consumption associated with lifestyles and, as a result, the binary identities between men and women are less clear cut. But this is both liberating and constraining and most especially in relation to health, it provides scope for the marketization of products - such as alcohol or cigarettes - to women. Women are presented ambiguously at one and the same time embracing girl power and yet succumbing to ladette culture - exemplified in the moral panic associated with binge drinking and the inability to cope with the new demands brought by these new 'freedoms'. Annandale cites the example of the book and film *Bridget Jones Diary*, which 'paints a rather bleak picture of women who are not really sure that they want to be "empowerd", cannot cope - Bridget is frequently seen drinking and smoking - and for whom all that matters ultimately is finding a "knight in shining armour"' (p. 121). In sum,

> But the most important point in all this is the potent metanarrative within these mixed messages: liberation has let women down and in the process generated a lucrative market of unstable identities and individual women who need to be shown in this light. (Annandale, 2009: 121)

In a context where the major causes of death are cancers and heart-related conditions which are largely preventable and associated with ways of living, the targeting of unhealthy products and the construction of gendered consumers is salient to our understanding of shifting patterns of gendered health inequalites.

The complexities of gender differences in health are further evident when examined in relation to different ethnic groups. As we noted above, the idea that women are 'sicker' than men is no longer supported by evidence in the general population. However, H. Cooper (2002) finds that women's health fares less well than men's does amongst minority ethnic groups. Overall, self-reported ill health is greater for ethnic minority groups, and, in addition, there are marked gender differences amongst minority ethnic groups, with women being 'sicker' than men. For example, Pakistani and Bangladeshi women report significantly worse health than Pakistani and Bangladeshi men do. Occupational class plays a limited role in explaining these differences; by contrast, educational qualifications and being in paid employment play a greater role. Thus there are associations between 'ethnicity' and health, and it is to these that we now turn.

'Race' and health

As with gender and class, there is considerable debate about the terminology, measures and explanations associated with ethnicity and health. Terminology varies over time (Aspinall, 2002). The term 'race' is expressed with quotation marks to highlight the fact that the attribution of genetically distinct groups is socially and politically constructed. 'Ethnicity' is often taken to refer to cultural traditions that provide boundaries between 'groups'. The term 'ethnic minority' (e.g., Pakistani or Irish) is used to highlight their statistical minority and, for some, disadvantage in terms of institutionalized power relations. Bartley (2004: 151) helpfully adopts the term '"racial or ethnic minority" to refer to any group of people who are likely to be at risk of unfavourable treatment because of their national origins, shared social histories, or religion'. As Karlsen and Nazroo (2002: 2) point out, ethnicity represents more than a social structural location; it also represents an identity which is in turn influenced by agency.

Since the 1970s there has been a growing epidemiological literature on 'race' and health. This has shown that health status is 'racially' patterned. Only relatively recently has there been a comparable growth in sociological research (Ahmad, 1993). This imbalance in the literature has resulted in a number of consequences. First, those studies which have been carried out tend to adopt a biomedical approach, in that they focus on the biological and individual characteristics of different social groups. Second, there has been a tendency to focus on certain conditions which are more common among some ethnic groups, such as sickle cell anaemia, thalassaemia and rickets, to the exclusion of more common health problems. Third, 'race' has in some instances come to be treated as an independent variable, which in itself is taken to be a cause of health and illness. Fourth, the concepts of 'race' and 'ethnicity' are treated as discrete and unproblematic concepts, and the fact that they are socially created categories often goes unacknowledged. Finally, the extent to which 'race' is an indicator of social relations which are shaped by nationalism, colonialism, imperialism and racism tends to go unexplored. For this reason the epidemiological 'evidence' on 'race' and health needs to be treated with some caution.

More recent sociological analyses of 'race' and health have begun to reveal the complexities of the topic. Although, overall, ethnic minority groups have higher rates of mortality and morbidity, there is considerable variation between ethnic groups and between conditions (Nazroo, 2001).

The evidence

Some of the main contours of the patterning of health by 'racial or ethnic minority group' have been summarized *inter alia* by Smaje (1995), Nazroo (2001) and Davey Smith et al. (2002). People who were born in the Indian subcontinent have higher than average rates of heart disease, diabetes and tuberculosis. However, they have lower rates of certain cancers and bronchitis. People born in African and Caribbean countries have higher rates of strokes, high blood pressure and diabetes. Whilst around a third of all male deaths in the UK are from circulatory diseases, this rises to around one half of all deaths of men under 50 who were born in the Indian subcontinent. SMRs for both men and women vary according to their country of birth for all causes of death. For example, men who were born in Bangladesh, Ireland, Scotland and West/South Africa have higher levels of mortality for all causes of death. However, whilst the SMRs from lung cancer are high for both men and women born in Scotland and Ireland, they are relatively low for those born in the other regions. Ischaemic heart disease, by contrast, is a major cause of death amongst all groups with the exception of those born in West/South Africa (Davey Smith et al., 2002).

Significant differences have also been found when birth statistics have been analysed in relation to the country of origin of mothers. Data on low birth weight, still births, perinatal and infant mortality rates are important indicators of health status more generally, and especially of the health status of women. The perinatal mortality rate for babies born to mothers who themselves were born in the UK in 2002 was 7.8 per 1,000 live births; this rises to 10.5 for mothers born in Bangladesh, 10.8 for mothers born in India, 14.5 for mothers born in Pakistan, and 15.4 for mothers born in the Caribbean (ONS, 2005). The picture created by the analysis of birth statistics is, however, very complex (Parsons et al., 1993: 59–60). In 1990 still births and infant mortality rates for babies born to mothers in the New Commonwealth were 40 per cent higher than for those born to mothers born in the UK. However, whilst still birth rates are considerably higher for mothers from Bangladesh than from the UK, their neonatal rates are lower.

Problems with measurement

Collating data on 'race' and health is extremely problematic. There are no universally agreed definitions or categories of 'ethnic' or 'racial' groups (Aspinall, 2002). Aggregate headings such as 'Asian' tend to conflate a wide range of factors which might include skin colour, place of birth, religion, language and so on, which might better be treated in terms of their own specificity. Reporting data using place of birth as an indicator of 'race' or 'ethnicity' can add further confusion; about 40 per cent of the UK black population were born in the UK, so such data are bound to be misleading. It is possible, therefore, that they tell us more about the health of people who have migrated than about the health status of black people living in Britain.

Perhaps the most significant problem of measurement in relation to 'race and ethnicity' and health is the lack of conceptual clarification about the concept itself. Is race presumed by the researchers to be a biological or a social characteristic? What the selected indicators purport to measure, and how they are interpreted, influence the type of explanations that are offered for health inequalities patterned by 'race' and 'ethnicity'.

Explaining racial and ethnic inequalities

Davey Smith and his colleagues (2002) have usefully identified seven 'models of explanation' for the 'racial' and 'ethnic' patterning of health from the ongoing debates. As we noted in the section on class and health, '*artefact*' explanations draw attention to the processes involved in the data collection and measurement. One of the strengths of this interpretation is that it reminds us that we need to be vigilant about the ways in which concepts and indicators are used and constructed. As we have seen, trying to collect data on 'ethnicity' is highly complex, and it is likely that some data may, at the very worst, be spurious or misleading. However, the weight of evidence now is such that most accept that variations in health status and life chances do exist between ethnic groups.

Biological factors such as genetic variations are sometimes cited as the reasons for differences in the prevalence of conditions such as diabetes and hypertension. It is important to recognize here that genetic factors, and indeed other physiological characteristics, are meshed within and shaped by social and environmental factors.

Such explanations may have a ready appeal in the face of less tangible social explanations. McDermott (1998), for example, describes how the so-called thrifty genotype hypothesis was developed to explain the high levels of diabetes amongst 'post-colonial indigenous societies', with the result that alternative explanations went unexamined. A consequence is that public health measures to manage and alleviate the disease were not pursued. She concludes her analysis of these debates thus:

> Thus diabetes in Aborigines has been defined, by non-Aboriginal scientists, simply as a problem of 'race' and 'genes' in a changing environment. Race becomes a biological entity and an independent risk factor, reified over and over again in repeated studies of disease which take no account of socio-economic status, history or culture. (1998: 1194)

Although genetic explanations may have some influence in the prevalence of inherited blood disorders (e.g., thalassaemia), and may also play a role in other diseases and infant mortality rates, they are unable to account for the wider 'racial and ethnic' patterning of health status. The '*migration*' mode of explanation suggests that the social processes associated with migration itself may contribute to the apparent differences in the health status of different groups. It may be that only those who are healthy tend to migrate; or conversely, the experience of migration itself may be stressful and damaging to health. However, such explanations are likely to have limited impact upon people's health status over time, so can only form part of the story.

A third set of explanations are those which suggest that *socio-economic factors* such as occupational class, income, housing tenure and so on may account for the differences. Certainly, some ethnic minorities – for example, Bangladeshis, Pakistanis and Carribeans – are over-represented in the relatively disadvantaged socio-economic groups and are more likely to be unemployed (Nazroo, 1997). Moreover, there are significant variations in terms of income between ethnic groups. For example, the mean income of Pakistani and Bangladeshi households which are in social classes I and II is less than the mean income of 'White' households who are classified as being in social classes IV and V (Davey Smith et al., 2002: 268). It is claimed, therefore, that it is not ethnicity *per se* that accounts for the differences, but the socio-economic factors that are experienced by those in particular groupings.

A fourth, 'popular' category of explanations is that linked to the '*culture, beliefs and behaviour*' of different social groups. As we have already seen in relation to social class, cultural accounts explain differences in health in terms of people's behaviours. Just as the working classes are presumed to lead more unhealthy lifestyles than the middle classes and are less likely to undertake health-related activities, so there is a presumption that some groups have unhealthy lifestyles, which are shaped by their religious or cultural beliefs. Most commonly in these types of explanations, patterns of health-related behaviours such as diet, smoking, exercise, child-rearing practices and low uptake of screening services are invoked. For example, higher rates of rickets have been found among Asian children, and this may be due to a lack of vitamin D. Ahmad (1989) has pointed out that this is invariably explained in terms of inappropriate dietary practices and the wearing of clothes which restrict the amount of sunlight which may be absorbed by the skin. Another cultural explanation which is drawn upon is consanguinity – marriages between individuals who are second cousins or more closely related (*The Lancet*, 1991). It has been argued that this results in higher levels of autosomal recessive diseases. There are, however, two main problems with this explanation. First, its effects tend to be overemphasized; Ahmad (1993: 21; 1996) has noted that '[h]igher rates of consanguinity among Asians, particularly Pakistanis, in Britain has become the ultimate "explanatory hypothesis" within medicine', and a growing number of researchers have begun 'to hang anything from poor birth "outcome" to blood disorders, cancers, diseases of the eye, and much more onto this new-found explanatory peg'. Second, the health and social benefits of marriages between relatives are ignored. For example, marriages between relatives may be due to a lack of suitable partners because of geographical or cultural isolation; the preservation of property, especially land; wives may feel more comfortable and receive more social support by marrying into a family where their mother-in-law is also their aunt; and it is alleged that immigration officials are more likely to consider planned marriages genuine if they involve marrying a relative (*The Lancet*, 1991).

Epidemiological studies which concentrate only on the relationship between 'race' and health differences to the exclusion of other social factors tend to explain their findings in cultural terms. This is because it is often assumed that the differences are due to the characteristics of an 'ethnic group' rather than the wider social context. The need for health education campaigns is therefore seen as the obvious conclusion (see chapter 10). For example, Balarajan's (1991: 563) study of different rates of heart disease concludes that: 'Particularly worrying is the increase in ischaemic heart disease among immigrants of Indian origin; it calls for further research as well as specially targeted public health campaigns.'

The problem with this approach is that it blames individuals, pathologizes cultures, and fails to address the main causes of health differences. The solutions offered will be circumscribed.

> In this perspective, racialized inequalities in both health and access to health care are explained as resulting from cultural differences and deficits. Integration on the part of the minority communities, and cultural understanding and ethnic sensitivity on the part of the health professional, then become the obvious solution; personal and institutional racist and racial discrimination have no part in this equation. (Ahmad, 1993: 2)

It is certainly the case that rates of smoking and drinking alcohol vary between '"racial" and ethnic groups'. Forty-four per cent of Bangladeshi men smoke cigarettes, followed by 39 per cent of Irish men and 35 per cent of Black Caribbean men. This compares with 27 per cent of men in the general population and 17 per cent of Chinese men (Department of Health, 1999). The picture for women, however, is very different; although in the general population there is little difference between men and women, only a tiny minority of Bangladeshi women smoke. Healthy behaviours and 'healthy' cultural practices tend to be overlooked. For example, among 'Asian' women there are lower rates of smoking and alcohol consumption. A consultative study carried out to elicit the views of the community on an English Health Authority's Strategy to improve health was told by a group of Asian women living in a run-down area of a northern city that 'this doesn't affect any of them because they don't smoke and they don't drink alcohol'. They identified social isolation, fear and frequency of racist attacks, and cold and damp housing as the main causes of their poor physical and mental health (Nettleton, 1993: 25).

Proponents of the cultural explanations also point to the associations between religion and health. Muslims, followed by Sikhs, for example, experience worse reported health status than members of other religions such as Jews and Christians. Whilst religious beliefs are often associated with health-related activities, they are far from straightforward, and can change over time and place. But it is extremely difficult to disaggregate these factors, and evidence of associations with health outcomes tends to be contradictory. As we saw in our 'heat wave' example at the beginning of this chapter, cultural explanations are often based on crude assumptions, stereotypes and myths, rather than evidence.

The fifth 'model of explanation' highlights *racism*, which affects health status in a number of ways. There is growing empirical evidence from both the USA and the UK that both the direct experiences of racism and fear of racism affect health. Karlsen and Nazroo (2004) found that those people who were worried about racial harassment were 61 per cent more likely to report that their health was less good than those who did not. There is a close interaction between this model of explanation and the socio-economic one noted above which suggests that one of the main reasons why ethnic minorities have been found to experience higher rates of disease and illness is that they are more likely to be materially deprived. This in turn is often associated with institutional racism. Blackburn (1991: 36–7) summarizes this view when she points out that 'people from minority ethnic groups, particularly black people, are more likely to be unemployed, or be in low paid jobs, living in poor housing and live in areas that lack adequate social and educational resources than white people. Black people share the disadvantages of white working-class people and more.' The 'more' that she refers to includes the racism and discrimination which black people routinely experience. Racism occurs at both institutional and individual levels. Black people are more likely to live in areas which are materially deprived, and as the 2001 Census shows, ethnic minority communities are concentrated in inner city areas and are unevenly distributed regionally. They are also more likely to face discrimination when trying to secure housing (Ginsberg and Watson, 1992). Furthermore, whilst 2 per cent of white groups live in overcrowded conditions, 7 per cent of Indian households, 9 per cent of black households, and 23 per cent of Pakistani and Bangladeshi groups do so (Harrison with Phillips, 2003).

Such experiences have been shaped by Britain's colonial heritage (F. Williams, 1989). Whilst black people have lived in the UK for more than 500 years, a significant proportion were encouraged to come during the post-war years when labour was in short supply. There was active recruitment, supported by the British government, by the NHS, London Transport and the British Hotels and Restaurants Association (Patel, 1993: 116). Black people are still over-represented in low-paid manual occupations, in hazardous industries such as textiles and clothing, and in domestic work, and are more likely to have to do shift work. They are also over-represented in those industries which are especially vulnerable in times of recession, and so job insecurity is high (Bhat et al., 1988). This history is captured by one elderly Asian woman in a study of mine (Nettleton, 1993: 38): 'These parents, once they were wanted, they brought them; they brought us here when they wanted us, now we are here and we are old and crippled, they have left us to die.' Indeed, the health needs of black elders have been neglected, and service delivery can be overtly racist (Patel, 1993). Part of the neglect may be born of racist stereotyping; for example, it is sometimes assumed that all Asian people live in extended families, and so do not require support, whereas, as seen above, a prime concern for some Asian women is in fact social isolation, loneliness and fear of crime (Nettleton, 1993).

Health service access and use is the final category of explanation offered by Davey Smith and his colleagues. Proponents of these explanations point to the unequal access to care, with people from ethnic groups being placed at a disadvantage. Certainly the routes to health care are complex, and inequalities in the provision and use of health services are well documented (Acheson Report, 1998).

It is evident from these seven sets of explanations that the issue of ethnic variations in health status is complex. It is unlikely that any one explanation could account for the differences found in the data on ethnic variations and health. When assessing the merits and de-merits of these explanations, it is important to pay careful attention to the available empirical evidence. It is all too easy to conjecture on the basis of the data and to conclude that apparent differences between ethnic minority groups may be intrinsically associated with a given group's 'ethnicity' or 'race' – their genes, their culture, their behaviours – and so may fail to see that these in turn are shaped by other social, economic or political factors.

The racial patterning of health and illness cannot be understood without an appreciation of the wider experiences of black people, which are shaped by a society which has been historically, and indeed remains, inherently racist. When we find links between 'ethnicity', 'race' and health status, it is therefore not something inherent in 'race', 'identity' or 'culture' that shapes people's health trajectory, but something inherent to the social context within which we must live our lives.

Place and health

One of the striking findings with respect to the heat-related deaths in Chicago was the extent to which they varied between two adjacent localities. You may recall Klinenberg's argument that the social and physical environment was critical to the precipitation of heat-related deaths. No doubt you will have walked around contrasting social and physical environments in urban localities and become aware of the variable exposure to health risks, which in turn may have induced differential feelings and experiences. But is there any evidence that the area in which one lives in and of itself can affect one's health?

The evidence

Mortality and morbidity are in fact spatially patterned. Obviously differences in the geographical distribution of social factors known to be associated with health, such as social class, 'race', gender and age, will be reflected in marked regional differences in health. Certainly those areas which score high on indices of deprivation are found to have higher levels of mortality. Within the UK there is a clear north–south divide in terms of health status. The life chances of those living in wealthy and relatively poor areas also reveal significant disparities. Premature deaths are much higher in Scotland than they are in England and Wales and in areas of multiple deprivation (Palmer et al., 2004). People resident in the north of England are a fifth more likely to experience premature (<75 years) death than those in the south, a difference that has endured and changed little between 1965 and 2008 (Hacking et al., 2011). In the north-east the male SMR is 114, whereas in the east and south-east it is 91. This divide is also found between regions in England and Wales. In 2003 the SMR for men in Norfolk, Suffolk and Cambridgeshire was 90, compared to 130 in Merthyr Tydfil (ONS, 2005). What is striking is the persistence of these geographical patterns:

> When considered by tenth of poverty, by the year 2007 for every 100 people under the age of 65 dying in the best-off areas, 199 were dying in the poorest tenth of areas. This is the highest relative inequality recorded since at least 1921. When we looked at people aged under 75, for every 100 people dying in the best-off areas, 188 were dying in the poorest tenth of areas. That is the highest ratio of inequality recorded since at least 1990. (Thomas et al., 2010)

The differences between mortality and morbidity rates between the so-called industrialized and developing nations are staggering. It is likely that the data on developing countries underestimate rates of disease and deaths because of the difficulties in obtaining reliable data (Timaeus et al., 1988). Nevertheless, it is evident that life expectancies vary throughout the world (United Nations, 2004). Life expectancies in countries such as Sierra Leone and Malawi are around half those of the rich post-industrial countries. But the geographical picture is more complex. In India the state of Kerala has an infant mortality rate of 17 per 1,000 live births, yet in Uttar Pradesh the rate is 99 per 1,000, and in Rajasthan it is 84. Although these areas have comparable incomes, they vary in terms of medical facilities, and crucially, women have greater participation in education and are less likely to marry under the age of 18 (Marmot, 2004: 186). The locally elected Communist councils have invested in the quality of the social environment and worked to buffer the effects of free markets. This is in contrast to the USA, as Marmot observes elsewhere:

> Walk the slums of Dhaka, in Bangladesh, or Accra, in Ghana, and it is not difficult to see how the urban environment of poor countries could be responsible for bad health. Walk north from Manhattan's museum district to Harlem, or east London's financial district to its old East End, and you will be struck by the contrast between rich and poor, existing cheek by jowl. It is less immediately obvious why there should be health differences between rich and poor areas of the same city. It is even less obvious, from casual inspection of the physical environment, why life expectancy for you black men in Harlem should be less than in Bangladesh. (2001: 134)

Explanations

The extent to which geographical location affects health independently of these other factors is extremely difficult to ascertain. Analytically, it is necessary to distinguish between what are called 'compositional factors' of individuals who live in an area (such as gender, age and material circumstances) and the 'contextual factors' of the area itself, although in practice they are inextricably interlinked (Curtis, 2004: 101). Studies of health inequalities have focused on the former, however, not least because of the hazards of committing the 'ecological fallacy' whereby individual-level relationships are inferred from aggregate-level data (MacIntyre, 2004). It may also be to do with a world-view which is inherently individualistic. As MacIntyre points out:

> Although sociology is supposed to focus on social structures and social relationships, all too often in the field of social inequalities in health we have tended to focus on individuals and their behaviours rather than on the environments to which they are exposed (perhaps because health and illness is expressed in individuals). (2000: 18)

Through a comparison of two areas of Glasgow, MacIntyre and her colleagues (2002) found that individuals who have similar compositional factors are likely to have better health if they live in more affluent and 'attractive' areas.

> Even for individuals who are similarly situated in terms of their personal circumstances (for example with the same income, family size, and tenure of house), it seems likely that living in the NW [the better-off area] would be more conducive to health than living in the SW [the worse-off area]; healthy foodstuffs are available, and cheaper, locally, there are more sporting recreation facilities within easy reach, better public transport, more extensive primary health services and a less threatening local environment. (2002: 288)

A growing number of studies endorse the thesis that the area in which one lives affects one's health even after other individual characteristics such as education, ethnicity and employment are taken into account (Wiggins et al., 2002; Stafford and Marmot, 2003). These findings support the view that policies to overcome health inequalities need to be orientated towards places as well as people.

Interestingly, regional variations in mortality rates do not reflect variations in the provision of health care (Eames et al., 1993). Indeed, this would support the McKeown thesis, discussed above, that in general significant improvements in overall health status lie beyond the scope of health care services. Taking an international perspective, Kim and Moody (1992) examined the impact of expenditure on health resources in 117 countries, and found that the amount of resources invested did not make a significant contribution to infant mortality rates, although, by contrast, greater investment in other socio-economic resources (such as levels of education, calorific intake, safe water supplies, etc.) did.

The causes of death and disease throughout the world also vary considerably. Demographers and epidemiologists speak of a *health transition*, which refers to the changes in the nature and extent of ill health throughout geographical regions. Essentially they have identified a shift in causes of mortality and morbidity which is associated with socio-economic changes (Lopez, 1990). The health transition refers to improved levels of health, with a decline in infectious diseases and a relative increase in non-communicable degenerative diseases such as circulatory conditions, neoplasms (cancers), diseases of the digestive system and congenital conditions (D. R. Phillips, 1990: 35; Kjellstrom and Rosenstock, 1990; Curtis, 2004). Infectious and parasitic diseases such as leprosy, diarrhoeal disease, tuberculosis and malaria have specific viral or bacterial causes, but resistance to them is mediated by socio-economic factors. They are not simply 'tropical' diseases, as they were previously prevalent in Western countries (Doyal with Pennell, 1979).

Related to this is the notion of *epidemiological transition*, which suggests that improved social, economic and health conditions cause a transition from short life expectancy, with high rates of infant mortality from infectious diseases, to increased survival, with a greater proportion of deaths from degenerative diseases. Paradoxically, those factors such as industrial development which have often been associated with the decline of infectious diseases also contribute to the relative increase of non-communicable disease. Kjellstrom and Rosenstock (1990: 194), for example, have described the impact of tobacco smoking, exposure to asbestos, traffic accidents and pesticide production, and point out that 'As countries evolve through economic development, there is a progressive change in the type of environmental and occupational hazards of poor sanitation, indoor air pollution and agricultural accidents to the modern hazards of urban air pollution, toxic chemicals and traffic accidents.' The underdevelopment of health in the Third World must be understood in terms of Western colonialism and imperialism (Doyal with Pennell, 1979). Commercial investment and exploitation by the 'North' of the 'South' has resulted in ecological destruction and a Third World debt crisis wherein countries in debt pay more in interest than they ever receive in aid.

A further puzzle evident in nations that have undergone the *epidemiological transition* and have relatively generous welfare regimens is the fact the health inequalities persist. Mackenbach (2012) addresses this conundrum when he asks the question: 'What explains the persistence and even widening of socio-economic inequalities in health in the highly developed welfare states of Western Europe, and the lack of association between generousness of welfare policies and the magnitude of health inequalities?' (p. 762). Sympathetic to the neo-materialist and psychological theories, he finds evidence to support the case for significant redistribution; that is, radical reform to shift resources from the wealthy to those less well off in concert with policies that focus on personal and cultural determinants of health. This is because of the increased homogeneity of unhealthy lifestyle practices amongst lower social groups are especially salient in welfare-rich societies which mean that consumption behaviours are important determinants of ill-health. However, the neo-liberal consensus means that radical redistributive policies are far-fetched and interventions designed to change behaviour are limited in their effectiveness. Mackenbach (2012) concludes that 'those who want to reduce health inequalities will have to be satisfied with small steps forward' (p. 769). This may also explain why they remain so stubborn and persistent.

Conclusion

There is a vast literature on health inequalities, and it is impossible to do justice to it in one chapter. However, it is clear that systematic inequalities in health status exist across a range of variables such as social class, gender, ethnicity or 'race', and geographical location. Further, we have seen that these variables interact, producing a complex social pattern of differences in health and illness across populations. However, the response of health care services does not seem to correspond to these patterns of inequality. As Tudor-Hart (1971: 412) noted decades ago, 'the availability of good medical care tends to vary inversely with the need of the population served'. This 'inverse-care law' means that those people who experience the greatest material deprivation also tend to live in areas with lower levels of health care service provision. Nevertheless, even if this were rectified, inequalities in health cannot be overcome simply by increased provision of health care, because, as we have seen, they are related to factors which exist largely beyond the domain of health and medical care. As we have seen throughout this chapter, much of the research in this field relies on studies undertaken by social epidemiologists and their findings are crucial to developing a sociological appreciation of health inequalities. But there are some further sociological questions that remain puzzling. For example: Why is evidence on health inequalities invariably presented as novel and surprising in the news media? Why do academics disagree so much about the empirical statistical data and the linking explanations? Why do health inequalities persist in wealthy societies?

FURTHER READING

Annandale, E. (2009), *Women, Health and Social Change*, London: Routledge.

Bartley, M. (2004), *Health Inequality: An Introduction to Theories, Concepts and Methods*, Cambridge: Polity.

Klinenberg, E. (2002), *Heat Wave: A Social Autopsy of Disaster in Chicago*, Chicago, IL: University of Chicago Press. A Durkheimian analysis of the social determinants of heat-wave deaths, discussed in this chapter.

Mackenbach, J. P. (2012), 'The Persistence of Health Inequalities in Modern Welfare States: The Explanation of a Paradox', *Social Science & Medicine*, 75, 4: 761–9. This article provides a lucid overview of the main explanations of health inequalities and gives clues to the question: Why do health inequalities persist in wealthy, welfare rich societies?

Nettleton, S. and Gustaffson, U. (eds) (2002), *The Sociology of Health and Illness Reader*, Cambridge: Polity. The chapters in Part IV, 'Social Patterning of Health and Illness' examine issues of class, gender, ethnicity and place.

Wilkinson, R. G. and Pickett, K. (2009), *The Spirit Level: Why More Equal Societies Almost Always Do Better*, London: Allen Lane.

This chapter has focused on the sociology of health inequalities in post-industrial societies and does not address the major social and health inequalities on a global scale. For an update on statistics on mortality and morbidity in the UK, see <http://www.statistics.gov.uk/>.

Globally poverty is the most significant cause of mortality and morbidity. Some useful resources include: The World Health Organization, <http://www.who.int/en/>; the Food and Agriculture Organization of the United Nations, <http://www.fao.org/>; and Unicef, <http://www.unicef.org/>.

8 Late Modernism and the Changing Social Relations of Formal Health Care Work

Introduction

As the second millennium drew to a close, many sociologists turned their attention to the dominant social formations that appeared to be emerging. Some conceptualized the changes that were taking place as being part of a process of *post*modernization (Crook et al., 1992), in which the social structures of modernity were superseded by radically new sets of arrangements (Lash and Urry, 1994). Other writers, such as Giddens (1990, 1991), argued that it is more appropriate to think about the contemporary period as being one wherein the central aspects of modernity are becoming significantly more dynamic and accentuated: 'The modern world is a "runaway world": not only is the *pace* of social change much faster than in any prior system, so also is its *scope* and the *profoundness* with which it affects pre-existing social practices and behaviour' (Giddens, 1991: 16, emphasis original). Giddens argues that it is therefore more appropriate to talk about the contemporary period as being one of *late* modernism or *reflexive modernization* (Beck et al., 1994). Although rather different in emphasis (Lupton, 1999), essentially these terms imply that existing social relations and social structures are in an inherent state of flux. Social organizations are becoming increasingly subject to constant reorganization and change. And the consequences of modernity are 'reflexive,' in that the effects of environmental, technological, social and economic 'developments' are rebounding - often with very negative effects. This chapter examines the manner in which some of these changes are manifesting in the social relations of formal health care work. In the UK the NHS has been subject to reorganizations throughout its history and health policies are permanently in a state of flux (R. Klein, 2010). Health care reforms are a feature of most welfare regimes and are politically emotive (Stevens, 2010). In the USA, valiant attempts to reform health care have been thwarted for decades. President Obama and the US Congress successfully passed a reform package in 2010 that will extend the access to health insurance to a significant proportion of the previously uninsured population. But opposition was intense. Health and health care is nothing but political and the pace of change is fast. For this reason this chapter will focus less on the details of policies, politics and reforms and instead focus on the conceptual resources that are useful for making sense of changes. Health policy reforms, working practices and social relations in formal health care settings are not only important in and of themselves, but they are also inextricably linked with the wider social and cultural shifts associated with late modernism.

In order to examine changing social relations of formal health care work in this context, we need to be familiar not just with recent changes, but with the major historical antecedents of the contemporary period. Thus, for example, to understand fully the changing role of health professional groups in the restructured NHS, it is crucial to appreciate some of the socio-historical processes of professionalization. We begin the chapter by considering the literature on professions under conditions of both modernity and late modernity. We next examine the evidence for the decline of professional dominance under late modernism and the concurrent rise of complementary and alternative forms of health care and healing. These changes have to be understood in relation to the broader restructuring of the NHS. After outlining the major contours of this restructuring, which some authors have conceptualized as being post-Fordist in nature, the chapter examines the changing social relations of, and innovations in, formal health service work, paying close attention to the rise of the 'new managerialism' and 'clinical governance'. These developments in health policy have led to tensions in practice. Economic and managerialist perspectives that emphasize efficiency and effectiveness can be at odds with the core business of health and social care work, which is in essence work by bodies on the bodies of others. We end the chapter reflecting on these issues using the concept of 'body work' as a prism that usefully helps us make sense of formal health care work.

Sociology of the health professions

Professions have long been of interest to sociologists, who have addressed questions such as: What constitutes a profession? Why have some occupational groups been more successful in achieving professional status than others? What strategies do occupational groups adopt to ensure professional recognition? To what extent are professional strategies mediated by class, gender and race? What can we say about the social relations between different professional groups? To what extent are we witnessing the demise of professionals in late modern societies? In many ways these questions, more or less, reflect a chronology which can be identified in the professions literature.

What constitutes a profession?

Given that sociology in the early twentieth century was preoccupied with work, the division of labour, industrialization and social order, it is hardly surprising that professions were given a considerable amount of attention. Professions such as law and medicine were presumed to possess specialized knowledge and to manifest a collective altruism, and as such, were regarded as a mainstay of liberal democratic societies (Carr-Saunders and Wilson, 1933). What taxed sociologists was the question: What makes an occupation a profession? In response, researchers endeavoured to produce exhaustive lists of professional attributes or traits.

It is generally agreed, however, that there are four core characteristics of a profession: first, *specialized knowledge and lengthy training*. To become accepted into a profession, an individual must undergo a long period of vocational training and thereby possess a specialized knowledge that is not accessible to the lay person, who becomes reliant on the 'expert'. Second, because of this dependency, a professional must work in the best interests of his or her clients; that is, they must be *altruistic*. Third, because it is deemed illegal for non-professionals to carry out certain defined tasks, a profession has a *monopoly over practice*. Fourth, only the professional can assess who is competent to practise; hence professions are *self-policing* and therefore *autonomous*. From a functionalist perspective, occupations which possess these attributes are crucial to the effective functioning of modern, complex societies (Parsons, 1951). For example, the medical profession ensures that healing will be carried out by those who have specialist technical knowledge and by those who will place the interests of their clients above their own. Professions, from this perspective, are therefore rightly accorded the privileges of status, higher pay and self-regulation.

This approach is of limited value, however. First, simply listing characteristics that are identified by the professions themselves merely reflects and reinforces their ideals and values. Second, this uncritical approach is static and ahistoric, and fails to capture the social, economic and political factors that precipitated the emergence of some occupations as professions and the subsequent division of labour between professional groups. Third, it is presumed that professions serve the good of society in general, rather than their own self-interest. This is not necessarily the case, however, and functionalist Marxists have argued both that the professions have contributed to, and that their emergence has been facilitated by, the advent of capitalism (T. Johnson, 1977; Navarro, 1978). Finally, the trait approach presumes that there is something inherent in the occupations themselves that facilitates their progress to professional status. In the case of medicine, the assumption is that success is associated with specialist knowledge of biomedical science. Critics, however, have argued that the medical profession latched on to medical science as a means to convince the state and the public of their superior product, and hence it was actually used to facilitate their strategies of occupational closure (Larson, 1977).

It is clear that professions did not emerge out of necessity; nor are they socially legitimated simply because of their altruism. The social positioning of the medical profession, the nature of their work, and relations between professions within the health care division of labour has attracted much interest from sociologists. There are now a range of theoretical perspectives available to us to explore the power and practices of the institution of medicine. In a lucid and comprehensive review, Riska (2010) has identified four broad theoretical frameworks: functionalist, interactionist, social constructionist and poststructuralist.

We have already explored the functionalist approach, and she places medicalization as a prime example of the social constructionist perspective (see chapter 2 of this volume). Within interactionist approaches she includes the dramaturgical approach of Goffman, Freidson's notions of professional autonomy and other Weberian modes of analysis. We turn to these now in more detail and consider the gendered nature of health care professions.

Strategies of social closure and occupational control

Rather, from a Weberian perspective, it is recognized that professions are formed as the result of historically specific socio-political processes (Parkin, 1974). Occupational groups have pursued strategies of social closure by securing a legal monopoly over their practice and the ability to restrict access to their ranks. Medicine secured not only the autonomy to regulate itself, but also the authority to define the tasks and boundaries of other, what Freidson (1970a) calls, paramedical professions, such as nursing and midwifery. Strategic success is most likely to be achieved by those occupations whose structural characteristics in terms of class, gender and race most closely approximate the characteristics of those in power at the level of the state and wider civil society (T. Johnson, 1977; Witz, 1992).

There are two important issues in the occupational control literature: first, the relationship between professionals and their 'markets', and second, the relationship between professional groups themselves. The nature of these relationships will determine the degree of *professional dominance* (Freidson, 1970b) enjoyed by an occupational group. With reference to its market, a profession's strategic success will be contingent on its ability to control and define the needs of the consumer. The extent to which consumers are dependent on an occupational group is not a function of professional expertise and lay ignorance; it is more a function of social distance between them and their relative access to socio-economic resources. The social distance between the doctor and the consumer is enhanced by clinical judgement which is claimed to be more of an art than a science. If there is a high indeterminacy/technicality ratio (I/T ratio) - that is, if doctors have relatively more intuitive and non-routinized intelligence than codified and openly accessible knowledge - then there will be greater social distance (Jamous and Peloille, 1970). According to T. Johnson (1972), this means that doctors operate a *collegiate* type of occupational control: that is, the provider defines the needs of the consumer and how they should be met. Consumers of medicine have little say about their health and illness, because it is presumed that they will have limited understanding and knowledge of medical science. This is in contrast to the other two dominant forms of occupational control identified by Johnson: *patronage*, where the client defines the need, as was the case in eighteenth-century medicine (Jewson, 1976), and *mediation*, where a third party, such as the state, intercedes in the relationship between the producer and the consumer.

The second dimension of occupational control is professional autonomy; the legitimated control that an occupation has over the content of its own work. Elston (1991: 61) distinguishes between three types of autonomy: *economic* autonomy - the right of professionals to determine their remuneration; *political* autonomy - the right to make policy decisions as the legitimate experts on health matters; and *clinical* autonomy - the right to set standards and control clinical performance. Related to the notion of autonomy is professional dominance, which refers to the way in which certain professions not only control the content of their own work but can also define the limits of the work of other occupational groups (Freidson, 1970b).

Larkin's (1980) historical study of the dental profession's control of dental dressers serves to illustrate professional dominance and shows how it may reinforce self-interest rather than collective altruism. Dentistry became a 'closed' profession in 1921, when entry became regulated through schools recognized by the General Medical Council (it did not become a fully autonomous profession until 1956). An exemption in the 1921 Act was for the dental nurse (dental dresser), who was employed in public service and was limited by statute to perform 'minor dental work'. The British Dental Association (BDA) pressured the Ministry of Health to interpret this at its most minimal, that is, non-surgical work and very minor dental surgery. In 1923 Derbyshire, Shropshire and Sheffield authorities employed dental dressers to perform minor dental surgery, and argued that total closure would ruin the newly born school dental service, because there was a huge amount of untreated dental disease. The Ministry of Health took advice from the BDA without even inspecting the scheme, and made it illegal for dental dressers to diagnose or carry out surgical treatments, however routine. The Ministry stated that the Derbyshire scheme 'involved diluting qualified professional men by their enforced co-operation with unqualified women with nothing more than a short empirical training' (cited in Larkin, 1980: 225). This example reveals another dimension of occupational control, although Larkin does not make it explicit: the fact that professional projects are gendered (Witz, 1992).

Gendered professional projects

Despite the marked gendered segregation of health care professions, Weberian analyses have, until recently, been gender-blind. Consequently we have only had a very partial picture of professionalization within health care. Alongside the emergence of professions was the transfer of healing from the hands of women to the control of men. As Witz (1992: 74–5) notes, it was 'the institutional relocation of medical practice from the domestic to the market arena, that sounded the death knell for women's participation in healing practices'. Of course women still participated in healing, in that it was they who carried out most health care (Stacey, 1988), but in the market arena their healing activities came to be controlled by men.

Developing the neo-Weberian accounts of professionalization, Witz (1992) has examined the gendered nature of occupational strategies. Professional projects are gendered in three ways. First, the agents are men or women. Second, gender may form a basis of solidarity. Third, strategies of occupational closure are located in patriarchal structures which historically have constituted the facilitating or constraining parameters of these strategies. In other words, the resources which men and women can strategically draw upon are different. Thus there is an interplay between strategy and structure, 'between strategic courses of action, which are gendered, and facilitating or constraining structures, which are patriarchal' (Witz, 1992: 52).

Witz identifies four strategies of occupational closure, reproduced in figure 8.1. Dominant groups exercise both *exclusionary strategies* – that is, intra-occupational control over their internal affairs which enables them to restrict access to their ranks – and *demarcatory strategies* – that is, inter-occupational control over the affairs of related para-professions. An example of a *gendered exclusionary strategy* is the barring of women from entering educational institutions required for access to a profession. *Gendered demarcatory strategies* are evident where dominant occupations encircle women within a related sphere of competence, as in the case of dentists and dental dressers already discussed. Subordinate groups, by contrast, employ *inclusionary strategies* – that is, they seek to become members of an occupation from which they are excluded (for example, women gaining entry to the medical profession) – and *dual closure strategies* – that is, they both challenge the dominant group's intra-occupational control of their competencies and strive to consolidate their own position by means of exclusion (for example, midwifery). Thus women, from their structurally subordinate location, pursued these two types of strategy.

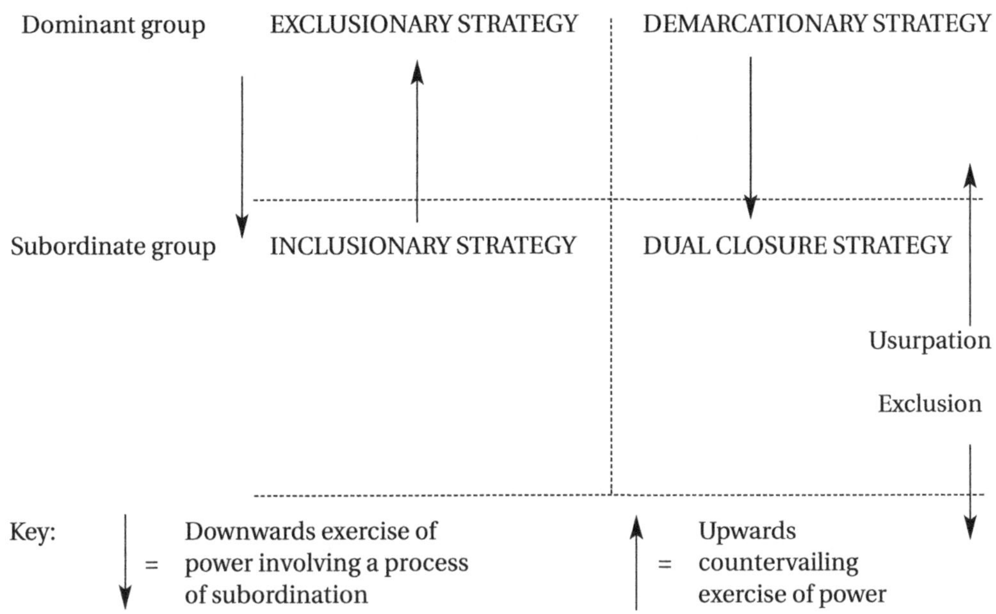

Figure 8.1 Strategies of occupational closure: a conceptual model
Source: Witz (1992: 45).

Women and medicine: an inclusionary strategy

It was the 1858 Medical Registration Act that legitimated the autonomous profession of medicine, in that only a legally or duly qualified medical practitioner could practise. The Act spoke of persons, and did not in itself exclude women. In fact, Elizabeth Blackwell, who had received her MD in the USA, was entered on the first register issued by the General Medical Council in this same year. However, in the UK women were excluded from medicine, in that they were not permitted to study and qualify in any of the recognized educational institutions. Thus the resources of male power were most effectively institutionalized in the modern university and professional co-operations, rather than in the state legislature. It was only through the tenacity of a number of women that these sites of power were ultimately challenged. The story of women's fight to become medical practitioners has been documented in graphic detail (Jex-Blake, 1886; Stacey, 1988; Witz, 1992; S. Roberts, 1993). Those women, such as Elizabeth Garrett Anderson, Sophia Jex-Blake and Edith Petchy, faced a whole series of battles, discrimination and abuse from professional men. For example, when a group of women finally managed to attend an examination in Edinburgh, they reported how a 'dense crowd had gathered outside the hall and the gates were slammed in their faces by a number of young men "who stood within, smoking and passing about bottles of whisky, while they abused us in the foulest possible language"' (Witz, 1992: 90, citing Jex-Blake, 1886: 92). During the examination the rioters even stooped to pushing a sheep into the examination hall!

Pursuing a separatist tactic, the London School of Medicine for Women was founded in 1874. This tactic was initially thwarted by the fact that access was required into teaching hospitals, and its examinations had to be recognized by one of the existing examining boards. It was finally recognized by the Kings and Queens College of Physicians in Ireland in 1876. It was also in Dublin that the five women, led by Jex-Blake, who had studied in Edinburgh, presented themselves for examination and were entered on to the register in 1877. This potted history illustrates Witz's thesis that it was civil institutions, colleges and co-operations that were the main sites of patriarchal power. Men's strategy of occupational closure was predominantly about securing support and recognition from the state. By contrast, women's professional project required challenging male power that was deeply embedded in civil society.

Women and midwifery: a dual closure strategy

The history of the struggle between midwives and medical men has been documented in some considerable detail (Oakley, 1976; Donnison, 1977; Versluysen, 1981). Prior to the emergence of modern medicine in the nineteenth century, many women earned a living from practising midwifery, and women in labour were almost invariably attended by other women. Most midwives were unlicensed practitioners, and learned their skills through oral traditions. Nevertheless, from as early as the seventeenth century, male midwives began to edge their way on to the scene. They tried to restrict the activities of female midwives by advocating that they attend only 'normal births', whilst they, with the aid of their instruments, such as forceps, intervened when there was any sign of abnormality.

As we have discussed, it was with the 1858 Medical Registration Act that medicine became a unified and autonomous profession. As such it was keen to regulate the activities of other related health care practitioners. Midwifery was no exception. Female midwives, however, were keen to ensure the continuation of their profession, and therefore pursued strategies to counter its demise. Witz (1992) analyses this struggle sociologically in terms of the gendered professional projects sketched out above. Neither the medical men nor the midwives were unified in their strategies. Medical men adopted demarcationary strategies: that is, they sought to secure inter-occupational control, of two types. General practitioners followed an incorporatist strategy, in that they wanted to have control of the whole process of childbirth and relegate midwives to the position of obstetric nurses. Obstetricians, on the other hand, were keen to support midwives in their pursuit of registration, so long as they could define their sphere of competence and ensure that they attended only normal births. Thus they pursued a strategy of de-skilling. It was this latter strategy which was successful; obstetricians supported the Midwives Act of 1902, which introduced compulsory registration. Midwives did not, however, achieve full professional autonomy. They were to be instructed by medical men, and they were licensed by a board appointed by the General Medical Council. Significantly, they could be struck off the register if they transcended occupational boundaries and undertook the more interventionist and medicalized tasks associated with delivery.

The 1902 Midwives Act was not brought about simply as a result of the activities of the medical profession. Midwives fought to secure their future. In particular, they were instrumental in challenging the incorporationist strategy which would have resulted in their demise as an occupational group. According to Witz, the female professional projects comprised two types: 'revolutionary dual closure' and 'accommodative dual closure'. The former, and chronologically earlier (around the 1860–1870s), was adopted by the Female Medical Society and the Obstetrical Association of Midwives, who sought to extend their sphere of competence and attend both normal and abnormal labours. They used credentialist tactics, in that they were keen to extend the education and examination of midwives to raise their levels of competence and knowledge, so that they could practise on an equal level with medical men. However, it was the accommodative strategy which led to the 1902 Act. In the 1880s the Midwives Institute followed legalist rather than credentialist tactics, to bring about registration. They broadly accepted the Obstetrical Society's scheme for the education and registration of midwives. Although forgoing full professional autonomy, they did at least secure some, in that they were free to supervise normal labour without any help from the medical profession. The male, medical Obstetrical Society was keen to go along with this for two reasons. First, there was a high demand for attendance at labour which they could not possibly have met. Moreover, even if they had been able to, most births would be time-consuming and straightforward, and therefore not particularly 'exciting' to medical men. Second, most of the women who called upon midwives were poor, and so there was no significant monetary gain to be had from attending them.

In sum, the outcome of the history of midwifery was one of partial autonomy from the medical profession. This was gained not purely as an outcome of political negotiations with the state, because midwives' relationship with the state was mediated by the medical profession (Witz, 1992: 126). These struggles over sphere of competence and the nature of occupational boundaries were not, however, laid to rest by the 1902 Act. On the contrary, disputes over the control of childbirth and the demarcation of tasks remain hotly debated. For example, in 1992 a Social Services Select Committee investigated maternity services and found that they were overly medicalized and dominated by a predominantly male obstetric medicine (Winterton Report, 1992). It found no evidence to justify the continuation of this state of affairs, and recommended that the role of midwives be enhanced. Needless to say, the debates still rage between and amongst obstetricians, midwives and women concerned with such matters.

'Race' and the health professions

The division of labour in the health service is patterned not only by gender but also by 'race'. Within and between occupations, men and women of colour have been systematically disadvantaged. They are proportionately more likely to be employed in the lower-paid jobs. They are more likely to be employed in domestic and catering work than in positions of management, or if they are trained professionals, they are more likely to be State Enrolled Nurses (SENs) than State Registered Nurses (SRNs), and they are more likely to be working in lower-status specialisms such as geriatrics or psychiatry (Rashid, 1990). Historically, in the UK and the USA, migrant workers have sustained health care by taking jobs in times of acute labour shortages (Bradby and Nazroo, 2010). The global market place means that 'wealthy' countries can benefit from skilled workers who have been trained elsewhere leaving other nations with labour shortages. Whilst we have data on the numbers of doctors and nurses coming to work for the NHS from overseas, we have only limited information on their subsequent careers.

An appreciation of racial inequalities within the NHS requires an understanding of imperialism and colonialism (F. Williams, 1989). After the foundation of the NHS in 1948, and during the expansionist period of the 1950s and 1960s, there was a labour shortage. The government therefore looked to the New Commonwealth to recruit cheap labour, and senior British nurses were sent overseas specifically for this purpose. In 1971 there were 15,493 student nurses from overseas, of whom over 40 per cent were from the West Indies, 29 per cent from Asia, 27 per cent from Africa and Mauritius, and 3 per cent from countries such as Fiji, Tonga, the Seychelles and the Virgin Islands (Akinsanya, 1988). The recruitment of nursing staff for the NHS bypassed the restrictions of the 1962 and 1965 Commonwealth Immigration Acts and reached a peak in 1970 (Pearson, 1987; Baxter, 1988). A political economy of migrant labour is therefore essential if we are to understand the nature of stratification within the context of health work. The exploitation of a migrant work-force is rooted in a historically specific colonial past, but this does not in itself explain the extent and perpetuation of both institutional and personal racism that is experienced within the Health Service by men and women of colour.

Equal opportunities have often taken the form simply of official statements rather than changes in actual practice. Indeed, it is evident from studies of employment relations in the Health Service that racial discrimination is widespread. 'By "discrimination" we mean that individuals have been denied employment, promotion and deployment opportunities on the basis of skin colour, ethnicity or place of origin rather than genuine occupational reasons of ability, training and so on' (Ward, 1993: 168). Although the Race Relations Act of 1976 enabled employers to take positive action to improve the training of any particular group under-represented in certain positions, by the mid-1980s very little had been done to improve the situation (Akinsanya, 1988). For example, a survey of six health authorities found that very few black nurses made it to the 'top' (Agbolegbe, 1984). There were no black district nursing officers, and of sixty directors of nursing, only two were black. In the UK following the publication of the Macpherson Report (1999), which highlighted the prevalence of institutional racism within public services, ethnicity and equality were placed high on policy agendas. However, studies reveal that difficulties in interpretation of policies on 'ethnic diversity' and 'equal opportunities' hinder their implementation (Johns, 2004). Studies carried out within medical schools have also found significant discriminatory practices which have limited opportunities for medical training on the basis of 'race', both at the level of entry and in subsequent careers (Anwar and Ali, 1987; McKeigne et al., 1990; Esmail and Everington, 1993). This may explain why doctors are over-represented in the least popular specialties and under-represented in teaching hospitals (Ward, 1993; Coker, 2001). For example, geriatric medicine from its inception in the 1950s was a lower status specialty in which overseas trained doctors were over-represented. Between 1964 and 1991, 23 per cent of all geriatric consultants were non-white and had trained outside the UK compared to 3 per cent in general medicine and 9 per cent of all consultants (Goldacre et al., 2004).

Kyriakides and Virdee (2003) provide a detailed analysis of the history of migrant medical labour in the UK, which reveals a dialect between immigration controls and the ideologies of racism and nationalism. They argue that migrant doctors – predominantly 'non-white' doctors from the New Commonwealth – were constructed as both 'saviours' and 'pariahs'. During the expansionist era of welfare, they were proactively recruited in order to overcome the clinical shortage in the NHS; yet they were also marginalized and widely regarded as 'inferior' to white doctors. 'The delicious irony, . . . is that an institution [the NHS] established with the express purpose of maintaining the Empire and "white supremacy", could only sustain itself by drawing heavily on the skilled labour of the "inferior races" in the postcolonial era' (Kyriakides and Virdee, 2003: 287). When immigration controls became more restrictive, as a result of popular political agitation, there were exemptions for medical doctors who nevertheless, in turn, arrived to face a racist society. Racist discourses were laced with talk of 'overseas doctors' – a euphemism for 'non-white' doctors, who were purported to have 'inferior' medical standards (Kyriakides and Virdee, 2003). Doctors migrating from the New Commonwealth had to undergo additional assessments in order to practise and maintain their registration. These practices resonate with contemporary concerns about the shortage of health professionals and the need to expand recruitment. Such issues are discussed alongside 'popular' and political demands for the regulation of immigration.

Immigrant medical practitioners are part of an occupationally elite group and yet can find themselves marginalized within the medical division of labour. This was especially so for those recruited from the Commonwealth countries in the years of welfare expansion, and serves as a reminder of how racism is bound up with colonialism and is historically mediated. Recollections of experiences of medicine amongst South Asian doctors reveal these complexities. Bornat et al. (2009) undertook an oral historical approach to this issue by interviewing 60 doctors trained in South Asia who worked, and still work in geriatric medicine in the UK. Oral history accounts of their experiences are nuanced, and although there is mention of overt discrimination, such references were relatively rare and presented in conjunction with other aspects of difference and diversity. Although working in racist environments, the doctors also reported careers that revealed their professional achievements. There is a complex interplay between class, race and gender that manifests differentially throughout the health care division of labour.

Baxter's (1988) study of black nurses found that they faced discrimination at the stages of recruitment, deployment and promotion, and that racism was experienced at both institutional and personal levels. Her study is important not only because it provides an insight into the experiences of the thirty-three women interviewed, but also because it gives a voice to those who would otherwise remain unheard. The nurses reported how they had been encouraged to become SENs rather than SRNs. The SEN qualification is not recognized internationally, which meant that some nurses could not easily find jobs outside the UK: 'I wanted to change over to the SRN but my tutor was not interested, even after I told her that I could not get a job at home with this qualification' (cited in Baxter, 1988: 26). It was found that there was a general lack of support for black nurses, from both nursing schools and trade unions, avenues which we might suppose should exist to support the needs of nurses. The nurses also reported how they were deployed into the least pleasant aspects of nursing work, such as having to do disproportionate amounts of night shift work, and were encouraged to enter the lower-status specialties. The nurses articulated how they were subjected to racist stereotyping. This occurred both in their everyday working practices and at interviews for training or promotion, as the following experience illustrates:

> After doing psychiatric training I applied to do general nurse training. At the interview the matron told me, we do not take too many Commonwealth girls here. We are prepared to take one in each year. This is a prestigious hospital where doctors, teachers and lawyers send their daughters. We believe in good standards of dress, self presentation and a high academic standard. I will offer you a place in the school on a six-week trial. If you are not up to our standard, you will be asked to leave. (Cited in Baxter, 1988: 51)

Structural inequalities within the Health Service are therefore as significant in terms of 'race' as they are in terms of class and gender. They can be understood only in the historical and colonial context in which the NHS emerged, together with the perpetuation of racist ideologies and practices. There have been persistent denials of the existence of racism in the Health Service and a reluctance to implement monitoring of equal opportunities. Already disadvantaged in terms of recruitment and deployment, black health workers have been further disadvantaged as a result of the many health service reorganizations. As Akinsanya (1988: 447) points out:

> since its inception in 1948, the NHS has undergone considerable restructuring in order to respond to developments in medical technology and demographic changes. The role of ethnic minority nurses has not, however, kept pace with these changes. In one important respect – that of upward professional mobility – this group has lost out as these changes have taken place.

In sum, we have seen that professionalization in health work under conditions of modernity has involved struggles over occupational control and professional autonomy. We have also seen how the struggles between, and the social relations within, professional groups have been indelibly marked by class, gender and 'race'. We shall now consider how issues of professional autonomy and dominance are being shaped by the conditions of late modernity.

Is professional medical dominance in decline?

Within the NHS it is the medical profession which has remained the dominant occupational group; however, the boundaries of occupational control are fluid, in that they are mediated by wider socio-economic and political processes. The extent to which the medical profession retains its control over related para-professions is likely to change, as is its control over the content of its terms of work. Thus professional dominance is a relative concept. Freidson (1986) has emphasized this relativity in the face of critics who have suggested that such dominance is in decline. These challenges take the form of the *deprofessionalization* and the *proletarianization* theses. Together, these theorize that doctors are increasingly being subjected to external forms of regulation, and are losing control over the content of their work. In sum, it is suggested, we are witnessing the demise of professional autonomy and therefore professional dominance.

The *de-professionalization* thesis (Haug, 1988) draws attention to the changing nature of the relationships between professionals and their clients: in particular, the cultural crisis of modern medicine and doubts about its efficacy which have led to increasing consumer scepticism. The *proletarianization* thesis (Oppenheimer, 1973; McKinlay and Stoeckle, 1988), sometimes called the *corporatization* thesis (McKinlay and Marceau, 2002), presumes that medicine, like all other occupations, will become increasingly incorporated into the capitalist system, with the inevitable consequence that it will be stripped of its control over the means of production. Further, as they become subjected to management control, medical and related professions will become increasingly alienated from their work. These arguments are important, because they remind us of the equivocal nature of professional power. Professional dominance and professional autonomy are therefore concepts which are historically contingent. We shall examine this issue by first considering the changing nature of medical work, and second, the rise of alternative medicine.

The changing nature of medical work

Commenting on medical work in the USA, McKinlay and Marceau (2002), themselves proponents of the corporatization thesis, claim that eight interrelated developments have contributed to what they call 'the decline of the golden age of doctoring'. Six of these are 'extrinsic factors', in that they are beyond the control of the profession, and two are 'intrinsic factors', and could be amenable to control by the institutions of medicine.

The first factor is '*the changing nature of the state and loss of its partisan support for doctoring*'. The political pluralism of the mid-twentieth century, they argue, has given way to the politics of the New Right, whereby governments have shifted their allegiances from adjudicating between a multiplicity of political and institutional interests to supporting global corporate interests. As we have seen earlier in this chapter, state support is crucial for securing medical autonomy. In the early years of the NHS, its organizational configuration was the result of a compromise between politicians and doctors (R. Klein, 2010). More recently, however, the influence of medicine at the level of domestic politics has declined (Harrison and Ahmed, 2002).

The second factor is '*the bureaucratization (corporatization) of doctoring*', which refers to the changing nature of employment relations and to the growing control over the content of doctors' work. Aspects of medical work such as treatment decisions, prescribing practices and medical referrals are monitored to assess the performance of practitioners. Practitioners are being made aware of the cost implications of their actions, and their decisions are now increasingly influenced by economic considerations (Paton, 1992). For example, in the UK the introduction of 'indicative drug budgets' and guidelines from bodies such as the National Institute for Clinical Excellence (NICE) may limit doctors' scope for prescribing drugs or treatments of their choice. Such monitoring alters the I/T ratio (discussed above), and relatedly creates a space for the control of doctors by managers rather than doctors themselves. The I/T ratio, T. Johnson (1977: 106) has argued, is facilitated by structural conditions: 'Professionalism, involving the collegiate control of work activities, can arise only where the ideological and political processes sustaining indeterminization coincide with the requirements of capital.' However, during the last two decades clinical knowledge has become increasingly codified. For example, computerized expert systems have been developed for diagnostic purposes. Hence decisions about diagnosis and prognosis are based on the systematic application of logic to a given knowledge base, rather than on the 'intuitive clinical judgements' which might rely upon more opaque interpretative procedures. Thus there has been a clear shift in the I/T ratio.

In turn, this relates to *'globalization and the information revolution'* (McKinlay and Marceau, 2002), which is associated with an increase in transnational corporations and supranational bodies which are emerging alongside the rise of information and communication technologies. The power of the medical profession has been superseded by both global agencies that influence policy and information systems which not only track the work and performance of practitioners but also, they claim, 'empower patients'. The extent to which patients are empowered by access to such information is contested, however, by others (Nettleton and Hanlon, 2006). Nevertheless, lay people and health care 'consumers' are becoming more knowledgeable and articulate about many health and health care issues. As we saw in chapter 6, people are also increasingly likely to voice their dissatisfaction with the care that they receive.

'The emerging competitive threat from other health workers' is another factor which erodes the 'golden age of doctoring'. The relative rise in status, autonomy and number of professions allied to medicine has been noted in most developed countries (Elston, 1977, 1991). Stacey captures this point when she writes:

> Developments in medical knowledge, advances in technology and the conditions which pertain in advanced capitalist societies have all been involved in the increased number of divisions in health labour. Specialisms and sub-specialisms have burgeoned in the last forty years, as have the number and range of non-medical workers, scientists and technicians – workers in the paramedical professions ... upon all of whom the doctors rely. (Stacey, 1988: 182)

This greater complexity and division of labour of knowledge results in fragmentation and undermines unity. Related to this is the shift of some tasks, once practised exclusively by doctors, to other practitioners, such as nurses or podiatrists.

The fifth reason McKinlay and Marceau offer for the demise of the golden age of doctoring is *'the epidemiologic transition and changes in the public conception of the body'*. With the rise of chronic conditions and the relative decline in curable conditions, curing is being replaced by caring and palliative measures – which are less 'glamorous' (McKinlay and Marceau, 2002: 402). Caring work can also be performed by a range of other providers.

The sixth extrinsic factor implies *'changes in the doctor–patient relationship and the erosion of trust'* – an issue we explored in detail in chapter 6. For McKinlay and Marceau, the key to this change is the extent to which corporate and commercial interests have pervaded the relationship.

The two factors which are 'intrinsic' to the profession itself relate to the *'weakening of physicians' labour market position through oversupply'* and *'the fragmentation of the physicians' union'*. The first factor is of more relevance to the USA, but the latter has some basis in most developed countries. In particular, the increase in medical specialization and fragmentation has undermined the unity of the professional associations, with separate associations being established for surgeons, general practitioners, obstetricians, oncologists and so on (Krause, 1996). Each is increasingly reliant on the knowledge and expertise of other professional groups.

Although the quasi-Marxist tone of McKinlay and Marceau's (2002) thesis is not necessarily shared by others, there is a growing body of opinion that supports the view that medicine is less powerful than it was during the previous century, this view being expressed within the medical profession (Horton, 2003; Irvine, 2003). Some analysts (Harrison and Ahmad, 2002) support the view that medical work is becoming more 'Fordist' than 'post-Fordist' (see below), as doctors have to adhere to more stringent regulations concerning their working practices, and the key to clinical autonomy - the idea that doctors are to respond to the needs of each individual patient - is being undermined. Writing in a UK context, Harrison and Ahmad assess the demise of medical dominance at the *micro* level by examining the content of doctors' day-to-day work; at a *meso* level by exploring the institutionalized relationships between the medical profession and the state; and at a *macro* level by considering the salience of the ideology of biomedicine. Like McKinlay and Marceau, they conclude that at the micro and meso levels, medicine's power is on the wane; however, the ideology of biomedicine, they claim, remains intact.

The enduring nature of biomedicine has, ironically perhaps, turned out to be a source of weakness for the medical profession. This is an argument developed by Stephen Harrison (2009) who points out that the reductionism and individualism that are inherent in biomedicine (see chapter 1 of this volume) are congruent with a managerialist ethos. The assumption that ill health can be reduced to specific causes 'allows cases to be standardised, categorised, and allocated specific protocols or pathways' (p. 192). Furthermore, the conceptualization of patients as homogeneous 'cases' rather than individuals with unique needs facilitates a bureaucratic form of management. The result of this 'conceptual commodification is that the occupiers of managerial roles are more easily able to control medical work' (p. 192). This is a novel view. Rather than presuming biomedicine enhances medical dominance, it argues that the dominance of biomedicine undermines the autonomy and independence of the profession.

Within the context of the UK the introduction of quasi-markets and the encouragement of public–private partnerships has been found to impact on the work of health care practitioners. Waring and Bishop (2011) examined the impact on what they called the 'healthcare identities' of health professionals working in Independent Sector Treatment Centres (ISTCs). These are private service providers who deliver services that are commissioned by the NHS. They are characteristic of the diversity of welfare provision and the standardization and commercialization of the public sector. The clinicians (doctors and nurses) working in one of these centres were acutely aware of the discontinuities with the NHS and pointed to 'the emphasis of profit, efficiency and productivity' (p. 672). However, they had differential responses to these new organizational forms. Waring and Bishop conceptualized three such responses or emerging identities: the 'pioneer identity' - those who embraced the opportunities that they felt working in the independent sector gave them for advancing high-quality services; the 'guardian identity' - those who perceived the values of the private sector were eroding the public nature of provision and undermining traditional occupational hierarchies; and the minority 'marooned identity' who were uncomfortable with the new forms of working and experienced a growing isolation from their professional colleagues. What is important here is the extent to which organizational and sectoral context is critical for healthcare identities and can give rise to 'new forms of clinical identity' and any one designing health policies must be sensitive to this.

Modernization and organizational changes may also impact on the intrinsic nature and content of medical work, medical practice and even medical knowledge (see also discussion of Jewson's work in chapter 1). As discussed above, health care professionals have been subjected to a whole assemblage of regulatory practices that form part of modernization agendas. New forms of inter- and intra-organizational governance have been devised to scrutinize workers, make institutions more accountable, sensitive to their consumers, and become more transparent in their procedures and decision making. This, in tandem with reforms in medical education and training (Bolton et al., 2011), has led to a shift in the balance of the I/T ratio favouring technicality over intuition. These developments have meant that 'becoming' and 'being' a doctor relies less and less on experiential knowledge and more and more on encoded and formal knowledge. Examining doctors' accounts of their work through the frame of the sociology of embodiment, Nettleton and her colleagues (2008) found that consultants worry that this may lead to a reduction of what Polanyi (1966) refers to as 'tacit knowledge' amongst the new generation of doctors. Much of medical work, Polanyi argued, is learned through hands-on experience and the knowledge tends to be intuitive rather than explicit - a view echoed by the doctors interviewed in Nettleton et al.'s study. The consultants spoke about the importance of 'instinct', 'pattern recognition' and 'intuition' which could only be gained by hands-on training. Limits on doctors working hours combined with a tick-box approach to training has meant that fitness for medical practice may be characterized by competences rather than embodied knowledge skills. Claims to the importance of clinical 'judgement' and intuitive knowledge are critical to the need for self-regulation and the view of the medical profession that external regulation of the profession is intolerable. This may then form another process by which the position of doctors in society is challenged.

There is a degree of ambivalence, then, surrounding the ideology of biomedicine. It has served as both a resource for the medical profession through its association with scientific method and objectivity to legitimate its authority, and yet more recently the ideology has played into the hands of policy makers and mangers keen to commodify and standardize medical work. But this is matched by another trend in health care and healing and this is the growing popularity of *complementary and alternative medicines.*

The rise of complementary and alternative medicines

The last two decades have seen a proliferation of 'alternative health care practitioners' (Cant and Sharma, 2000; Cant, 2009; Thomson et al., 2011). The existence of a range of healing systems and therapies is by no means a new phenomenon. Indeed, prior to the nineteenth century the provision of health care in the UK was characterized more by its diversity and plurality than by any kind of uniformity (Stacey, 1988: 33–46). However, with the development of biomedicine and the associated hegemony of the medical profession, alternative forms of healing fell into relative decline. Today, the situation is beginning to look rather different; there has been a recent upsurge in the use of, and interest in, non-orthodox therapies and a corresponding increase in alternative healers. What has also changed in recent years is the response of orthodox medicine to non-orthodox practitioners, a change which may be characterized as a shift from open hostility to one of reluctant co-option.

The appropriate terminology for non-orthodox health care is the subject of some debate. Terms such as 'non-orthodox', 'alternative', 'complementary', 'holistic', 'traditional' and 'unconventional' are often used interchangeably, although some authors express specific preferences for certain terms because of their political and pragmatic implications. Saks (1992: 4), for example, opts for 'alternative medicine', which he says

> can be taken to encompass all the health care practices that at any specific point in time generally do not receive support from the medical establishment in the British context, whether this be through such mechanisms as orthodox medical research funding, sympathetic coverage in the mainstream medical journals, or routine inclusion in the mainstream medical curriculum.

He rejects the term 'complementary medicine' because, he argues, the label 'excludes therapies like homoeopathy which in their purest form are based on philosophies that fundamentally conflict with medical orthodoxy' (Saks, 1992: 3). Sharma (1992: 6), on the other hand, prefers this latter term, 'implying as it does the possibility of cooperation with orthodox medicine', and this, according to her empirical research, 'is a more general reflection of the views of patients' actual behaviour and practitioners' views'. With the growth of provision and use of non-orthodox health care, the nature of relations between it and orthodox medicine in the 1980s became increasingly vexed. However, more recently, the medical profession has become more accommodative. There are now some efforts being made by policy makers to facilitate the use of complementary and alternative medicines. For example, *The NHSTA Directory of Complementary and Alternative Practitioners* <http://www.nhstadirectory.org/>, managed and maintained by and for health care professionals and the NHS Trusts Association, provides information and guidance about complementary medicines for both health professionals and the public.

It is difficult to estimate the precise numbers of people who consult alternative practitioners. In the USA, 4 in 10 adults reported using a complementary alternative medicine (CAM) in 2007 (Barnes et al., 2008). In Ireland in 2002, one study found that 27 per cent of the population had seen a CAM practitioner and their review suggests that this indication is in keeping with international comparisons (Fox et al., 2010). It is also difficult to estimate how many alternative healers are currently practising, because the surveys have tended not to include the same range of practitioners.

Various explanations have been postulated for the rise in popularity of alternative medicine (Bakx, 1991; Sharma, 1992; Saks, 2003). These include changes in advanced capitalism, which is moving from a Fordist to a post-Fordist phase, with a concomitant rise in consumer influence over production; a decline of faith in scientific orthodoxy and biomedicine; a more active search for information about one's own health and a confidence to make choices about appropriate care and treatment; and attempts by individuals to seek solutions to problems which biomedicine cannot cure. Bakx (1991: 33) summarizes some of these arguments when he writes:

> biomedicine is in danger of losing both its actual and ideological hegemony because: firstly, it has culturally distanced itself from the consumers of its services; secondly, it has failed to match its propaganda promises with real breakthroughs in combating the disease created by modernism itself; thirdly, patients have become further alienated by negative physical and psychological experiences at the hands of biomedical practitioners themselves.

We must, however, be cautious here and not overstate the level of dissatisfaction with biomedicine; as already indicated, Sharma found from her interviews with users that they were not so much seeking alternatives as a result of direct dissatisfaction as using alternative healers in parallel. This is summed up by one of her respondents who said: 'The thing is about herbalism you cannot do without your doctor and your hospitals. It's a thing you can combine because if you want quick pain relief you can't get it from herbs but for such things like high blood pressure or stress then it is very good' (quoted in Sharma, 1992: 82).

It is clear that alternative health care practitioners are likely to play a more significant role in health care and healing in the future. They are clearly securing a market of users, and are offering genuine alternatives to those proffered by conventional practitioners. Not surprisingly, therefore, the medical profession has in recent years paid closer attention to their activities. Although a very small minority of the medical profession has used alternative therapies alongside more conventional approaches, for the most part the medical profession has long been at best dismissive and at worst hostile towards alternative medicines. Two main reasons are offered for this. First, the theoretical basis of many of the approaches is completely at odds with conventional medical science, and so represents a challenge to their knowledge base. It is argued, quite simply, that they cannot possibly be based on 'truth'. The BMA, in response to the growing interest in alternative medicine, set up a Working Party on Alternative Therapy in 1983, which produced the subsequent report *Alternative Therapy*, published in 1986 (BMA, 1992). Significantly, the largest section of the report (thirty of its seventy-eight pages) was devoted to a detailed account of the merits of scientific methods and the rigours and achievements of biomedicine, which are 'free from overriding social values and political bias' and have 'become inevitably and increasingly separated from doctrines embracing superstition, magic, and the supernatural' (BMA, 1992: 212). The scientific basis of modern medicine is contrasted to those alternative therapies which involve 'a reversion to primitive beliefs and outmoded practices, almost without basis' (BMA, 1992: 216).

Second, the medical profession sees itself as the rightful guardian of public health. It expresses concern that the lay public may be in danger from 'the so-called alternative therapies' (BMA, 1992: 215), and therefore the medical profession must ensure that patients are made aware of the risks: 'The patient should also be helped to understand that consultation with the practitioners of some alternative therapies may be attended by the risk of great harm' (BMA, 1992: 228). For this reason, they argue, alternative forms of healing must be subjected to the rigours of scientific evaluation, which are in turn rooted within the paradigm of conventional science.

We can see, therefore, that in 1986 the BMA had little sympathy with alternative medicine and appeared keen to discredit it. The report did little to stop the tide, however, and more people appear to be seeking and benefiting from diverse forms of healing and healers. It may be for this reason that the BMA felt bound to carry out a further investigation, which culminated in a second report, *Complementary Medicine: New Approaches to Good Practice* (BMA, 1993). As the change in title suggests, the BMA no longer implied that non-orthodox healing systems were simply at odds with orthodox medicine, but rather that they could function alongside, or indeed 'complement', conventional medical practice. This report sets out quite clearly the appropriate boundaries between orthodox and non-orthodox practitioners. Indeed, it aims to demarcate the sphere within which alternative practitioners can legitimately function. Whilst it advocates professionalization and self-regulation as beneficial for both alternative practitioners and public alike, it also states that those who gain state recognition as professionals must have the support of the medical profession. It also highlights the need for 'good practice' among what it terms 'discrete clinical disciplines', which include systems such as acupuncture, chiropractice, homoeopathy, herbalism and osteopathy:

> for all therapies, good practice would demand that each body representing a therapy demonstrate: an organized structure; a single register of members; guide-lines on relationships with medical practitioners; sound training at accredited institutions; an effective ethical code; agreed levels of competence; and a proven commitment to research. (BMA, 1993: 141)

It seems, therefore, that whilst the medical profession appears keen to see alternative practitioners become increasingly professionalized and autonomous, it is also keen to set the parameters in which they can work. For example, the report reiterates throughout the need for alternative practitioners to be well versed in medical sciences, so that they know when to refer patients to orthodox practitioners.

> Practitioners should show an awareness of the limits of competence and the scope of their particular therapy, together with a knowledge of absolute and relative contra-indications to therapy. With this goes the ability to recognize conditions where a particular treatment is inappropriate, and also when a patient is suffering from a condition that requires immediate referral to the patient's GP. (BMA, 1993: 136–7)

The report also emphasizes that the use of alternative therapies must not delay seeking help from conventional therapists. GPs should also be kept informed of any treatments being followed by users of alternative therapies.

Saks (2003) adopts a Weberian approach when theorizing the shifting relationship between orthodox and non-orthodox medicine. He accounts for the professionalization of these groups in terms of processes of occupational exclusion and inclusion (see above), his central thesis being 'that interest-based politics, rather than scientific logic *per se*, is central to the understanding of health care in general and the relationship between orthodox and alternative medicine in particular' (2003: 6). The relationships between the occupational players are dynamic and transforming. Undoubtedly, orthodox medicine remains the dominant profession, but the expansion of alternative medicine is such that Cant and Sharma (1999) have suggested that there is some evidence of medical pluralism.

The hegemony of the medical profession has thus been subject to some profound changes in both the internal organization of conventional health care and the rise of competing paradigms of health care. These changes are perhaps indicative of broader socio-economic and cultural shifts associated with late modernism. We shall now turn to consider how these shifts impact upon the NHS more generally.

The restructuring of the National Health Service

The changes and developments outlined in the previous section have not occurred in a vacuum. They reflect broader transformations in wider society, which are often characterized in the literature as shifts from modernism to post- or late modernism at the socio-cultural level, from Fordism to post-Fordism at the level of the economy, and from an industrial to an 'information society' at a socio-technical level. These terms refer to the changes that we have witnessed since the 1970s, wherein, within the context of welfare, there has been a shift from mass, universal needs being met by monolithic, paternalistic, professionally led bureaucracies to a situation of welfare pluralism, quasi-markets and consumer sovereignty (Harrison and McDonald, 2008). Such social transformations are evidenced in the restructuring of the NHS. This restructuring has had a significant impact on the nature of health care work, and this is an important area of study within the sociology of health and illness. In the next section we will examine the nature and impact of these changes in more detail.

Historically the process of the restructuring of the Health Service is seen as a response to the 'crisis' in welfare provision that occurred in advanced capitalist societies in the mid-1970s. According to Offe (1984) there are inherent contradictions in the state system, which will make the current provision of health and welfare untenable (Fitzpatrick, 1987). Offe argues that the state is not simply an instrument of capital, as traditional Marxist theory would have it, but rather is a system which comprises three elements: the political administrative system, the economic system and the legitimation system. The government, or the political administrative system, continually attempts to reconcile the other two elements. On the one hand, it must facilitate capital accumulation, and on the other, it must ensure social cohesion and political support. The NHS exemplifies this problem. On the one hand, it is a drain on resources, and so constitutes a threat to capital accumulation, whilst, on the other hand, it is extremely popular. The key to Offe's analysis is the idea that social policies should not concentrate only on class demands, or the needs of capital, but should consider 'answers to what can be called the *internal* problem of the state apparatus, namely how it can react *consistently* to the two poles of the "needs" of labour and capital . . . The problem is that of the precarious compatibility of its own institutions and performances' (Offe, 1984: 104, cited in Fitzpatrick, 1987: 231).

One response at the level of institutions is that of restructuring. Throughout the 1980s the NHS underwent significant changes in relation to the organization and provision of health care. Some authors, such as R. Klein (2010), have highlighted the fact that the main principles on which it was founded (that is, to be predominantly funded by taxation and to be, for the most part, free at the point of access) are still intact. Others, by contrast, argue that significant transformations have taken place, and such changes are commonly referred to as restructuring. Flynn (1992: 4) defines this as 'a process by which significant changes are made in established arrangements in resource allocation, in the division of labour and organizational structure, and the criteria and objectives of service provision'. The restructuring of the Health Service involves new corporate planning procedures, the enforcement of cash limits, performance indicators, compulsory tendering for contracts, efficiency savings, the hiving off of statutory services, private finance initiatives, greater use of market and consumer relations techniques, a challenge to professional dominance, and the formation of an enterprise culture.

Since the late 1990s, New Labour and Coalition governments continued to place 'patient choice' at the heart of their policies. For example, *The NHS Plan* (Department of Health, 2000: 88–95) put structures in place to ensure that patients have greater choices about their treatment, professionals respond to their needs, and patients are more fully informed. Subsequent Coalition governments in the UK extended these strategies using the language or choice and ridding the health service of provider led bureaucracy. For example, a White Paper setting out the government's plans for reform, titled *Liberating the NHS: Greater Choice and Control*, states:

> The White Paper, *Equity and Excellence: Liberating the NHS*, sets out the Government's vision of an NHS that puts patients and the public first – where patients, service users, carers and families have far more influence and choice in the system, and the NHS is more responsive to their needs and wishes. (Department of Health, 2010)

Governments of various political hues appear to articulate something of a consensus that taps into neo-liberal notions of choice and freedom. Health policies, structures and modes of delivery change rapidly. It is useful therefore to have analytic tools and a historical context in order to make sense of these changes. For example, the concepts of professional autonomy and accountability are helpful to appreciate the impact of organizational developments on health care workers and the relations between occupational groups.

Post-Fordism and health care

In the second half of the twentieth century, the crisis in capitalism, which exhibited itself in the fiscal crisis of the welfare state in the 1970s, is now understood by some commentators to have been a manifestation of the shift from a Fordist to a post-Fordist regime of accumulation. These terms refer to the methods of organizing production and the social, political and cultural consequences of this. A Fordist regime is one in which there is a system of mass production of standardized products, which is matched by sustained levels of mass consumption. This is typified by Henry Ford's black car. The production process is large-scale, inflexible and capital-intensive; it is characterized by rigid hierarchical and bureaucratic management structures; and workers' tasks are routine and repetitive, and are subjected to the principles of scientific management.

Post-Fordism, by contrast, is characterized by production techniques which are designed to respond to consumer demand and fragmented market tastes. Consumers no longer satisfied with the 'black car' have become more discerning. More flexible production processes require more decentralized forms of labour process and work organization. There needs to be a skill-flexible core of employees and a time-flexible periphery of low-paid and therefore insecurely employed workers. This involves a decline in manual occupations and a concurrent expansion of service and professional occupations. In terms of consumption, it involves the promotion of more varied types of goods and services and an ever-increasing range of individually chosen lifestyles and tastes. With the help of information technologies, data are assimilated on the characteristics of consumers which have now become fundamental to the niche marketing of goods. These principles were articulated by the NHS Management Executive (1993), which cites the Ford motor company's present-day marketing slogan – 'Everything we do is driven by you' – as providing a rationale for the way forward in the NHS. The anthropologist Emily Martin (1994) has argued that 'flexibility' is *the* dominant motif of organizational culture in the new millennium. But one of the unintended consequences of organizations being flexible in order to be ever vigilant and responsive to 'consumers' needs' is that employees have to be on hand on a 24-hour basis. Of course, this has always been the case for occupational groups within health care, but the growth of services designed to meet patients' needs has implications for staff. Theories of post-Fordism can provide a heuristic device by which we might understand the current changes within the NHS, and direct our attention to the changing nature of both the labour process and organizational dynamics.

'Modernization' and new managerialism

During the 1980s there was a radical shift in the way in which the Health Service was managed. From the 1960s to 1983, Health Service management took the form of what Harrison et al. (1990) call a 'diplomacy model'. In this model the Health Service manager's role was not to lead or change the direction of the Health Service, but to smooth out conflicts and enable professionals to get on with their job of caring for patients. The diplomacy model had four key characteristics (Harrison et al., 1990: 103–4). First, doctors had more influence than managers, in that they were clinically free to make decisions about individual patients, and so through the aggregation of their decisions they determined the shape of the service. Second, managers were reactive rather than proactive, and were problem-solvers rather than innovators. Third, managers concentrated on problems that were internal to the organization, rather than considering the wider environment and the needs of consumers. Fourth, the pattern of change was slow and incremental, with little critical analysis of the *status quo*.

The term *new managerialism* emerged in the 1980s and involved the displacement of diplomatic management with a more interventionist, dynamic and innovative style derived from models of private sector management, considered to be more appropriate to the needs of late modern, post-Fordist organizational life. This was a consequence of the then Conservative government's more interventionist approach to the service. Despite espousing a rhetoric of devolving power from the centre to the periphery when they came into office in 1979, the Conservatives soon began to be dictatorial about the direction the Health Service should take. In 1983 the government appointed a team of business leaders, led by Griffiths, the managing director of Sainsbury's supermarkets, to review management in the NHS. Griffiths (DHSS, 1983) concluded that 'private sector' styles of management were what the NHS needed and, in particular, that there was a need for continuous evaluation of performance against defined objectives, outputs and standards. The key recommendation was that the 'consensus management teams' introduced in the 1974 reorganization of the NHS, which consisted of representatives from the medical, nursing and administrative staff, should be replaced by a clearly defined general 'line' manager at every tier of the service. The report summed up the problem thus: 'In short, if Florence Nightingale were carrying her lamp through the corridors of the NHS today she would almost certainly be searching for the people in charge' (DHSS, 1983: 12). Strong management and a private sector ethos would both 'stimulate initiative, urgency and vitality' and ensure 'a constant search for major change and cost improvement'. Indeed, the government's promotional video which accompanied its White Paper on the reforms, *Working for Patients* (Department of Health, 1989), stated that 'the NHS is not a business run for profit, but it can certainly become more businesslike.' Thus the change was not simply one of the structural arrangements of the Health Service, as the previous reorganizations had been, but also involved a transformation in its values and culture.

With this new type of management, the structures of control in the Health Service have shifted, and managers have tackled head-on the government's crucial dilemma: that is, 'how to impose its political priorities on an organization where professional judgement determined the local delivery of services' (Cousins, 1988: 211). A whole series of experiments and initiatives have been developed to refine measures of activities and outputs. As Elston (1991: 69) puts it:

> Demands for greater 'value for money' have spawned a plethora of techniques for managerial evaluation and control over clinical activity. The new acronyms, QA, PIs, DRGs, QALYs, promise a new era in which doctors' clinical freedom of action within the NHS might be progressively circumscribed through bureaucratic assessment.

These acronyms stand for quality assurance, performance indicators, diagnostic-related groups and quality-adjusted life years, respectively. These, and other associated managerial procedures, 'represent a radical departure from previous arrangements concerning professional autonomy, because they entail managerial encroachment on the determination of work content, productivity, resource use and quality standards' (Flynn, 1992: 183). The aim, then, is to increase the productivity and efficiency of clinicians by encouraging them to consider factors other than their clinical judgement when making decisions.

Green et al. (2011) usefully described three 'interconnected changes' to welfare provision that occurred under the rubric of 'modernization' (see also Kuhlmann, 2006). The first of these is the exponential growth of 'the audit society' (Power, 1997) and the application of accounting techniques and auditing procedures in order to make outcomes explicit and measurable. The work of health practitioners and professionals is subject to regulation; for example, their practice is assessed against a number of measures or 'indicators' of performance. In addition their clinical decision making is shaped by protocols which in turn are presumed to be underpinned by a sound evidence base, although the validity of such evidence is sometimes called into question (Power, 1997; Flynn, 1992, 2004). Related to this was the rise of what in the 1980s was referred to as the 'New Public Management' which involved a more hands-on style to monitoring performance and the replication of market structures into the public sector whereby services were in effect 'bought' and 'sold' by 'commissioners' and 'providers' of services. Third, in concert with the introduction of market mechanisms was the promulgation of consumerism: the patient, as a consumer, was bestowed with choice. Patients, citizens, clients, consumers, call them what you will, were to be placed – rhetorically at least – as the drivers of health care (Martin, 2008). Finally, Green and her colleagues point to the ways in which modernization encourages shared working practices evident in the vocabulary of 'partnerships' and 'networks', and the 'replacement of hierarchical arrangements and "silos" of activity with more fluid and cross-cutting arrangements' (2011: 819).

Whilst the organizational costs of professionals having discretion and control over their work have become untenable, at the same time, because of the high I/T ratio of medical practice, managers still have to grant them a considerable amount of freedom. Hunter (1991) argues that attempts to shift the boundaries of control from medicine to management remain varied, with doctors resisting direct involvement in management activity, which they fear will pave the way for a further reduction in clinical freedom. Thus, throughout the Health Service, organizational settings function as 'locales of politics' (Clegg, 1989), where negotiation, contestation and struggle between groups are routine. According to Clegg, power increasingly takes the form of surveillance characteristic of Foucault's disciplinary or panoptic power (see chapter 5), wherein professionals are overseen with the aid of information technology and are thereby encouraged to monitor their own behaviour, a component of the 'audit society', where there is an increase of monitoring as opposed to other forms of control. Through the techniques of monitoring, a new system of knowledge is generated, which in turn may be used to assess the activities of auditees. Just as public health officials collated and disseminated knowledge about the habits of the general population, mechanisms are now being devised for assessing health professionals. Audit is justified in terms of empowering popular control, in that those who use collective resources are placed under scrutiny (Power, 1992).

Clinical governance and evidence-based medicine

Clinical governance – a term introduced by New Labour in the late 1990s – forms a central strand of contemporary health management and a key feature of New Labour's modernization programme. The term implies a set of governing mechanisms, rather than a unified central mode of command. The term is variously defined, but Harrison (2004: 180–1) usefully delineates its five key features. First, chief executives of Health Trusts are responsible for financial *and* clinical performance – which implies that managers can challenge doctors. Trusts and Health Authorities have a statutory duty to assure and improve quality. Second, clinical governance involves the activities of a number of institutions whose remit involves standard setting, inspection and surveillance. The National Institute of Clinical Excellence (NICE) issues guidance on treatments and the cost-effectiveness of drugs and therapies. National Service Frameworks (NSFs) set out models for service delivery of particular care groups, services and conditions. The Commission for Health Audit and Inspection (CHAI) monitors standards and carries out reviews of local services. Third, in concert with these developments, doctors have to revalidate their registration with the General Medical Council (GMC). Fourth, implementation of clinical governance is based on 'explicit policies and procedures'. Finally, and relatedly, clinical governance is inextricably linked with – although not identical to – 'evidence-based medicine' (EBM). EBM involves the creation and dissemination of guidelines for clinicians on the relative effectiveness of health care interventions. We discuss EBM in more detail in the following chapter. In essence, then, clinical governance comprises a number of means of ensuring accountability and uniformly good standards of care.

Flynn (2004) cogently argues that new forms of management are more appropriately understood as Foucauldian than Fordist or post-Fordist, as some analysts have suggested. In particular, the mechanisms of clinical governance have been devised in an attempt to reconcile two key tensions: the need to regulate doctors, yet ensure that the public still trust them; and the need to achieve collective objectives, yet allow for 'tacit knowledge and individual expertise' (2004: 16). Clinical governance forms a neat illustration of what Foucault (1991) terms 'governmentality', a means of governing at a distance, 'so that actors come to perceive problems in similar ways *and* accept a responsibility to seek ways of transforming their position themselves' (Flynn, 2004: 18). Flynn draws on Courpasson's (2000) concept 'soft bureaucracy', which refers to forms of organizational governance that rely on mechanisms of both external surveillance and self-surveillance, and is especially apposite for dealing with indeterminate knowledge. He also makes use of Lam's (2000) typology of organizational forms to suggest that the implementation of clinical governance involves a shift from a 'professional bureaucracy' – wherein professionals are free to apply their knowledge – to a 'machine bureaucracy' – where professionals' knowledge is monitored and made explicit through codification and guidelines.

An important sociological question is if, and if so how, these changes are consequential for medical knowledge and practice. One study of hospital doctors working in the the UK (Nettleton et al., 2008) found that clinicians voiced concerns that processes of modernization and what felt to them like excessive audit was curtailing their scope for recourse to their clinical judgement which is rooted in their tacit and experiential, or as Jamous and Peloille (1970) would call it, indeterminate knowledge. Of course the 'art of medicine' rather than the evidence base of medicine has long been criticized for being subjective, and historically has been used by the profession to preclude external evaluation of practice. But there may be issues here that beg consideration, for example, this tacit knowledge the medical doctors argued was gained through prolonged and extensive 'hands-on' training whereby they learned through doing. The feared that reforms in medical education and training that limited their working hours and gave way to tick-box 'audits' and assessments of competencies would undermine the intuitive and practical qualities of clinical work. Such views echoed the thesis articulated by the doctor turned philosopher Polanyi (1959, 1966), who in his book *The Tacit Dimension* argues that practical knowledge, such as making a clinical diagnosis, requires intuitive bodily awareness. Such awareness, or 'knowledge' is achieved through what he calls 'indwelling' – the process of both observing empathetically and doing. Tacit knowledge fundamentally relies on 'hands-on' experience and the technological instruments deployed in scientific explorations are inseparable from the body. And of course much of medical work and health care generally comprises work by bodies and work on bodies. Much of health work can therefore be conceptualized as body work.

'Body work'

What characterizes paid health care practitioners – be they doctors, dentists, health care assistants, domiciliary care workers, nurses, or CAM therapists – is that they undertake *body work*. This concept was initially devised by Wolkowitz (2002, 2006) and then usefully applied by Twigg and her colleagues (2011) to the health care sector. It elucidates some of the unique qualities of work associated with working on the bodies of others. It is a valuable concept because it sharpens the focus of a lens through which we are able to examine the day-to-day work and political context of those people who are paid to provide hands-on health care.

Body work is defined as,'work that focuses directly on the bodies of others: assessing, diagnosing, handling, treating, manipulating, and monitoring bodies, that has thus become the object of the worker's labour' (Twigg et al., 2011: 171). It has a number of interrelated characteristics. First, it is ambivalent work in that normal social codes or mores associated with touch, proximity and emotional intimacy can be violated. Uniforms or other markers are sometimes used to demarcate roles in order to counter any unease that can arise from these ambivalences. Relatedly, body work lies at the border of the erotic, 'mimicking sexuality' (p. 172) in a way that can trouble normal social encounters. We saw evidence of this in our discussion of Lawler's analysis of nursing work in chapter 5 and the way in which props may be used to overcome any embarrassment. Third, body work can be 'dirty work', having to negotiate body boundaries and most especially those instances where bodily fluids transcend the boundaries of the body. Fourth, body work involves not only working on a material body but also a person – the recipient of body work is both object and subject – thus it can give rise to a complex play of inter-subjectivities. Consequently the body worker has to have at least some appreciation of the physical body and the personhood that is present in that body. Body workers must be skilled in emotional labour, they can sooth, cause pain or pleasure, cure, care and communicate. Thus micro social relations between the worked on and the worker are critical. Body work requires co-presence (Twigg et al., 2011; Cohen, 2011), thus limiting the spatial and temporal ordering of its provision. Providers and recipients have to be in the same place and at the same time. It is therefore labour intensive and relatively inflexible work. The needs of the worked upon may not easily fit into normal 'working hours', and bodies are notoriously unpredictable and capricious.

Body work also gives us some analytic purchase into macro social relations, providing insight as to why divisions of labour in health care are so durable. Co-presence means that the work is labour hungry; body workers cannot be replaced by machines or their labour offshored. Body work maps onto status hierarchies and is startlingly gendered and racialized. Those further up the social hierarchy, such as doctors or dentists, tend to have a mediated contact with the bodies they work upon; the patient's body may be prepared prior to any interaction, and contact tends to be limited to discrete interventions or investigations. This is in contrast to those with less socio-economic status who tend to undertake physically demanding and sometimes socially demeaning tasks associated with mopping up bodily mess and attending to 'dependent' bodies. Body work is gendered, racialized and (as we saw in our discussion of 'race' and medicine above) reliant on migrant workers. In the global north, ageing populations, increased numbers of women participating in paid employment, and transformations in familial relations have generated an increase in the need for care workers. Consequently 'the care worker is usually a woman, sometimes a migrant worker, holding an ill-paid job, with little social status, and moreover one that is often stigmatized because of the dirty work it involves' (Twigg et al., 2011: 180).

Conclusion

This chapter has dealt with processes of social change as they are manifesting in the restructuring of both work practices and organizational forms in the context of formal health care. It began by examining changes in the health professions, and how they are being shaped by contemporary developments in the social relations of class, gender and 'race'. The evidence for the decline of professional dominance was considered, especially in relation to both the changing nature of medical work and the rise of alternative medicine, both of which are in turn associated with a set of broader socio-economic and cultural changes. This led to a discussion of the restructuring of the NHS more generally. Theorizations based upon the idea of the development of a post-Fordist regime of accumulation were introduced and illustrated by the emergence of new managerialism, clinical governance, health economics, and the implementation of a labour market strategy designed to create a more 'flexible' ancillary work-force. The changes in formal health work which have been detailed are broadly consistent with the dynamics associated with both late modern and post-Fordist theorizations of contemporary Western liberal democracies. These socio-cultural changes are being accelerated by technological transformations, most notably information and communication technologies which are a key feature of the 'information society' (Castells, 2000) and which are evident in some of the contemporary developments in UK health policy, to which we now turn.

FURTHER READING

Freidson, E. (2001), *Professionalism: The Third Logic*, Cambridge: Polity. Freidson's sociological critiques of the medical profession have dominated the literature for decades. This book comprises a review, reflection and revision of many of his earlier ideas in the light of socio-economic changes.

Harrison S. R. and McDonald E. R. (2008), *The Politics of Healthcare in Britain*, London: Sage.

Nettleton, S. and Gustaffson, U. (eds) (2002), *The Sociology of Health and Illness Reader*, Cambridge: Polity. The chapters in Part V, 'Health Care Work', are relevant here.

Riska, E. (2010), 'Health Professions and Occupations', in W. Cockerham (ed.), *The New Blackwell Companion to Medical Sociology*, London: Wiley-Blackwell.

Saks, M. (2003), *Orthodox and Complementary Medicine: Politics, Professionalization and Health Care*, London: Sage. A Weberian analysis of the changing circumstances of complementary and alternative practitioners in the UK and the USA.

Witz, A. (1992), *Professions and Patriarchy*, London: Routledge. Another Weberian account, one which is gendered and examines the salience of patriarchy for the nursing, midwifery and medical professions. An excellent read both conceptually and historically.

9 The Sociology of Innovative Health Technology

Introduction

Technologies play a central role in health care. Testing and screening procedures, inhalers, surgical instruments, imaging techniques, prosthesis, reproductive technologies and pharmaceutical developments are only a few of the many forms of technology that are routinely used within contemporary medical practice. A visit to a museum of medical history reveals a myriad of instruments that can, to our eyes, appear as curious and even barbaric inventions. Some technologies have endured. The stethoscope invented in 1816 remains perhaps *the* most iconic marker of Western biomedicine. Medical consultations are more often than not concluded with the doctor prescribing some form of drug to alleviate symptoms. Complementary and alternative medicines are also reliant on technologies such as the needles used by an acupuncturist or the remedies issued by a homeopath. Technologies then have long been central to the practice of health care, but there is a sense that the pace of technological innovation accelerated as we moved into the twenty-first century.

When the first edition of this book was published in 1995, the idea that lay people like you or I might look up symptoms on the Internet, or 'Google' the drugs we had been prescribed by our doctor would have been thought of as at best absurd, or at worse, a cause for concern. The prospect of surveillance technologies being placed into the homes of frail men and women would have connoted thoughts of 'big brother', and the idea that the Human Genome Project initiated in 1990 might have successfully mapped the human genome (the sequencing of the long chains of deoxyribonucleic acid (DNA) that make up the human genome) was a mere aspiration. These and related innovations, Casper and Morrison (2010) observe, comprise a shift 'from large "machines at the bedside" to tiny pills and devices that enter into and transform human bodies' (p. 121). The lexicon of a 'biotechnological revolution' in the context of an 'information age' of digitized technologies contributes to an impression that health and medical work is being transformed.

The pace of technological innovation has given rise to a plethora of health practices and conundrums that sociologists are keen to study. There is a significant body of empirical work on how technologies are used in practice and a growing convergence between the theoretical traditions of medical sociology and 'science and technology studies' (referred to by the acronym STS). Novel theories that span these subfields enable researchers to think critically about 'technology', and indeed even the consequences for the politics of life itself (Rose, 2001). Biotechnologies associated with genetics, pharmaco-genetics, tissue engineering, stem cell research, nanotechnologies and so on generate a raft of moral and ethical questions giving rise to a relatively new field of study known as bio-ethics (De Vries et al., 2007; Petersen, 2011a, 2011b).

The testing of bodies for possible biomarkers of disease, or the extraction of body tissue for sale or exchange, are as much social and political as they are biotechnological practices, and the concepts of 'bio-politics', 'bio-value' and 'bio-socialities' help us make sense of them.

The sociological literature on health technologies is now substantial and so in order to try to communicate some of the key parameters of the debates within one chapter, we will first provide a brief description of sociological approaches to medical technology. We will then take three distinct examples of health technologies: medical imaging, tissue transfer and genetics. The fine tuning of technologies to visualize the interiority of bodies prompts interesting questions as to how the images are interpreted and by whom, and so speaks to debates on the socially constructed and negotiated nature of medical knowledge (see chapter 2). The transfer of body tissue serves as a neat reminder that the use and implementation of technological procedures are muddied by the practical matters of extracting, exchanging and moving body parts through health care contexts and systems. The infiltration of genetic medicine into everyday health discourses and routine clinical practices provokes questions of identity, responsibility and citizenship. We explore these implications and concepts below, but first let us foreground these examples in the theoretical perspectives that are influential for sociological analyses of medical technologies.

Sociological approaches to medical technology

Contemporary scholars are critical of those sociological approaches that fail to grasp the emergent properties of technologies and so fail to confront the complex and nuanced issues that their use gives rise to (Webster, 2008). There is a continuum of perspectives on medical technologies; at one end there are those that see technologies as discrete, inert tools that can be used, abused or neglected by groups or organizations, and at the other end there are those who seek to collapse the distinction between the properties of technological and organizational forms. Timmermans and Berg (2003) usefully identify three sociological approaches to understanding technology in medicine which have gained prominence over time and figure on this continuum.

'Technological determinism' is an approach that tends to bracket off and so exclude technologies from the analytic endeavour, seeing them as neutral arbiters in medical practice. Technological innovations, distanced from analysis bolster medicalization and are presumed to influence social change often with detrimental consequences. Technological iatrogenesis disproportionately affects the socially and politically disadvantaged. For example, information and communication technologies are criticized for extending surveillance; reproductive technologies for reinforcing patriarchal control over childbirth; and screening practices for giving rise to stigma and discrimination. This view is akin to the political economy variant of medicalization that we discussed in chapter 2.

Timmermans and Berg (2003) find technological determinism wanting on three counts. First, this reductionist view invests '"super technological" powers to tools and practices; powers that do not hold up in empirical analysis' (p. 100). Second, technological procedures such as medication for the relief of pain, contraceptive technologies that allow women to control fertility, reproductive technologies that overcome infertility and so on are overlooked. Third, technological determinism is 'fuelled by a suspicious blend of case selection and conspiracy theories' and so has limited analytic purchase. Nevertheless, this approach, although uniformly criticized, reminds us of the significance of the broader politico-economic context in which technologies are produced, most particularly the way financial investments in health technologies can yield substantial profits. In turn this gives us some clues as to why increasingly complex technological solutions may be privileged over less 'high-tech' ones associated with public health interventions to address issues associated with material disadvantage and inequality.

A second 'social essentialist' approach focuses on the ways in which medical technologies 'function as sociological *catalysts* . . . The key characteristic of a social essentialist perspective is that the technology is a passive, non communicable device requiring social interpretations to be rendered meaningful' (Timmermans and Berg, 2003: 101, 102). Again technologies are presumed to be neutral and seen as a tabula rasa on which actors impose their meanings or interpretations. Aspirins or acupuncture, for example, will be understood differently by people in differing contexts and so rendered meaningful through the process of individuals or groups making sense of them. The medical profession may use complex high-tech equipment to enhance their status or expertise, or more benignly the equipment may be used to improve the quality of care for their patients. Patients deploy technologies to alleviate pain, treat symptoms and prolong life. Thus this approach to understanding medical technology, like the previous one, sees technologies as separate from people. What is of sociological interest is how the technologies are deployed and used, and how meanings are invested in them. In keeping with conventional sociological preoccupations, these analyses examine the interests of social groups who benefit from the use of technologies and gloss over 'what is technological in medical technologies' (p. 103). For this reason, Timmermans and Berg favour a third approach labelled 'technology in practice.'

Technology-in-practice combines the interests of medical sociology and STS and treats technologies as active players within the health care setting. This idea is rooted in Actor Network Theory (ANT), an approach within science studies that examines technologies and humans as if they have an equivalence, both having a kind of agency (Law, 2009). ANT has infiltrated the sociology of health and illness during the last decade and is ontologically and epistemologically challenging. In terms of ontology, it questions what 'things' are. For example, we conventionally regard technological artefacts as asocial tools that can only be effective when 'used' by humans. ANT scholars, on the other hand, presume that both human and non-human 'actors' can create or 'enact' outcomes. This is because of the way in which they mesh within contexts and networks which in turn exist in relation to each other. Hence they use the term '*actants*' to capture the notion that both human and non-human actors have the capacity to be consequential. All things – tools, technologies, individuals, groups etc. – exist in relation to each other and are constantly altering and refracting.

Epistemologically a form of social constructionism, ANT offers a distinctive methodological approach with an emphasis upon detailed descriptions of specific objects as they travel through settings. Law (2009) argues that ANT is not so much a theory but a 'material semiotic' approach that offers a 'toolkit' for undertaking 'grounded empirical case studies' (p. 141). Herein lies the value of ANT for sociologists researching medical technologies. The approach involves undertaking detailed, ethnographic, case studies that examine how machines, humans, things, objects and text co-construct realities. The focus is upon how these actants function in relation to each other; they do not have intrinsic stable qualities but each is troubled through its dynamic interplay with other material and non-material entities, be they tools, clinicians, professional groups, carers or patients.

Annemarie Mol's (2002) book *The Body Multiple* is one of the pioneering examples of this approach which spans STS and medical sociology. As the title suggests, she argues that it might be more appropriate to think of individual patients having 'multiple bodies', a view she arrived at while undertaking an ethnography of clinical pathways experienced by patients as they acquired a diagnosis of lower limb atherosclerosis which, in conventional medicine, refers to the blocked arteries in the leg. Her thesis is that the 'body' of a single patient is differentially 'enacted' as it moves through the health care system. In consultations with a general practitioner the patient presents with symptoms of leg pain; in the vascular clinic a pressure cuff and scanning technologies generate readings of blood flow and blood pressure; in radiography x-rays provide images of blocked blood vessels and ultrasound readings record blood flow in narrowed sections of the vessels; and in the operating theatre the surgeon 'de-clogs' blood vessels. Thus each health practitioner enacts or performs in relation to a specific material reality. However, the reality of the body is constantly shifting. Mol uses the term 'patchwork singularity' to capture the idea that any coherence or any one reading of the body is a temporary stitching together of these multiple enactments.

Taking Mol's (2002) thesis as a point of departure, Gardner et al. (2011) undertook a case study of a man presenting with chest pains, observing him as he moved through three clinical settings: a consultation in primary care, an ECG test in hospital and a follow-up outpatient meeting with a consultant. During the first consultation, the doctor suspects heart disease, and yet during the second consultation, results of the ECG give him the 'all clear'. During the third outpatient consultation, the consultant explains away the test results and advises the patient that the ECG is not necessarily a comprehensive arbiter and the patient's clinical profile indicates he is 'at risk' of heart disease. Monitoring and measuring technologies thus carry particular conceptions of health risks and, in collaboration with practitioners, point to not only disease but symptoms of 'pre-disease'. Normative public health discourses then come into play, and the patient is encouraged to undertake 'healthy' behaviours to reduce his risk status. Thus diagnostic procedures have temporal and affective dimensions and are located in wider health discourses. What is interesting in this case is that the results of the tests confirmed the patient as having a normal heart with no identifiable problems, and yet the presentation of his symptoms, his age, his gender, give cause for concern. There is no clear correspondence between technological procedures and outcomes; rather these are mediated by the clinical and wider social processes in which they are embedded.

In sum, those who subscribe to the technology-in-practice approach do not so much see disease as socially constructed but as 'enacted' through practices carried out in a variety of clinical settings with a variety of technologies and players. The importance of this distinction is that, while the former implies that a stable category may be forged, the latter emphasizes the frailty of assemblages which in turn are contingent upon the context, be it the clinic, the laboratory, the home and so on. Technologies are consequential within given settings and are not tools that are deployed in order to exert social control or to reproduce social divisions. Contemporary approaches that combine STS and medical sociology go some way to bridging the gulf between political economy perspectives that see innovations in medical technologies as a means to perpetuate the hegemony of powerful groups and interactionist studies that focus on the social relations that exist alongside technologies. Their strength lies in the pursuit of empirical and especially ethnographic explorations into health care and medical practice, and so dovetail well with medical sociology's empirical tradition. It is to one such empirical case study that we now turn as we begin to think about another tranche of technologies used for visualizing bodies.

Medical imaging: visualizing bodies and vanishing patients?

Mildred Blaxter, a leading authority in medical sociology, published an autobiographical account of her own clinical case history the year before she died at the age of 85 (Blaxter, 2009). Drawing on both STS and other sociological perspectives, her analysis explores the consequences of technological procedures for patient care and medical practice. Her article also highlights the merits of longitudinal approaches over cross-sectional studies and her range of data include: fieldnotes, records of consultations, reports, test results, and letters spanning the 141 days, from an initial consultation to the beginning of her treatment for cancer. In the article entitled, 'The Case of the Vanishing Patient? Image and Experience', she reflects upon her experiences of 'high-tech medicine' and explores three themes: the place of the image in a diagnosis, the embodied experience of technology, and the extent to which she – as the patient – is a 'co-producer of the diagnosis' (p. 766). Overall, she did not experience technologies as alienating and dehumanizing as a technological determinist approach might indicate. On the contrary, the images produced by the CT scans (computerized tomography) and PETs (positron emission tomography) were intriguing; seeing the inside of her own body was a fascinating opportunity. However, the way in which the images interpreted by clinicians in different specialties produced multiple, often conflicting accounts of her body did invoke a sense of alienation. Blaxter's own interpretation of her symptoms tended to be marginalized. Take the following extract from her fieldnotes reporting on an exchange about a 'slipped disc':

DATA EXTRACT 5 – The slipped disc: extracts from P diary

Day 119 [A few days before being admitted for the (aborted) surgery, P developed severe pain in the back. On arrival at the surgical ward, the nurses and Mr. S were consulted, since it might have relevance to the proposed surgery. Mr. S ordered an immediate scan]

Mr. S: The scan is back – as I thought it's a slipped disc.

P: This won't affect the surgery?

Mr. S: No, not at all. We'll give you some oral morphine so that you can lie more comfortably now, and you'll have analgesia afterwards anyway.

P: It doesn't quite feel like . . . (relapses into silence, not wanting to introduce complications which might delay the surgery in any way)

Day 124 (After returning home following the node biopsy, the pain increased. P consulted Dr. GP2, since her 'own' doctor, GP1, was away)

Dr. GP2: I see they scanned this and found a slipped disc. Let me show you what has happened. (GP produces plastic model of the spine and demonstrates its construction.) Try to keep moving, and carry on with the oral morphine.

P: I don't think it feels quite like a slipped disc - look, I can lift my leg.

Dr. GP2: But the scan showed it was.

Day 125 (Not liking the effect of the continued medication, and doubtful of the diagnosis, P consulted an osteopath, who spent half an hour in a careful physical examination)

Mrs. O: And they said it was a slipped disc? No. What the scan was seeing was that old slipped disc you had some years ago. This often happens - it shows up on scans. This is a flare-up of the PMR [polymyalgia] you had a year ago - not surprising, it does flare up with stress. You didn't recognise it because it was a different part of the body. Did anyone actually examine you?

P: No

Mrs. O: Right. Or ask about your history? The PMR would be in the notes. Well, there you are. A blood test and seeing the response to '[specific drug]' will make it clear.

(Subsequently the condition responded immediately to the correct medication)

Four observations are apparent from this example. First, the consultant and GP's readings of the scan result carry a weight of authority that overrides the patient's interpretation. When Blaxter recruits an osteopath to consider her symptoms, a different diagnosis is made. Thus she does not passively accept the clinician's reading of the scan but proactively reinterprets it, drawing both on her embodied experience and the expertise of an alternative practitioner. These activities are what the anthropologist Cussins (1998) refers to as 'ontological choreography', a concept she developed when undertaking an ethnography of an infertility clinic. She reports how women undergoing treatment were not passive in the face of technologies, but rather they creatively navigate the system to ensure that their hopes, aspirations and health outcomes were met. She writes that it is not 'forms of objectification *per se* that make these technologies so threatening, but rather the various outcomes of those objectifications' (Cussins, 1998: 600).

A second issue is the way in which scan images are (re)read and (re)interpreted in different contexts. This is in line with other studies of imaging techniques. Kelly Joyce's (2008) North American ethnography of MRI scans reveals how 'MRI scans do not provide a transparent "window" into the inner body but instead *produce* the body' (p. 63). For example, she details how scan images can contain inexplicable traces that clinicians may or may not feel warrant attention. Physicians refer to these as 'unidentified bright objects' (UBOs) or 'old friends', that is, there are marks on the images that they cannot explain but their 'tacit knowledge' (p. 68) leads them to conclude that they are unimportant. As one physician put it, 'Well, I don't know what it is but I know that it's not important. It's an old friend' (p. 66). However, practitioners routinely make decisions as to whether an observed abnormality is *problematically* abnormal or *normally* abnormal. Returning to Blaxter's paper, we learn that an abnormality on her x-ray indicated 'mild heart disease' to a cardiologist, was seen as a lung tumour by a clinician in respiratory medicine, and then subsequently confirmed as cancer by an oncologist.

This relates to a third issue; the way in which Blaxter's body 'begins to be divided up into different organs and systems, each of which has to be looked at separately and serially' and is differentially scrutinized by 'different specialists, departments, outpatient clinics, places within a hospital and even different hospitals' (p. 768). Although the patient takes her whole body in to the hospital, as Mol (2002) suggests (above), its organs are examined in different departments. Thus, her body becomes re-contexualized and remade as it moves through the spaces and places of the hospital. The multiplicity of encounters involved in a patient's pathway to a diagnosis relates to a fourth point evident in Blaxter's work. Satisfactory encounters with health professionals do not merely rest on the quality of communication within a single consultation so much as the overall quality of care over series of meetings. A longitudinal study that followed oncology patients through their care (Schaepe, 2011) found that the impact of receiving 'bad news' on both carers and patients was 'tied only tangentially to one well-executed disclosure'. What is important to the outcome are 'initial impressions about the coordination of care within the medical system [which] led to positive or negative expectations brought to subsequent clinic visits and proved integral to the level of trust patient and caregivers had in their providers' (p. 919). Thus organizational procedures and institutional systems are crucial for good quality health care. Research that simply focuses on one-off consultations or particular technological procedures is at risk of overlooking this point.

In sum, visualization technologies form a critical role in the contemporary diagnostic process. The images produced tend to take precedent over the patient's view, but imaging technologies in and of themselves are not alienating. The ways in which the images are interpreted and crucially the way the readings are translated and written up in the patient's medical record may be. Although the patient medical record is a much more 'traditional' and low-tech medical procedure, it is, ironically perhaps, the space where the patient herself vanishes.

> It was the *translation* of the images into records and decisions that was felt as alienating. It can be argued that the most sustainable image is not in fact the picture or the instrument reading, but the written report or record into which it is translated. (Blaxter 2009: 771 italics in original)

The patient is not involved in the drafting of her own record, and is marginalized from the process, offering her little scope for her to be a co-producer of the diagnosis. Blaxter's auto-ethnography therefore adds weight to the view that it is organizational processes that can lead to the objectification of bodies by a complex choreography of devices used by practitioners and experienced by patients. This is because technologies do not exist in a vacuum but are embedded in relations between actors, practitioners and locations. Their embedded nature means that seemingly inert objects can take on a life of their own and have the capacity to impact upon social practices and reconfigure human bodies. As Casper and Morrison (2010) put it, detailed studies of technologies have opened up 'previously black-boxed medical technologies' in order to dissect 'their historical, cultural, and political innards' (2010: 123). Ethnographies of the removal and transfer of body parts provide particularly apposite examples of how we can usefully prise open black-boxed technologies, because there are numerous sites of negotiation and exchange as anatomical materials weave through the health care system.

Tissue transfer and bio-economies

While imaging technologies refine the visualization of bodies, other medical devices enable the transfer, redistribution and exchange of body parts and body tissue. While such a statement might conjure up images of dark alley sales of kidneys, the reality is usually more banal. Blood, organs, bones, sperm, embryos and so on can be removed, studied, manipulated, transformed and even reinserted in bodies for purposes of research and therapy. Thus medical procedures rely on the transfer and redistribution of body parts and body tissue. Waldby and Mitchell (2006: 6–7) usefully identify types of transplantation, reminding us that some modes of transfer have longer histories than others. Blood transfusion has been practised for over a hundred years (Wailoo, 1997), and the transplantation of whole organs became part of routine medical practice in the latter half of the twentieth century along with the development of drugs that enable immunological suppression and so reduce the risks of rejection of foreign tissue. Other components of bodies such as skin, bone, heart valves and saliva are now routinely harvested and can be manipulated to yield commercial value. Waldby and Mitchell (2006: 32) refer to this process as 'technicity'.

> These tissues can be leveraged biotechnically so that they become more prolific or useful, through processes like the fractioning of blood, the use of polymerase chain reaction (PCR) to amplify genetic sequences, the creation of cell lines, genetic engineering and cell nuclear transfer. A great deal of medical biotechnology is devoted to this amplification and modification of the biological capacities of tissue fragments. Biotechnical procedures induce the tissue fragment to unfurl or recapacitate, to produce new substances or develop along new pathways, to recombine with other fragments and swap properties. This biovaluable engineering is often associated with the requirements for patent, so that surplus in vitro vitality may eventually be transformed into surplus commercial profits, as well as in vivo therapies. In this way, the productivity of tissues intersects with the productivity of markets, entering into the circuits of national and transnational capital economies. (2006: 33)

'Biovalue' denotes the profit accrued from biological material; in other words, sources of capital generated when biotechnology and digital information economies collide (see chapter 6). Waldby and Michell (2006) refer to these systems of production and consumption of human tissue as 'tissue economies.' The mechanisms deployed for harvesting, sourcing, storing and distributing components of bodies within these economies are complex, and touch on questions of identity and citizenship. The notions of tissue economy and biovalue usefully complement politicized perspectives on organ donation and the transfer of biological material. For example, Donna Dickenson's (2008) book *Body Shopping: The Economy Fuelled by Flesh and Blood* documents the nature and extent of international trade in body parts, the scale of financial capital involved and the potential and actual exploitation of those who provide or sell bits of the body. This builds on a tradition of work led by the anthropologist and activist Nancy Scheper-Hughes (2008) whose investigative activities through her organization 'Organ Watch' exposed the global trafficking of body parts from 'poor' to 'rich' countries. But there is another concurrent, more mundane, aspect to the fragmentation and circulation of biological material that can be seen each and every day within localized health care settings. Taking a technology-in-practice perspective, we might ask: How are bits of bodies extracted for use and exchange? How are the associated organizational processes played out? Can fragments of bodies be bought and sold? Does this clash with moral imperatives that body parts should not be exchanged for financial gain? What forms of value can be attributed to body matter?

Circumventing trade: a case study

Klaus Hoeyer's (2009) STS-inspired study of the micro-practices of exchange associated with the relatively commonplace intervention hip replacement provides a fascinating example of trading tissue. He 'explores how the *not trade dictum* performs, shapes and formats exchanges of objects thought of as too human to trade' (p. 240). To this end, he follows two objects called 'femoral heads' (i.e., prosthetic hips) as they pass through the system. One is a metal prosthetic hip and the other made of human bone. The bone is procured from patients undergoing prosthetic hip replacements or from cadavers. When the procedure was relatively rare, surplus hip bones were stored in freezers in the hospital ward for use when needed. Today, however, in order to meet growing demand, hips are stored in bone banks ready for distribution. The bone bankers source hip bones from hospitals, encourage practitioners to extract and deposit the bones, and pay 'expenses' to cover the costs. In other words, they *compensate* the hospitals for their efforts. Compensation is the critical term here, as this transactional form solves the conundrum involved when trading that which cannot be bought and sold. Hoeyer (2009) concludes thus: 'the notion of "compensation of expenses" provides legitimacy to the setting of a price where no price is supposed to be'; furthermore, 'reference to "compensation" can imply that it remains unexplored how the price is calculated and who gains in the process' (p. 253). Thus separating or 'disentangling' the bone from the body and distributing it comprise a series of pragmatic compromises rather than a trading of goods on an open market. Compensation functions as a palatable ethical solution to circumvent the tensions that arise in those countries where it is legally and morally unacceptable to buy and sell body parts.

As we can see, the transfer of organs and tissue for therapy and research requires modes of exchange that do not readily fit in purely economic or altruistic transactions. However, debates on donation are dominated by the language of neo-classical economics and most especially the imbalance between supply and demand. This is a topical conundrum with media reports of high 'need'/demand and limited supply fuelling the dilemma. Rhetorics of compensatory payments are deployed to redress this problematic imbalance. Roberts and Throsby's (2008) analysis of a Human Fertilization and Embryo Authority (HFEA) ruling that granted permission for a UK-based stem cell research team to contribute to the costs of IVF treatments for patients in exchange for women's eggs provides an illustrative example of this. The press release that accompanied the decision reported that these compensatory payments would increase the supply of eggs available for 'path-breaking' stem cell research, which in turn would advance medical treatments. Thus the media coverage about the decision juxtaposed two contradictory claims. On the one hand, compensating women for their eggs extended the existing practice of paying women for their 'spare embryos' and 'failed to fertilize' eggs. On the other hand, by focusing on the innovative nature of the research, the novelty of the scheme was highlighted. Roberts and Throsby argue that this compensatory mechanism serves to blur distinctions between: eggs and embryos; donation and selling; and research and treatment. Equating 'spare embryos' with 'fresh eggs' in this justificatory discourse glosses over the important distinction between eggs that are potentially useful for the donor's own treatment and 'failed-to-fertilize' eggs which cannot benefit the donors themselves. Being 'paid' to 'share' eggs, they point out, is paradoxical and complicates donating and selling. Women are asked to volunteer their eggs and yet they are being paid - albeit in kind - by the stem cell research team. Roberts and Throsby (2008) are especially troubled by the way in which women are positioned as sources of 'valuable' biological material and therefore find themselves:

> in some important ways responsible for the (potential) development of stem cell research itself. This representation creates a significant additional burden for infertile women (or women in infertile couples) in particular. Because 'fresh' eggs are never 'spare' within IVF treatment, asking women patients to donate them is a serious and complex request. (p. 168)

Within the context of stem cell research, women are therefore the main tissue donors and this new trade rests on women's corporeal productivity. Organizations are reliant upon what Waldby and Cooper (2010) call 'regenerative labour' defined as the way 'female bodily productivity is mobilized to support bioeconomic research, [and] yet this economic value remains largely unacknowledged' (pp. 4–5).

Biological waste and biological value

Ian Hacking (2006) argues that as a result of technological innovations and new modes of biomedical engineering, our bodies are 'becoming more Cartesian' because 'we now treat the body as an assemblage of replaceable parts, a veritable machine, exactly what Descartes said it was'. 'At present' he continues 'there is a fairly sharp boundary between mechanical spare parts, made of non-organic materials, and spare parts taken from donors, or the patient's own. But hybrids between the two are on the way' (pp. 13–14). Others, however, suggest that hybrids have been with us for some time (Haraway, 1991) and indeed this does seem a persuasive observation. Returning to our example of the hip, we can see how the metal hip takes on human qualities when it comes to the disposal of bodies. The titanium metal does not melt during cremation and so 'metal agency of the prosthesis poses a particular problem for the crematoria: it can break the urn' (Hoeyer, 2009: 253). Then there is a further problem: what to do with the metal?

> The metal hip is indeed in-between humanness and the commodity realm. It is too human to be sold but not human enough to follow the remains of the deceased into the urn and ruin the principle of total decomposition. (Hoeyer, 2009: 253)

Hoeyer describes various creative solutions developed to handle the unwanted and yet potentially useful devices. Although the metal prosthesis is of no use to the dead person and this waste material could be converted for use elsewhere, there is hesitancy when it comes to acceptable modes of recycling. While some crematoria sold the metal, others were less confident in doing so for fear of violating social and ethical boundaries.

Thus we see what constitutes 'waste' in one context can regain 'value' in another and within the complex and ever fluid environments of medical technologies notions of waste and value become muddied. Body matter such as blood, a kidney or an embryo is essential for maintaining or reproducing life and is unlikely to be classified as waste. The act of giving such tissue to other humans is seen to epitomize altruism, as the author Richard Titmuss articulated in his classic treatise, *The Gift Relationship: from Human Blood to Social Policy* (1970). Other tissue such as hair, nail clippings, urine, faeces, sweat and so on are not imbued with the same symbolic significance and are classified as by-products and waste. In fact they are often regarded as 'dirt' in the sense that they are matter that has to be cleaned up and disposed of. However, this clinical waste can become commercially valuable material. For example, genetic knowledge may be extracted from saliva or hair samples. Hormonal material may be extracted from urine, tissue from tumours can be valuable to researchers investigating cancer treatments, and placentas can provide raw research material for pharmaceutical companies. Waldby and Mitchell (2006) distinguish between clinical and ontological waste and clinical and ontological value to capture the differing meanings of these body tissues. While hair may not carry an ontological significance and it can have a clinical value, an embryo has an ontological value in that donations are associated with altruism and corporeal citizenship, and would not be regarded as waste. Embryos are, however, classified as 'spare' when they are produced as part of IVF treatments.

Thus tissue economies are nuanced and intricate, and there are features of contemporary technologies that give rise to this. Polarized debates between those who point to the exploitative potential of technologies to extract capital from bodies, and those who see the giving of human material to be a marker of civic solidarity and public trust are overly crude in the context of twenty-first-century health care. In contrast to the era when Titmuss (1970) wrote his classic study comparing North American (free market) and British (collectivist) approaches to the exchange of blood, today elements of each combine to form complex systems of exchange. There is no pure gift economy and no pure free market. The case of umbilical cord blood demonstrates this well.

Umbilical cord blood is tissue extracted moments after the delivery of a baby and its therapeutic value has come to be recognized. Rich in hematopoietic stem cells, it is useful for regenerative medicine, is used as an alternative to bone marrow for the treatment of cancers, immune system disorders and for gene therapies. Thus the value of cord blood has shifted over time and context. It is of little 'use value' to the mother at the time of birth and historically would have been disposed of as 'clinical waste'. However, it now has a 'clinical use value' for the development of therapies and therefore has latent commercial value for research (Brown et al., 2011; Brown, 2012). Like hips, cord blood is sourced, stored and distributed and, like hips, this is done through a system of banking. Public banks store cord blood on a basis of allogeneic transfer (one individual to another), that is they retrieve cord blood from individuals for use by immunologically matched recipients unknown to the donors. Individuals can also deposit cord blood in commercial banks for their children's use should the need arise; this is referred to as autologous (self-to-self or biological kin) transfer of biological material. Marketing strategies of private cord blood banks rest on the insurance principle, offering parents assurances that the banked blood will be available in the event of life-threatening diseases. Waldby (2006) argues that private cord blood banking fosters a 'neo-liberal medical subjectivity', one which is 'orientated towards the entrepreneurial maximization of future health' (p. 67). Just as individuals invest in their financial futures through pensions and savings,

> [S]o too they may provide for the future of their bodies through the investments of autologous biological material. Each practice suggests a personalised, demutualised vision of the future, in which prudential self-management and self-investment will yield enduring financial and biological security. (p. 68)

Currently, the therapeutic use of cord blood is limited but it appears that parents are swayed by the speculative value. In other words, the expectation is that the pace of scientific progress is so great that should their child contract a life-threatening condition in the future, the blood may – in effect – save its life (Waldby, 2006). Thus expectations about the future use of technologies have consequences for the present. A sociology of expectations (Brown and Michael, 2003) examines the performative play of hopes and aspirations associated with medical progress. Ideals inherent in tropes such as 'the race for cure' and 'the medical breakthrough' are mobilized by research scientists, parents, commercial companies and politicians to garner support for biotechnological investment and innovation. Future promise impacts upon the present. But such hopes are situated, and detailed observational studies have revealed how the translation of medical research from the 'bench to bedside' comes to be complicated by the practicalities of implementation. This is perhaps nowhere more evident than in relation to genetics and medicine.

Sociology of genetics

In the 'Introduction' to this book, we discussed how the canon of medical sociology arose through a critical engagement with the biomedical model, which in turn contributed to the articulation of a social model of health, illness and the body. Hacking's claim (2006) that the Cartesian body is reasserting a hegemonic status and Conrad's (2002) thesis that the 'new genetics' are consolidating reductionist and medicalized interpretations of health and illness inclines to the view that biomedicine is regaining ideological prominence. Certainly the language of genes, genetics and the human genome has infiltrated popular discourses of health and illness in recent decades and attracted much interest from sociologists. Amongst sociologists, however, there are two contrastive positions. On the one hand, there are, as we have just noted, those who point to a resurgence of the biomedical model with a concomitant privileging of biological explanations for the causes and manifestations of disease. On the other hand, there are those who argue that adherence to genetic notions of disease are generating new forms of sociality. This second approach has given rise to concepts such as 'biosociality' and 'vital politics' (Rabinow, 1999; Rose and Novas, 2005; Rose, 2007) that stand in opposition to notions of medicalization. These writers argue that the intensification of the biological engenders a strengthening of the social. We explore these tensions below, but first let us reflect very briefly on what we mean by genetics or more appropriately, the 'new genetics.'

The new genetics

> refers specifically to the body of knowledge and techniques arising since the invention of recombinant DNA technology in 1973. It involves research into the genetic

> components of human disease and behaviour, which may have clinical applications through the provision of genetic testing or screening for disease or risk factors for disease, and through treatments such as gene therapy or new pharmaceuticals. (Cunningham-Burley and Boulton, 2000: 174)

There has been an exponential growth of research to determine the genetic bases of disease, and a concomitant development of techniques and services to identify 'genetic' conditions. While geneticists have long recognized monogenic conditions (where variations in an individual gene lead to the onset of specific diseases and children who inherit a dominant gene from a parent or a recessive gene from both parents will develop the condition), developments in recombinant DNA technologies in the 1980s have given rise to more complex, predispositional models of association between genes and disease pathologies. This distinction has important social implications. For example, the distinction between recessive conditions where individuals who inherit a faulty gene from both parents will inevitably develop a condition (e.g., cystic fibrosis) and late-onset dominant conditions where the inheritance of a single copy gene puts an individual *at risk* of contracting a condition (e.g., breast cancer) will carry different biological, social and psychological consequences, not least because the latter carries a greater degree of uncertainty and unpredictability than does the former. Indeed, it is paradoxical that the production of greater medical knowledge and the 'success' of the human genome project itself gives rise to uncertainties associated with the management of health, illness and disease. Inherent to the processes of testing for genetic conditions is a panoply of doubts and responsibilities in terms of what to do with the test results.

Biological citizenship and genetic responsibility

Testing for genetic conditions alters the temporality of diagnosis and disease. Being diagnosed with a genetic predisposition or genetic risk of a condition has the potential to transform an otherwise healthy person into a 'patient without symptoms', a body that has greater likelihood of developing a condition: a kind of partial diagnosis. Research into people's responses to genetic testing does indicate that on the whole men and women are able to rationalize positive test results and recognize that they are not definitive. At the risk of sounding crass, they appreciate that life is uncertain. Whitmarsh et al. (2007), for example, found that men and women interviewed recognized the indeterminate nature of their genetic-based diagnoses, appreciating that their genetic status is embedded within the broader context of their everyday lives. They did not see their disease trajectory as an inevitable or irreversible one but simply an aspect of life's multiple trajectories. Similarly, Lock and her colleagues (2007) found that families and carers of kin who have Alzheimer's disease were not overly troubled by positive test results. Individuals simply added this information to their multifaceted theories of causation. The authors found that family history was held to be as good as, if not a better indicator of, future disease than were the results of genetic tests. Thus relatives 'make sense' of kin ties in ways that do not crudely conform to clinical genetics. This and similar research reminds us of the need to look for the intersections between biological and social categories of kinship; a 'family' sense of inheritance is likely to be mapped onto a 'biological' one in a messy rather than linear way (Featherstone et al., 2005). Furthermore, the indeterminacy associated with predispositional genetics serves to amplify the uncertainty inherent in genetics and health:

> The very complexity of molecular genetics has brought about a dethroning of the gene, ensuring that the certainties that many scientists and members of the public alike thought was within our grasp will not come about in the near future, if ever. Molecular genomics fit comfortably into the postmodern condition. (Lock et al., 2007: 272)

It seems that medical practitioners, like lay people do not necessarily privilege the genetic markers of biological predisposition to disease. For example, a study of clinicians' accounts of genetic testing for familial hypercholesterolaemia found that doctors rely on cholesterol results and patients' reported symptoms rather than results of DNA tests when making diagnoses (Will et al., 2010). In concert, findings from these and other studies challenge a concept that has become influential in medical sociology, namely, the person who is 'genetically at risk'. They suggest that the concept gives too much credence to the role that genetic information plays in shaping social actions.

To recap, genetic predisposition to disease is where individuals are diagnosed as having an increased biological propensity of contracting a condition. This genetic information may or may not be accepted as significant or used to alter ways of living in order to counter the increased chance of contracting cancer, heart disease, diabetes or whatever. There is, however, a thesis proposed that groups who share the 'at risk' status may develop a 'risky genetic self' as a result of being 'genetically at risk' (Novas and Rose, 2000: 504–5). These biological markers thus form a basis of identity which propels individuals to undertake associated actions. As Novas and Rose (2007) argue:

> individuals and their families have taken unto themselves the responsibility for the government of their risky genes, in relation not merely to a secular norm of the individual health, but an obligation to one's kin, to those one loves and to the future. (Novas and Rose, 2007: 507)

Once testing is available individuals may feel an ethical obligation to seek out such procedures to become better informed so that they might pursue appropriate life strategies such as following health-related behaviours and informing kin of their health status. 'Individuals act upon the inscriptions of clinical risk which mark their bodies and define them as particular kinds of subjects' (Novas and Rose, 2007: 507). This thesis runs counter to those who argue that the contemporary focus on genetics forms an extension of medicalization and associated reductionism and determinism. It also challenges the 'geneticization thesis', a theory proposed by Abby Lippman (1991) in a discussion on prenatal genetic testing. Her claim is that genetic explanations have come to dominate discourses of health and illness and that genetic technologies have become a ubiquitous feature of Western health care with deleterious effects. One concern is the way in which individual differences are reduced to their codes of DNA to the relative neglect of the societal influences (Lippman, 1992: 1470). In contrast Novas and Rose point to the creative and productive effects of genetic technologies and associated practices rather than their repressive tendencies. For example, individuals are propelled to proactively develop 'life strategies' to manage their bodies, their selves and their social relationships. Observing the impact of genetic discourses, they claim to see not resignation to biological predispositions but rather 'emergence of complex ethical technologies for the management of biological existence' (Novas and Rose, 2000: 488). Furthermore, a genetic condition forges a 'a web of genetic connectedness', potentially altering relations with kin, reshaping ways of (healthy) living, undergoing counselling to manage genetic selfhood, establishing networks of interaction patient groups, participating in trials of therapies and even sociological research. Rights, duties and responsibilities associated with vitality: a politics of the biological.

> [W]e use the term biological citizenship descriptively, to encompass all those citizenship projects that have linked their conceptions of citizens to beliefs about the biological existence of human beings, as individuals, as families and lineages, as communities, as population and races and as a species. And like other dimensions of citizenship, biological citizenship is undergoing transformation and re-territorialising itself along national, local and transnational dimensions. (Rose and Novas, 2005: 440)

Central to citizenship is, of course, the notion of responsibility and there is a growing body of empirical research that has examined how men and women manage the responsibility of communicating information about their genetic status to kin. To be diagnosed as a carrier of a genetic condition has consequences for family members and so invariably confounds relations between kin. In a series of studies of men and women carriers of BRACA genes for breast cancer, Hallowell found that they experience a profound yet complex sense of moral responsibility to kin (Hallowell, 1999; Hallowell et al., 2006). The will to know about genetic status can be an intricate process and more information can be constraining as well as empowering, not least because bodies, individuals and knowledge exist in fields of power relations that are shaped by gender, 'race', class, age and so on. In a considered appraisal of the implications of genetic testing in relation to ethnicity, Atkin (2003) captures these challenges well:

> Citizenship rights might, therefore, imply the responsible use of genetic information and compliance with medical advice. This issue raises important dilemmas. If a person reasonably suspects that he or she should carry or is 'at risk' of a genetic condition, do they have a responsibility to be tested? What preventative strategies should they take? Do they have an obligation to tell other family members who might also be 'at risk'? Should they tell employers and insurance companies? If they are likely to give birth to an affected child should they, as responsible citizens (and parents), abort the affected child? Does their non-compliance or refusal to abort shift them into the category of the undeserving in terms of access to state welfare? If they do not choose abortion should they then be responsible for the costs of bringing up the affected child? (p. 96)

Thus the practices of biological citizenship not only concretize shared corporeal concerns, the formation of social groupings and momentum to collective action, but they also problematize responsibility and decision making. Such decisions are socially and politically charged and are public issues as well as private matters.

The anthropologist Paul Rabinow (1992) developed the term 'biosociality' to describe the way in which people with shared biological concerns begin to group together. From his study of patients and their relatives affected by the dystrophies in France, he documents how they established the organization Association Française contre les Myopathies (AFM) to share experience, offer social support and lobby for further research (Rabinow, 1999). His point is that these collective identities and forms of political engagement are rooted in genetic or other biolological markers. Biology is therefore not destiny but something that groups, often forging alliances with scientists and clinicians, can work on to improve or change. Here again we can see how expectations come to play a performative role; the promise of progress may be deployed by actors and stakeholders bringing together those located in commercial enterprises, research scientists, media and patient groups to lobby for investment into research, treatments and so on.

Sociology and bioethics

We began this chapter by pointing to the increased pace of change and innovation in medical technologies. We noted too that, since the turn of the millennium, there appears to be significant political and popular optimism associated with research into the new genetics, nanotechnologies, imaging techniques and so on. As our discussion progressed, we can begin to see that the application of these novel methods gives rise to moral and ethical questions that demand consideration. During the last few decades a subfield of philosophy called 'bioethics' has developed which deliberates these matters. Sociologists (DeVries, 2003; 2007; Hedgecoe, 2010; Petersen, 2011a; 2011b) question the assumptions underpinning this field of study, predominantly because it tends to focus on the individual and eclipse the social and political context. Bioethics is rooted in moral philosophy and its epistemological underpinnings tend to privilege the individual. Like medical ethics more generally, thinking has been dominated by an approach developed by Beauchamp and Childress (2008) that identifies four principles: autonomy, beneficence (do good), non-maleficence (do no harm), and justice that can be balanced in relation to clinical practice. Petersen (2011b) argues that the demand for bioethical analyses and research is easy to understand. First, because it offers a ready tool for assessing dilemmas associated with the introduction of new medical practices. Second, because it serves as a useful 'tool of governance' and can help to legitimize innovations. Third, it limits debates to the application of technologies rather than questioning the rationale for their development or existence. Finally, in so doing it 'offers no threats to dominant interests'. Preoccupation with principles such as 'respect for autonomy', the 'right to know' and informed choice, has resulted in bioethics developing:

> a body of principles and frameworks, and ways of reasoning, that have found congruence with bureaucratic, formal procedures and the neo-liberal policies that dominate contemporary healthcare and other spheres of life. (Petersen 2011b: n.p.)

A critical sociology of bioethics is important not least to enable us to think critically as to why particular ethical, social and legal issues appear worthy of consideration and others do not. What constitutes an ethical issue? What is intriguing is the way in which bioethics has emerged in conjunction with the increased pace of change in medical technologies. It seems that the application of technical procedures raises moral questions in a way that other health and illness issues do not. As Nicolas Rose questions:

> Why should informed consent in reproductive technology be 'bioethical' and the rising rate of female infertility not? Why should the 'dignity' of the person at the end of life be a bioethical issue, but not the massive 'letting die' of millions of children under five each year from preventable causes? Why does contemporary biopolitics seem to require bioethical authority yet circumscribe the issues to which such ethical concerns appear relevant? (2007: 16)

This reminds us that the main causes of morbidity and mortality throughout the world are associated with factors such as poverty, nutrition and conflict. Investments into technological solutions are vast in comparison to economic and political investment into low-tech and public health interventions. Curiously, these are rarely conceptualized or debated in ethical terms. Bioethics forms another technological device, along with the tools of evidence-based medicine or measures of quality of life, that beg critical sociological engagement. What are the ideological underpinnings of these tools and technologies? What forms of knowledge do they produce? How is the knowledge deployed and in what contexts? Why are some spheres of medical science thought to offer such promise and others not? These questions lie at the heart of the sociology of health and illness. How as a society do we respond to, define, prioritize, make sense of health, illness and disease? For the sociologist, medical technologies yield novel questions rather than invariably offering innovative solutions.

Conclusion

Although the pace of technological change in health care is fast, many of the sociological questions and issues endure. What is the interplay between the construction of medical knowledge and technological practices? How are medical interventions experienced and deployed by patients and practitioners? How do novel readings of the physical body invoke shifts in social relations, responsibility and notions of the self? To what extent are relationships within medical care settings mediated by innovative technological forms? These are long-standing concerns for medical sociologists. Although technological advances may feel dramatic, it is worth reflecting that health and medical care, perhaps more than any other aspect of welfare, has long relied on more or less complex technologies, many of which have been aligned with particular professional groups or experts. In this chapter in order to explore novel conceptualizations and theoretical approaches we selected only three forms of technology: imaging, tissue transfer and genetics. Through these we demonstrated the merits of the technology-in-practice approach and in particular the gains to be made from the marriage between STS and medical sociology. Both these subfields privilege empirical investigations and, through close analytic scrutiny of medical settings, illuminate our appreciation of health care practices. These detailed studies of technology in practice confirm the thesis proposed in chapter 2 of this volume that medical knowledge is a dynamic ongoing accomplishment that is produced through the interplay of technical procedures and those who apply, use and interpret them. A technological device may produce a knowledge of the body but it is only meaningful when read by those trained to understand them and able to arrive at a consensus as to their significance. Such activities remain fraught with negotiation and debate and are of continued fascination for sociologists of health and illness.

FURTHER READING

Featherstone, K., Clarke, A., Bharadwaj, A. and Atkinson, P. (2005), *Risky Relations: Family, Kinship and the New Genetics*, Oxford: Berg.

Martin, P. and Dingwall, R. (2010), 'Medical Sociology and Genetics', in W. Cockerham (ed.), *The New Blackwell Companion to Medical Sociology*, Oxford: Blackwell.

Webster, A. (2008), *Health Technology and Society: A Sociological Critique*, Basingstoke: Palgrave Macmillan.

10 Sociological Analyses of Developments in UK Health Policy: A New Paradigm for Health Care?

Introduction

This chapter will explore three strands of health policy which are associated with the changing nature of contemporary health and medical care: health promotion and the 'New Public Health' (NPH), the shift from hospital to community care, and the rise of consumerism and patient choice. These three aspects of health policy have been selected, as they form part of what Armstrong refers to as a 'new regime of total health' or 'surveillance medicine' (2002). That is, people are increasingly being encouraged to monitor and maintain their own health; patients are increasingly being cared for in non-institutional environments; and people are being invited to voice their views and exercise their choices in relation to health and health care. These policy trends, which incorporate patients and people within their social context, may help to reinforce a relatively social model of health and illness. However, other, concurrent developments in health policy may, rather paradoxically, be contributing to the perpetuation of the biomedical model: most especially, those policies and practices associated with increased use of e-health informational technologies. We take the examples of 'evidence-based medicine' and consumer informatics by way of illustration, and argue that these are features of the new paradigm of medicine and health – namely, e-scaped medicine – that we outlined in chapter 2.

The sociology of health and illness has contributed to developments in health policy in three main ways. First, it provides analyses of their contemporary emergence; second, it can provide critiques of the content of the policies themselves; and third, as practitioners, sociologists may well be involved in studies which assess or evaluate the merits or de-merits of particular health programmes or forms of care. A feature of health policy is that it is characterized by change and for those working within health care settings organizational flux may feel like the norm. Although this chapter details developments that have taken place since the second half of the twentieth century, the main aim is to try to discern underlying trends that have shaped these policies. Excellent comprehensive accounts of health policy in the UK, which complement this chapter, are detailed elsewhere (see Greener, 2008; Klein, 2010).

Perhaps the defining feature of contemporary health care both in the UK and other post-industrial nations is the grip of neo-liberalism, most particularly the emphasis on choice, individualism, commercialism and competition. Although modern health care systems have distinct characteristics shaped by national social, cultural and political histories, there is some evidence that they are converging not least because they face similar problems. Stevens (2010) lists these as rising costs and concerns to achieve value for money, changing demographics in particular ageing populations, continued increase in chronic illnesses, many of which are amenable to prevention, and an encouragement of technological innovation. In addition there is a challenge to adhere to the values of equity (the idea that health care should be accessible to all), efficiency (the premise that resources are spent effectively) and autonomy (the belief in self-determination and free choice) (Stevens, 2010: 436). A further feature of modern health care systems is a seemingly continued appetite for reform. In the UK the most radical health policy reform was the establishment of the NHS in 1948. This socialized system was based on the principle that health care should be available to all on the basis of need not ability to pay. A second more protracted and ongoing phase of reform can be traced to the late 1980s and 1990s. Although health care was still funded out of taxation and free (for the most part) at the point of use, new principles and practices were ushered in. Most notably, internal market systems were established whereby purchasing authorities (known as commissioners) negotiated to buy services from health care providers, managerial practices were reformed and relied on performance management, targets and monitoring, and patients became reconceptualized as consumers. A detailed study of a number of northern European countries identified common justifications for health care reform at the turn of the millennium which the authors argue can be understood in relation to processes of globalization (Tritter et al., 2010). Globalization in this context is understood in terms of the processes of both economic integration and the transmission and mediation of ideas (p. 4). In relation to health policy this is evident in two distinct discourses: first, the merits of competition between service providers and the separation of funding from the provision of health services, which in turn creates opportunities for public, private and voluntary sectors to provide care and it is argued can contain costs; and second, the sovereignty of the individual patient articulated in terms of patient's rights and obligations as citizens and also in terms of quality care is encouraged to be patient centred. There appears to be a common emphasis on the 'co-production of health with individuals' (Dixon, 2012: 343) both in relation to their responsibility to maintain and monitor their own health and in terms of the receipt of care whereby patients have been redrawn as consumers (Tritter et al., 2010). Policies designed to encourage people to maintain their own health fall under the orbit of health promotion and public health.

Health promotion and the new public health

During the latter decades of the twentieth century, there was a shift in the emphasis of health care from cure to prevention. From the mid-1970s, health policy documents began to emphasize the need to promote good health rather than treat illness and disease (DHSS, 1976, 1977). The reasons for this change are fourfold. First, influenced by the efficacy debate (see chapter 7), policy makers came to recognize that increasing investments in technological medicine resulted in diminishing returns. Second, the disease burden has changed; the decline in infectious diseases has been matched by an increase in chronic conditions that are often caused by social and behavioural factors. Third, a growing elderly population places a greater stress on an already overburdened Health Service. Finally, the financing of a Health Service which has to deal with a seemingly infinite demand in a period of retrenchment became untenable.

In relation to the financing of the NHS, C. Davies (1987) identifies three stages in policy since its inception. The first twenty years of the NHS allowed the supply and demand of health care to grow untrammelled, with the result that more and more money was simply pumped into the system; the next ten years involved efforts to control the supply side by making the provision of health care more efficient and therefore more cost-effective; whereas in the third and present stage, there are now attempts to manage and control both the supply and the demand side factors. The control of the demand side has seen attempts to encourage people to modify their behaviours and to lead increasingly healthy lives. Indeed, a central theme of consecutive Labour and Conservative policy documents has been that individuals must take more responsibility for their own health, and must adopt more healthy behaviours. For example, the Labour Party's White Paper *Prevention and Health* (DHSS, 1977: 39) stated:

> Much ill health in Britain today arises from over-indulgence and unwise behaviour. Not surprisingly, the greatest potential and perhaps the greatest problem for preventive medicine now lies in changing behaviour and attitudes to health. The individual can do much to help himself [*sic*], his family and the community by accepting more direct personal responsibility for his own health and well-being.

During the 1980s and 1990s a series of major health policy documents continued to emphasize the role of disease prevention and health promotion. For example, *Promoting Better Health: The Government's Programme for Improving Primary Health Care* (DHSS, 1987) stated that 'the shift from an illness service to a health service' was the 'next big challenge for the NHS'. Carrying this a stage further, both the Conservative and New Labour governments outlined a strategic approach to raising the health status of the population by way of reducing the prevalence of preventable premature deaths from major diseases (Department of Health, 1992, 2004b). In an attempt to differentiate their approach from previous Conservative governments, New Labour policies focused on three elements of public health. These were tackling health inequalities; community development and neighbourhood regeneration (with special attention to the health of disadvantaged children); and a 'Third Way' philosophy, which maintains that the responsibility for health comprises a 'contract' between individuals, communities and government (Secretary of State for Health, 1999; Department of Health, 2000, 2002b).

Keen not to be tarred with the criticisms of public health policies of the earlier decades, New Labour emphasized the fact that a range of institutions play a key role in enabling people to make 'healthy choices' rather than simply exhorting them to do so. *Choosing Health: Making Healthy Choices Easier* (Department of Health, 2004a) states:

> At the start of the twenty-first century England needs a new approach to health [*sic*] of the public, reflecting the rapid and radical transformation of English society in the latter half of the twentieth century, responding to the needs and wishes of its citizens as individuals . . . That means an approach which respects the freedom of individual choice in a diverse, open more questioning society; which recognises the realities of the impact of the consumer society on those choices; which addresses the fact that too many people and groups have been left behind or ignored in the past.

The Conservative and Liberal coalition government similarly talk about a 'responsibility deal', with Andrew Lansley, the Minister for Health, echoing demands of previous administrations that 'Public health is everyone's responsibility and there is a role for all of us, working in partnership, to tackle these challenges' (Department of Health, 2011). The underlying principles are articulated as 'informed choice for all', 'personalization of support to make healthy choices', and 'working in partnership to make health everyone's business'. We return to these issues below; but first we examine how the emergence of health promotion is bound up with a broader shift in health care – a reorientation of power from secondary to primary care.

Prevention, primary health care and the role of GPs

Primary health care has long been recognized to be a key site for the effective prevention of illness (WHO, 1978). In the UK primary health care trusts (PCTs) until recently have been considered to be key functionaries in the promotion of better health. Although PCTs have been abolished, they are in effect metamorphosing into Clinical Commissioning Groups who purchase services on behalf of their patients. As well as commissioning hospital services from other NHS trusts, they are encouraged to commission other welfare services or work in partnership with local services both within and beyond the public sector. A feature of health care systems during the latter half of the twentieth century has been the attempt to shift resources from secondary to primary care and from intervention to prevention. General practitioners were able to capitalize on these developments to enhance their relative status in relation to those sectors of the medical profession who hitherto had commanded greater socio-economic status and political clout.

In effect, GPs used prevention to establish their professional identity (Armstrong, 1979; C. Davies, 1984). This was because after the NHS had been established, GPs found themselves in an insecure position. The emphasis in the NHS was on curing, intervention and technology, with the result that doctors working within hospitals achieved a more secure position and a higher social status. Consequently, both local authority medical officers and GPs found themselves 'out in the ideological cold' (C. Davies, 1984: 281). Floundering in the face of hospital medicine, they searched for a distinct body of knowledge on which they could base their own professional expertise. Clinicians working in primary care articulated the potential for prevention within general practice. Three spheres for prevention were identified (Calnan, 1991). First, within the consultation itself, where the GP should not only manage the patient's presenting problems but should also include a preventive component such as opportunistic screening, advice on smoking, and the promotion of healthy lifestyles. Second, the GP is well placed to monitor the health of his or her practice population, as the age/sex register provides GPs with a database from which they can identify certain groups for screening, immunizations and health checks. Thus the GP can pursue a life-cycle approach by offering screening and interventions at crucial stages throughout the life-course. Finally, the GP could possibly become involved with the local community by working with other institutions, such as schools.

GPs found their alternative to the biomedical approach in the form of biographical and holistic medicine (Armstrong, 1979). The biographical approach asserts the individuality of the patient, the unity of psyche and soma, and the need to get beyond the presenting symptoms to explore the history and circumstances of the patient's life. A theoretical basis for this approach was developed by Balint, a doctor and psychoanalyst, and his followers (Balint, 1956). Thus prevention provided an important rationale for GPs' existence and raised their status in relation to hospital medicine. This was made explicit by New Labour in *Shifting the Balance of Power within the NHS* (Department of Health, 2002b), which claimed to devolve power within health care to patients and 'front line' providers of care, a trend that has been extended (at the level of rhetoric at least) with the Coalition government's Health and Social Care Bill 2011, which gives responsibility for commissioning health care to GPs and their practice teams working together with and for their patients. How this will work out remains to be seen. Furthermore, some public health and health promotion functions may be diluted. The medical speciality of public health, meanwhile, from 2013 will be relocated from the NHS to local authorities from whence it came in the early 1970s. Public health and public health practitioners have had a chequered history, with governments never quite clear where they might best be located.

The new public health

The emergent interest in the prevention of illness and the promotion of health in primary care during the latter decades of the twentieth century was matched by a renewed interest in public health (Bunton and Macdonald, 2002; Bunton et al., 1995). An outcome of the 1974 reorganization of the NHS was the integration of local authority medical officers of health into the NHS and the establishment of the new discipline of community medicine. Throughout the 1980s, however, there was growing concern about the function of a discipline that had lost its way (Lewis, 1986). Following an inquiry into its future development, Acheson (1998) produced a report, *Public Health in England*, which made a number of recommendations which facilitated the revival of the public health doctor, as have more recent reports into the public health function by successors to his role of Chief Medical Officer (Chief Medical Officer, 2001). Public medicine plays a key role in implementing public health strategies, such as those designed to address health inequalities. From 2013 public health will be transferred back to local authorities, which could have the potential to enhance primary prevention through a social rather than medical model of health and illness.

The reappearance of public health medicine in the 1980s was referred to as 'the new public health', in order to distinguish it from older forms of public health. Ashton and Seymour (1988) have identified four phases in public health in Europe and North America. The first phase was in response to the health threats which occurred with the rapid growth of industrialization and urbanization. The Public Health Acts of 1848 and 1870 were concerned with housing, sanitation and food. From the 1870s the attention of medical officers became oriented towards individuals, and the main concerns were personal hygiene and immunization. The advent of new drugs and the decline of infectious diseases from the 1930s are described by Ashton and Seymour as 'the therapeutic era'. It was at this time, they point out, that the departments of public health were weakened in comparison to the rising importance of hospital-based, therapeutic medicine. However, in the 1970s, when the assumptions on which curative medicine were based began to be challenged (see chapter 1), public health medicine entered its fourth phase – the phase of the new public health. To capture the essence of this new form of public health, and to locate its advent in their chronological account, Ashton and Seymour (1988) cite the influential report produced by Marc Lalonde (1974), the Canadian Minister for Health, as a marker of change. They describe the new approach to health care in the following way:

> What is emerging as the New Public Health is an approach which brings together environmental change and personal preventative measures with appropriate therapeutic interventions, especially for the elderly and disabled. However the New Public Health goes beyond an understanding of human biology and recognises the importance of those social aspects of health problems which are caused by lifestyles . . . Many contemporary health problems are therefore seen as being social rather than solely individual problems; underlying them are concrete issues of local and national public policy, and what are needed to address these problems are 'Healthy Public Policies' - policies in many fields which support the promotion of health. (Ashton and Seymour, 1988: 21)

We can begin to appreciate that the new public health 'shifts the focus from patients and hospitals to people and their everyday life' (Martin and McQueen, 1989: 2). Whilst public health tends to focus on specific diseases and risk factors, the approach is also one which takes into account the social basis of these issues. According to Lalonde (1974), any effective health policy must work at four levels: health care provision; lifestyle or behavioural factors, environmental pollution and biophysical factors.

Health promotion

The term 'health promotion' emerged out of these debates in the 1980s. The First International Conference on Health Promotion held in Ottawa produced the Ottawa Charter (WHO, 1986), which set out its aims and philosophy. The WHO concept of health promotion sees health and lifestyles as being inextricably linked to the socio-economic environment. However, it has been criticized, because the emphasis is on the empowerment of individuals and communities rather than on any commitment to challenge the socio-economic context in which people live out their lives (Navarro, 1984; Strong, 1986).

We can begin to see that throughout the 1980s two distinct, but related, concepts emerged at both national and global levels. These were *health promotion* and the *new public health* (Bunton and Macdonald, 2002). The two concepts are clearly related, as Baggot notes (1991: 194): 'Health promotion . . . is seen as a key feature of the modern public health approach.' Thus there would appear to be an alliance between health promotion and public health, the former both giving impetus to, and being usurped by, the latter. Although health promotion is based on a grass-roots approach to health, within the UK health promotion has become a core function of the health authorities and primary care trusts, who are required to work with a variety of welfare organizations, local authorities and private businesses. Although health promotion and the new public health have now become incorporated into government health policies and mainstream health care, the concepts actually emerged from radical critiques of policies on the prevention of illness and 'conventional' approaches to health education. These critiques came from both academic social scientists and the community health movement.

Sociological critiques of health promotion

Thorogood (2002) has distinguished between a sociology *as applied to* health promotion and a sociology *of* health promotion. The former refers to the ways in which sociology can refine and develop the techniques and practices of health promotion, whilst the latter alludes to a critical analysis of the assumptions underpinning health promotion itself. In other words, sociology can both extend the health promotion project and/or be critical of it. Thorogood has identified three ways in which sociology contributes to the health promotion project: analyses of power, an understanding of social stratification, and studies of lay health beliefs. In contrast, a critique of the project of health promotion itself would address the failure to reconcile the individual versus structure debate, its ideological underpinnings, the way in which health promotion may reinforce structural divisions and forms of discrimination, the fallacy of empowerment, and the articulation of new forms of social regulation.

Sociology as applied to health promotion

The concept of health promotion emerged, in part, out of critiques of conventional approaches to health education. The conventional approach worked with a simplistic model of behavioural change that assumed that if you give people information, they will act upon it. Such a model fails to incorporate the structural dimensions of social action and may therefore be counter-productive (Naidoo and Wills, 2009). It is inherently individualistic and reinforces the ideological assumptions of capitalism. Rather than acknowledging the complexities of the social causation of illness, it blames the victim: 'The victim-blaming ideology . . . instructs people to be individually responsible . . . [and] tends to obscure the reality of class and the impact on the social inequality of health' (Crawford, 1977: 672).

It is further argued that such a model is elitist, in that it adopts a 'top-down' approach to the planning and implementation of health education, and fails to take account of the views of those it seeks to inform and the socio-cultural variations in health beliefs and practices. This prescriptive style tends to reflect the dominant value system, which in our society is white and middle class, with the consequence that the agenda for health education is not determined by the health needs of the whole population. A fundamental premise of health promotion is that people ought to be encouraged to take control over their actions, so that they can lead healthy lives. Thus there has been a move from what are now seen to be naïve assumptions about the relationship between knowledge, attitudes and behaviours (KABs) to the concept of *empowerment* – that is, the facilitation of decision-making skills and the promotion of social and political action through the acknowledgement of structural constraints on free choice.

Sociology's analyses of power and the relationship between social structure and action are clearly crucial if health promotion is to acknowledge the constraints on, and potential for, social change (Thorogood, 2002: 60). Indeed, research into those behaviours which are considered to be risk factors has documented the extent to which they are woven into the fabric of social life.

Central to conventional health education is the idea that once people are informed, they can make healthy choices. Graham (1984) has suggested that, instead, they make *healthy compromises*, given the socially structured context in which they live out their lives. This has important implications for prevention policies more generally, which have tended to be oriented more towards the consumers than the producers of cigarettes, alcohol and food. For example, governments have been reluctant to take on the tobacco industry because of the vested interests and revenue from taxation (Casswell, 2012).

The further way in which Thorogood (2002) suggests that sociology can contribute to health promotion is through the study of lay health beliefs. As we saw in chapter 3, non-professional people do not accept medical advice uncritically; similarly, it is likely that they will not simply absorb passively the advice of health promoters. Lay health beliefs have been found to be more akin to those of epidemiologists than health educators (Davison et al., 1991; Frankel et al., 1991). Whilst within the discipline of epidemiology there are many acknowledged uncertainties and debates about the relationship between, let us say, cholesterol and heart disease, these tend to be glossed over by health promoters, who favour simple, straightforward unequivocal messages (see chapter 3). The danger is that health promotion will be ineffective unless it takes into account the full complexities of lay health beliefs.

Sociological analyses of health promotion activities have therefore thrown light on the structural factors that constrain people's lives. In response, sociologists have both advocated and provided critiques of the idea of 'social capital'. The notion was brought to prominence through the work of the American sociologist Putnam (2000), who popularized his argument with the reference to the powerful imagery of 'bowling alone' - the title of his book. Social capital refers to the degree of trust, integration, participation and cohesion within a society or a community. Putnam's argument is that social capital is on the decline, a thesis which concurs with the psycho-social explanation of inequalities in health (see chapter 5 above). Putnam's arguments added a further fillip to urban regeneration programmes. These are explicitly associated with attempts to foster relationships between communities, citizens and the state. Although formulated and adopted by some sociologists to further the promotion of health and reduce inequality, the concept of social capital is criticized by others both methodologically and substantively. Not only is it notoriously difficult to operationalize (for example, how do we measure trust, community and so on), but it may also serve to shift victim blaming from individuals in poor communities to the communities themselves (Song et al., 2010).

Sociology of health promotion and new public health

The underlying rationale of health promotion and the NPH is that they adopt a broader socio-structural approach (Martin and McQueen, 1989) than did conventional approaches to health education. The sociological critiques outlined above have contributed to these changes, and have welcomed these developments. Nevertheless, a sociology *of* health promotion has questioned the premisses - the norms and values - on which these new and apparently more radical approaches are based (Thorogood, 2002).

First, the individual versus structure debate (which revolves around the extent to which structural changes are required if individuals are to be able to change lifestyles) continues. Within the supposedly radical discourse and practice of health promotion and the NPH, terms such as lifestyles, risks and behaviours still proliferate. Policy and practice are dominated by the 'risk factor approach'; an approach 'whereby individuals' presumed probability of developing a particular disease is characterized in terms of their profile with respect to specific behavioural or lifestyle factors' (Martin and McQueen, 1989: 4). There is a 'holy trinity' of risk factors: smoking, diet and exercise. These are evident in the UK with initiatives such as 'Change 4 Life' which advises that children should 'eat well', 'move more' and so 'live longer'. McQueen (1989) attempts to understand the reasons for this, and he draws attention to the fact that the collective concept of health promotion emerged at a time when the dominant ideology was one of individualism. The two concepts, however, fit together well,

> because the rhetoric of health promotion and the New Public Health is social, but the actions, the behavioural base, are at the individual level. How else can one explain a public health rhetoric which argues that social conditions affect health outcomes and then, in turn, argues that the appropriate solution is to eat better, exercise more, drink less and give up smoking. (McQueen, 1989: 342)

Second, a critical sociology of health promotion is able to articulate its underlying ideologies. These are those associated with scientific medicine and rationality. The collective concept of health promotion presumes that once the socio-structural constraints on people's lives are removed, they will be able to make rational healthy choices. However, what is 'rational' and what is 'healthy' is informed by scientific medicine: 'Thus healthy behaviour is seen to be synonymous with rational behaviour. This discourse of rationality belongs within the medico-scientific paradigm which itself defines health and disease. This focus therefore privileges the health choice and obscures decisions made in other discourses' (Thorogood, 2002: 73). This observation is very important in the light of contemporary health promotion policies which are underpinned by the notion of 'choice'. It is explored in more detail in chapter 3.

A third criticism of health promotion is that it reinforces sexist, racist and homophobic ideologies. Whilst prevention has been hailed as being 'everybody's business' (DHSS, 1976), much of the advice is oriented towards women, and especially mothers, and so might be more aptly phrased as 'every mother's business' (Graham, 1979). The idea that women ought to take responsibility for not only their own health but that of others is thereby reinforced (Nettleton, 1996).

A fourth problem is what we might term the fallacy of empowerment. Those people who have the worst health status within society are also those with the least power. Health education, and now health promotion, have long been oriented towards women and the working classes. However, those very groups to which health education has been oriented traditionally have contested the attempts to control and change their behaviours. This is evident from the emergence of the community health movement in the 1970s. Farrant (1991) suggests that this movement was linked to the women's movement, health action by black and ethnic minority groups, increasing public dissatisfaction with conventional approaches to health care, community workers involved in local health issues, and health workers keen to tackle the social, economic and political determinants of health. Watt and Rodmell (1993) have identified three main sectors of the community health movement. What they all have in common is a challenge to medical dominance. First, there are self-help groups – that is, groups of people who come together because they have a shared concern about a given condition or illness. Second, there are community health groups which are interested in health issues which are beyond the remit of health professionals and formal health care - matters such as housing conditions or safe play areas for children. Third, there are community development projects which are supported by paid community health workers who assist residents of a neighbourhood to identify their health needs and organize themselves collectively to get these needs met. Whilst the first two sectors of the movement are 'supplementary' to the work of health professionals, the third may be characterized as 'oppositional', in that health is placed firmly in the political arena, and the prevailing power structures are challenged.

Community participation, community empowerment and community development are deemed to be crucial to the success of the contemporary locality-based policies on social exclusion and neighbourhood regeneration. There is therefore a danger that community development may become appropriated by those whom it seeks to challenge. As it becomes absorbed into the professional structures of formal health care, it thereby loses its political potential. This is compounded by the fact that community development projects may be dependent on the state for funding. If they successfully mobilize communities to challenge authority, they run the risk that they will bite the hand that feeds them (Beattie, 1991: 178). Nevertheless, there are examples of people living within particular localities working together effectively to create opportunities which may help to mitigate disadvantage (Adams et al., 2002).

A further problem within community development is the notion of empowerment itself. Grace (1991) argues that health promotion and community development activities are both empowering *and* controlling. Empowerment implies that people within a community have the power to take action to control and enhance their own lives. People are encouraged to find ways of meeting their self-defined needs. However, these needs, Grace points out, are frequently set by those with an a priori agenda. The process of identifying needs itself serves to construct people as 'consumers' who have a need and a desire for health status. 'Health promotion, rather than fulfilling its promise of empowerment, effectively constructs the individual as a "health consumer" in accordance with the model of consumer capitalism' (Grace, 1991: 330). From interviews with twenty-one health promoters in New Zealand, two themes emerged which have direct parallels in the discourse of marketing. These themes were, first, providing and serving, and second, planning, changing and controlling. Health promoters want to enable people to recognize that they have needs; yet at the same time they want people to come to identify their needs themselves. It would appear, therefore, that the public is supplied with the language of needs in relation to health. Indeed, social marketing (the use of marketing techniques for social issues and causes, rather than products and services) is considered to be a key technique within health promotion (Lefebvre, 1992).

A final concern critical to a sociology of health promotion and the NPH is the extent to which these practices are emerging as a new form of social regulation (Thorogood, 2002). Whilst conventional health education was taken to task, not least by sociologists, for being too narrow in its focus, health promotion and the NPH expound a broader perspective, which incorporates many aspects of people's lives and a wider range of social agencies. Recipients of advice about health are not simply informed but are encouraged to co-operate, to indicate how they feel about, for example, their drinking, or their eating, or their smoking (Bunton, 1990; Nettleton, 1992). Under the auspices of health promotion, aspects of people's lives are coming under closer scrutiny, and in turn people are encouraged to account for their behaviours in relation to health. It is possible to identify a shift in the form of social regulation in relation to health from an external to an internal approach. Rather than simply being told how to act, or being treated by medical interventions when ill, people are increasingly being induced to monitor their own health and are being instilled with healthy attitudes. The control of health must therefore come from *within* the person.

Conceptualizing health promotion and the new public health

From our discussion of the debates associated with the emergence of health promotion and the NPH, it is apparent that there are a number of inherent tensions. They would appear to fit with the ideologies of both collectivism and individualism; they are policies which are favoured by political parties of both the left and the right; and they are discourses supported by the establishment and community groups. It would appear to be an emergent policy form that transcends traditional political boundaries. In this respect it is sociologically interesting (Bunton et al., 1995). There are also epistemological differences pertaining to how health might best be conceptualized, measured and promoted (McKinlay, 1998: 371). On the one hand, there is the dominant 'natural science (mechanistic view)', which focuses on disease states, risk factors and causal mechanisms. On the other hand, there is the 'holistic view', which regards health as a multifaceted concept, not just an absence of disease, but a state of 'existential equilibrium'. The disproportionate attention on the former has led to a greater reliance on 'downstream' rather than 'upstream' policy interventions. The former include patient health education, rehabilitation, counselling, screening and so on. Upstream approaches, by contrast, are orientated towards institutions rather than individuals, and are directed at entire populations – for example, legislation and fiscal policies.

Lewis et al. (2000) outline 'six simple truths' that explain why shifting policy upstream is so notoriously difficult. First, 'health-care systems want to grow', and this invariably includes expansion of technologies and treatments. Second, 'higher health spending does not necessarily lead to higher health status', but this is not presumed to be popular with the electorate. Third, 'universal access to health care does not lead to universally good health'; this is because much wider determinants shape health. However, this is unlikely to be acknowledged by the 'medical-industrial complex'. Fourth, 'public awareness of health risks has greatly improved'. Downstream health education has no doubt contributed to this. Fifth, 'health care almost always wins out in the competition for resources'; despite public awareness of health risks, the provision of more health care gains political popularity. Finally, 'changing the distribution of health status through "upstream" strategies is extraordinarily difficult'.

Beattie (1991: 167) has provided a conceptual schema which enumerates the logical possibilities of health promotion approaches and enables us to appreciate the wide political appeal of prevention policies (see figure 10.1). Beattie's schema is based on two dichotomies: the 'mode of intervention', which may be authoritative or negotiated, and the 'focus of intervention', which may be individual or collective. First, there are health persuasion techniques. These are interventions which employ the authority of public health expertise to redirect the behaviour of individuals in

PRESCRIPTIVE

	HEALTH PERSUASION TECHNIQUES 'PROFESSIONALIST' – agenda determined by expert – validated by colleagues (peers in the craft)	*LEGISLATIVE ACTION FOR HEALTH* 'MANAGERIALIST' – agenda determined by bureaucratic rules – validated by scientific-legal authority	
PRIVATE			PUBLIC
	PERSONAL COUNSELLING FOR HEALTH 'CONSUMERIST' – agenda determined by the enterprising patron/customer	*COMMUNITY DEVELOPMENT FOR HEALTH* 'SYNDICALIST' – agenda determined by collective negotiation among allies	

PARTICIPATIVE

Figure 10.1 Strategies of health promotion: Beattie's typology
Source: Beattie (1991: 167).

'top-down' prescriptive ways. This strategy has a long history, and traditional forms of health education would fall into this category – for example, the VD campaigns during the First World War and the mass media AIDS campaigns in the 1980s. Governments favour this approach because of its high profile, and persist in pursuing it despite evidence which suggests that it has only a limited impact on people's behaviours.

The second strategy is 'legislative action for health'. Whilst the first approach is favoured by the political Right, this second approach is within the domain of the left. Here the authority of public health expertise is drawn upon to influence legislation: for example, Clean Air Acts, compulsory fluoridation of water supplies, or the control over advertising of cigarettes. One of the most important examples of this in recent decades is legislation that prevents smoking in public places. These changes have reduced the numbers of people smoking and provided opportunities to support those who wish to desist smoking cigarettes (Ritche et al., 2010) and there is growing evidence that the legislation is impacting on health outcomes (Mackay et al., 2012).

The 'personal counselling for health' approach is likely to transcend political boundaries, although being inherently individualistic, it is likely to be favoured by the Right. This approach involves the use of individual or group counselling to encourage people to reflect upon and thereby be encouraged to alter their lifestyles.

Finally, the 'community development for health' approach involves group-based action which aims to challenge conventional forms of health care and identify alternative means to promote health. Whilst falling firmly within the boundaries of the collectivist tradition, as we have seen, there is potential for community development to be appropriated by the Right.

Clearly, these four strategies of health promotion have implications for the role of health professionals. Within the health persuasion approach expertise is enhanced, whilst within the community development approach expertise is challenged, and new, more egalitarian forms of professional–client relationships could be envisaged. Further, each approach implies a different form of governance. Just as different strategies of health promotion create different experiences and objects of medical attention, so too do different health policies. For example, health and illness that are dealt with in the context of the hospital are different from those found in the community. It is to this topic that we now turn.

Hospital to community care

In the early nineteenth century, formal medical care was primarily concerned with diseased bodies, which were most suitably treated within the domain of the hospital. By contrast, contemporary health and medical care are dispersed throughout multiple locations, and involve the maintenance and the promotion of health throughout the community. This section describes these policy changes briefly, and then examines some explanations for this shift in approach.

Policy analysts have pointed to a post-war 'precarious consensus' (Walker, 1993) between political parties which were committed to community care. For children, elderly people, those with learning difficulties, people with physical disabilities and those experiencing mental illness, care in the community was considered to be preferable to care within institutions. In the case of mental health, for example, the 1959 Mental Health Act outlined the intention to increase the range of community services such as homes, hostels and social clubs. In relation to policies for the elderly, the Minister for Health stated in 1958 that the 'underlying principle of our services for the old should be this: that the best place for old people is in their own homes, with help from home services if need be' (Townsend, 1962: 196).

The policy of running down large hospitals dates back to the 1962 Hospital Plan, which was complemented by the Ministry of Health's *Health and Welfare: The Development of Community Care*, which stressed the need to expand community care rather than hospital care (Ham, 2004). The post-war consensus was, 'precarious' because, although this was the officially stated view, in practice until the 1980s there was little change at the level of actual delivery of services. Since that time the process of de-hospitalization has been accelerated, with more and more people living in their homes, in hostels or with relatives (Tomlinson, 1992). Whilst the precarious consensus advocated care *in* the community (that is, through the provision of support services), the period post-consensus was characterized by a shift to care *by* the community (DHSS, 1981: 3), by friends, relatives, voluntary agencies, private residential homes and social service departments, all of which were to be managed by local authorities. Hence local authorities became enablers and co-ordinators of care rather than providers. The central thrust of social policy was that, wherever possible, people should remain in their own homes or in 'homely' settings within the community. Debates on community care policies have focused on the merits and de-merits of the policy and provision of community care. These centre on the relationships between gender, ethnicity, poverty and community care policies; the lack of opportunities for participation in decision making by user groups; and the gap between policy rhetoric and the reality of provision in the light of the chronic underfunding of community care services (Dalley, 1988; Rogers et al., 1992). Sociological analyses, by contrast, have theorized about the general trend of the move from hospital to community care.

Explanations for the shift from hospital to community care

Sociological accounts of the post-war policy shift towards community care have focused primarily on psychiatric care and mental illness. Three explanations for this change have been offered: therapeutic, economic and a reconceptualization of the medical model (Busfield, 1986). The therapeutic, or technological, explanation points to the contribution of neuroleptic drugs, which appeared on the scene in the 1950s. Pharmaceutical innovations meant that patients were considered both able and safe enough (to themselves and those around them) to live in the community. This liberal-scientific explanation is far from adequate, however. First, there is a problem of timing: Busfield (1986: 326) has pointed out that there was a decline in the population in psychiatric beds before chemically synthesized drugs were introduced. Second, the effectiveness of the drugs has been overestimated. Psychiatrists, some have suggested (Treacher and Baruch, 1981), have overplayed the effectiveness of drugs in their bid to become more integrated into mainstream medicine, and to end their perceived isolation and thereby enhance their status and careers. Third, the use of drugs to permit people to live in the community would not account for the change in patterns of care for other groups of people.

An alternative suggestion is that long-stay in-patient care was expensive, and so moving people into the community was thought to provide a cheaper alternative. In its Marxist variant, this argument draws attention to the fact that pouring money into large institutions must surely threaten the interests of capital. When money was found to be short, community care solutions looked attractive (P. Brown, 1988). Whilst economic considerations undoubtedly form part of the explanation for shifts in policy, they remain partial. For example, cross-national comparisons have indicated that there is no correlation between financial crises and reduced rates of institutionalized care (Rose, 1986: 56). Furthermore, as is becoming increasingly evident, the extent to which community care is the cheaper alternative is questionable.

The third explanation is one which examines the content of the medical model or medical knowledge itself. These accounts suggest that what the existing critiques of mental health policies have failed to take into account is the transformation in psychiatric knowledge, which in turn is inextricably interrelated to psychiatric practice. In other words, we need to examine the discursive context of psychiatry – that is, what those who speak about psychiatry and mental illness are saying, what they are doing, and, through these activities, what objects they are constructing. As Prior (1991: 486) argues, 'each discourse carries with it different objects of focus as well as its own techniques for observing, measuring and organizing such objects'. In light of a detailed observational study of a long-stay psychiatric hospital, Prior (1991: 487) concludes that 'the old asylums have been destroyed from within rather than without the walls'. The central object within hospital was the patient's behaviour. Prior found that both nursing policy on a psychiatric ward and assessments of patients focused on activities for daily living (ADL). Care plans, for example, were directed less at illness and more at patients' behaviours, which were observed, assessed and rectified. Behavioural scales, which focused on things such as the management of money, personal bodily care and clarity of speech, were devised for assessment purposes. Of course, other forms of assessment would also be undertaken, but the behavioural ones appeared to be ubiquitous throughout the hospital. Clearly the best place to assess normal behaviour is within a normal setting. In this respect institutions are not considered to be particularly conducive, and so the community would be a preferable location for those with behavioural problems. This is the nub of Prior's (1991: 487) argument:

> in choosing behaviour as an object of therapeutic focus psychiatry and psychiatric nursing have lost the rationale they once had for confining themselves within the grounds of a psychiatric hospital. Indeed, the new object of focus has necessitated an extension of professional psychiatric practice into the world 'outside'.

Medicine and nursing do not have a monopoly over behaviour; other kinds of professional involvement become just as legitimate in the management and control of mental illness. Working at the level of behaviour, there is no need to make reference to the underlying organic malfunctions. Indeed, there has been an expansion of behaviour therapies since the Second World War, together with a 'proliferation of sites for the practice of psychiatry', which has involved 'the psychiatrization of new problems and the differentiation of the psychiatric population' (Rose, 1986: 83). There is a whole range of targets, from alcoholics to anorexics to the simply anxious. In fact, psychiatry is concerned not only with mental illness, but with the whole domain of mental health, the potential for which can be realized only within the community.

It is important to point out that this argument does not assume that all those involved in psychiatric care are enthusiastic about care in the community. There are the old guard who prefer the biomedical approach and are sceptical about new forms of care and new types of health professional. However, alternative strategies and techniques are established as a result of debates between the traditionalists and the reformists. 'Hospitals using psychotropic medications, therapeutic communities, feminist self-help groups, social work group homes, community nurses and many other strange bed fellows have combined to chart the domain of mental health and develop technologies for its management' (Rose, 1986: 83). Thus the critiques of custodial and institutional care have actually contributed to the reorganization of psychiatry and the creation of new forms of mental health practice.

What unifies the accounts within this explanation is the idea that the objects of the medical or social sciences are an effect of the practices that surround them (see chapter 2). If we are to understand changes in the organization of health and medical care, we must begin by exploring how the objects of its focus are constructed. The prime object of medical care located within the hospital was a diseased anatomy; the central object of health care located in the community is a whole person who simultaneously manifests a potential to be ill and a potential to be increasingly healthy. Whilst care and control within institutions were described by Foucault as panoptic power (see chapter 5), care and control of people in the community have been characterized by what Armstrong (1983a) has called 'Dispensary power'.

Panoptic to Dispensary power

Dispensaries were founded towards the end of the nineteenth century, initially for the screening, diagnosis and treatment of patients with tuberculosis. In this respect they formed an interface between the hospital and the community. But for Armstrong (1983a: 8), the Dispensary was not only a building that housed a new form of health care, it was 'also a new perceptual structure – a new way of seeing illness which manifested itself in different ways'. It 'was a new way of construing illness' in three respects. First, it involved a new way of organizing health care that radiated into the community. Functioning beyond the walls of the hospital, it acted as a co-ordinating centre for those who sought out and monitored disease. Second, the medical gaze was diverted from the interior of the physical body to the spaces between bodies. Pathology was not only localized and static, but was found to travel throughout the social body, and so there was a need to focus on contacts, relationships and home visits (Rose, 1985; Nettleton, 1991). Third, as surveillance extended throughout the community, the emphasis began to shift from those who were ill to those who were potentially ill. Consequently, there was a demise of the binary separation between the normal and abnormal, the ill and the healthy, the mad and the sane. Thus the Dispensary involved a reorganization of care, a new conceptualization of illness, and new forms of observation. Thus, from a Foucauldian perspective '[c]omprehensive health care in Britain, from 1948, and the contemporary invention and importance of community care are simply manifestations of a new diagram of power which spreads its pervasive gaze throughout a society' (Armstrong, 1983a: 100). Both the promotion of health and the provision of health care in the community have impacted upon the patients and recipients of health care. No longer is the passive body treated in hospital; rather, the active person is encouraged to participate in their own health, as we have discussed in relation to health promotion above. Given the dominance of consumer culture within late modern societies, it is perhaps no surprise that issues surrounding health and health care are increasingly being articulated in terms of this discourse (Hugman, 1994). Indeed, a third strand of health policy which has contributed to the 'new regime of total health' is that of consumerism.

Consumerism, choice and the National Health Service

The last few decades have seen a shift in emphasis in the health policy from paternalism to consumerism (Klein, 2010). Patients are increasingly being treated as consumers who make demands and have needs which the Health Service must strive to meet. In the context of the health care reforms that have taken place, consumerism has come to mean the maximization of patient choice, the provision of adequate information, raising the standards of health care, ensuring the quality of services by taking into account the views of consumers, carrying out surveys to ensure consumer satisfaction, developing tools for the assessment of needs, reducing waiting times for treatment, and encouraging consumers to complain if they are not satisfied with the service they receive. Clearly these concerns reflect a certain model of consumerism, one which is congruent with the market and the enterprise culture. It is about the rights of individual consumers, rather than collective representation and participation. This was evident in the publication in the early 1990s of the *Patient's Charter* (Department of Health, 1991b), which implies that people ought to be treated as 'customers' of care. Since the 1980s the tone of policy statements is that health care provision should be tailored to the preferences of the individual; terms such as 'personal service' and 'personal attention' are used, and there is a 'drive' to develop a service which is 'responsive, convenient and personalised' (Department of Health, 2004b). Recent reforms in the UK centre on expanding patient choice and using competition between providers to enhance performance.

During the 1990s the means by which health care provision could become more consumer orientated was the introduction of the 'internal market', wherein the Health Service came to comprise both providers and purchasers of care. At the heart of the Conservative government reforms was the notion of patient choice: 'to give patients, wherever they live in the UK, better health care and greater choice of the services available' (Department of Health, 1991a: 3). However, as many authors pointed out, within the context of a quasi-market, individual consumers were not able to exercise their choice (Paton, 1992; Walker, 1993), as it was the purchasing authorities (for example, primary care trusts or clinical commissing groups) who bought the services, and not the consumers themselves. Moreover, once services are contracted between purchasers and providers, there is limited scope for manoeuvre if the individual consumer prefers to go elsewhere. Patient choice figures prominently in the health policies of New Labour and Coalition governments, and is claimed to be *the* central driver for policy change (Milburn, 2003; Tritter et al., 2010). The internal market was modified in the late 1990s, and was replaced by partnerships. The provider of the care can be public, private or not-for-profit. Appleby et al. (2003) point out that 'improving choice has tremendous popular and political appeal: who could argue against the desirability of allowing patients more say in decisions concerning their health care?' However, further consideration reminds us that individual needs and wants can be at odds with the needs of the majority. In addition, some people may be better able - due to their financial, educational, and informational resources - to exercise choice than others.

The rationale for the changes is to overcome paternalism, increase professional accountability, and to improve efficiency. The privileging of patient choice also serves as a justification for the need to provide more flexible and responsive services. Examples of consumer-orientated health care in the UK include 24-hour 'walk-in' health centres, tailored to the needs of the patients, not the professionals; the telephone and on-line services NHS Direct and NHS On-line; and single electronic patient records which enable patients to move more effectively between the various services on offer.

Sociologists have theorized the emergence of this shift from paternalism to consumerism and have argued that it may be suggestive of more significant aspects of social change. Bakx (1991), for example, suggests that the rise of consumerism and growth of alternative forms of consumption and health are part of a cultural transformation, a move from modernism to late modernism. Biomedicine was a fundamentally modernist project, in that it was based on scientific orthodoxy, claimed a superior knowledge and thereby secured a monopoly of provision. Today, however, faith in the modernist project has diminished (see chapter 8). As a consequence of this alienation from medicine, people are once again wanting to regain control over their bodies and have a say in the types of interventions that are administered and the general care which they receive.

In this respect there is a congruence between notions of consumerism and patient choice and the sociological concept of reflexivity (Giddens, 1990). The 'reflexive self', like the 'consumer', presumes that individuals act in calculated ways to further their own interests (Lupton, 2002). Although sociologists are in general agreement that we live in a consumer society, the extent to which individuals invariably behave in rational and entrepreneurial or 'reflexive' ways is an empirical question. Lupton's (2002) analysis of the views of Australian health care users finds some evidence to suggest that people are indeed discerning and questioning of medical practice. But she also finds that in general people still retain a considerable degree of faith in and respect for medical practitioners. This, she suggests, may be to do with the nature of the doctor-patient relationship itself, where on occasion patients may have a 'felt desire' to take on a 'passive patient' role and appreciate the opportunity to be dependent on others, especially those whom they trust.

There is no doubt, however, that a fundamental shift has occurred in health care policy which involves a reorientation - at the levels of both rhetoric and practice - towards the patient, consumer or user. This involves a growing diversity of health care provision and mechanisms which will permit patients to exercise their 'choice', even if some patients are better placed to exercise choice than others. It is likely that changes in the NHS are part of a more profound transformation that is taking place in advanced capitalist societies which are both economically and ideologically driven. Commenting on the changes within the Health Service, Jefferys (1991: 231) states:

> If I am right, the changes now in progress in the National Health Service are not merely cosmetic or historically trivial. They are the outcome, at least in part, of some more fundamental changes in the nature of the capitalist system in Britain, themselves occasioned by its destabilization in the network of world economies.

Jefferys' observation is indeed an accurate observation. These policy changes are manifestations of what we might call Western fundamentalism and that is an unshakable belief in the neo-liberalism which gives primacy to choice and competition. In health care it is difficult to argue with aspirations of person-centred care, patient choice, and accountability. But if we broaden the lens and place patients within a broader canvas, we can begin to see that their individual choices and preferences are articulated in terms of wants rather than needs, and in a neo-liberal context have come to take precedence over social rights such as access to care and the provision of services of good quality for all (Tritter et al., 2010: 170).

A new paradigm for health?

Reflecting on contemporary health care, Castel (1991) has suggested that we are currently experiencing a transformation or revolution in health care. This change will see the demise of the practitioner-patient relationship, a new role for health professionals as health strategists, an increasing emphasis on the profiling of populations and the potential marginalization of those groups which are not able to consume and thereby participate in late modern society.

Castel (1991) conceptualizes these changes in terms of a shift from 'dangerousness' to 'risk'. Hitherto doctors and psychiatrists – those who have been able to diagnose and prescribe – have treated mental and physical illness. If there was any doubt as to the presence of illness, they were likely to err on the side of caution to prevent manifestation of disease. That is, the patient was potentially 'dangerous'. Now, the target of medical care is not merely symptoms but also a person's characteristics, which the specialists of prevention policy have constituted as risk factors. The 'clinic of the subject' is being replaced by the 'epidemiological clinic': that is, 'a system of multifarious but exactly located expertise which supplants the old doctor–patient relation. This certainly does not mean the end of the doctor, but it does definitely mark a profound transformation in medical practice' (Castel, 1991: 282). Thus we are witnessing the advent of a new mode of surveillance, aided by technological advances which make the calculus and probabilities of 'systematic predetection' more and more sophisticated.

There are two very real consequences of this profound change to medical practice. First, 'the separation of diagnosis and treatment, and the transformation of the caring function into an activity of expertise' (Castel, 1991: 290). Practitioners' key function will be to assess their clients and then, on the basis of this assessment, to identify the appropriate route that they should take. Populations are thereby managed on the basis of their profiles; that is, their age, social class, occupation, gender, lifestyle, relationships, where they live, who they live with, and so on. It is factors such as these which form their 'risk'. A second consequence is that practitioners become subordinate to administrators. The managers of health care are increasingly taking the role of health strategists rather than managing health workers.

> Administration requires an almost complete autonomy because it has virtually absolute control of the new technology. The operative on the ground now becomes a simple auxiliary to a manager who he or she supplies with information derived from the activity of the diagnosis expertise . . . These items of information are then stockpiled, processed and distributed along channels completely disconnected from those of professional practice, using in particular the medium of computer data handling. (Castel, 1991: 293)

Indeed, this is evident in the changing nature of health care which is now focusing on needs assessments based on epidemiological and survey data. The work of the Public Health Observatories, established by the government in the UK in the early 2000s, is illustrative of one of a number of institutional sites which aim to collate and disseminate data in order to improve collective health status rather than that of individuals. The creation of information about individuals and communities is a key element of what Armstrong calls surveillance medicine. Today, however, information is not limited to statistical data; within the context of the 'Information Age' it appears to permeate medicine in more fundamental ways.

Medicine in the Information Age

The notion of the Information Age now has a wide currency within sociology and beyond. It can be defined in any number of different ways, but perhaps the most influential conceptualization comes from Manuel Castells. For Castells, the Information

Age refers to a historical period in which societies organize their activities in what he calls a 'technological paradigm' (Castells, 2000), a cluster of related technologies articulated around ICTs and genetic engineering. As such, it is conceived as a mode of social organization that subsumes the Industrial Age, a technological paradigm organized around the production and distribution of energy.

Webster (2002: 450) argues that medicine can be conceptualized in terms of 'information'. He writes:

> The rapid spread of both genetics and health informatics within clinical science and medicine, as well as their development for health management purposes (as in DNA registers, or in health information management systems such as the electronic patient record [EPR]), suggest that the contemporary medical portfolio is becoming increasingly 'informaticized'.

He identifies three aspects of this informaticization. First, in terms of the 'language and practice of biology', this is itself becoming an information science. Bio-informaticists map and manage information about cells, proteins and genes. The Human Genome Project (an international consortium which identified all the genes in human DNA and aims to determine the sequences of the chemical bases that make up human DNA) was made possible only by massive computing capacity. Indeed, a number of writers (Haraway, 1991; Fox Keller, 1995) suggest that information is '*the* dominant motif in modern biology' (Birke, 1999). The commercial consequences of these technological developments are immense, and the ethical and social implications associated with privacy and confidentiality are likely to be profound.

A second way in which medicine is becoming informaticized is through 'its delivery and management through telecare, telemedicine, and health informatics' (Webster, 2002: 452). Patients and practitioners no longer have to be in the same locality to access and exchange information. Telecare, for example, enables 'a much faster roll out of patients from hospitals to their own homes where their blood pressure, respiratory rate and images of healing wounds can be taken electronically and downloaded to physicians' (Webster 2002: 450).

Third, the rise of informaticized medicine is associated with an increase in 'risk-laden diagnosis and clinical understanding'. The collation of information about risks, be it associated with genetic or lifestyle risk factors, results in the generation of information which can be used to assess the likelihood of illness and disease, and this adds a 'greater provisionality to medical diagnosis' (Webster, 2002: 452). Communication between patients and professionals will increasingly be about probabilities and possibilities rather than determining the presence or absence of disease (see chapter 6).

Two further examples of the ways in which the work of health care practitioners and the patients is being influenced by the assimilation and proliferation of information are worthy of consideration; these are the rise of evidence-based medicine (EBM) and consumer informatics.

Evidence-based medicine (EBM)

Contemporary health policy dictates that clinical practice should be based on evidence about the effectiveness of the interventions used. Over three decades ago, a medical epidemiologist named Archie Cochrane observed that many routine clinical interventions had never actually been tested or evaluated, and that doctors tended to rely on their practice-based experience or knowledge they had acquired – often many years ago – at medical school (Cochrane, 1972). He subsequently developed research tools that are used to systematically collate and review evidence of the effectiveness of interventions. The legacy of his work can be found in the work of the Cochrane Collaboration, an international network of centres which undertake systematic reviews to collate available research evidence, which in turn are used to develop clinical guidelines by institutions such as the National Institute of Clinical Excellence (NICE) in the UK. EBM is defined as 'The conscientious, explicit, and judicious use of current best evidence in making decisions about the care of individual patients' (Sackett et al., 1996).

The *raison d'être* for EBM is that the reviews and guidelines will inform both practitioners and policy makers about the most effective diagnostic or therapeutic procedures; this in turn will benefit patients, who will receive medical care which is proven in its effectiveness. Thus care packages, drug regimens and so on are subjected to systematic evaluation, and the individual clinician is encouraged to take these findings into account in her daily practice. The evidence is collated and disseminated not only by clinically trained practitioners but also by experts in information science. Thus the art of clinical medicine is being displaced by health 'intelligence'. Information scientists who specialize in this health-related work comprise a relatively new occupational group, who have their own journals and methodologies and are increasingly able to influence health policy and practice.

The emergence of EBM has not escaped sociological scrutiny. Harrison (1998) suggests that although 'ostensibly rational *and* politically appealing', EBM is based on 'three serious naïveties'. First there is the problem of *implementation*. There is an assumption that clinicians will act upon guidelines. Yet Harrison points out (somewhat ironically) that there is plenty of 'evidence' which suggests that clinicians are unlikely to act on the basis of information unless it is patient-specific or linked to incentives or disincentives. However, as medical education comes to encompass training in EBM, this may alter, and practitioners may become more proficient at combining research-based and experientially derived knowledge and develop what Timmermans and Angell (2001) call 'evidence based clinical judgment'.

The second 'naïvety' underpinning EBM relates to its *political* appeal; politicians can draw on seemingly objective evidence to justify rationing and resource allocation. They are let off the hook, as it were. After all, who would want to receive, or see resources being invested in, ineffective care? However, in practice it is not so straightforward; evidence-based decisions about medications for conditions such as multiple sclerosis and Alzheimer's disease have been challenged by both clinicians and patient groups, and have secured much media attention.

Although assessments of effectiveness are derived systematically through the collation of objective studies, this can mean that certain groups can be systematically excluded. Rogers (2004), for example, reveals how at each stage of the EBM process there are a series of biases against women. Health issues studied tend to be influenced by 'biological essentialism' and so, when it comes to women's health issues, the focus is disproportionately on reproductive health. The gendered nature of other health matters tends to be overlooked as a result of 'gender blindness'; for example, although globally one million more women than men die of cardiovascular diseases, the evidence reviewed derives disproportionately from studies of men. For example, there is significant gender bias in clinical trials. Rogers (2004: 60) claims that 'in the US 85 per cent of research participants are male; this rises to 95 per cent in Canada'.

Harrison's third critique relates to the *epistemological* underpinnings of EBM. The proponents of EBM maintain that 'evidence' is based on authoritative scientific studies, some of which have more 'authority' than others, and this in turn depends on their positioning on a 'hierarchy of evidence'. The pinnacle of the hierarchy is the randomized controlled trial (RCT) wherein patients are randomly assigned to either 'experimental' or 'control' groups. The former receive intervention, the latter do not, and if the RCT is double blind, then neither the clinicians nor the patients know who is in which group. The RCT is therefore a tool of epidemiology; it relies on statistical methods, and as such is a 'probabilistic model' derived from collective rather than individual-level data. This is in contrast to the 'traditional model' wherein clinicians seek to understand the natural history of the disease by observing how 'disease processes develop over time and impact upon normal physiological processes' (Harrison, 1998: 25). Harrison suggests that clinicians are more likely to act on their experience and observations of their own patients. Their reasonings about treatment tended to be rooted in their knowledge of the workings of the body, rather than on the 'publication of meta-analyses of large numbers of cases' (1998: 26).

In many ways EBM arose out of some of the early criticisms of the biomedical model, most especially the charge that the institution of medicine paid insufficient attention to its efficacy (see chapters 1 and 5). EBM continues to gain momentum and is a specific example of processes of standardization that are a central feature of contemporary life (Timmermans and Epstein, 2010). Standardization processes are appealing because they appear to be politically neutral in that the setting of research informed standards ensure uniformity of quality. Health practitioners, the criticism goes, were relying on tradition or were duped by the pharmaceutical industry. However, this belies the observation that the creation and implementation of standards are not neutral activities. For analytic purposes, Timmermans and Epstein (2010) usefully disaggregate standards into four components: design of standards (e.g., the properties of tools and protocols); terminological standards (e.g., International Classification of Diseases); performance standards (e.g., outcomes of operations); and procedural standards (e.g., how care practices should be performed). Taking these in turn it is clear that there is scope for negotiation when it comes to determining each of them. This makes them ripe for sociological scrutiny to unearth the processes involved in their production and their intended and unintended consequences. Certainly sociologists have, for example, found how the application of protocols and treatments enshrined in evidence-based guidelines are resisted in practice as clinicians tailor treatments to what they perceive the needs of their individual patients are rather than what the official evidence would prescribe.

Critics of EBM, and in particular RCTs, suggest that these techniques tend to focus on clinical interventions and outcomes to the relative - though not exclusive - neglect of other determinants of health. Indeed, the evidence-based turn is extremely influential in social policy and health promotion interventions in the form of evidence-based social policy and evidence-based health care (Oakley, 2000).

Nevertheless, some argue that within the health care context the biomedical model is reinforced. Rogers concludes her analysis of the implications of EBM and women thus:

> Evidence of efficacy is best proved by changes in well defined outcomes such as weight of babies, number of deaths or level of blood pressure; where it is not possible to define these kind of outcomes, it is more difficult for research to demonstrate effectiveness. A narrowly biomedical research programme receiving much of its funding from the pharmaceutical industry is unlikely to embrace research into effective social interventions, such as income support, or programmes to decrease violence against women. (2004: 69)

EBM does not in and of itself reinforce the biomedical model, but an unintended consequence of its use in practice may be to reinforce a biomedical mentality.

Consumer informatics

It has been reported that 61 per cent of adults in the USA have gone on-line for medical advice which is more than those who actually visit health professionals (Fox and Jones, 2009). The availability of interactive information that is accessible to consumers through the Internet and related technologies such as digital television and web television is vast. There is much debate about the pros and cons of such a vast array of information being available (Nettleton and Hanlon, 2006). Some commentators are concerned about lay people being misled by dubious information, whilst other observers point to the empowering potential of e-health information sources. In terms of Webster's (2002) notion of the informaticization of medicine, however, *medical knowledge* is being metamorphosed into information; crucially, it is circulating beyond the walls of medical schools, hospitals and laboratories. It is available to anyone who cares, or is able, to access it. Patients and practitioners alike can access the findings of the Cochrane Collaboration's latest systematic review. Medical knowledge can be accessed, and indeed is now increasingly produced, by health consumers and health users (Hardey, 2010). A consequence is that throughout the media there is a juxtaposition of diverse types of knowledge or, rather, information. Experiential knowledge may be read alongside biomedical knowledge, and commercial companies vie with independent research sites.

The availability of such vast amounts of information must invariably contribute to a diversity and plurality of knowledge, ideas and interpretations of health and illness – a process, which one might suppose would serve to counter the dominance of biomedicine. Yet, there is some – albeit still rather suggestive – evidence that this may not necessarily be the case. Seale (2005) advances the sociological 'media convergence' thesis to suggest that on-line information is becoming structured in ways which are congruent with more traditional forms of media. In relation to health and medicine, this means that conventional health and medical material has become foregrounded on the Internet. Although it is undoubtedly the case that there is a staggeringly wide range of information on just about any health matter potentially available on the Internet, unconventional and less mainstream sources are not necessarily all that easy to find, and the structure of the Internet is such that it does not immediately surface when users go on-line. Seale undertook an analysis of information sources about cancer and found that search engines invariably prioritized 'biomedical' sources of health information. He concludes, therefore, that the initial diversity of health information on the Internet has become curtailed as more traditional 'producer' interests - governmental, biomedical and charitable sites - have come to dominate. Indeed, there is a convergence in content between the 'old' and 'new' media that is undercutting earlier celebrations, and concerns about the Internet as a medium that promotes a complex diversity of perspectives on health and illness are borne out by empirical evidence. He states: 'where the trustworthiness of information is a major issue . . . consumer reliance on . . . mainstream sites is more likely . . . [and] . . . is encouraged by the ways in which search engines structure the experience for most users'.

Nettleton et al. (2005) scrutinized parents' accounts of their experiences of seeking on-line health information for themselves and their children. Their findings complemented those of Seale, in that they identified a 'concordance' between the macro-structural foregrounding of health resources on the web - as suggested by media convergence theory - and the accounting practices that lay people use to accomplish the 'trustworthiness' (or otherwise) of health information on the web. From the accounts of the everyday use of the Internet to access health information, we identified a number of ways in which people 'accomplish' the legitimacy of information sources. Individuals articulate the need to manage a tension which is inherent in Internet use. On the one hand, it comprises a useful and practical resource; but on the other hand, there is awareness that it may be a harbinger of danger. People appear to manage this tension by drawing upon a range of rhetorical devices, or 'rhetorics of reliability', which articulate why they trust some on-line sources of information and not others.

Six 'rhetorics of reliability' were discerned from the parents' accounts. These are 'real rather than virtual organizations', 'UK versus other', 'commercial versus non-commercial', 'professional/official versus non-professional', 'codified versus experiential knowledge' and 'replication - going with the majority view'. Such assessments implicitly reinforce the discourses of professionalism and biomedicine, and led us to conclude that the future of medicine, and biomedicine in particular, is not so 'on the line' in the Information Age as is sometimes suggested (Loader et al., 2002).

Conclusion

This chapter has examined sociological analyses of three areas of late modern health policy: the emergence of health promotion of the NPH, the shift from hospital to community care, and the rise of consumerism and patient choice. It has been suggested that these three areas of policy are emblematic of a wider transformation of health care. This change towards a new regime of 'total health' implies a demise of the traditional professional-patient relationship and a concurrent rise in health surveillance strategies and the profiling of healthy populations. It also involves a shift from traditional forms of formal institutionalized health care to a broader range of informal and community-based alternatives. Associated with these changes is a blurring of a distinction between the 'expert' providers and the consumers of health care, who are also presumed to be experts on their own health and illness. In terms of the health policy rhetoric, at least, the contribution of the latter must help to shape the provision of health care. It has also been argued that the sociology of health and illness has not only analysed these changes, but has contributed to them. The sociology of health and illness, as we have seen throughout this text, has helped to forge an alternative to the traditional biomedical approach to health care. It has highlighted the importance of the patient as a whole person, the merits of community care as opposed to institutional care, the importance of health as well as disease and illness, and the importance of lay views on health and illness and health care. This critique of medicine and societal responses to health, illness and disease remains important, not least in the light of socio-material changes associated with innovative health-related technologies which in themselves may help to reinforce the primacy of biomedicine.

FURTHER READING

Gabe, J. and Calnan, M. (eds) (2009), *The New Sociology of the Health Service*, Abingdon: Routledge.

Hunter, D. J. (2008), *The Health Debate*, Bristol: The Policy Press.

Klein, R. (2010), *The New Politics of the NHS*, 6th edn, London: Prentice-Hall. A clear and informed classic which is a must for those interested in health policy.

Lupton, D. (1995), *The Imperative of Health: Public Health and the Regulated Body*, London: Sage. A sociological analysis of the promotion of health.

Tritter, J., Koivusalo, O. and Dorfman, P. (2010), *Globalization, Markets and Health Care Policy: Redrawing the Patient as Consumer*, Abingdon: Routledge.

Bibliography

Acheson, P. (1998), *Independent Inquiry into Inequalities in Health, The Acheson Report*, London: The Stationery Office.

Adams, L., Amos, M. and Munro, J. (2002), *Promoting Health: Politics and Practice*, London: Sage.

Agbolegbe, G. (1984), 'Fighting the Racist Disease', *Nursing Times*, 18 April, 18–20.

Ahmad, W. I. U. (1989), 'Policies, Pills and Political Will: Critique of Policies to Improve the Health Status of Ethnic Minorities', *The Lancet*, 8630: 148–50.

Ahmad, W. I. U. (ed.) (1993), *Race and Health in Contemporary Britain*, Buckingham: Open University Press.

Ahmad, W. I. U. (1996), 'Consanguinity and Related Demons: Science and Racism in the Debate on Consanguinity and Birth Outcome', in S. Samson and N. South (eds), *Conflict and Consensus in Social Policy*, Basingstoke: Macmillan.

Akinsanya, J. A. (1988), 'Ethnic Minority Nurses, Midwives and Health Visitors: What Role for them in the National Health Service?', *New Community*, 14, 3: 444–51.

Annandale, E. (2009), *Women's Health and Social Change*, Abingdon: Taylor and Francis.

Anwar, A. and Ali, A. (1987), *Overseas Doctors: Experience and Expectations*, London: Commission of Racial Equality.

Appleby, J., Harrison, A. and Devlin, N. (2003), *What is the Real Cost of More Patient Choice?* London: Kings Fund.

Arber, S. (1990), 'Revealing Women's Health: Re-Analysing the General Household Survey', in H. Roberts (ed.), *Women's Health Counts*, London: Routledge.

Arber, S. and Cooper, H. (2000), 'Gender Inequalities in Health across the Life Course', in E. Annandale and K. Hunt (eds), *Gender Inequalities in Health*, Buckingham: Open University Press.

Arber, S. and Thomas, H. (2001), 'From Women's Health to Gender Analysis of Health', in W. C. Cockerham (ed.), *The Blackwell Companion to Medical Sociology*, Oxford: Blackwell.

Arber, S., Dale, A. and Gilbert, N. (1986), 'The Limitations of Existing Social Class Classifications for Women', in A. Jacoby (ed.), *The Measurement of Social Class*, London: Social Research Association.

Arber, S., Bote, M. and Meadows, R. (2009), 'Gender and Socio-Economic Patterning of Self Reported Sleep Problems in Britain', *Social Science & Medicine*, 68, 2: 281–9.

Arksey, H. (1998), *RSI and the Experts: The Construction of Medical Knowledge*, London: UCL Press.

Armstrong, D. (1979), 'The Emancipation of Biographical Medicine', *Social Science & Medicine*, 13A: 1–3.

Armstrong, D. (1983a), *Political Anatomy of the Body: Medical Knowledge in Britain in the Twentieth Century*, Cambridge: Cambridge University Press.

Armstrong, D. (1983b), 'The Fabrication of Nurse–Patient Relationships', *Social Science & Medicine*, 17: 457–60.

Armstrong, D. (1984), 'The Patient's View', *Social Science & Medicine*, 18: 737–44.

Armstrong, D. (1993), 'Public Health Spaces and the Fabrication of Identity', *Sociology*, 27, 3: 393–410.

Armstrong, D. (2000), 'Social Theorizing about Health and Illness', in G. L. Albrecht, R. Fitzpatrick and S. C. Scrimshaw (eds), *The Handbook of Social Studies in Health and Medicine*, London: Sage.

Armstrong, D. (2002), 'The Rise of Surveillance Medicine', in S. Nettleton and U. Gustaffson (eds), *The Sociology of Health and Illness Reader*, Cambridge: Polity.

Arney, W. R. (1982), *Power and the Profession of Obstetrics*, London: University of Chicago Press.

Arney, W. R. and Bergen, B. (1984), *Medicine and the Management of Living: Taming the Last Great Beast*, London: University of Chicago Press.

Aronowitz, R. (2001), 'When do Symptoms become a Disease?', *Annals of Internal Medicine*, 134, 9: 803–8.

Aronowitz, R. (2009), 'Converged Experience of Risk and Disease', *The Milbank Quarterly*, 87, 2: 417–22.

Ashton, J. and Seymour, H. (1988), *The New Public Health*, Milton Keynes: Open University Press.

Aspinall, P. J. (2002), 'Collective Terminology to Describe the Minority Ethnic Population: The Persistence of Confusion and Ambiguity in Usage', *Sociology*, 36, 4: 803–16.

Atkin, K. (2003), 'Ethnicity and the Politics of the New Genetics: Principles and Engagement', *Ethnicity and Health*, 8, 2: 91–109.

Atkin, K. and Ahmad, W. (2002), 'Pumping Iron: Compliance with Chelation Therapy among Young People who have Thalassaemia Major', in S. Nettleton and U. Gustaffson (eds), *The Sociology of Health and Illness Reader*, Cambridge: Polity.

Atkin, K., Ahmad, W. and Anionwu, E. (1998), 'Screening and Counselling for Sickle Cell Disorders and Thalassaemia: The Experience of Parents and Health Professionals', *Social Science & Medicine*, 47, 11: 1639–51.

Atkinson, P. (1981), *The Clinical Experience: The Construction and Reconstruction of Medical Reality*, Aldershot: Gower.

Atkinson, P. (1988), 'Discourse, Descriptions and Diagnoses: Reproducing Normal Medicine', in M. Lock and D. Gordon (eds), *Biomedicine Examined*, London: Kluwer Academic Publishers.

Atkinson, P. (2002), 'Reading the Body Major', in S. Nettleton and U. Gustaffson (eds), *The Sociology of Health and Illness Reader*, Cambridge: Polity.

Baggott, R. (1991), 'Looking Forward to the Past? The Politics of Public Health', *Journal of Social Policy*, 20, 2: 191–213.

Bakx, K. (1991), 'The "Eclipse" of Folk Medicine in Western Society', *Sociology of Health and Illness*, 13, 1: 20–38.

Balarajan, R. (1991), 'Ethnic Differences in Mortality from Ischaemic Heart Disease and Cerebrovascular Disease in England and Wales', *British Medical Journal*, 302: 560–4.

Balint, M. (1956), *The Doctor, his Patient and the Illness*, London: Pitman.

Barcan, R. (2011), *Complementary and Alternative Medicine Bodies, Therapies, Senses*, Leamington Spa: Berg Publishers.

Barker, R. and Roberts, H. (1986), 'Social Classification Scheme for Women', Working Paper No. 51, London: Social Statistics Research Unit, City University.

Barnes, P., Bloom, B. and Nahin, R. (2008), 'Complementary and Alternative Medicine Use among Adults and Children: United States, 2007', *National Health Statistics Reports*, 12: 1–9.

Barry, C., Stevenson, F., Britten, N., Barber, N. and Bradley, C. (2001), 'Giving Voice to the Lifeworld: More Humane, More Effective Medical Care? A Qualitative Study of Doctor–Patient Communication in General Practice', *Social Science & Medicine*, 53: 487–505.

Bartley, M. (1990), 'Do We Need a Strong Programme in Medical Sociology?', *Sociology of Health and Illness*, 12, 4: 371–90.

Bartley, M. (1992), *Authorities and Partisans: Debate on Unemployment and Health*, Edinburgh: Edinburgh University Press.

Bartley, M. (2004), *Health Inequality: An Introduction to Theories, Concepts and Methods*, Cambridge: Polity.

Bauman, Z. (1990), *Thinking Sociologically*, Oxford: Blackwell.

Baxter, C. (1988), *The Black Nurse: An Endangered Species*, Cambridge: Training in Health and Race.

Beattie, A. (1991), 'Knowledge and Control in Health Promotion: A Test Case for Social Policy and Social Theory', in J. Gabe, M. Calnan and M. Bury (eds), *The Sociology of the Health Service*, London: Routledge.

Beauchamp, T. and Childress, J. (2008), *Principles of Biomedical Ethics*, 6th edn, Oxford: Oxford University Press.

Beck, U. (1992a), *Risk Society: Towards a New Modernity*, London: Sage.

Beck, U. (1992b), 'From Industrial Society to Risk Society: Questions of Survival, Social Structure and Ecological Enlightenment', in M. Featherstone (ed.), *Cultural Theory and Cultural Change*, London: Sage.

Beck, U., Giddens, A. and Lash, S. (1994), *Reflexive Modernization: Politics, Tradition and Aesthetics in the Modern Social Order*, Cambridge: Polity.

Becker, M. H. (1974), 'The Health Belief Model and Personal Health Behaviour', *Health Education Monographs*, 2: 324–508.

Bellaby, P. (2003), 'Communication and Miscommunication of Risk: Understanding UK Parents' Attitudes to Combined MMR Vaccination', *British Medical Journal*, 327: 725–7.

Bendelow, G. (2000), *Pain and Gender*, Harlow: Prentice-Hall.

Bendelow, G., Carpenter, M., Vautier, C. and Williams, S. (2002), *Gender, Health and Healing: The Public/Private Divide*, London: Routledge.

Bennett, T., Savage, M., Silva, E., Warde, A., Gayo-Cal, M. and Wright, D. (2009), *Culture, Class and Distinction*, London: Routledge.

Benson, J. and Britten, N. (2002), 'Patients' Decisions about Whether or not to Take Antihypertensive Drugs: Qualitative Study', *British Medical Journal*, 325: 873.

Berger, P. L. and Luckmann, T. (1967), *The Social Construction of Reality*, London: Allen Lane, Penguin.

Berridge, V. (1996), *AIDS the Making of a Policy, 1981–1994*, Oxford: Oxford University Press.

Bhaskar, R. (1979), *The Possibility of Naturalism*, Brighton: Harvester.

Bhat, A., Carr-Hill, R. and Ohri, S. (1988), *Britain's Black Population*, 2nd edn, Aldershot: Gower/Radical Statistics Group.

Birke, L. (1999), *Feminism and the Biological Body*, Edinburgh: Edinburgh University Press.

Birke, L. (2003), 'Shaping Biology: Feminism and the Idea of "the Biological"', in S. Williams, L. Birke and G. Bendelow (eds), *Debating Biology: Sociological Reflections on Health, Medicine and Society*, London: Routledge.

Bissell, P., May, C. and Noyce, P. (2004), 'From Compliance to Concordance: Barriers to Accomplishing a Re-framed Model of Health Care Interactions', *Social Science & Medicine*, 58: 851–62.

Blackburn, C. (1991), *Poverty and Health: Working with Families*, Milton Keynes: Open University Press.

Blane, D. (1990), 'Real Wages, the Economic Cycle, and Mortality in England and Wales, 1870–1914', *International Journal of Health Services*, 20, 1: 43–52.

Blane, D. (1999), 'The Life Course, Social Gradient and Health', in M. Marmot and R. G. Wilkinson (eds), *Social Determinants of Health*, Oxford: Oxford University Press.

Blaxter, M. (1978), 'Diagnosis as Category and Process: the Case of Alcoholism', *Social Science & Medicine*, 12, 9: 9–17.

Blaxter, M. (1983), 'Health Services as a Defence against the Consequences of Poverty in Industrialized Societies', *Social Science & Medicine*, 17, 16: 1139–48.

Blaxter, M. (1990), *Health and Lifestyles*, London: Routledge.

Blaxter, M. (1993), 'Why Do Victims Blame Themselves?', in A. Radley (ed.), *Worlds of Illness: Biographical and Cultural Perspectives on Health and Disease*, London: Routledge.

Blaxter, M. (1997), 'Whose Fault Is It? People's Own Conceptions of the Reasons for Health Inequalities', *Social Science & Medicine*, 44, 6: 747–56.

Blaxter, M. (2009), 'The Case of the Vanishing Patient? Image and Experience', *Sociology of Health and Illness*, 31, 5: 762–78.

Blaxter, M. (2010), *Health*, 2nd edn, Cambridge: Polity.

Blaxter, M. and Peterson, L. (1982), *Mothers and Daughters: A Three Generation Study of Health Attitudes and Behaviour*, London: Heinemann Educational Books.

Bleier, R. (1984), *Science and Gender: A Critique of Biology and its Theories on Women*, New York: Pergamon Press.

Bloor, M. (2000), 'The South Wales Miners Federation, Miners' Lung and the Instrumental Use of Expertise 1900–1950', *Social Studies of Science*, 30, 1: 125–40.

Bloor, M. and Horobin, G. (1975), 'Conflict and Conflict Resolution in Doctor–Patient Relationships', in C. Cox and A. Mead (eds), *A Sociology of Medical Practice*, London: Collier Macmillan.

Bloor, M. and McIntosh, J. (1990), 'Surveillance and Concealment: A Comparison of Techniques of Client Resistance in Therapeutic Communities and Health Visiting', in S. Cunningham-Burley and N. McKeganey (eds), *Readings in Medical Sociology*, London: Routledge.

Bloor, M., Samphier, M. and Prior, L. (1987), 'Artefact Explanations of Inequalities in Health: An Assessment of the Evidence', *Sociology of Health and Illness*, 9, 3: 231–64.

Bolton, S. C. (2001), 'Changing Faces: Nurses as Emotional Jugglers', *Sociology of Health and Illness*, 32, 1: 85–100.

Bolton, S. C., Muzio, D. and Boyd-Quinn, C. (2011), 'Making Sense of Modern Medical Careers: The Case of the UK's National Health Service', *Sociology*, 45, 4: 682–99.

Bordo, S. (1990), 'Reading the Slender Body', in M. Jacobus, E. Fox Keller and S. Shuttleworth (eds), *Body/Politics: Women and the Discourses of Science*, London: Routledge.

Bornat, J., Pereira, C., Pilgrim, D. and Williams, F. (1993), *Community Care: A Reader*, London: Macmillan.

Bornat, J., Henry, L. and Raghuram, P. (2009), '"Don't Mix Race with the Speciality": Interviewing South Asian Overseas-trained Geriatricians', *Oral History*, Spring, 74–84.

Boston Women's Health Book Collective (2011), *Our Bodies, Ourselves, for the New Century*, Boston, MA: Simon and Schuster.

Bourdieu, P. (1984), *Distinction: A Social Critique of Judgement and Taste*, London: Routledge.

Bowker, G. and Starr, S. L. (1999), *Sorting Things Out: Classification and its Consequences*, Cambridge, MA: MIT Press.

Bowling, A. (2005), *Measuring Health: A Review of Quality of Life Measurement Scales*, Maidenhead: Open University Press.

Bradby, H. and Nazroo, J. Y. (2010), 'Health, Ethnicity and Race', in W. Cockerham (ed.), *The New Blackwell Companion to Medical Sociology*, London: Wiley-Blackwell, pp. 113–29.

British Medical Association (BMA) (1992), 'Report on an Alternative Medicine' (partially reproduced version of BMA (1986), *Alternative Therapy*, London: BMA), in M. Saks (ed.), *Alternative Medicine in Britain*, Oxford: Clarendon Press.

British Medical Association (BMA) (1993), *Complementary Medicine: New Approaches to Good Practice*, London: BMA.

Brown, G. and Harris, T. (1978), *The Social Origins of Depression*, London: Tavistock.

Brown, N. (2012), 'Contradictions of value: between use and exchange in cord blood bioeconomy', *Sociology of Health and Illness*, in press.

Brown, N. and Michael, M. (2003), 'A Sociology of Expectations: Retrospecting Patients and Prospecting Retrospect', *Technology Analysis & Strategic Management*, 15, 1: 3–18.

Brown, N. and Webster, A. (2004), *New Medical Technologies and Society: Reordering Life*, Cambridge: Polity.

Brown, N., Machin, L. and McLeod, D. (2011), 'Immunitary Bioeconomy: The Economization of Life in the International Cord Blood Market', *Social Science & Medicine*, 72: 1115–22.

Brown, P. (1988), 'Recent Trends in the Political Economy of Mental Health', in C. J. Smith and J. A. Giggs (eds), *Location and Stigma: Perspectives on Mental Health and Mental Health Care*, London: Unwin Hyman.

Brown, P. (1995), 'Naming and Framing: the Social Construction of Diagnosis and Illness', *Journal of Health and Social Behavior*, 35 (Extra Issue), 34–52.

Brown, P. and Zavestoski, S. (2004), 'Social Movements in Health: An Introduction', *Sociology of Health and Illness*, 26, 6: 679–94.

Bunton, R. (1990), 'Regulating Our Favourite Drug', in P. Abbott and G. Payne (eds), *New Directions in the Sociology of Health*, London: Falmer Press.

Bunton, R. and Crawshaw, P. (2002), 'Consuming Men's Health: Ritual and Ambivalence in Men's Lifestyle Magazines', in S. Henderson and A. Petersen (eds), *Consuming Health: The Commodification of Health Care*, London: Routledge.

Bunton, R. and Macdonald, G. (2002), *Health Promotion: Disciplines, Diversity, and Developments*, 2nd edn, London: Routledge.

Bunton, R., Murphey, S. and Bennet, P. (1991), 'Theories of Behaviour Change and their Use in Health Promotion: Some Neglected Areas', *Health Education Research*, 6, 2: 153–62.

Bunton, R., Nettleton, S. and Burrows, R. (eds) (1995), *The Sociology of Health Promotion: Critical Analyses of Consumption, Lifestyle and Risk*, London: Routledge.

Bury, M. R. (1982), 'Chronic Illness as Biographical Disruption', *Sociology of Health and Illness*, 4: 167–82.

Bury, M. R. (1986), 'Social Constructionism and the Development of Medical Sociology', *Sociology of Health and Illness*, 8: 137–69.

Bury, M. R. (1988), 'Meanings at Risk: The Experience of Arthritis', in R. Anderson and M. Bury (eds), *Living with Chronic Illness: The Experience of Patients and their Families*, London: Unwin Hyman.

Bury, M. R. (1991), 'The Sociology of Chronic Illness: A Review of Research and Prospects', *Sociology of Health and Illness*, 13, 4: 451–68.

Bury, M. R. (2001), 'Illness Narratives: Fact or Fiction?', *Sociology of Health and Illness*, 23, 3: 263–85.

Busfield, J. (1986), *Managing Madness: Changing Ideas and Practice*, London: Unwin Hyman.

Busfield, J. (1994), *Women and Mental Health*, London: Macmillan.

Busfield, J. (2010), '"A Pill for every Ill": Explaining the Expansion in Medicine Use', *Social Science & Medicine*, 70, 6: 934–41.

Byrne, P. and Long, B. (1976), *Doctors Talking to Patients*, London: DHSS.

Calnan, M. (1984a), 'Women and Medicalization: An Empirical Examination of the Extent of Women's Dependence on Medical Technology in the Early Detection of Breast Cancer', *Social Science & Medicine*, 18, 7: 561–9.

Calnan, M. (1984b), 'The Health Belief Model and Participation in Programmes for the Early Detection of Breast Cancer: A Comparative Analysis', *Social Science & Medicine*, 19: 823–30.

Calnan, M. (1987), *Health and Illness: The Lay Perspective*, London: Tavistock.

Calnan, M. (1991), *Preventing Coronary Heart Disease: Prospects, Policies and Politics*, London: Routledge.

Cant, C. (2009), 'Mainstream Marginality: "Non Orthodox" Medicine in an "Orthodox" NHS', in J. Gabe and M. Calnan (eds), *The New Sociology of the NHS*, London: Routledge.

Cant, S. and Sharma, U. (1999), *A New Medical Pluralism: Complementary Medicine, Doctors, Patients and the State*, London: Taylor and Francis.

Cant, S. and Sharma, U. (2000), 'Alternative Health Practices and Systems', in G. L. Albrecht, R. Fitzpatrick and S. C. Scrimshaw (eds), *The Handbook of Social Studies in Health and Medicine*, London: Sage.

Carr-Hill, R. (1987), 'The Inequalities in Health Debate: A Critical Review of the Issues', *Journal of Social Policy*, 14, 4: 509–42.

Carr-Saunders, A. M. and Wilson, P. A. (1933), *The Professions*, London: Oxford University Press.

Cartwright, A. and Anderson, R. (1981), *General Practice Revisited: A Second Study of Patients and their Doctors*, London: Tavistock.

Casper, M. J. and Morrison, D. R. (2010), 'Medical Sociology and Technology: Critical Engagements', *Journal of Health and Social Behaviour*, 31, 5: S120–32.

Casswell, S. (2012), 'Current Status of Alcohol Marketing Policy – An Urgent Challenge for Global Governance', *Addiction*, 107, 3: 478–85.

Castel, R. (1991), 'From Dangerousness to Risk', in G. Burchell, C. Gordon and P. Miller (eds), *The Foucault Effect: Studies in Governmentality*, Brighton: Harvester Wheatsheaf.

Castells, M. (2000), 'Materials for an Exploratory Theory of the Network Society', *British Journal of Sociology*, 1, 1: 5–24.

Chandola, T., Bartley, M., Sacker, A., Jenkinson, C. and Marmot, M. (2003), 'Health Selection in the Whitehall II Study, UK', *Social Science & Medicine*, 56: 2059–72.

Charles, N. and Kerr, M. (1988), *Women, Food and Families*, Manchester: Manchester University Press.

Charles-Jones, H., Latimer, J. and May, C. (2003), 'Transforming General Practice: The Redistribution of Medical Work in Primary Care', *Sociology of Health & Illness*, 25: 71–92.

Charmaz, K. (1983), 'Loss of Self: A Fundamental Form of Suffering in the Chronically Ill', *Sociology of Health and Illness*, 5: 168–95.

Charmaz, K. (1987), 'Struggling for a Self: Identity Levels of the Chronically Ill', in J. A. Roth and P. Conrad (eds), *Research in the Sociology of Health Care*, vol. 6, *The Experience and Management of Chronic Illness*, Greenwich, CT: JAI Press.

Charmaz, K. (2000), 'Experiencing Chronic Illness', in G. L. Albrecht, R. Fitzpatrick and S. C. Scrimshaw (eds), *The Handbook of Social Studies in Health and Medicine*, London: Sage.

Chief Medical Officer (2001), *Report of the Chief Medical Officer's Project to Strengthen the Public Health Function*, London: Department of Health.

Clark, D. (ed.) (1993), *The Sociology of Death*, Oxford: Blackwell.

Clarke, J. (1981), 'A Multiple Paradigm Approach to the Sociology of Medicine, Health and Illness', *Sociology of Health and Illness*, 3, 1: 89–103.

Clegg, S. (1989), *Frameworks of Power*, London: Sage.

Cochrane, A. L. (1972), *Effectiveness and Efficiency: Random Reflections on Health Services*, Leeds: Nuffield Provincial Hospital Trust.

Cohen, R. L. (2011), 'Time, Space and Touch at Work: Body Work and Labour Process and Reorganisation', *Sociology of Health and Illness*, 33, 2: 19–35.

Coker, N. (2001), *Racism in Medicine: An Agenda for Change*, London: Kings Fund.

Collins, J. and Lee, K. (2003), *Globalization and Transborder Risk in the UK: Case Studies in Tobacco Control and Population Mobility*, London: Nuffield Trust.

Comaroff, J. (1978), 'Medicine and Culture: Some Anthropological Perspectives', *Social Science & Medicine*, 12B: 247–54.

Comaroff, J. (1982), 'Medicine, Symbol and Ideology', in P. Wright and A. Treacher (eds), *The Problem of Medical Knowledge: Examining the Social Construction of Medicine*, Edinburgh: Edinburgh University Press.

Connell, R. (1987), *Gender and Power*, Cambridge: Polity.

Conrad, P. (1985), 'The Meaning of Medication: Another Look at Compliance', *Social Science & Medicine*, 20: 29–37.

Conrad, P. (1987), 'The Experience of Illness: Recent and New Directions', in J. Roth and P. Conrad (eds), *Research in the Sociology of Health Care*, vol. 6, *The Experience and Management of Chronic Illness*, Greenwich, CT: JAI Press.

Conrad, P. (1997), 'The Social Nature of Disease', in P. Conrad (ed.), *The Sociology of Health and Illness: Critical Perspectives*, New York: St Martin's Press.

Conrad, P. (2002), 'A Mirage of Genes', in S. Nettleton and U. Gustaffson (eds), *The Sociology of Health and Illness Reader*, Cambridge: Polity.

Conrad, P. (2007), *The Medicalization of Society: On the Transformation of Human Conditions into Treatable Disorders*. Baltimore, MD: Johns Hopkins University Press.

Conrad, P. and Barker, K. (2010), 'The Social Construction of Illness: Key Insights and Policy Implications', *Journal of Health and Social Behavior*, 51, Supplement, S67–79.

Conrad, P. and Schneider, J. W. (1980), *Deviance and Medicalization: From Badness to Sickness*, St Louis, MO: C. V. Mosby.

Cooper, H. (2002), 'Investigating Socio-economic Explanations for Gender and Ethnic Inequalities in Health', *Social Science & Medicine*, 54: 693–706.

Cooper, L. (2002), 'Myalgic Encephalomyelitis and the Medical Encounter', in S. Nettleton and U. Gustaffson (eds), *The Sociology of Health and Illness Reader*, Cambridge: Polity.

Corbin, J. and Strauss, A. (1985), 'Managing Chronic Illness at Home: Three Lines of Work', *Qualitative Sociology*, 8, 3: 224–47.

Corea, G. (1985), *The Mother Machine*, New York: Harper & Row.

Cornwell, J. (1984), *Hard-Earned Lives: Accounts of Health and Illness from East London*, London: Tavistock.

Coulter, A. (2002), *The Autonomous Patient: Ending Paternalism in Medical Care*, London: Nuffield Trust.

Coulter, A. and Magee, H. (eds) (2003), *The European Patient of the Future*, Maidenhead: Open University Press.

Coulthard, M., Huang Chow, Y., Dattani, N., White, C., Baker, A. and Johnson, B. (2004), 'Health', in P. Babb, J. Martin and P. Haezewindt (eds), *Focus on Social Inequalities*, London: Office for National Statistics (ONS), pp. 69–84.

Courpasson, D. (2000), 'Managerial Strategies of Domination: Power in Soft Bureaucracies', *Organization Studies*, 21, 1: 141–61.

Cousins, C. (1988), 'The Restructuring of Welfare Work: The Introduction of General Management and the Contracting Out of Ancillary Services in the NHS', *Work, Employment and Society*, 2: 210–28.

Craddock, C. and Reid, M. (1993), 'Structure and Struggle: Implementing a Social Model of a Well Woman Clinic in Glasgow', *Social Science & Medicine*, 36, 1: 67–76.

Craddock, S. (2004), 'Introduction: Beyond Epidemiology: Locating AIDS in Africa', in E. Kalipeni, S. Craddock, J. R. Oppong and J. Ghosh (eds), *HIV and AIDS in Africa: Beyond Epidemiology*, Oxford: Blackwell.

Crawford, R. (1977), 'You are Dangerous to Your Health: The Ideology and Politics of Victim Blaming', *International Journal of Health Services*, 7: 663–80.

Crawford, R. (1984), 'A Cultural Account of Health: Control, Release, and the Social Body', in J. McKinlay (ed.), *Issues in the Political Economy of Health Care*, London: Tavistock.

Crawford, R. (2000), 'The Ritual of Health Promotion in the US', in S. J. Williams, J. Gabe and M. Calnan (eds), *Health Medicine and Society: Key Theories, Future Agendas*, London: Routledge.

Crawford, R. (2006), 'Health as a Meaningful Social Practice', *Health*, 10: 401–20.

Crook, S., Pakulski, J. and Waters, M. (1992), *Postmodernization: Change in Advanced Society*, London: Sage.

Crossley, M. L. (2002), 'Could you Please Pass one of those Health Leaflets Along? Exploring Health, Mortality and Resistance through Focus Groups', *Social Science & Medicine*, 55: 1471–83.

Crossley, N. (2001), *The Social Body: Habit, Identity and Desire*, London: Sage.

Crossley, N. (2003), 'Prozac Nation and the Biochemical Self: A Critique', in S. Williams, L. Birke and G. Bendelow (eds), *Debating Biology: Sociological Reflections on Health, Medicine and Society*, London: Routledge.

Crossley, N. (2006), *Reflexive Embodiment in Contemporary Society*, Maidenhead: Open University Press.

CSO (Central Statistical Office) (1994), *Social Trends*, London: HMSO.

Cunningham-Burley, S. and Boulton, M. (2000), 'The Social Context of the New Genetics', in G. Albrecht, R. Fitzpatrick and S. Scrimshaw (eds), *Handbook of Social Studies in Health and Medicine*, London: Sage.

Curtis, S. (2004), *Health and Inequality*, London: Sage.

Cussins, C. (1998), 'Ontological Choreography: Agency for Women in an Infertility Clinic', in M. Berg and A. Mol (eds), *Differences in Medicine: Unravelling Practices, Techniques and Bodies*, Durham, NC: Duke University Press.

Dalley, G. (1988), *Ideologies of Caring: Re-thinking Community and Collectivism*, London: Macmillan.

Davenas, E. et al. (1988), 'Human Basophil Degranulation Triggered by Very Dilute Antiserum against IgE', *Nature*, 333 (June): 816–18.

Davey, B. and Hart, G. (2002), 'HIV and AIDS', in B. Davey and C. Seale (eds), *Experiencing and Explaining Disease*, Buckingham: Open University Press.

Davey Smith, G., Bartley, M. and Blane, D. (1990), 'The Black Report on Socioeconomic Inequalities in Health 10 Years On', *British Medical Journal*, 301: 373–7.

Davey Smith, G., Chaturvedi, N., Harding, S., Nazroo, J. and Williams, R. (2002), 'Ethnic Inequalities in Health: A Review of UK Epidemiological Evidence', in S. Nettleton and U. Gustaffson (eds), *The Sociology of Health and Illness Reader*, Cambridge: Polity.

Davies, C. (1984), 'General Practitioners and the Pull of Prevention', *Sociology of Health and Illness*, 6, 3: 267–89.

Davies, C. (1987), 'Viewpoint: Things to Come – the NHS in the Next Decade', *Sociology of Health and Illness*, 9, 3: 302–17.

Davies, K. (1995), *Reshaping the Female Body: The Dilemma of Cosmetic Surgery*, New York: Routledge.

Davis, M. (2008), 'The "Loss of Community" and Other Problems for Sexual Citizenship in Recent HIV Prevention', *Sociology of Health and Illness*, 30, 2: 182–96.

Davis, M. and Squire, C. (eds) (2010), *HIV Treatment and Prevention in International Perspective*, Basingstoke: Palgrave Macmillan.

Davison, C., Davey Smith, G. and Frankel, S. (1991), 'Lay Epidemiology and the Prevention Paradox: The Implications of Coronary Candidacy for Health Education', *Sociology of Health and Illness*, 13, 1: 1–19.

Davison, C., Frankel, S. and Davey Smith, G. (1992), 'The Limits of Lifestyle: Re-assessing "Fatalism" in the Popular Culture of Illness Prevention', *Social Science & Medicine*, 34, 6: 675–85.

De Mul, J. (1999), 'The Informatization of the World View', *Information, Communication and Society*, 2, 1: 69–94.

Dean, M. (1993), 'Self-Inflicted Rationing', *The Lancet*, 341: 1525.

Department of Health (1989), *Working for Patients*, London: HMSO, Cm 555.

Department of Health (1991a), *The Health of the Nation*, London: HMSO, Cm 1523.

Department of Health (1991b), *The Patient's Charter*, London: HMSO.

Department of Health (1992), *The Health of the Nation*, London: HMSO.

Department of Health (1999), *The Health of Minority Ethnic Groups, Health Survey for England 1999*, London: Department of Health.

Department of Health (2000), *The NHS Plan*, London: The Stationery Office, Cm 4818.

Department of Health (2001), *The Expert Patient: A New Approach to Chronic Disease Management for the 21st Century*, London: Department of Health.

Department of Health (2002a), *Health Survey for England*, London: Department of Health.

Department of Health (2002b), *Health Improvement and Prevention*, National Service Framework, London.

Department of Health (2004a), *Choosing Health: Making Healthy Choices Easier*, London: HMSO, Cm 6374.

Department of Health (2004b), *NHS Improvement Plan 2004: Putting People at the Heart of Public Services*, London: Department of Health.

Department of Health (2010), *Healthy Lives, Healthy People: Our Strategy for Public Health in England*, London: Department of Health.

Department of Health (2011), *Public Health Responsibility Deal*, London: Department of Health.

De Vries, R. (2003), 'How Can We Help?: From "Sociology in" to "Sociology of" Bioethics', *Journal of Law, Medicine & Ethics*, 32: 279–92.

De Vries, R., Turner, L., Orfali, K. and Bosk, C. (eds) (2007), *The View From Here: Bioethics and the Social Sciences*, Malden, MA: Blackwell Publishing.

DHSS (1976), *Prevention and Health: Everybody's Business*, London: HMSO.

DHSS (1977), *Prevention and Health*, London: HMSO, Cm 7047.

DHSS (1981), *Care in the Community*, London: HMSO.

DHSS (1983), *NHS Management Inquiry (Griffiths Report)*, London: HMSO.

DHSS (1987), *Promoting Better Health*, London: HMSO, Cm 249.

Dickens, P. (2001), 'Linking the Social and Natural Sciences: Is Capital Modifying Human Biology in its own Image?', *Sociology*, 35, 1: 93–101.

Dickenson, D. (2008), *Body Shopping: The Economy Fuelled by Flesh and Blood*, London: One World Publications.

Dillon, T. (2004), 'Looking Straight at Gay Parents', *USA Today*, September. www.usatoday.com.

Dingwall, R. (1976), *Aspects of Illness*, Oxford: Martin Robertson.

Dingwall, R. and Murray, T. (1983), 'Categorization in Accident Departments: "Good" Patients, "Bad" Patients and "Children"', *Sociology of Health and Illness*, 5, 2: 127–48.

Dixon, J. (2012), 'Reform and the National Health Service', *The Political Quarterly*, 83, 2: 343–51.

Dolan, A. (2011), '"You can't ask for a Dubonnet and lemonade!": Working-class Masculinity and Men's Health Practices', *Sociology of Health & Illness*, 33: 586–601.

Donkin, A., Huang Lee, Y. and Toson, B. (2002b), 'Implications of Changes in the UK Social and Occupational Classifications in 2001 for Vital Statistics', *Population Trends*, 107 (spring): 23–9.

Donnison, J. (1977), *Midwives and Medical Men: A History of Inter-Professional Rivalries and Women's Rights*, London: Heinemann.

Douglas, M. (1966), *Purity and Danger: An Analysis of the Concepts of Pollution and Taboo*, London: Routledge & Kegan Paul.

Douglas, M. (1970), *Natural Symbols: Explorations in Cosmology*, London: Barrie and Rockliff, the Cresset Press.

Douglas, M. (1986), *Risk Acceptability According to the Social Sciences*, London: Routledge & Kegan Paul.

Douglas, M. (1992), *Risk and Blame: Essays in Cultural Theory*, London: Routledge.

Doyal, L. (ed.) (1998), *Women and Health Services: An Agenda for Change*, Buckingham: Open University Press.

Doyal, L. and Anderson, J. (2005), '"My fear is to fall in love again . . .": How HIV-Positive African Women Survive in London', *Social Science & Medicine*, 60: 1729–38.

Doyal, L. with Pennell, I. (1979), *The Political Economy of Health*, London: Pluto Press.

Doyal, L., Anderson, J. and Paparini, S. (2009), '"You are not yourself": Exploring Masculinities among Heterosexual African Men Living with HIV in London', *Social Science & Medicine*, 68, 10: 1901–7.

Draper, A. and Green, J. (2002), 'Food Safety and Consumers: Constructions of Choice and Risk', *Social Policy and Administration*, 36, 6: 610–25.

Drew, P. (2006), 'Mis-alignments in "After-Hours" Calls to a British GP's Practice: A Study of Telephone Medicine', in J. Heritage and D. Maynard (eds), *Communication in Medical Care: Interaction between Physicians and Patients*, Cambridge: Cambridge University Press.

Dubos, R. (1959), *Mirage of Health*, New York: Harper & Row.

Duden, B. (1991), *The Woman beneath the Skin: A Doctor's Patients in Eighteenth-Century Germany*, London: Harvard University Press.

Dumit, J. (2000), 'When Explanations Rest: "Good-enough" Brain Science and the New Socio-medical Disorders', in M. Lock, A. Young and A. Cambrosio (eds), *Living and Working with the New Medical Technologies*, Cambridge: Cambridge University Press.

Eames, N., Ben-Shlomo, Y. and Marmot, M. (1993), 'Social Deprivation and Premature Mortality: Regional Comparison across England', *British Medical Journal*, 307: 1097–102.

Ebeling, M. (2011), '"Get with the Program!": Pharmaceutical Marketing, Symptom Checklists and Self-diagnosis', *Social Science & Medicine*, 73, 6: 825–32.

Edwards, C. and Imrie, R. (2003), 'Disability and Bodies as Bearers of Value', *Sociology*, 37, 2: 239–56.

Edwards, C., Staniszweska, S. and Crichton, N. (2004), 'Investigation of the Ways in which Patients' Reports of their Satisfaction with Health Care are Constructed', *Sociology of Health and Illness*, 26, 2: 159–83.

Edwards, J. (2000), *Born and Bred: Idioms of Kinship and New Reproductive Technologies in England*, Oxford: Oxford University Press.

Ehrenreich, B. and English, D. (2011), *Complaints and Disorders: The Sexual Politics of Sickness*, 2nd edn, New York: The Feminist Press.

Elford, J. and Hart, G. (2005), 'HAART, Viral Load and Sexual Risk Behaviour', *AIDS*, 19: 205–7.

Elias, N. (1978), *The Civilizing Process*, vol. 1: *The History of Manners*, Oxford: Blackwell.

Elias, N. (1982), *The Civilizing Process*, vol. 2: *State Formation and Civilization*, Oxford: Blackwell.

Elstad, J. J. (2002), 'The Psycho-social Perspective on Social Inequalities in Health', in S. Nettleton and U. Gustaffson (eds), *The Sociology of Health and Illness Reader*, Cambridge: Polity.

Elster, A., Jaroski, J., VanGeest, J. and Fleming, M. (2003), 'Racial and Ethnic Disparities in Health Care for Adolescents: A Systematic Review of the Literature', *Archives of Pediatric and Adolescent Medicine*, 157: 850–1.

Elston, M. A. (1977), 'Medical Autonomy: Challenge and Response', in K. Bernard and K. Lee (eds), *Conflicts in the National Health Service*, London: Croom Helm.

Elston, M. A. (1991), 'The Politics of Professional Power: Medicine in a Changing Health Care Service', in J. Gabe, M. Calnan and M. Bury (eds), *The Sociology of the Health Service*, London: Routledge.

Emslie, C., Hunt, K. and Macintyre, S. (1999), 'Problematising Gender, Work and Health: The Relationship between Gender, Occupational Grade, Working Conditions and Minor Morbidity in Full-Time Bank Employees', *Social Science & Medicine*, 48: 33–48.

Emslie, C., Hunt, K. and Watt, G. (2002), 'Invisible Women? The Importance of Gender in Lay Beliefs about Heart Problems', in S. Nettleton and U. Gustaffson (eds), *The Sociology of Health and Illness Reader*, Cambridge: Polity.

Engel, G. L. (1981), 'The Need for a New Medical Model: A Challenge to Bio-medicine', in A. L. Kaplan, H. T. Engelhardt and J. J. McCartney (eds), *Concepts of Health and Disease: Interdisciplinary Perspectives*, London: Addison-Wesley.

Esmail, A. and Everington, S. (1993), 'Racial Discrimination against Doctors from Ethnic Minorities', *British Medical Journal*, 306: 691–2.

Ettorre, E. (2002), 'Reproductive Genetics, Gender and the Body: "Please Doctors May I have a Normal Baby?"', in S. Nettleton and U. Gustafsson (eds), *The Sociology of Health and Illness Reader*, Cambridge: Polity.

Fagerhaugh, S. Y. and Strauss, A. (1977), *Politics of Pain Management: Staff–Patient Interaction*, Menlo Park, CA: Addison-Wesley.

Fair, B. (2010), 'Morgellons: Contested Illness, Diagnostic Compromise and Medicalization', *Sociology of Health and Illness*, 32, 4: 597–612.

Farrant, W. (1991), 'Addressing the Contradictions: Health Promotion and Community Health Action in the United Kingdom', *International Journal of Health Services*, 21, 3: 423–39.

Faulkner, W. and Arnold, E. (1985), *Smothered by Invention: Technology in Women's Lives*, London: Pluto Press.

Fausto-Sterling, A. (2000), *Sexing the Body: Gender Politics and the Construction of Sexuality*, New York: Basic Books.

Fausto-Sterling, A. (2003), 'The Problem of Sex/Gender and Nature/Nurture?', in S. Williams, L. Birke and G. Bendelow (eds), *Debating Biology: Sociological Reflections on Health, Medicine and Society*, London: Routledge.

Featherstone, K., Clarke, A., Bharadwaj, A. and Atkinson, P. (2005), *Risky Relations: Family, Kinship and the New Genetics*, London: Berg.

Featherstone, M. (1991a), *Consumer Culture and Postmodernism*, London: Sage.

Featherstone, M. (1991b), 'The Body in Consumer Culture', in M. Featherstone, M. Hepworth and B. S. Turner (eds), *The Body: Social Processes and Cultural Theory*, London: Sage.

Featherstone, M. (2010), 'Body, Image and Affect in Consumer Culture', *Body and Society*, 16, 1: 193–221.

Featherstone, M., Hepworth, M. and Turner, B. S. (eds) (1991), *The Body: Social Process and Cultural Theory*, London: Sage.

Figlio, K. (1982), 'How Does Illness Mediate Social Relations? Workman's Compensation and Medico-Legal Practices 1890–1940', in P. Wright and A. Treacher (eds), *The Problem of Medical Knowledge: Examining the Social Construction of Medicine*, Edinburgh: Edinburgh University Press.

Finch, J. and Mason, J. (1992), *Negotiating Family Responsibilities*, London: Routledge.

Fisher, S. (1986), *In the Patient's Best Interest: Women and the Politics of Medical Decisions*, New Brunswick, NJ: Rutgers University Press.

Fitzpatrick, R. (1984), 'Lay Concepts of Illness', in R. Fitzpatrick, J. Hinton, S. Newman, G. Scambler and J. Thompson (eds), *The Experience of Illness*, London: Tavistock.

Fitzpatrick, R. (1987), 'Political Science and Health Policy', in G. Scambler (ed.), *Sociological Theory and Medical Sociology*, London: Tavistock.

Fleck, L. (1935a), 'On the Question of the Foundations of Medical Knowledge', *Journal of Medicine and Philosophy*, 6: 237–56.

Fleck, L. (1935b), *Genesis and Development of a Scientific Fact*, Chicago, IL: University of Chicago Press.

Flick, U. (2000), 'Qualitative Inquiries into Social Representations of Health', *Journal of Health Psychology*, 5, 3: 315–24.

Flowers, P. (2001), 'Gay Men and HIV/AIDS Risk Management', *Health*, 5, 1: 50–75.

Flynn, R. (1992), *Structures of Control in Health Management*, London: Routledge.

Flynn, R. (2004), '"Soft Bureaucracy" Governmentality and Clinical Governance: Theoretical Approaches to Emergent Policy', in A. Gray and S. Harrison (eds), *Governing Medicine: Theory and Practice*, Maidenhead: Open University Press.

Foster, P. (1995), *Women and the Health Care Industry*, 2nd edn, Maidenhead: Open University Press.

Foucault, M. (1976), *The Birth of the Clinic: An Archaeology of Medical Perception*, London: Tavistock.

Foucault, M. (1979), *Discipline and Punish: The Birth of the Prison*, Harmondsworth: Penguin.

Foucault, M. (1980a), 'The Eye of Power', in C. Gordon (ed.), *Power/Knowledge: Selected Interviews and Other Writings 1972–1977 by Michel Foucault*, Brighton: Harvester.

Foucault, M. (1980b), 'The Politics of Health in the Eighteenth Century', in C. Gordon (ed.), *Power/Knowledge: Selected Interviews and Other Writings 1972–1977 by Michel Foucault*, Brighton: Harvester.

Foucault, M. (1980c), 'Body/Power', in C. Gordon (ed.), *Power/Knowledge: Selected Interviews and Other Writings 1972 1977 by Michel Foucault*, Brighton: Harvester.

Foucault, M. (1981), *The History of Sexuality: An Introduction*, Harmondsworth: Penguin.

Foucault, M. (1991) [original in French 1978], 'Governmentality', in G. Burchill, C. Gordon and P. Miller (eds), *The Foucault Effect*, Hemel Hempstead: Harvester Wheatsheaf.

Fox, P., Coughlan, B., Butler, M. and Kelleher, C. (2010), 'Complementary Alternative Medicine (CAM) Use in Ireland: A Secondary Analysis of SLAN Data', *Complementary Therapies in Medicine*, 18, 2: 95–103.

Fox, S. and Jones, S. (2009), *The Social Life of Internet Users*, Washington, DC: Pew Internet & American Life Project.

Fox Keller, E. (1995), *Refiguring Life*, New York: Columbia University Press.

Frank, A. (1990), 'Bringing Bodies Back In: A Decade Review', *Theory, Culture and Society*, 7, 1: 131–62.

Frank, A. (1995), *The Wounded Storyteller: Body, Illness and Ethics*, Chicago, IL: University of Chicago Press.

Frankel, S., Davison, C. and Davey Smith, G. (1991), 'Lay Epidemiology and the Rationality of Responses to Health Education', *British Journal of General Practice*, 41: 428–30.

Freidson, E. (1970a), *Profession of Medicine: A Study of the Sociology of Applied Knowledge*, New York: Harper & Row.

Freidson, E. (1970b), *Professional Dominance*, New York: Atherton.

Freidson, E. (1975), 'Dilemmas in the Doctor–Patient Relationship', in C. Cox and A. Mead, *A Sociology of Medical Practice*, London: Collier Macmillan.

Freidson, E. (1986), *Professional Powers: A Study of the Institutionalization of Formal Knowledge*, London: University of Chicago Press.

Freund, P., McGuire, M. B. and Podhurst, L. B. (2002), *Health, Illness and the Social Body: A Critical Sociology*, 4th edn, Upper Saddle River, NJ: Prentice-Hall.

Fukuyama, F. (1989), 'The End of History?', *The National Interest*, 16: 3–18.

Gabbay, J. (1982), 'Asthma Attacked? Tactics in the Reconstruction of a Disease Concept', in P. Wright and A. Treacher (eds), *The Problem of Medical Knowledge: Examining the Social Construction of Medicine*, Edinburgh: Edinburgh University Press.

Gabe, J. and Calnan, M. (1989), 'The Limits of Medicine: Women's Perception of Medical Technology', *Social Science & Medicine*, 28, 3: 223–31.

Gabe, J. and Lipshitz-Phillips, S. (1984), 'Tranquillizers as Social Control?', *Sociological Review*, 32, 3: 524–46.

Gadamer, H. (1996), *The Enigma of Health: The Art of Healing in a Scientific Age*, Cambridge: Polity.

Garcia, J., Kilpatrick, R. and Richards, M. (1990), *The Politics of Maternity Care: Services for Childbearing Women in Twentieth-Century Britain*, Oxford: Clarendon Paperbacks.

Gardner, J., Dew K., Stubbe, M., Dowell, T. and Macdonald, L. (2011), 'Patchwork Diagnoses: The

Production of Coherence, Uncertainty, and Manageable Bodies', *Social Science & Medicine*, 73, 6: 843–50.

Garfinkel, H. (1967), *Studies in Ethnomethodology*, Englewood Cliffs, NJ: Prentice-Hall.

Gerhardt, U. (1989), *Ideas about Illness: An Intellectual and Political History of Medical Sociology*, Basingstoke: Macmillan.

Giddens, A. (1990), *The Consequences of Modernity*, Cambridge: Polity.

Giddens, A. (1991), *Modernity and Self-Identity: Self and Society in the Late Modern Age*, Cambridge: Polity.

Giddens, A. (1994), *Beyond Left and Right: The Future of Radical Politics*, Cambridge: Polity.

Gifford, S. M. (2002), 'The Meaning of Lumps: A Case Study in the Ambiguities of Risk', in S. Nettleton and U. Gustaffson (eds), *The Sociology of Health and Illness Reader*, Cambridge: Polity.

Gillett, J. (2003), 'Media Activism and Internet Use by People with HIV/AIDS', *Sociology of Health and Illness*, 25, 6: 608–24.

Gilman, S. (1999), *Making the Body Beautiful: A Cultural History of Aesthetic Surgery*, Princeton, NJ: Princeton University Press.

Ginsberg, N. and Watson, S. (1992), 'Issues of Race and Gender Facing Housing Policy', in J. Birchall (ed.), *Housing Policy in the 1990s*, London: Routledge.

Glassner, B. (1989), 'Fitness and the Postmodern Self', *Journal of Health and Social Behaviour*, 30: 180–91.

Goffman, E. (1961), *Asylums*, Harmondsworth: Penguin.

Goffman, E. (1968), *Stigma: Notes on the Management of Spoiled Identity*, Harmondsworth: Penguin.

Goldacre, M. J., Davidson, J. and Lambert, T. (2004), 'Country of training and ethnic origin of UK doctors: database and survey studies', *British Medical Journal*, 329: 597.

Goode, J., Greatbatch, D., O'Cathain, A., Luff, D., Hanlon, G. and Stangleman, T. (2004), 'Risk and the Responsible Health Consumer: The Problematics of Entitlement amongst Callers to NHS Direct', *Critical Social Policy*, 24, 2: 210–32.

Grace, V. M. (1991), 'The Marketing of Empowerment and the Construction of the Health Consumer: A Critique of Health Promotion', *International Journal of Health Services*, 21, 2: 329–43.

Graham, H. (1979), 'Prevention and Health: Every Mother's Business, A Comment on Child Health Policies in the 1970s', in C. Harris (ed.), *Sociology of the Family: New Directions for British Sociology*, Sociological Review Monograph 28, Keele: University of Keele.

Graham, H. (1984), *Women, Health and the Family*, Brighton: Harvester Wheatsheaf.

Graham, H. (1987), 'Women's Smoking and Family Health', *Social Science & Medicine*, 25, 1: 47–56.

Graham, H. (1992), 'Budgeting for Health: Mothers in Low-Income Households', in C. Glendinning and J. Millar (eds), *Women and Poverty in Britain in the 1990s*, London: Harvester Wheatsheaf.

Graham, H. (2002), 'Socio-economic Change and Inequalities in Men and Women's Health Risk in the UK', in S. Nettleton and U. Gustaffson (eds), *The Sociology of Health and Illness Reader*, Cambridge: Polity.

Graham, H. and Oakley, A. (1986), 'Competing Ideologies of Reproduction: Medical and Maternal Perspectives on Pregnancy', in C. Currer and M. Stacey (eds), *Concepts of Health, Illness and Disease*, Leamington Spa: Berg.

Graham, H., Hawkins, S. and Law, C. (2009), 'Lifecourse Influences on Women's Smoking before, during and after Pregnancy', *Social Science & Medicine*, 30: 1–6.

Gray, N., Klein, J., Noyce, P., Sessleberg, T. and Cantrill, J. (2005), 'Health Information-Seeking Behaviour in Adolescence: The Place of the Internet', *Social Science & Medicine*, 60, 7: 1467–78.

Green, G. (2009), *The End of Stigma?: Changes in the Social Experience of Long-term Illness*, Abingdon: Routledge.

Green, G. and Smith, R. (2004), 'The Psychosocial and Health Care Needs of HIV-Positive People in the United Kingdom: A Review', *HIV Medicine*, 5: 5–46.

Green, J., Draper, A. and Dowler, E. A. (2003), 'Short Cuts to Safety: Risk and "Rules of Thumb" in Accounts of Food Choice', *Health, Risk and Society*, 5, 1: 33–52.

Green, J., Durand, M. A., Hutchings, A. and Black, N. (2011), 'Modernization as a Professionalising Strategy: The Case of Critical Care in England', *Sociology of Health & Illness*, 33: 819–36.

Greene, J. (2004), 'Therapeutic Infidelities: "Noncompliance" Enters the Medical Literature, 1955–1975', *Social History of Medicine*, 17, 3: 327–343.

Greener, I. (2008), *Continuity and Change in the NHS*, Bristol: Policy Press.

Gustafsson, U. (2004), 'The Privatization of Risk in School Meals Policies', *Health, Risk and Society*, 6, 1: 53–65.

Habermas, J. (1970), 'On Systematically Distorted Communication and Towards a Theory of Communicative Competence', *Inquiry*, 13: 205–18, 360–75.

Hacking, I. (2006), 'The Cartesian Body', *Biosocieties*, 1: 13–15.

Hacking, J., Muller, S. and Buchan, I. (2011), 'Trends in Mortality from 1965 to 2008 across the English North-South Divide: Comparative Observational Study', *British Medical Journal*, 342: d508.

Hallowell, N. (1999), 'Advising on the Management of Genetic Risk: Offering Choice or Prescribing Action', *Health Risk and Society*, 1: 267–80.

Hallowell, N., Arden-Jones, A., Eeles, R., Foster, C., Lucassen, A., Moynihan, C. and Watson, M. (2006), 'Guilt, Blame, Responsibility: Men's Understanding of their Role in the Transmission of BRCA1/2 Mutations with their Family', *Sociology of Health and Illness*, 28: 969–88.

Ham, C. (2004), *Health Policy in Britain: The Politics and Organization of the NHS*, 4th edn, New York: Palgrave Macmillan.

Hanmer, J. (1985), 'Transforming Consciousness: Women and the New Reproductive Technologies', in G. Corea and R. Duelli Klein (eds), *Man-Made Women: How New Reproductive Technologies Affect Women*, London: Hutchinson.

Hannay, D. R. (1979), *The Symptom Iceberg: A Study of Community Health*, London: Routledge & Kegan Paul.

Haraway, D. (1991), *Simians, Cyborgs, and Women: The Reinvention of Nature*, London: Free Association Books.

Hardey, M. (1999), 'Doctor in the House: The Internet as a Source of Lay Knowledge and the Challenge to Expertise', *Sociology of Health and Illness*, 21: 820–35.

Hardey, M. (2002), 'The Story of my Illness: Personal Accounts of Illness on the Internet', *Health*, 6: 31–46.

Hardey, M. (2010), 'Consuming Professions: User-Review Websites and Health Services', *Journal of Consumer Culture*, 10, 1: 129–49.

Harrison, M. with Phillips, D. (2003), *Housing and Black and Minority Ethnic Communities. Review of the Evidence Base*, London: Office of the Deputy Prime Minister.

Harrison, S. (1998), 'The Politics of Evidence-Based Medicine in the United Kingdom', *Policy and Politics*, 26, 1: 15–30.

Harrison, S. (2004), 'Governing Medicine: Governance, Science and Practice', in A. Gray and S. Harrison (eds), *Governing Medicine: Theory and Practice*, Maidenhead: Open University Press.

Harrison, S. (2009), 'Co-option, Commodificication and the Medical Model: Governing UK Medicine since 1991', *Public Administration*, 87, 2: 184–97.

Harrison, S. and Ahmed, W. (2002), 'Medical Autonomy and the UK State 1975 to 2025', in S. Nettleton and U. Gustaffson (eds), *The Sociology of Health and Illness Reader*, Cambridge: Polity.

Harrison, S. and McDonald, R. (2008), *The Politics of Healthcare in Britain*, London: Sage.

Harrison, S., Hunter, D. and Pollit, C. (1990), *The Dynamics of British Health Policy*, London: Unwin Hyman.

Hart, G. and Carter, S. (2000), 'A Sociology of Risk Behaviour', in S. J. Williams, J. Gabe and M. Calnan (eds), *Health Medicine and Society: Key Theories, Future Agendas*, London: Routledge.

Hartley, H. (2006), 'The "Pinking" of Viagra Culture: Drug Industry Efforts to Create and Repackage Sex Drugs for Women', *Sexualities*, 9: 363–78.

Haug, M. (1988), 'A Re-examination of the Hypothesis of Deprofessionalization', *Milbank Quarterly*, suppl. 2: 48–56.

Health Commission (2008), *Towards better Birth: a Review of Maternity Services in England*, London: Health Commission.

Healy, D. (2006), 'The Last Mania: Selling Biopolar Disorder', *PLoS Medicine*, 3, 4: e185.

Heath, C. (1984), 'Participation in the Medical Consultation: The Coordination of Verbal and

Non-Verbal Behaviour between the Doctor and the Patient', *Sociology of Health and Illness*, 6, 3: 311–38.

Hedgecoe, A. (2010), 'Bioethics and the Reinforcement of Socio-Technical Expectations', *Social Studies of Science*, 40, 2: 163–86.

Heitman, E. (2002), 'Social and Ethical Aspects of *in vitro* Fertilization', in S. Nettleton and U. Gustafsson (eds), *The Sociology of Health and Illness Reader*, Cambridge: Polity.

Helman, C. (1978), '"Feed a Cold and Starve a Fever" – Folk Models of Infection in an English Suburban Community and their Relation to Medical Treatment', *Culture, Medicine and Psychiatry*, 2: 107–37.

Heritage, J. and Robinson, J. (2006), 'Accounting for the Visit: Giving Reasons for Seeking Medical Care', in J. Heritage and D. Maynard (eds), *Communication in Medical Care: Interaction between Physicians and Patients*, Cambridge: Cambridge University Press.

Herzlich, C. (1973), *Health and Illness*, London: Academic Press.

Herzlich, C. and Pierret, J. (1987), *Illness and Self in Society*, Baltimore, MD: Johns Hopkins University Press.

Hinze, S. (2004), '"Am I being oversensitive?" Women's Experience of Sexual Harassment during Medical Training', *Health*, 8, 1: 101–27.

Hislop, J. and Arber, S. (2003), 'Sleepers Wake! The Gendered Nature of Sleep Disruption amongst Mid-life Women', *Sociology*, 37, 4: 695–711.

Hobson-West, P. (2003), 'Understanding Vaccination Resistance Moving beyond Risk', *Health, Risk and Society*, 5, 3: 274–83.

Hockey, J. and James, A. (2003), *Social Identities across the Life Course*, Basingstoke: Palgrave Macmillan.

Hockey, J. and James, A. (2007), *Embodying Health Identities*, Basingstoke: Palgrave Macmillan.

Hoeyer, K. (2009), 'Tradable Body Parts? How Bone and Recycled Prosthetic Devices Acquire a Price without Forming a "Market"', *Biosocieties*, 4: 239–56.

Horobin, G. (1985), 'Medical Sociology in Britain: "True Confessions of an Empiricist"', *Sociology of Health and Illness*, 7: 94–107.

Horton, R. (2003), *Second Opinion: Doctors, Diseases and Decisions in Modern Medicine*, London: Granta Books.

Horwitz, A. and Wakefield, J. (2007), *The Loss of Sadness: How Psychiatry Transformed Normal Sorrow into Depressive Disorder*, New York: Oxford University Press.

Howlett, B. C., Ahmad, W. I. and Murray, R. (1992), 'An Exploration of White, Asian and Afro-Caribbean Peoples' Concepts of Health and Illness Causation', *New Community*, 18, 2: 281–92.

Hsai, S. et al. (1984), 'Unregulated Production of a Virus and/or Sperm Specific Antiidiotypic Antibodies as a Cause of AIDS', *The Lancet*, 2: 212–14.

Hugman, R. (1994), 'Consuming Health and Welfare', in R. Keat, N. Whiteley and N. Abercrombie (eds), *The Authority of the Consumer*, London: Routledge.

Humphrey, C. (2000), 'Antibiotic Resistance: An Exemplary Case of Medical Nemesis', *Critical Public Health*, 10, 3: 353–8.

Hunt, K. (2002), 'A Generation Apart? Gender-Related Experiences and Health in Women in Early and Mid-life', *Social Science & Medicine*, 54: 663–76.

Hunt, S. (1989), 'The Public Health Implications of Private Cars', in C. J. Martin and D. V. McQueen (eds), *Readings for a New Public Health*, Edinburgh: Edinburgh University Press.

Hunter, D. (1991), 'Managing Medicine: A Response to Crisis', *Social Science & Medicine*, 32: 441–8.

Hyden, L. (1997), 'Illness and Narrative', *Sociology of Health and Illness*, 19, 1: 48–69.

Illich, I. (1976), *Limits to Medicine*, London: Marion Boyars.

Illsley, R. (1986), 'Occupational Class, Selection and the Production of Inequalities in Health', *Quarterly Journal of Social Affairs*, 2, 2: 151–65.

Illsley, R. and Le Grand, J. (1987), 'The Measurement of Inequality in Health', in A. Williams (ed.), *Economics and Health*, London: Macmillan.

Imrie, R. (2004), 'Demystifying Disability: A Review of the International Classification of Functioning, Disability and Health', *Sociology of Health and Illness*, 26, 3: 287–305.

Ingleby, D. (ed.) (1980), *Critical Psychiatry*, Harmondsworth: Penguin.

Irvine, D. (2003), *The Doctor's Tale: Professionalism and Public Trust*, Oxford: Radcliffe Medical Press.

Jacobus, M., Fox Keller, E. and Shuttleworth, S. (1990), *Body/Politics: Women and the Discourses of Science*, London: Routledge.

James, N. (1989), 'Emotion Labour: Skill and Work in the Social Regulation of Feelings', *Sociological Review*, 37, 1: 15–42.

Jamous, H. and Peloille, B. (1970), 'Changes in the French University Hospital System', in J. A. Jackson (ed.), *Professions and Professionalization*, Cambridge: Cambridge University Press.

Jefferys, M. (1991), 'The Agenda for Sociological Health-Policy Research for the 1990s', in J. Gabe, M. Calnan and M. Bury (eds), *The Sociology of the Health Service*, London: Routledge.

Jeffrey, R. (1979), 'Normal Rubbish: Deviant Patients in Casualty Departments', *Sociology of Health and Illness*, 1: 90–107.

Jewson, N. (1976), 'The Disappearance of the Sick Man from Medical Cosmology 1770–1870', *Sociology*, 10: 225–44.

Jex-Blake, S. (1886), *Medical Women: A Thesis and History*, Edinburgh: Oliphant, Anderson and Ferrier.

Jobling, R. (1988), 'The Experience of Psoriasis under Treatment', in R. Anderson and M. Bury (eds), *Living with Chronic Illness: The Experience of Patients and their Families*, London: Unwin Hyman.

Johanson, R., Newburn, M. and Macfarlane, A. (2002), 'Has Medicalization of Childbirth Gone Too Far?', *British Medical Journal*, 324: 892–5.

Johns, N. (2004), 'Ethnic Diversity Policy: Perceptions within the NHS', *Social Policy and Administration*, 38, 1: 73–88.

Johnson, S. (2001), *Emergence: The Connected Lives of Ants, Brains, Cities and Software*, Harmondsworth: Penguin.

Johnson, T. (1972), *Professions and Power*, London: Macmillan.

Johnson, T. (1977), 'Professions in the Class Structure', in R. Scase (ed.), *Industrial Society: Class, Cleavage and Control*, London: Allen Unwin.

Johnson, T., Dandeker, C. and Ashworth, C. (1984), *The Structure of Social Theory*, Basingstoke: Macmillan.

Joyce, K. (2008), *Magnetic Appeal: MRI and the Myth of Transparency*, Ithaca, NY: Cornell University Press.

Jutel, A. (2009), 'Sociology of Diagnosis: A Preliminary Review', *Sociology of Health and Illness*, 31, 1: 278–99.

Jutel, A. (2011), *Putting a Name to It: Diagnosis in Contemporary Society*, Baltimore, MD: Johns Hopkins University Press.

Jutel, A. and Nettleton, S. (2011), 'Towards a Sociology of Diagnosis: Reflections and Opportunities', *Social Science & Medicine*, 73: 793–800.

Kaler, A. (2004), 'AIDS-Talk in Everyday Life: The Presence of HIV/AIDS in Men's Informal Conversation in Southern Malawi', *Social Science & Medicine*, 59: 285–97.

Kalipeni, E., Craddock, S., Oppong, J. R. and Ghosh, J. (eds) (2004), *HIV and AIDS in Africa: Beyond Epidemiology*, Oxford: Blackwell.

Karlsen, S. and Nazroo, J. (2002), 'Agency and Structure: The Impact of Ethnic Identity and Racism on the Health of Ethnic Minority People', *Sociology of Health and Illness*, 24, 1: 1–20.

Karlsen, S. and Nazroo, J. (2004), 'Fear of Racism and Health', *Journal of Epidemiology and Community Health*, 58: 1017–18.

Kasl, S. V. and Cobb, S. (1966), 'Health Behaviour, Illness Behaviour and Sick Role Behaviour', *Archives of Environmental Research*, 12: 246–7.

Keeley, B., Wright, L. and Condit, C. M. (2009), 'Functions of Health Fatalism: Fatalistic Talk as Face Saving, Uncertainty Management, Stress Relief and Sense Making', *Sociology of Health & Illness*, 31: 734–47.

Kelleher, D. (1988), *Diabetes*, London: Tavistock.

Kelly, M. (1992), *Colitis*, London: Routledge.

Kelman, S. (1975), 'The Social Nature of the Definition Problem in Health', *International Journal of Health Services*, 5: 625–42.

Kent, J. (2000), *Social Perspectives on Pregnancy and Childbirth for Midwives, Nurses and the Caring Professions*, Buckingham: Open University Press.

Kerr, A. (2004), *Genetics and Society: A Sociology of Disease*, London: Routledge.

Kim, K. and Moody, P. (1992), 'More Resources Better Health?: A Cross National Perspective', *Social Science & Medicine*, 34, 8: 837–42.

Kjellstrom, T. and Rosenstock, L. (1990), 'The Role of Environmental and Occupational Hazards in the Adult Health Transition', *World Health Statistics Quarterly*, 43: 188–96.

Klawiter, M. (2004), 'Breast Cancer in Two Regimes: The Impact of Social Movements on Illness Experience', *Sociology of Health and Illness*, 26, 6: 845–74.

Klein, R. (2010), *The New Politics of the NHS*, 6th edn, London: Prentice-Hall.

Klein, R. D. (1984), 'Doing it Ourselves: Self-Insemination', in R. D. Arditti, R. D. Klein and S. Minden (eds), *Test-Tube Women: What Future for Motherhood?* London: Pandora.

Kleinman, A. (1988), *The Illness Narratives: Suffering, Healing and the Human Condition*, New York: Basic Books.

Klinenberg, E. (2002), *Heat Wave: A Social Autopsy of Disaster in Chicago*, Chicago, IL: University of Chicago Press.

Korp, P. (2010), 'Problems of the Healthy Lifestyle Discourse', *Sociology Compass*, 4: 800–10.

Krause, E. (1996), *Death of the Guilds*, New Haven, CT: Yale University Press.

Kroker, A. and Kroker, M. (1988), *Body Invaders: Sexuality and the Postmodern Condition*, London: Macmillan.

Kuh, D. and Ben-Shlomo, Y. (eds) (1997), *A Life Course Approach to Chronic Disease Epidemiology*, Oxford: Oxford University Press.

Kuh, D. and Ben-Shlomo, Y. (2002), 'A Life Course Approach to Chronic Disease Epidemiology: Conceptual Models, Empirical Challenges and Interdisciplinary Perspectives', *International Journal of Epidemiology*, 31, 2: 285–93.

Kuhlmann, E. (2006), *Modernising Health Care: Reinventing Professions, the State and the Public*, Bristol: Policy Press.

Kuhn, T. (1962), *The Structure of Scientific Revolutions*, Chicago, IL: Chicago University Press.

Kunst, A. E., Groenhof, F. and Makenbach, J. (1998), 'Mortality by Occupational Class among 30–64 years in 11 European Countries', *Social Science & Medicine*, 46, 11: 1459–76.

Kyriakides, C. and Virdee, S. (2003), 'Migrant Labour, Racism and the British National Health Service', *Ethnicity and Health*, 8, 4: 282–305.

Lacey, C. J. N. and Waugh, M. A. (1983), 'Cellular Immunity in Male Homosexuals', *The Lancet*, 2: 464.

Lahelma, E., Arber, S., Martikainen, P., Rahkonen, O. and Silventoinen, K. (2001), 'The Myth of Gender Differences in Health: Social Structural Determinants across Adult Ages in Britain and Finland', *Current Sociology*, 49, 3: 31–54.

Lalonde, M. (1974), *A New Perspective on the Health of Canadians*, Ottawa: Ministry of Supply and Services.

Lam, A. (2000), 'Tacit Knowledge, Organizational Learning and Societal Institutions – An Integrated Framework', *Organization Studies*, 21: 487–513.

The Lancet (1991), 'Consanguinity and Health', *The Lancet*, 338: 85–6.

Laqueur, W. (1990), *Making Sex, Body and Gender from the Greeks to Freud*, Cambridge, MA: Harvard University Press.

Larkin, G. (1980), 'Professionalism, Dentistry and Public Health', *Social Science & Medicine*, 14: 223–9.

Larson, M. (1977), *The Rise of Professionalism*, Berkeley, CA: University of California Press.

Larsson, A. T. and Grassman, E. J. (2012), 'Bodily Changes among People Living with Physical Impairments and Chronic Illnesses: Biographical Disruption or Normal Illness?', *Sociology of Health & Illness*. DOI: 10.1111/j.1467-9566.2012.01460.x.

Lash, S. and Urry, J. (1994), *Economics of Signs and Space*, London: Sage.

Lau, R. and Ware, J. (1981), 'Refinements in the Measurement of Health Specific Locus of Control Beliefs', *Medical Care*, 19: 1147–57.

Law, J. (2009), 'Actor Network Theory and Material Semiotics', in B. S. Turner (ed.), *The New Blackwell Companion to Social Theory*, Oxford: Blackwell.
Lawler, J. (1991), *Behind the Screens: Nursing, Somology and the Problem of the Body*, London: Churchill Livingstone.
Lawrence, C. (1979), 'The Nervous System and Society in the Scottish Enlightenment', in B. Barnes and S. Shapin (eds), *Natural Order*, London: Sage.
Lawrence, F. (2004), 'Food Watchdog's Safety Limits on Eating Fish', *Guardian*, 25 June.
Lawrence, S. C. and Bendixen, K. (1992), 'His and Hers: Male and Female Anatomy in Anatomy Texts for US Medical Students, 1890–1989', *Social Science & Medicine*, 35, 7: 925–34.
Lawton, J. (2000), *The Dying Process: Patients' Experiences of Palliative Care*, London: Routledge.
Lawton, J. (2002a), 'Colonising the Future: Temporal Perceptions and Health Relevant Behaviours across the Adult Lifecourse', *Sociology of Health and Illness*, 24: 714–33.
Lawton, J. (2002b), 'Contemporary Hospice Care: The Sequestration of the Unbounded Body and "Dirty Dying" England', in S. Nettleton and U. Gustaffson (eds), *The Sociology of Health and Illness Reader*, Cambridge: Polity.
Lawton, J. (2003), 'Lay Experiences of Health and Illness: Past Research and Future Agendas', *Sociology of Health and Illness*, 25: 23–40.
Le Grand, J. (1985), *Inequalities in Health: The Human Capital Approach*, Welfare State Programme Pamphlet no. 1, London: London School of Economics.
Leder, D. (1992), 'Introduction', in D. Leder (ed.), *The Body in Medical Thought and Practice*, London: Kluwer Academic.
Lefebvre, C. (1992), 'Social Marketing Health Promotion', in R. Bunton and G. Macdonald (eds), *Health Promotion: Disciplines and Diversity*, London: Routledge.
Lew-Ting, C.-Y. and Chen, L.-H. (2008), 'The Surrogate Marker and its Discontents: Pluralism in Immunity Maintenance among HIV-infected Persons in Taiwan', *Sociology of Health & Illness*, 30: 1039–54.
Lewis, J. (1986), *What Price Community Medicine? The Policy and Practice of Public Health 1918–1980*, Brighton: Wheatsheaf.
Lewis, S., Saulnier, M. and Renaud, M. (2000), 'Reconfiguring Health Policy: Simple Truths, Complex Solutions', in G. L. Albrecht, R. Fitzpatrick and S. C. Scrimshaw (eds), *The Handbook of Social Studies in Health and Medicine*, London: Sage.
Lippman, A. (1991), 'Prenatal Genetic Testing and Screening: Constructing Needs and Reinforcing Inequities', *American Journal of Law & Medicine*, 17 (1–2): 15–50.
Lippman, A. (1992), 'Led (Astray) by Genetic Maps: The Cartography of the Human Genome and Health Care', *Social Science & Medicine*, 35: 1469–76.
Loader, B. D., Muncer, S., Burrows, R., Pleace, N. and Nettleton, S. (2002), 'Medicine on the Line? Computer-Mediated Social Support and Advice for People with Diabetes', *International Journal of Social Welfare*, 11, 1: 53–65.
Lock, M. (1988), *Biomedicine Examined*, London: Kluwer Academic.
Lock, M., Freeman, J., Chilibeck, G., Beveridge, B. and Padolsky, M. (2007), 'Susceptibility Genes and the Question of Embodied Identity', *Medical Anthropology Quarterly*, 21, 3: 256–76.
Lonsdale, S. (1990), *Women and Disability: The Experiences of Physical Disability among Women*, London: Macmillan.
Lopez, A. D. (1990), 'Causes of Death: An Assessment of Global Patterns of Mortality around 1985', *World Health Statistics Quarterly*, 43: 91–104.
Lowy, I. (1988), 'Ludwik Fleck on the Social Construction of Medical Knowledge', *Sociology of Health and Illness*, 10, 2: 133–55.
Lupton, D. (1996), *Food, the Body and the Self*, London: Sage Publications.
Lupton, D. (1999), *Risk*, London: Routledge.
Lupton, D. (2000), 'The Social Construction of Medicine and the Body', in G. L. Albrecht, R. Fitzpatrick and S. C. Scrimshaw (eds), *The Handbook of Social Studies in Health and Medicine*, London: Sage.
Lupton, D. (2002), 'Consumerism, Reflexivity and the Medical Encounter', in S. Nettleton and U. Gustafsson (eds), *The Sociology of Health and Illness Reader*, Cambridge: Polity.

Lupton, D. and Tulloch, J. (2002), '"Life would be Pretty Dull without Risk": Voluntary Risk-Taking and its Pleasures', *Health Risk and Society*, 4, 2: 113–24.

Lutfey, K. E., Campbell, S. M., Renfrew, M. R., Marceau, L. D., Roland, M. and McKinlay, J. B. (2008), 'How are Patient Characteristics Relevant for Physicians' Clinical Decision Making in Diabetes?: An Analysis of Qualitative Results from a Cross-national Factorial Experiment', *Social Science & Medicine*, 67, 9: 1391–9.

Lynch, J. W., Kaplan, G., Pamuk, E. R., Cohen, R. D., Heck, K. E., Balofour, J. L. and Yen, I. H. (1998), 'Income Inequality and Mortality in Metropolitan Areas of the United States', *American Journal of Public Health*, 88: 1074–80.

Lynch, J. W., Davey Smith, G., Kaplan, G. A. and House, J. S. (2000), 'Income Inequality and Mortality: Importance to Health of Individual Income, Psychosocial Environment, or Material Conditions', *British Medical Journal*, 320: 1200–4.

MacFarlane, A. (1990), 'Official Statistics and Women's Health', in H. Roberts (ed.), *Women's Health Counts*, London: Routledge.

MacIntyre, S. (2000), 'The Social Patterning of Health: Bringing the Social Context Back In', plenary address, British Medical Sociology Annual Conference; reproduced in *Medical Sociology News*, 26, 1: 14–19.

MacIntyre, S. (2004), 'Place', in J. Gabe, M. Bury and M. A. Elston (eds), *Key Concepts in Medical Sociology*, London: Sage.

MacIntyre, S., Annandale, E., Ecob, R., Ford, G., Hunt, K., MacIver, S., West, P. and Wyke, S. (1989), 'The West of Scotland Twenty-07 Study: Health in the Community', in C. Martin and D. McQueen (eds), *Readings for a New Public Health*, Edinburgh: Edinburgh University Press.

MacIntyre, S., Reilly, J., Miller, D. and Eldridge, J. (1998), 'Food Choice, Food Scares, and Health: The Role of the Media', in A. Murcott (ed.), *The Nation's Diet: The Social Science of Food Choice*, London: Longman.

MacIntyre, S., MacIver, S. and A. Sooman (2002), 'Area, Class and Health: Should we be Focusing on Places or People?', in S. Nettleton and U. Gustafsson (eds), *The Sociology of Health and Illness Reader*, Cambridge: Polity.

Mackay, D. F., Nelson, S. M., Haw, S. J. and Pell, J. P. (2012), 'Impact of Scotland's Smoke-Free Legislation on Pregnancy Complications: Retrospective Cohort Study', *PLoS Med*, 9, 3: e1001175. doi:10.1371/journal.pmed.1001175.

Mackenbach, J. P. (2012), 'The Persistence of Health Inequalities in Modern Welfare States: The Explanation of a Paradox', *Social Science & Medicine*, 75, 4: 761–9.

Macpherson, W. (1999), *The Stephen Lawrence Inquiry*, London: The Stationery Office, Cm 4262-I.

Marinker, M., Blenkinsopp, A., Bond, C., Britten, N., Feely, M., George, C. et al. (1997), *From Compliance to Concordance: Achieving Shared Goals in Medicine Taking*, London: Royal Pharmaceutical Society of Great Britain.

Marmot, M. (2001), 'Inequalities in Health', *New England Journal of Medicine*, 345: 134–6.

Marmot, M. (2004), *Status Syndrome: How your Social Standing Directly Affects your Health and your Life Expectancy*, London: Bloomsbury Publishing.

Marmot, M. (2010), *Fair Society, Healthy Lives: A Strategic Review of Health Inequalities in England Post-2010*, London: The Marmot Review.

Marsh, A., Gordon, D., Pantazis, C. and Heslop, P. (1999), *Home Sweet Home?* Bristol: Policy Press.

Marshall, W. E. (2005), 'Aids, Race and the Limits of Science', *Social Science & Medicine*, 60: 2515–25.

Martin, C. J. and McQueen, D. V. (1989), *Readings for a New Public Health*, Edinburgh: Edinburgh University Press.

Martin, E. (1989), *The Woman in the Body: A Cultural Analysis of Reproduction*, Milton Keynes: Open University Press.

Martin, E. (1994), *Flexible Bodies: The Role of Immunity in American Culture from the Days of Polio to the Age of AIDS*, Boston, MA: Beacon Press.

Martin, E. (2000), 'Flexible Bodies and Health in the US', in S. J. Williams, J. Gabe and M. Calnan (eds), *Health, Medicine and Society: Key Theories, Future Agendas*, London: Routledge.

Martin, G. P. (2008), '"Ordinary People Only": Knowledge, Representativeness and the Publics of Public Participation in Healthcare', *Sociology of Health & Illness*, 30, 1: 35–54.

Mauss, M. (1973 [1934]), 'Techniques of the Body', *Economy and Society*, 2, 1: 70–88.

May, C. (1992), 'Nursing Work, Nurses' Knowledge, and the Subjectification of the Patient', *Sociology of Health and Illness*, 14, 4: 472–87.

May, C. (2007), 'The Clinical Encounter and the Problem of Context', *Sociology*, 41, 1: 29–45.

McDermott, R. (1998), 'Ethics, Epidemiology and the Thrifty Gene: Biological Determinism as a Health Hazard', *Social Science & Medicine*, 49, 9: 1189–95.

McFadyean, M. (2005), 'Who Knew?', *The Guardian Weekend*, 22 January: 15–20.

McKeigne, P. M., Richards, J. D. and Richards, P. (1990), 'Effects of Discrimination by Sex and Race on the Early Careers of British Medical Undergraduates 1981-1987', *British Medical Journal*, 301: 961–4.

McKeown, T. (1976), *The Role of Medicine: Dream, Mirage, or Nemesis*? London: Nuffield Provincial Hospitals Trust.

McKie, R. (2004), 'Food Defect could make Thousands Mentally Ill', *Observer*, 27 June: 13.

McKinlay, J. B. (1998), 'Paradigmatic Obstacles to Improving the Health of Populations - Implications for Health Policy', *Salud Publica de Mexico*, 40, 4: 369–79.

McKinlay, J. B. and Marceau, L. (2002), 'The End of the Golden Age of Doctoring', *International Journal of Health Services*, 32, 2: 379–416.

McKinlay, J. B. and Stoekle, J. (1988), 'Corporatization and the Social Transformation of Doctoring', *International Journal of Health Services*, 18: 191–205.

McNeill, M., Varcoe, I. and Yearley, S. (eds) (1990), *The New Reproductive Technologies*, Basingstoke: Macmillan.

McQueen, D. (1989), 'Thoughts on the Ideological Origins of Health Promotion', *Health Promotion*, 4, 4: 339–42.

Mead, N. and Bower, P. (2000), 'Patient-Centredness: A Conceptual Framework and Review of the Empirical Literature', *Social Science & Medicine*, 51: 1087–110.

Meadows, R. (2005), 'The Negotiated Night: An Embodied Conceptual Framework for the Sociological Study of Sleep', *The Sociological Review*, 53, 2: 240–54.

Merleau-Ponty, M. (1962), *Phenomenology of Perception*, London: Routledge & Kegan Paul.

Milburn, A. (2003), 'Choice for All', speech to NHS Chief Executives, 11 February.

Mishler, E. G. (1984), *The Discourse of Medicine: Dialectics of Medical Interviews*, Norwood, NJ: Ablex Publishing.

Mol, A. (2002), *The Body Multiple: Ontology in Medical Practice*, Durham, NC: Duke University Press.

Monaghan, L. (1999), 'Challenging Medicine? Body Building, Drugs and Risk', *Sociology of Health and Illness*, 21, 6: 707–34.

Monaghan, L. (2001a), *Bodybuilding Drugs and Risk*, London: Routledge.

Monaghan, L. (2001b), 'Looking Good, Feeling Good: The Embodied Pleasures of Vibrant Physicality', *Sociology of Health and Illness*, 23, 3: 330–56.

Mort, M., May, C. and Williams, T. (2003), 'Remote Doctors and Absent Patients: Acting at a Distance in Telemedicine', *Science, Technology and Human Values*, 28, 2: 274–95.

Moss, N. (2002), 'Gender Equity and Socioeconomic Inequality: A Framework for the Patterning of Women's Health', *Social Science & Medicine*, 36: 649–61.

Moyle, G. and Boffito, M. (2004), 'Unexpected Drug Interactions and Adverse Events with Antiretroviral Drugs', *The Lancet*, 364 (3 July): 8–9.

Moynihan, R. and Cassels, A. (2005), *Selling Sickness: How Drug Companies are Turning us all into Patients*, London: Allen and Unwin.

Muntaner, C. and Navarro, V. (eds) (2004), *Political and Economic Determinants of Population Health and Well Being: Controversies and Developments*, Amityville, NY: Baywood.

Naidoo, J. and Wills, J. (2009), *Foundations for Health Promotion*, 3rd edn, London: Bailliere Tindall.

Navarro, V. (1978), *Class, Struggle, the State and Medicine*, London: Martin Robertson.

Navarro, V. (1984), 'A Critique of the Ideological and Political Positions of the Willy Brandt Report and the WHO Alma Ata Declaration', *Social Science & Medicine*, 18: 467–74.

Navarro, V. (2004), 'The Politics of Health Inequalities Research in the United States', *International Journal of Health Services*, 34, 1: 87–99.

Nazroo, J. (1997), *The Health of Britain's Ethnic Minorities*, London: Policy Studies Institute.

Nazroo, J. (2001), *Ethnicity, Class and Health*, London: Policy Studies Institute.

Nettleton, S. (1991), 'Wisdom, Diligence and Teeth: Discursive Practices and the Creation of Mothers', *Sociology of Health and Illness*, 13, 1: 98–111.

Nettleton, S. (1992), *Power, Pain and Dentistry*, Buckingham: Open University Press.

Nettleton, S. (1993), *How Do We Create a Healthy North? Consultation with People in the Community*, Newcastle upon Tyne: Northern Regional Health Authority.

Nettleton, S. (1996), 'Women and the New Paradigm of Health and Medicine', *Critical Social Policy*, 16, 3: 33–53.

Nettleton, S. (1997), 'Governing the Risky Self: How to Become Healthy, Wealthy and Wise', in R. Bunton and A. Petersen (eds), *Foucault, Health and Medicine*, London: Routledge.

Nettleton, S. (2004), 'The Emergence of E-Scaped Medicine', *Sociology*, 38, 4: 661–80.

Nettleton, S. (2007), 'Retaining the Sociology in Medical Sociology', *Social Science & Medicine*, 65, 12: 2409–12.

Nettleton, S. and Burrows, R. (1998), 'Mortgage Debt, Insecure Home Ownership and Health: An Exploratory Analysis', *Sociology of Health and Illness*, 20, 5: 731–53.

Nettleton, S. and Hanlon, G. (2006), '"Pathways to the Doctor" in the Information Age: The Role of ICTs in Contemporary Lay Referral Systems', in A. Webster and S. Wyatt (eds), *Innovative Health Technologies: New Perspectives, Challenge and Change*, London: Palgrave Macmillan.

Nettleton, S. and Harding, G. (1994), 'Protesting Patients: A Study of Complaints Made to a Family Health Service Authority', *Sociology of Health and Illness*, 16, 1: 38–61.

Nettleton, S. and Watson, J. (eds) (1998), *The Body in Everyday Life*, London: Routledge.

Nettleton, S., O'Malley, L., Watt, I. and Duffey, P. (2004), 'Enigmatic Illness: Narratives of Medically Unexplained Illness', *Social Theory and Health*, 2, 1: 47–66.

Nettleton, S., Burrows, R. and O'Malley, L. (2005a), 'The Mundane Realities of the Everyday Lay Use of the Internet for Health and their Consequences for Media Convergence', *Sociology of Health and Illness*, 27, 7: 972–92.

Nettleton, S., Watt, I., O'Malley, L. and Duffey, P. (2005b), 'Understanding the Narratives of People who Live with Medically Unexplained Illness', *Patient Education and Counselling*, 56: 205–10.

Nettleton, S., Burrows, R. and Watt, I. (2008), 'Regulating Medical Bodies? The Consequences of the "Modernization" of the NHS and the Disembodiment of Clinical Knowledge', *Sociology of Health and Illness*, 30, 3: 333–48.

Nettleton, S., Neale, J. and Pickering, L. (2011a), '"I don't think there's much of a rational mind in a drug addict when they are in the thick of it": Towards an Embodied Analysis of Recovering Heroin Users', *Sociology of Health and Illness*, 33, 3: 341–55.

Nettleton, S., Neale, J. and Pickering, L. (2011b), 'Techniques and Transitions: A Sociological Analysis of Sleeping Practices amongst Recovering Heroin Users', *Social Science & Medicine*, 72, 8: 1367–73.

Nettleton, S., Neale, J. and Stevenson, C. (2012), 'Sleeping at the Margins: a Qualitative Study of Homeless Drug Users who Stay in Emergency Hostels and Shelters', *Critical Public Health*, 22, 3: 319–28.

The NHS Information Centre (2011), *Statistics on Smoking: England, 2011*, London: The Health and Social Care Information Centre.

NHS Management Executive (1993), *The Quality Journey*, Leeds: NHS Management Executive.

Nicholson, M. (2009), 'Commentary: Nicholas Jewson and the Disappearance of the Sick Man from Medical Cosmology, 1770–1870', *International Journal of Epidemiology*, 38, 3: 639–42.

Nordqvist, P. (2011), '"Dealing with Sperm": Comparing Lesbians' Clinical and Non-clinical Donor Conception Processes', *Sociology of Health & Illness*, 33: 114–29.

Novas, C. and Rose, N. (2000), 'Genetic Risk and the Birth of the Somatic Individual', *Economy and Society*, 29, 4: 485–513.

Oakley, A. (1976), 'Wisewoman and Medicine Man: Changes in the Management of Childbirth', in J. Mitchell and A. Oakley (eds), *The Rights and Wrongs of Women*, Harmondsworth: Penguin.

Oakley, A. (1984), *The Captured Womb: A History of the Medical Care of Pregnant Women*, Oxford: Blackwell.

Oakley, A. (1987), 'From Walking Wombs to Test-tube Babies', in M. Stanworth (ed.), *Reproductive Technologies: Gender, Motherhood and Medicine*, Cambridge: Polity.

Oakley, A. (1989), 'Smoking in Pregnancy: Smokescreen or Risk Factor? Towards a Materialist Analysis', *Sociology of Health and Illness*, 11, 4: 311–35.

Oakley, A. (1993), *Essays on Women, Medicine and Health*, Edinburgh: Edinburgh University Press.

Oakley, A. (2000), *Experiments in Knowing: Gender and Method in the Social Sciences*, Cambridge: Polity.

Offe, C. (1984), *Contradictions of the Welfare State*, London: Hutchinson.

Olin Lauritzen, S. and Sachs, L. (2001), 'Normality, Risk and the Future: Implicit Communication of Threat in Health Surveillance', *Sociology of Health and Illness*, 23: 497–516.

ONS (2005), *National Statistics Online*, <http://www.statistics.gov.uk/>.

ONS (2007), *Trends in Life Expectancy by Social Class 1972–2005*, London: Office for National Statistics.

ONS (2012), *Intercensal Mortality Rates by NSSEC, 2001–2010*, London: Office for National Statistics.

Oppenheimer, M. (1973), 'The Proletarianization of the Professional', *Sociological Review Monograph*, 20: 213–37.

Oudshoorn, N. and Van Den Wijngaard, M. (1991), 'Dualism in Biology: The Case of Sex Hormones', *Women's Studies International Forum*, 14, 5: 459–71.

Pahl, J. (1990), 'Household Spending, Personal Spending and the Control of Money in Marriage', *Sociology*, 24, 1: 119–38.

Palmer, G., Carr, J. and Kenway, P. (2004), *Monitoring Poverty and Social Exclusion in Scotland 2004*, York: Joseph Rowntree Foundation.

Pamuk, E. R. (1985), 'Social Class Inequality in Mortality from 1921 to 1972 in England and Wales', *Population Studies*, 39: 17–31.

Pantazis, C. and Gordon, D. (2000), *Tackling Health Inequalities: Where are we Now and What can be Done?* Bristol: Policy Press.

Parker, R. and Aggleton, P. (2003), 'HIV and AIDS-Related Stigma and Discrimination: A Conceptual Framework and Implications for Action', *Social Science & Medicine*, 57: 13–24.

Parkin, F. (1974), 'Strategies of Social Closure and Class Formation', in F. Parkin (ed.), *The Social Analysis of Class Structure*, London: Tavistock.

Parsons, L., Macfarland, A. and Golding, J. (1993), 'Pregnancy, Birth and Maternity Care', in W. I. U. Ahmad (ed.), *Race and Health in Contemporary Britain*, Buckingham: Open University Press.

Parsons, T. (1951), *The Social System*, Glencoe, IL: Free Press.

Parsons, T. (1979), 'Definitions of Health and Illness in the Light of American Values and Social Structure', in E. Jaco and E. Gartley (eds), *Patients, Physicians and Illness: A Source Book in Behavioural Science and Health*, 3rd edn, London: Collier-Macmillan.

Patel, N. (1993), 'Healthy Margins: Black Elders' Care – Models, Policies and Prospects', in W. I. U. Ahmad (ed.), *Race and Health in Contemporary Britain*, Buckingham: Open University Press.

Paton, C. (1992), *Competition and Planning in the NHS: The Danger of Unplanned Markets*, London: Chapman Hall.

Pattenden, G., Watt, I., Lewin, R. and Stanford, N. (2002), 'Decision Making Processes in People with Symptoms of Acute Myocardial Infarction: Qualitative Study', *British Medical Journal*, 324: 1006.

Pavis, S., Cunningham-Burley, S. and Amos, A. (2002), 'Health Related Behavioural Change in Context', in S. Nettleton and U. Gustafsson (eds), *The Sociology of Health and Illness Reader*, Cambridge: Polity.

Pearson, M. (1987), 'Racism – the Great Divide', *Nursing Times and Nursing Mirror*, June.

Perren, K., Arber, S. and Davidson, K. (2004), 'Neighbouring in Later Life: The Influence of Socio-economic Resources, Gender Household Composition on Neighbourly Relationships', *Sociology*, 38, 5: 965–84.

Persson, A. (2004), 'Incorporating *Pharmakon*: HIV, Medicine and Body Shape Change', *Body and Society*, 10, 4: 45–67.

Petersen, A. (2011a), *The Politics of Bioethics*, London: Routledge.

Petersen, A. (2011b), 'Can and Should Sociology Save Bioethics?', *Medical Sociology News Online*.

Petersen, A. and Lupton, D. (1996), *The New Public Health: Health and Self in the Age of Risk*, London: Sage.

Petts, J. and Niemeyer, S. (2004), 'Health Risk Communication and Amplification: Learning from the MMR Vaccination Controversy', *Health, Risk and Society*, 6, 1: 7–23.

Pfeffer, N. (1987), 'Artificial Insemination, In-vitro Fertilization and the Stigma of Infertility', in M. Stanworth (ed.), *Reproductive Technologies: Gender, Motherhood and Medicine*, Cambridge: Polity.

Phillimore, P. (1989), *Shortened Lives: Premature Death in North Tyneside*, Bristol Papers in Applied Social Studies no. 12, Bristol: University of Bristol.

Phillips, D. R. (1990), *Health and Health Care in the Third World*, Harlow: Longman.

Pilgrim, D. and Rogers, A. (1993), *A Sociology of Mental Health and Illness*, Buckingham: Open University Press.

Pilnick, A. (2002), *Genetics and Society: An Introduction*, Buckingham: Open University Press.

Pinder, R. (1988), 'Striking Balances: Living with Parkinson's Disease', in R. Anderson and M. Bury (eds), *Living with Chronic Illness: The Experience of Patients and their Families*, London: Unwin Hyman.

Polanyi, M. (1959), *The Study of Man*, Chicago, IL: Chicago University Press.

Polanyi, M. (1966), *The Tacit Dimension*, New York: Anchor Books.

Pollock, K. (1993), 'Attitude of Mind as a Means of Resisting Illness', in A. Radley (ed.), *Worlds of Illness: Biographical and Cultural Perspectives on Health and Disease*, London: Routledge.

Popay, J. (2009), 'Equalizing People's Health', in J. Gabe and M. Calnan (eds), *The New Sociology of the Health Service*, London: Routledge.

Popay, J. and Bartley, M. (1989), 'Conditions of Labour and Women's Health', in C. Martin and D. McQueen (eds), *Readings For a New Public Health*, Edinburgh: Edinburgh University Press.

Popay, J. and Jones, G. (1990), 'Patterns of Health and Illness amongst Lone Parents', *Journal of Social Policy*, 19, 4: 499–534.

Popay, J., Williams, G., Thomas, C. and Gatrell, T. (1998), 'Theorising Inequalities in Health: The Place of Lay Knowledge', *Sociology of Health and Illness*, 20, 5: 619–44.

Popay, J., Bennett, S., Thomas, C., Williams, G., Gatrell, A. and Bostock, G. (2003), 'Beyond "Beer, Fags, Eggs and Chips"? Exploring Lay Understanding of Social Inequalities in Health', *Sociology of Health and Illness*, 25, 1: 1–23.

Porter, M. (1990), 'Professional–Client Relationships and Women's Reproductive Health Care', in S. Cunningham-Burley and N. P. McKeganey (eds), *Readings in Medical Sociology*, London: Routledge.

Potter, S. J. and McKinlay, B. (2005), 'From Relationship to Encounter: An Examination of Longitudinal and Lateral Dimensions in the Doctor–Patient Relationship', *Social Science & Medicine*, 61, 2: 465–79.

Potts, L. (2004), 'Mapping Citizen Expertise about Environmental Risk of Breast Cancer', *Critical Social Policy*, 24, 4: 550–74.

Pound, P., Gompertz, P. and Ebrahim, S. (1998), 'Illness in the Context of Older Age: The Case of Stroke', *Sociology of Health and Illness*, 20: 489–506.

Power, M. (1997), *The Audit Society: Rituals of Verification*, Oxford: Oxford University Press.

Powles, J. (1973), 'On the Limitations of Modern Medicine', *Science, Medicine and Man*, 1: 1–30.

Prior, L. (1985), 'The Social Production of Mortality Statistics', *Sociology of Health and Illness*, 7: 220–35.

Prior, L. (1989), *The Social Organization of Death: Medical Discourses and Social Practices in Belfast*, London: Macmillan.

Prior, L. (1991), 'Community versus Hospital Care: The Crisis in Psychiatric Provision', *Social Science & Medicine*, 32, 4: 483–9.

Prior, L. (1993), *The Social Organization of Mental Illness*, London: Sage.

Prior, L. (2003), 'Belief, Knowledge and Expertise: The Emergence of the Lay Expert in Medical Sociology', *Sociology of Health and Illness*, 25: 41–57.

Prior, L. (2009), 'Commentary: From Sick Men and Women, to Patients, and thence to Clients and Consumers – The Structuring of the 'Patient' in the Modern World', *International Journal of Epidemiology*, 38, 3: 637–9.

Prior, L., Chun, P. L. and Huat, S. B. (2002), 'Beliefs and Accounts of Illness: Views from Two Cantonese Communities in England', in S. Nettleton and U. Gustaffson (eds), *The Sociology of Health and Illness Reader*, Cambridge: Polity.

Prout, A. (1986), '"Wet Children" and "Little Actresses": Going Sick in Primary School', *Sociology of Health and Illness*, 8: 111–36.

Putnam, R. D. (2000), *Bowling Alone: The Collapse and Revival of American Community*, New York: Simon & Schuster.

Rabinow, P. (1992), 'Artificiality and Enlightenment: from Sociobiology to Biosociality', in J. Crary and S. Kwinter (eds), *Incorporations*, New York: Zone Books.

Rabinow, P. (1999), *French DNA: Trouble in Purgatory*, Chicago, IL: University of Chicago Press.

Radford, T. (1993), 'Code of Conduct', *Guardian*, 21 July: 1–2.

Radley, A. (1989), 'Style, Discourse and Constraint in Adjustment to Chronic Illness', *Sociology of Health and Illness*, 11: 231–52.

Radley, A. (1993), 'Introduction', in A. Radley (ed.), *Worlds of Illness: Biographical and Cultural Perspectives on Health and Disease*, London: Routledge.

Radley, A. and Billig, M. (1996), 'Accounts of Health and Illness: Dilemmas and Representations', *Sociology of Health and Illness*, 18, 2: 220–40.

Radley, A., Cheek, J. and Ritter, C. (2006), 'The Making of *Health*: a Reflection of the First 10 Years in the Life of a Journal', *Health*, 10, 4: 389–400.

Rapp, R. (2000), *Testing Women: The Social Impact of Amniocentesis in America*, London: Routledge.

Rashid, A. (1990), 'Asian Doctors and Nurses in the NHS', in B. R. McAvoy and L. Donaldson (eds), *Health Care for Asians*, Oxford: Oxford University Press.

Raz, A. E. (2009), 'Eugenic Utopias/Dystopias, Reprogenetics, and Community Genetics', *Sociology of Health and Illness*, 31, 4: 602–16.

Rhodes, D. (1985), *An Outline of History of Medicine*, London: Butterworth.

Rhodes, T. (1997), 'Risk Theory in Epidemic Times: Sex, Drugs and the Organization of Risk Behaviour', *Sociology of Health and Illness*, 19, 2: 208–27.

Rhodes, T. and Cusick, L. (2000), 'Love Intimacy in Relationship Management: HIV Positive People and their Sexual Partners', *Sociology of Health and Illness*, 22, 1: 1–26.

Rhodes, T., Singer, M., Bourgois, P., Friedman, S. and Strathdee, S. (2005), 'The Social Structural Production of HIV Risk among Injecting Drug Users', *Social Science & Medicine*, 61: 1026–44.

Riessmann, C. K. (1983), 'Women and Medicalization: A New Perspective', *Social Policy*, 1, Summer: 3–18.

Riska, E. (2010), 'Health Professions and Occupations', in W. Cockerham (ed.), *The New Blackwell Companion to Medical Sociology*, London: Wiley-Blackwell.

Ritche, D., Amos, A. and Martin, C. (2010), 'Public Places after Smoke-free – A Qualitative Exploration of the Changes in Smoking Behaviour', *Health and Place*, 16, 3: 461–9.

Roberts, C. and Throsby, K. (2008), 'Paid to Share: IVF Patients, Eggs and Stem Cell Research', *Social Science & Medicine*, 66, 1: 159–69.

Roberts, H. (1985), *Women: The Patient Patients*, London: Pandora Press.

Roberts, H. (1990), *Women's Health Counts*, London: Routledge.

Roberts, H. (1992), 'Professionals' and Parents' Perceptions of A&E Use in a Children's Hospital', *Sociological Review*, 40, 1: 109–31.

Roberts, S. (1993), *Sophia Jex-Blake: A Woman Pioneer in Nineteenth-Century Medical Reform*, London: Routledge.

Robinson, I. (1988a), *Multiple Sclerosis*, London: Routledge.

Robinson, I. (1988b), 'Reconstructing Lives: Negotiating the Meaning of Multiple Sclerosis', in R. Anderson and M. Bury (eds), *Living with Chronic Illness: The Experiences of Patients and their Families*, London: Unwin Hyman.

Rogers, A., Pilgrim, D. and Lacey, R. (1992), *Experiencing Psychiatry: Users' View of Services*, London: Macmillan.

Rogers, W. (2004), 'Evidence-Based Medicine and Women: Do the Principles and Practice of EBM Further Women's Health?', *Bioethics*, 18, 1: 50–71.

Rose, N. (1985), *The Psychological Complex: Psychology, Politics and Society in England 1869–1939*, London: Routledge & Kegan Paul.

Rose, N. (1986), 'Psychiatry: The Discipline and Mental Health', in P. Miller and N. Rose (eds), *The Power of Psychiatry*, Cambridge: Polity.

Rose, N. (2001), 'The Politics of Life Itself', *Theory, Culture and Society*, 18, 6: 1–30.

Rose, N. (2007), 'Molecular Biopolitics, Somatic Ethics and the Spirit of Biocapital', *Social Theory and Health*, 5: 3–29.

Rose, N. and Novas, C. (2005), 'Biological Citizenship', in A. Ong and S. J. Collier (eds), *Global Assemblages: Technology, Politics and Ethics as Anthropological Problems*, Oxford: Blackwell.

Rosengarten, M. (2004), 'Consumer Activism in the Pharmacology of HIV', *Body and Society*, 10, 1: 91–107.

Rosengarten, M. (2009), *HIV Interventions: Biomedicine and the Traffic between Information and Flesh*, London: University of Washington Press.

Rosengarten, M., Imrie, J., Flowers, P., Davis, M. and Hart, G. (2004), 'After the Euphoria: HIV Medical Technologies from the Perspective of their Prescribers', *Sociology of Health and Illness*, 26, 5: 575–96.

Rosenhan, D. (1973), 'On Being Sane in Insane Places', *Science*, 179: 250–8.

Rosenstock, I. M. (1974), 'Historical Origins of the Health Belief Model', *Health Education Monographs*, 2: 409–19.

Ross, N. A., Wolfson, M., Dunn, J. R., Berthelot, J.-M., Kaplan, G. A. and Lynch, J. W. (2000), 'Relation between Income Inequality and Mortality in Canada and the United States: Cross Sectional Assessment Using Census Data and Vital Statistics', *British Medical Journal*, 320: 898–902.

Rowland, R. (1985), 'A Child at Any Price?', *Women's Studies International Forum*, 8, 6: 539–46.

Sackett, D. L., Rosenberg, W. M. C., Gray, J., Haynes, R. and Richardson, W. S. (1996), 'Evidence Based Medicine: What it Is and What it Isn't', *British Medical Journal*, 312: 71–2.

Saks, M. (ed.) (1992), *Alternative Medicine in Britain*, Oxford: Clarendon Press.

Saks, M. (2003), *Orthodox and Complementary Medicine: Politics, Professionalization and Health Care*, London: Sage.

Sanders, C., Donovan, J. and Dieppe, P. (2002), 'The Significance and Consequences of Having Painful and Disabled Joints in Older Age: Co-existing Accounts of Normal and Disrupted Biographies', *Sociology of Health and Illness*, 24, 2: 227–53.

Saunders, P. (2010), *Beware False Prophets: Equality, the Good Society and The Spirit Level*, London: The Policy Institute.

Savage, M., Bagnall, G. and Longhurst, B. (2005), *Globalization and Belonging*, London: Sage.

Sawicki, J. (1991), *Disciplining Foucault: Feminism, Power and the Body*, London: Routledge.

Sayer, A. (1992), *Method in Social Science: A Realist Approach*, 2nd edn, London: Routledge.

Scambler, A., Scambler, B. and Craig, D. (1981), 'Kinship and Friendship Networks and Women's Demands for Primary Care', *Journal of Royal College of General Practitioners*, 26: 746–50.

Scambler, G. (1989), *Epilepsy*, London: Routledge.

Scambler, G. (2004), 'Re-framing Stigma: Felt and Enacted Stigma and Challenges to the Sociology of Chronic Disabling Conditions', *Social Theory and Health*, 2, 1: 29–46.

Scambler, G. and Higgs, P. (1999), 'Stratification, Class and Health: Class Relations and Health Inequalities in High Modernity', *Sociology*, 33: 275–96.

Scambler, G. and Hopkins, A. (1986), 'Being Epileptic: Coming to Terms with Stigma', *Sociology of Health and Illness*, 8, 1: 26–43.

Scanlan, J. P. (2006), 'Can we Actually Measure Health Disparities?', *Chance*, 19, 2: 47–51.

Schaepe, K. (2011), 'Bad News and First Impressions: Patient and Family Caregiver Accounts of Learning the Cancer Diagnosis', *Social Science & Medicine*, 73, 6: 912–21.

Scheper-Hughes, N. (2008), *The Last Commodity: Post-Human Ethics, Global (In)justice, and the Traffic in Organs*, Penang: Multiversity & Citizens International.

Schubert, C. (2011), 'Making Sure: A Comparative Micro-Analysis of Diagnostic Instruments in Medical Practice', *Social Science & Medicine*, 73: 851–7.

Schwartz, B. (1970), 'Notes on the Sociology of Sleep', *The Sociological Quarterly*, 11, 4: 485–99.

Scott, S. (2006), 'The Medicalization of Shyness: From Social Misfits to Social Fitness', *Sociology of Health and Illness*, 28, 2: 133–53.

Scott, S. and Morgan, D. (eds) (1993), *Body Matters: Essays on the Sociology of the Body*, London: Falmer Press.

Scott, S., Prior, L., Wood, F. and Gray, J. (2005), 'Repositioning the Patient: The Implications of being "at Risk"', *Social Science & Medicine*, 60, 8: 1869–79.

Seale, C. (2002), *Media and Health*, London: Sage.

Seale, C. (2005), 'New Directions for Critical Internet Health Studies: Representing Cancer Experiences on the Web', *Sociology of Health and Illness*, 27, 4: 515–40.

Seale, C. (2008), 'Mapping the Field of Medical Sociology: A Comparative Analysis of Journals', *Sociology of Health and Illness*, 30, 5: 677–95.

Secretary of State for Health (1999), *Saving Lives: Our Healthier Nation*, London: Stationery Office.

Sharma, U. (1992), *Complementary Medicine Today: Practitioners and Patients*, London: Routledge.

Shaw, I. (2004), 'Doctors, "Dirty Work", Patients and "Revolving Doors"', *Qualitative Health Research*, 24, 8: 1032–45.

Shilling, C. (1991), 'Educating the Body: Physical Capital and the Production of Social Inequalities', *Sociology*, 25: 653–72.

Shilling, C. (2002), 'Culture, the "Sick Role" and the Consumption of Health', *British Journal of Sociology*, 3: 621–38.

Shilling, C. (2003), *The Body and Social Theory*, 2nd edn, London: Sage.

Shortt, S. (1983), 'Physicians, Science, and Status: Issues in the Professionalization of Anglo-American Medicine in the Nineteenth Century', *Medical History*, 27: 51–68.

Shryock, R. (1979), *The Development of Modern Medicine*, Madison, WI: University of Wisconsin Press.

Shuttleworth, S. (1990), 'Female Circulation: Medical Discourse and Popular Advertising in the Mid-Victorian Era', in M. Jacobus, E. Fox Keller and S. Shuttleworth (eds), *Body/Politics: Women and Discourses of Science*, London: Routledge.

Sidell, M. (1992), 'The Relationship of Elderly Women to their Doctors', in J. George and S. Ebrahim (eds), *Health Care for Older Women*, Oxford: Oxford Medical Publications.

Siegrist, J. (2010), 'Work, Stress and Health', in W. C. Cockerham (ed.), *The New Blackwell Companion to Medical Sociology*, Oxford: Blackwell.

Siegrist, J. and Marmot, M. (2004), 'Health Inequalities and the Psychosocial Environment - Two Scientific Challenges', *Social Science & Medicine*, 58: 1463–73.

Silverman, D. (1987), *Communication and Medical Practice: Social Relations in the Clinic*, London: Sage.

Skolbekken, J. (1995), 'The Risk Epidemic in Medical Journals', *Social Science & Medicine*, 40, 3: 291–305.

Smaje, C. (1995), *Health, 'Race', and Ethnicity: Making Sense of the Evidence*, London: King's Fund Institute.

Smart, B. (1992), *Modern Conditions, Postmodern Controversies*, London: Routledge.

Smith, J. L. (2003), '"Suitable Mothers": Lesbian and Single Women and the "Unborn" in Australian Parliamentary Discourse', *Critical Social Policy*, 32, 1: 63–88.

Smith, R. (2003), 'The Future of Medical Education: Speculation and Possible Implications', accessed at <www.bmj.com/talks>.

Smith-Rosenberg, C. (1984), 'The Hysterical Women: Sex Roles and Role Conflict in 19th-Century America', in N. Black et al. (eds), *Health and Disease: A Reader*, Milton Keynes: Open University Press.

Snowdon, C. (2010), *The Spirit Level Delusion: Fact-checking the Left's New Theory of Everything*, London: Democracy Institute/Little Dice.

Song, L., Son, J. and Linm, N. (2010), 'Social Capital and Health', in W. C. Cockerham (ed.), *The New Blackwell Companion to Medical Sociology*, Oxford: Blackwell.

Sontag, S. (1988), *AIDS and its Metaphors*, Harmondsworth: Penguin.

Stacey, M. (1987), 'The Role of Information in the Development of Social Policy', *Community Medicine*, 9, 3: 216–25.

Stacey, M. (1988), *The Sociology of Health and Healing*, London: Unwin Hyman.

Stafford, M. and Marmot, M. (2003), 'Neighbourhood Deprivation and Health: Does it Affect us Equally?', *International Journal of Epidemiology*, 32: 357–66.

Stainton-Rogers, W. (1991), *Explaining Health and Illness: An Exploration of Diversity*, London: Harvester Wheatsheaf.

Stanworth, M. (ed.) (1987), *Reproductive Technologies: Gender, Motherhood and Medicine*, Cambridge: Polity.

Stevens, F. (2010), 'The Convergence and Divergence of Modern Health Care Systems', in W. Cockerham (ed.), *The New Blackwell Companion to Medical Sociology*, London: Wiley-Blackwell.

Stevenson, F. and Scambler, G. (2005), 'The Relationship between Medicine and the Public: The Challenge of Concordance', *Health*, 9: 5–21.

Stevenson, F., Barry, C., Britten, N., Barber, N. and Bradley, C. (2000), 'Doctor–Patient Communication about Drugs: The Evidence for Shared Decision Making', *Social Science & Medicine*, 50: 829–40.

Stimpson, G. (1976), 'General Practitioners: Trouble and Types of Patients', in M. Stacey (ed.), *The Sociology of the NHS*, Sociological Review Monograph 22, Keele: University of Keele.

Stimpson, G. and Webb, B. (1975), *Going to See the Doctor*, London: Routledge.

Strang, J. and Stimpson, G. (1990), *AIDS and Drug Misuse: The Challenge for Policy and Practice in the 1990s*, London: Routledge.

Strauss, A. L. (1975), *Chronic Illness and the Quality of Life*, St Louis, MO: C. V. Mosby and Co.

Strauss, A. L. (1978), *Negotiations: Varieties, Contexts, Processes and Social Order*, San Francisco, CA: Jossey Bass.

Strauss, R. (1957), 'The Nature and Status of Medical Sociology', *American Sociological Review*, 22: 200–4.

Streefland, P. H. (2001), 'Public Doubts about Vaccination Safety and Resistance against Vaccination', *Health Policy*, 55: 159–72.

Street, R. L. (1991), 'Information-Giving in Medical Consultations: The Influence of Patterns of Communicative Styles and Personal Characteristics', *Social Science & Medicine*, 32, 5: 541–8.

Strong, P. (1979a), 'Materialism and Medical Interaction: A Critique of "Medicine, Super-Structure and Micro-Politics"', *Social Science & Medicine*, 13A: 601–9.

Strong, P. (1979b), *The Ceremonial Order of the Clinic: Parents, Doctors and Medical Bureaucracies*, London: Routledge & Kegan Paul.

Strong, P. (1986), 'A New-Modelled Medicine: Comments on the WHO's Regional Strategy for Europe', *Social Science & Medicine*, 22: 193–9.

Strong, P. (1990), 'Epidemic Psychology: A Model', *Sociology of Health and Illness*, 2, 3: 249–59.

Sulik, G. (2010), *Pink Ribbon Blues: How Breast Cancer Culture Undermines Women's Health*, New York: Oxford University Press.

Szasz, T. (1970), *The Manufacture of Madness*, New York: Harper & Row.

Szreter, S, (2002), 'Rethinking McKeown: The Relationship between Public Health and Social Change', *Amercican Journal of Public Health*, 92, 5: 722–5.

Taussig, M. T. (1980), 'Reification and Consciousness of the Patient', *Social Science & Medicine*, 14B: 3–13.

Taylor, S. and Ashworth, C. (1987), 'Durkheim and Social Realism: An Approach to Health and Illness', in G. Scambler (ed.), *Sociological Theory and Medical Sociology*, London: Tavistock.

Tew, M. (1990), *Safer Childbirth: A Critical History of Maternity Care*, London: Chapman & Hall.

Thomas, B., Doring, D. and Davey Smith, G. (2010), 'Inequalities in Premature Mortality in Britain: Observational Study from 1921 to 2007', *British Medical Journal*, 341: 363–9.

Thomas, C. (1997), 'The Baby and the Bath Water: Disabled Women and Motherhood in Social Context', *Sociology of Health and Illness*, 19, 5: 622–43.

Thomson, P., Jones, J., Evans, J. M. and Leslie, S. L. (2011), 'Factors Influencing the Use of Complementary and Alternative Medicine and Whether Patients Inform their Primary Care Physician', *Complementary Therapies in Medicine*, 20, 1: 45–53.

Thorogood, N. (2002), 'What is the Relevance of Sociology for Health Promotion?', in R. Bunton and G. Macdonald (eds), *Health Promotion: Disciplines, Diversity and Developments*, London: Routledge.

Timaeus, I., Harpham, T., Price, M. and Gilson, L. (1988), 'Health Surveys in Developing Countries: The Objectives and Design of an International Programme', *Social Science & Medicine*, 27, 4: 359–68.

Timmermans, S. and Angell, A. (2001), 'Evidence Based Medicine, Clinical Uncertainty and Learning to Doctor', *Journal of Health and Social Behaviour*, 42: 342–59.

Timmermans, S. and Berg, M. (2003), 'The Practice of Medical Technology', *Sociology of Health and Illness*, 25 (silver anniversary edition): 97–114.

Timmermans, S. and Epstein, S. (2010), 'A World of Standards but not a Standard World: Towards a Sociology of Standards and Standardization', *Annual of Review of Sociology*, 36: 6–89.

Timmermans, S. and Haas, S. (2008), 'Towards a Sociology of Disease', *Sociology of Health and Illness*, 30, 5: 659–76.

Titmuss, R. (1970), *The Gift Relationship: From Human Blood to Social Policy*, New York: Pantheon Books.

Tomlinson, B. (1992), *Report of the Inquiry into London's Health Service, Medical Education and Research, Presented to the Secretaries of State for Health and Education by Sir Bernard Tomlinson*, London: HMSO.

Toombs, S. K. (1992), 'The Body in Multiple Sclerosis: A Patient's Perspective', in D. Leder (ed.), *The Body in Medical Thought and Practice*, London: Kluwer Academic.

Townsend, P. (1962), *The Last Refuge*, London: Routledge & Kegan Paul.

Townsend, P. (1990), 'Individual or Social Responsibility for Premature Death? Current Controversies in the British Debate about Health', *International Journal of Health Services*, 20, 3: 373–92.

Townsend, P. and Davidson, N. (1982), *Inequalities in Health: The Black Report*, Harmondsworth: Penguin.

Treacher, A. and Baruch, G. (1981), 'Towards a Critical History of the Psychiatric Profession', in D. Ingleby (ed.), *Critical Psychiatry*, Harmondsworth: Penguin.

Treichler, P. (1999), *How to Have Theory in an Epidemic*, Durham, NC: Duke University Press.

Tritter, J., Koivusalo, M., Ollila, E. and Dorfman, P. (2010), *Globalisation, Markets and Health Care Policy: Redrawing the Patient as Consumer*, London: Routledge.

Tuckett, D., Boulton, M., Olson, C. and Williams, A. (1985), *Meetings between Experts*, London: Tavistock.

Tudor-Hart, J. (1971), 'The Inverse Care Law', *The Lancet*, 27 February: 405–12.

Turner, B. S. (1991a), 'Recent Developments in the Theory of the Body', in M. Featherstone, M. Hepworth and B. S. Turner (eds), *The Body: Social Processes and Cultural Theory*, London: Sage.

Turner, B. S. (1991b), 'Missing Bodies, Towards a Sociology of Embodiment', *Sociology of Health and Illness*, 13: 265–72.

Turner, B. S. (1992), *Regulating Bodies: Essays in Medical Sociology*, London: Routledge.

Turner, B. S. (1995), *Medical Power and Social Knowledge*, 2nd edn, London: Sage.

Turner, B. S. (1996), *The Body and Society: Explorations in Social Theory*, 2nd edn, London: Sage.

Turner, B. S. (2003), 'Biology, Vulnerability and Politics', in S. Williams, L. Birke and G. Bendelow (eds), *Debating Biology: Sociological Reflections on Health, Medicine and Society*, London: Routledge.

Turner, B. S. (2004), *The New Medical Sociology*, New York: Norton.

Twigg, J., Wolkowitz, C., Cohen, R. and Nettleton, S. (2011), *Body Work: Critical Themes, New Agendas*, Oxford: Wiley-Blackwell.

Underwood, M. J. and Bailey, J. S. (1993), 'Should Smokers be Offered Coronary Bypass Surgery?', *British Medical Journal*, 306: 1047–50.

Ungerson, C. (1990), *Gender and Caring*, Hemel Hempstead: Harvester Wheatsheaf.

United Nations (2004), 'United Nations Statistics Division: Indicators of Men and Women', accessed at <http://unstats.un.org/unsd/demographic/sconcerns/health/>.

United Nations (2010), *Global Report: UNAIDS Report on the Global AIDS Epidemic 2010*, WHO Joint United Nations Programme on HIV/AIDS.

Versluysen, M. C. (1981), 'Midwives, Medical Men and the "Poor Labouring of Child": Lying-In Hospitals in Eighteenth Century London', in H. Roberts (ed.), *Women, Health and Reproduction*, London: Routledge & Kegan Paul.

Vines, G. (1988), 'Ghostly Antibodies Baffle Scientists', *New Scientist*, 14 July: 39.

Wadsworth, M. E. J. (1986), 'Serious Illness in Childhood and its Association with Later Life Achievement', in R. G. Wilkinson (ed.), *Class and Health: Research and Longitudinal Data*, London: Tavistock.

Wailoo, K. (1997), *Drawing Blood Technology and Disease Identity in Twentieth-Century America*, Baltimore, MD: Johns Hopkins University Press.

Waitzkin, H. (1984), 'The Micropolitics of Medicine: A Contextual Analysis', *International Journal of Health Services*, 14, 3: 339–77.

Waitzkin, H. (1989), 'A Critical Theory of Medical Discourses', *Journal of Health and Social Behaviour*, 30: 220–39.

Waitzkin, H. (2000), *The Second Sickness: Contradictions of Capitalist Health Care*, New York: Rowman and Littlefield.

Wakefield, A. J. and Montgomery, S. M. (2000), 'Measles, Mumps and Rubella Vaccine: Through a Glass Darkly', *Adverse Drug Reactions and Toxicology Review*, 19, 4: 265–83.

Wakefield, A. J. et al. (1998), 'Ideal-Lymphoid-Nodular Hyperplasia, Non-specific Colitis, and Pervasive Developmental Disorder in Children', *The Lancet*, 351: 637–41.

Waldby, C. (2000), *The Visible Human Project: Informatic Bodies and Post Human Medicine*, London: Routledge.

Waldby, C. (2002), 'Stem Cells, Tissue Cultures and the Production of Biovalue', *Health*, 6, 3: 305–23.

Waldby, C. (2006), 'Umbilical Cord Blood: From Social Gift to Venture Capital', *Biosocieties*, 1: 55–70.

Waldby, C. and Cooper, M. (2010), 'From Reproductive Work to Regenerative Labour: The Female Body in the Stem Cell Industries', *Feminist Theory*, 11, 1: 3–22.

Waldby, C. and Mitchell, R. (2006), *Tissue Economies: Blood, Organs and Cell Lines in Late Capitalism*, Durham, NC: Duke University Press.

Waldron, I. (2000), 'Trends in Gender Differences in Mortality: Relationships to Changing Gender Differences in Behaviour and Other Causal Factors', in E. Annandale and K. Hunt (eds), *Gender Inequalities in Health*, Buckingham: Open University Press.

Walker, A. (1993), 'Community Care Policy: From Consensus to Conflict', in B. Bornat, C. Pereira, D. Pilgrim and F. Williams (eds), *Community Care: A Reader*, Basingstoke: Macmillan.

Walsh, D. (2010) Childbirth Embodiment: Problematic Aspects of Current Understandings', *Sociology of Health and Illness*, 32, 3: 486–581.

Walter, T. (2004), 'Body Worlds: Clinical Detachment and Anatomical Awe', *Sociology of Health and Illness*, 26, 4: 464–88.

Wang, C. (1992), 'Culture Meaning and Disability: Injury Prevention Campaigns and the Production of Stigma', *Social Science & Medicine*, 35, 9: 1093–102.

Wanless, D. (2002), *Securing Our Future Health: Taking a Long-Term View*, London: HM Treasury.

Ward, L. (1993), 'Race, Equality and Employment in the NHS', in W. I. U. Ahmad (ed.), *Race and Health in Contemporary Britain*, Buckingham: Open University Press.

Waring, J., and Bishop, S. (2011), 'Healthcare Identities at the Crossroads of Service Modernization: The Transfer of NHS Clinicians to the Independent Sector?', *Sociology of Health and Illness*, 33, 5: 661–76.

Warnock Committee (1984), *Report of the Committee of Inquiry into Human Fertilization and Embryology*, London: HMSO, Cm 9314.

Washer, P. (2004), 'Representations of SARS in the British Newspapers', *Social Science & Medicine*, 59, 12: 2561–71.
Watt, A. and Rodmell, S. (1993), 'Community Involvement in Health Promotion: Progress or Panacea?', in A. Beattie, M. Gott, L. Jones and M. Sidell (eds), *Health and Wellbeing: A Reader*, London: Macmillan.
Weaver, J. (2002), 'Court-Ordered Caesarean Sections', in A. Bainhan, S. Sclater and M. Richards (eds), *Body Lore and Laws*, Oxford: Hart Publishing.
Webster, A. (2002), 'Innovative Health Technologies and the Social: Redefining Health, Medicine and the Body', *Current Sociology*, 50, 3: 443–57.
Webster, A. (2008), *Health Technology and Society: A Sociological Critique*, Basingstoke: Palgrave Macmillan.
West, C. (1984), *Routine Complications: Troubles with Talk between Doctors and Patients*, Bloomington, IN: Indiana University Press.
West, P. (1979), 'An Investigation into the Social Construction of Consequences of the Label Epilepsy', *Sociological Review*, 27, 4: 719–41.
West, P. (1991), 'Rethinking the Health Selection Explanation for Health Inequalities', *Social Science & Medicine*, 32, 4: 373–84.
White, C., van Galen, F. and Huang Chow, Y. (2003), 'Trends in Social Class Differences in Mortality by Cause', *Health Statistics Quarterly*, 20, Winter: 25–36.
White, K. (1991), 'The Sociology of Health and Illness', *Current Sociology*, 39, 2: 1–134.
White, K. (2009), *An Introduction to the Sociology of Health and Illness*, 2nd edn, London: Sage.
White, S. (2002), 'Accomplishing "the Case" in Paediatrics and Child Health: Medicine and Morality in Inter Professional Talk', *Sociology of Health and Illness*, 4: 409–35.
Whitmarsh, I., Davis, A., Skinner, D. and Bailey, D. B. (2007), 'A Place for Genetic Uncertainty: Parents Valuing an Unknown in the Meaning of Disease', *Social Science & Medicine*, 65: 1082–93.
WHO (1978), *Alma Ata 1977, Primary Health Care*, Geneva: UNICEF.
WHO (1986), *Ottawa Charter for Health Promotion*, Ottawa: Health and Welfare, Canada.
WHO (2008), *Closing the Gap in a Generation: Health Equity through Action on the Social Determinants of Health*, Geneva: WHO.
Wiggins, R., Joshi, M., Bartley, M., Gleave, S., Lynch, K. and Cullis, A. (2002), 'Place and Personal Circumstances in a Multilevel Account of Women's Long Term Illness', *Social Science & Medicine*, 54: 827–38.
Wilkinson, R. G. (1996), *Unhealthy Societies: The Afflictions of Inequality*, London: Routledge.
Wilkinson, R. G. (2000), *Mind the Gap: Hierarchies, Health and Human Evolution*, London: Weidenfeld & Nicolson.
Wilkinson, R. G. and Pickett, K. (2009), *The Spirit Level: Why More Equal Societies Almost Always Do Better*, London: Allen Lane.
Will, C. M., Armstrong, D. and Marteau, T. M. (2010), 'Genetic Unexceptionalism: Clinician Accounts of Genetic Testing for Familial Hypercholesterolaemia', *Social Science & Medicine*, 71, 5: 910–17.
Williams, C., Kitzinger, J. and Henderson, L. (2003), 'Media Reporting on the Ethical Debates on Stem Cell Research', *Sociology of Health and Illness*, 25, 7: 793–814.
Williams, F. (1989), *Social Policy*, Cambridge: Polity.
Williams, G. (1984), 'The Genesis of Chronic Illness: Narrative Reconstruction', *Sociology of Health and Illness*, 6: 175–200.
Williams, G. (1989), 'Hope for the Humblest? The Role of Self Help in Chronic Illness: The Case of Ankylosing Spondylitis', *Sociology of Health and Illness*, 11, 2: 135–59.
Williams, G. (1993), 'Chronic Illness and the Pursuit of Virtue in Everyday Life', in A. Radley (ed.), *Worlds of Illness: Biographical and Cultural Perspectives on Health and Disease*, London: Routledge.
Williams, G. and Busby, H. (2000), 'The Politics of "Disabled" Bodies', in S. J. Williams, J. Gabe and M. Calnan (eds), *Health, Medicine and Society: Key Theories, Future Agendas*, London: Routledge.
Williams, S. (1998), 'Capitalising on Emotions? Rethinking the Inequalities Debate', *Sociology*, 31, 1: 121–39.

Williams, S. (2000), 'Chronic Illness as Biographical Disruption or Biographical Disruption as Chronic Illness? Reflections on a Core Concept', *Sociology of Health and Illness*, 22, 1: 40–67.

Williams, S. (2011), *The Politics of Sleep: Governing (Un)Consciousness in the Late Modern Age*, Basingstoke: Palgrave Macmillan.

Williams, S. and Bendelow, G. (1998), *The Lived Body: Sociological Themes, Embodied Issues*, London: Routledge.

Williams, S. and Crossley, N. (2008), 'Introduction: Sleeping Bodies', *Body & Society*, 14, 4: 1–13.

Williams, S., Birke, L. and Bendelow, G. (eds) (2003), *Debating Biology: Sociological Reflections on Health, Medicine and Society*, London: Routledge.

Willis, E. (1990), *Medical Dominance*, Melbourne: George Allen & Unwin.

Winterton Report (1992), *Report of the Social Services Select Committee on Maternity Services*, London: HMSO.

Witz, A. (1992), *Professions and Patriarchy*, London: Routledge.

Wolfe, R. and Sharp, L. K. (2002), 'Anti Vaccinationists Past and Present', *British Medical Journal*, 325: 430–2.

Wolkowitz, C. (2002), 'The Social Relations of Body Work', *Work, Employment and Society*, 16, 3: 497–510.

Wolkowitz, C. (2006), *Bodies at Work*, London: Sage.

Wood, P. H. N. (1980), *The International Classification of Impairments, Disabilities and Handicaps*, Geneva: WHO.

Woolgar, S. (1988), *Science: The Very Idea*, London: Routledge.

Wright, P. (1979), 'A Study of the Legitimation of Knowledge: The "Success" of Medicine and the "Failure" of Astrology', in R. Wallis (ed.), *On the Margins of Science: The Social Construction of Knowledge*, Sociological Review Monograph 27, Keele: University of Keele.

Wright, P. and Treacher, A. (eds) (1982), *The Problem of Medical Knowledge: Examining the Social Construction of Medicine*, Edinburgh: Edinburgh University Press.

Young, A. (1980), 'The Discourse on Stress and the Reproduction of Conventional Knowledge', *Social Science & Medicine*, 14B: 133–46.

Young, J. T. (2004), 'Illness Behaviour: A Selective Review and Synthesis', *Sociology of Health and Illness*, 26, 1: 1–31.

Zborowski, M. (1952), 'Cultural Components in Response to Pain', *Journal of Social Issues*, 8: 16–30.

Ziebland, S. (2004), 'The Importance of Being Expert: The Quest for Cancer Information on the Internet', *Social Science & Medicine*, 59: 1783–93.

Zimmerman, D. H. and West, C. (1976), 'Sex Roles, Interruptions and Silences in Conversation', in B. Thorne and N. Hanley (eds), *Language and Sex: Difference and Dominance*? Rowley, MA: Newbury House Publishers.

Zipper, J. and Sevenhuijsen, S. (1987), 'Surrogacy: Feminist Notions of Motherhood Reconsidered', in M. Stanworth (ed.), *Reproductive Technologies: Gender, Motherhood and Medicine*, Cambridge: Polity.

Zola, I. K. (1966), 'Culture and Symptoms: An Analysis of Patients Presenting Complaints', *American Sociological Review*, 31: 615–30.

Zola, I. K. (1972), 'Medicine as an Institution of Social Control', *Sociological Review*, 20: 487–504.

Zola, I. K. (1973), 'Pathways to the Doctor: From Person to Patient', *Social Science & Medicine*, 7: 677–89.

Index